National Character

First published in 1927, *National Character* is based upon a course of ten lectures on citizenship, delivered, under the terms of the Stevenson Foundation, in the University and the City of Glasgow during the latter part of 1925 and the beginning of 1926. The author argues that to see how nations have become what they are may be the best way of discovering how they can make themselves other than what they are.

Divided into two parts-the material factors and the spiritual factors, the book discusses themes like race, territory and climate, population and occupation, growth of national spirit, law and government, influence of churches, role of literature and thought, and ideas and system of education to understand the factors behind the formation of national character. This is an important historical reference work for scholars and researchers of political studies and political philosophy.

National Character

And the Factors in its Formation

Ernest Barker

Routledge
Taylor & Francis Group

First published in 1927
by Methuen & Co. Ltd.

This edition first published in 2024 by Routledge
4 Park Square, Milton Park, Abingdon, Oxon, OX14 4RN

and by Routledge
605 Third Avenue, New York, NY 10017

Routledge is an imprint of the Taylor & Francis Group, an informa business

© 1927 Ernest Barker

Publisher's Note
The publisher has gone to great lengths to ensure the quality of this reprint but points out that some imperfections in the original copies may be apparent.

Disclaimer
The publisher has made every effort to trace copyright holders and welcomes correspondence from those they have been unable to contact.

A Library of Congress record exists under LCCN: 49014737

ISBN: 978-1-032-80333-3 (hbk)
ISBN: 978-1-003-49646-5 (ebk)
ISBN: 978-1-032-80334-0 (pbk)

Book DOI 10.4324/9781003496465

NATIONAL CHARACTER

AND THE FACTORS IN
ITS FORMATION

by

ERNEST BARKER

KING'S COLLEGE, LONDON

The Devereux Books

METHUEN PUBLISHERS LONDON
36 Essex Street Strand W.C.2

First Published . . . . . . May 19th 1927
Second Edition . . . . . . January 1928
Third Edition (Devereux Books)   1939

PRINTED IN GREAT BRITAIN

PREFACE

THIS book is based upon a course of ten lectures on Citizenship, delivered, under the terms of the Stevenson Foundation, in the University and the City of Glasgow during the latter part of 1925 and the beginning of 1926. Only the first and the last lectures are printed as they were actually delivered. The other lectures were delivered from notes which I have done my best to shape into a written text during the year of grace permitted to me, by the terms of my appointment, after the conclusion of the course. I have done what I could in such periods of leisure as I could command. But it has been difficult to reconcile the just claims of scholarship with the demands of other duties; and if the basis of induction is sometimes narrow, and the *ultima lima* is here and there missing, I can only beg the indulgence of my readers.

The theme of the courses of lectures delivered on the Stevenson Foundation is Citizenship, or some branch of the subject. I have sometimes asked myself, in the course of preparing these lectures and writing this book, whether I was actually dealing with citizenship or a branch of citizenship, or whether I was not rather attempting a series of historical observations on the making of England and the English type. I have comforted myself, when I have fallen into such moods of doubt, by the reflection that teachers are generally agreed that civics is best handled not as an abstract subject, but as something involved and immersed in the stream of historical processes. Our citizenship is an historical formation; and we shall best understand its nature and its obligations if we study its growth and examine its history. To see how nations have become what they are may be the best way of discovering how they can make themselves other than what they are ; and to know the instruments and the processes of our making during the past may throw some light upon the problems of our development in the future.

In any case (to make a frank confession), I thought it best to write something which would express such ideas as I had come to form, during a life spent in the teaching of history, and particularly of English history, about our civic life and national tradition. It is a tradition which is not peculiar to our island. If it arose there, it has now flowed far outside the place of its origin. It has crossed the Atlantic, and affected a great part of the north of the Continent of America ; it has crossed the Equator, and entered into the lives of peoples in the Southern Hemisphere. It seemed worth while to examine its nature and to study its growth. A national tradition is a spiritual fact ; and a study of its making is a study of one of the greatest achievements of the human spirit.

ERNEST BARKER

20 *March,* 1927

Note.—I desire to record my obligation to Miss Hall, of King's College, who deciphered my manuscript with unfailing insight and industry, and produced a typed text which greatly eased the labour of revision.

CONTENTS

NATIONAL CHARACTER

CHAPTER I

INTRODUCTORY: THE PROBLEM AND THE FACTORS, MATERIAL AND SPIRITUAL

"To trace the causes, whether for good or ill, that have made nations what they are, is the true philosophy of history. It is mainly in proportion as this is done, that history becomes a study of real value, and assuredly no historical school is more mischievous or misleading than that which evades the problem by treating all differences of national character as innate and inexplicable. . . ." [1]

I

SOME sixty years ago the Chair of Modern History in King's College, London, was held by C. H. Pearson. A little over thirty years ago he published a book on *National Life and Character*. It was a book written in a spirit of gentle and yet stoical melancholy—a book of the evening, and sunset, and soft grey clouds—in which he sought to analyse the effects of democratic institutions and socialistic tendencies, of urban agglomerations within and Asiatic industrial competition without, on the national characteristics of the British people. He saw the fibre of individualism slackened; reliance upon the State swelling in a steady tide; the family in decay; the springs of initiative, in art and literature and life, all drying up and failing. The motto of his book may be expressed in the refrain of Æschylus:

"Sing woe and well-a-day; yet may the good prevail."

To read it is to be stimulated to questionings. What is national character, and how shall we define its nature? Is it a natural and inherent datum, which falls within the sphere of what Aristotle calls "things that cannot be otherwise than as they are"? Or is it a growing product, like clay on the potter's wheel, which is being shaped by historic revolutions and the urging and pressing mind of man? If it has within itself both of these elements, how, and by what combination of nature and

[1] Lecky, *History of England in the Eighteenth Century*, vol. ii. p. 320.

I

human art, has it been made ?   By what influences, and in what direction, is it now being shaped ?   What forecast shall we make of its future turn and trend ?   Is the accumulated mass of the past so great that, though we may expect modifications, we cannot expect a revolution ?   Or may the character of a nation undergo a complete and general conversion ?   If we can answer, however imperfectly, some of these questions, we shall be able in some measure to judge, against a background of general and historical considerations, the justice of Pearson's analysis of the present and his prognostication of the future.   Nor is this all.   The better understanding of anything which lies, to any degree, in the sphere of human control, means the possibility of an increase and an improvement in such control.   So far, therefore, as the formation of national character lies in that sphere (and we shall see, as the argument proceeds, that it has always done so in part, and is coming to do so more and more), we may render practical service in our generation to the greatest process in our national life by attempting to understand and explain the conditions under which the character of a nation is formed, and the methods by which it is made.

The Material Factors

The theme and the plan of this work may be simply stated. We may assume, in a provisional and preliminary way, that a nation is a material basis with a spiritual superstructure.   The material basis consists of three elements.   The first of these is Race.   Under this head we are concerned with the physical bodies of the members of a nation, considered as belonging to this or that physical breed or breeds, and distinguished as such by the physical or anthropological criteria of stature, formation of skull, and colouring.   The racial blend which we find in a nation, and the relative proportions of the different races which constitute the blend, are the original and primary stuff or " matter " on which the " form " of a national character is subsequently imposed by the human spirit, under the limitations and according to the genius of that (and of other) given material. The second element in the material basis of any nation is Environment.   Under this head we have to consider the physical territory on which the physical bodies of the members of a nation move and have their being—its size and shape and external outline, and more particularly its coasts and frontiers ;   its internal content, or, in other words, the sum and distribution of its resources ;   its skies, its atmosphere, its climate.   These are all factors which play on the racial blend and affect the formation of national character—not, indeed, in the way of determining that character by a sort of fatality, but rather in the way of providing possibilities of development, among which the members of a nation must make their choice, and by their choice of which they determine themselves in this direction or that, according as they prefer the possibilities of the sea to those of the land, or this possibility of the land to that, or one combination of possibilities to another. The last of the three elements which constitute the material basis of national character is Population—population considered primarily in terms of mass or density, according as it is sown thickly or thinly on the soil, but secondarily, and in consequence, considered also in terms of occupation ; and this for the simple reason that the mass of a nation's population varies directly with its occupation, so that pastoral occupation accompanies one degree of density, agricultural another, and industrial another still. Population and occupation go so closely together that either word may designate the element we seek to express. Whichever word we choose, we are really concerned with the economic factor ; and what we have to examine is the influence of that factor—as expressed in the density, the distribution, and the occupations of a nation—on the type of its character. That influence is profound. It matters very greatly to the character of a country whether it is moderately populated, agricultural and rural, or is densely populated, industrial and urban. A nation may almost revolutionize its character, as we did ours in the nineteenth century, if it quadruples its population by industrializing its occupation. A dense population engaged in industrial pursuits in great urban areas will develop a new type, or, to speak more exactly, it will write a new and bold script on the ancient palimpsest of the national character.

THE SPIRITUAL FACTORS

It is not possible, at any rate in this matter, to draw any clear demarcation between the material and the spiritual. The material basis of national character is not a given and inevitable datum distinct from the spiritual forces of human thought and human will which play upon it. We can modify the material basis, within certain limits, by the course of our thought and the acts of our will. A nation, by taking thought, may modify the racial blend which is one of its bases ; it may seek, by immigration laws, or by other measures of eugenic policy, to mould the blend to its liking. A nation, again, is not only free to choose among the existing geographical possibilities of its territory : it may also modify its territory, and create new possibilities, by driving channels of irrigation or spreading tracts of afforestation. In the same way, too, nations have sought to regulate population, and governments have attempted to control the course of national occupations, throughout the course of recorded history. But, in spite of this interplay, by which the spiritual is infused into the material, we may none the less distinguish, and isolate for the purposes of inquiry, on the one hand the material basis, which is the foundation, and on the other the spiritual superstructure, which is the intimate essence, of nations and national characters. That superstructure, which we may now proceed to consider, is a mental organization connecting the minds of all the members of a national community by ties and connections as fine as silk and as firm as steel. It is a subtle spiritual cobweb of threads which are spun from mind to mind. If we seek to analyse these threads, we may distinguish four main kinds. There is the thread of Law and Government—the thread of political and legal organization, which regulates social action in the light, and as the expression, of a common set of ideas concerning the proper nature of social cohesion and conduct. There is the thread of Religion—a community of religious ideas and emotions, which may be compatible, as it is in our country to-day, with an actual division of creeds and churches, but which, during the early ages of the formation of nations and their characters, was a catholic community of one church and creed as well as of common ideas and emotions. There is the thread of Language, and of that child of language, Literature, which expresses a nation's sense of beauty and approach to truth, and which, if it expresses a nation, also impresses itself in turn upon it, and helps to form its genius and character. There is finally the thread of Education—a common system of training, which unites the minds of the members of a nation ; a system at first practised under the authority of the Church, and then under that of the State, but in either form serving not merely to imbue intelligences with a common content of ideas, but also to quicken characters towards the pursuit of common ideals. Of each of these four—Law and Government, Religion, Language and Literature, Education— we say that it is the creation of a nation, and at the same time the creator of a nation. Men make these great and august things, and these great and august things in turn make men. We are made by what we have made. We project our ideas into the world of reality, and when they have taken shape and form, they shape and form us by their reaction upon us. A nation makes a system of law and government ; and that system, in its measure, makes the character of that nation. We build more greatly than we know ; and our acts have consequences beyond our intentions.

Individual Character and National Character

The character of a nation, in its formation and its manifestation, has its analogies with the character of an individual man. Each of us, in his moral growth, starts from a raw stuff of original nature, which is partly a matter of temperament, as determined by bodily structure and its peculiarities, and partly a matter both of inherited instincts common to our general kind and of inherited predispositions common to our immediate stock or family. We shape that raw stuff into a settled form, partly by submission to social discipline, in all its phases, and partly by the repeated exercise of moral choice along lines which gradually become definite and marked. That settled form is character—" the sum of acquired tendencies built upon native bases " ; [1] and when it is achieved we have attained both unity of self and permanence of behaviour—we have built an identity which is constant, and expresses itself in what we may call " expectable " action. In much the same way a nation starts from the raw stuff of its material basis ; in much the same way it builds upon it a sum of acquired tendencies ; in much the same way it settles into the unity and permanence of form which we call by the name of national character. There are indeed differences between the nation and the individual. In the first place, we can see the individual as a single physical body, whose character goes, as it were, with his gait and face, and is expressed in obvious and visible actions, which are his, and his alone. We cannot see a nation. It has many members, divided by an infinity of differences ; and the unity of its character must be a matter rather of faith than of sight. Yet we can experience if we cannot see ; and we somehow know, as Eduard Meyer has said, that " in seizing or despising the possibilities given in each moment a people reveals its individuality, or, in a word, what we call its character." " It is," he adds, " something which we can never explain scientifically in detail, but must accept as a thing which is simply given ; and yet it is just this individual and particular element which determines the peculiarity and innermost essence of every historical process." [2]

In the second place, the formation of national character is less a matter of conscious effort and will than the making of individual character. The individual is a single will, acting in the space of a lifetime. The nation is a congeries of wills, acting through centuries. Even an individual, in his measure, moves unconsciously towards the settled form which is his character. He does things for a low purpose which come to serve a higher ; and he climbs without conscious knowledge of

[1] MacDougall, *Social Psychology*, p. 120.
[2] E. Meyer, *Geschichte des Altertums*, i. p. 83.

the steps and stages of his ascent. " Man, like Saul the son of Kish, goes out to find his father's asses, and finds a kingdom." This is even more true of the history of nations and their characters than it is of the individual man. They move, as it were, in a mist on the mountains, and grope their way upwards. They do this or that immediate thing, and it enures to purposes which they have not guessed. For long centuries of a nation's history its character is engaged in a process of development which is mainly unconscious. In our age of democratic self-determination, and in these days of national systems of education, things may be changed ; and nations at the long last may perhaps " see and choose " their way. From the stage of the making of national character by race and environment, by population and occupation ; through the stage in which nations made themselves what they were by the reaction upon them of the institutions, political and ecclesiastical, and of the literature, which they had made for themselves—they may now have moved to a stage at which they make themselves freshly by their own free choice of ideals (ideals consciously framed and consciously pursued) in the fields both of social organization and of national education. If it be so, it is a great and solemn thing. But if it be so now, it was not so in the centuries of the past. And as we look at those centuries, we must allow a large area for the working of man's unconscious mind.

Nature and Nurture

" Unconscious," we have said ; but it was none the less mind which was at work :

" totamque infusa per artus
Mens agitat molem et magno se corpore miscet."

Fundamentally, a nation makes its character by the minds and the wills of its members, as an individual makes his own character by the operation of his mind and his will. This is an assumption which many, and more particularly many men of science, may feel disposed to challenge. There is a familiar distinction between nature and nurture—between the innate and persistent basis, which is given, and the acquired and variable structure, which is not given, but made, and made by mental processes. Look at the two in the broadest sense, and you will say that nature is inherent and inevitable, and nurture is made and modifiable. Look at them in their bearing on human life, and you will say that nature is biologically inherited in the body through the protoplasm, and nurture is socially transmitted from mind to mind by a process which we may call, in the widest sense of the word, the process of education. The distinction between the two is clear ; but what is the relative weight of the two ? The answer to that question will depend, in the last resort, on the training and experience of life of the answerer. Has he been trained in natural science, or devoted himself to the study of eugenics, or come from a family stock with persistent qualities which he has himself inherited and maintained ? He will emphasize nature—persistent and ineluctable nature ; and he may be sceptical about the modifications and the progress which may be achieved by any process of nurture. Has he been trained in the record of human thought and human art and human action, or does he come from a stock from which he has varied and departed in the course of his own development ? He will emphasize the indomitable initiative of the human mind—the triumphs which it can win, and the progress which it can achieve, even in the face of natural handicaps. I must confess that my own bias lies in this latter direction ; and I would ask the reader to allow for that bias as he follows the course and the run of my argument. I shall not forget that there are natural elements of breed and environment and occupation which condition the development of national character. But I shall assume that the character of a nation belongs mainly, if not entirely, to the sphere of nurture, and that it is therefore made, and is also modifiable, by the creative mind of man.

It is possible to make this assumption the more readily because (as the subsequent argument may serve to show) a nation is essentially the unity which it is in virtue of that " spiritual superstructure " which it has built by its own hands for its own dwelling. It is not one by virtue of the natural fact of race ; for it generally contains different races. It is not one by virtue of the natural factor of territory or environment ; for that may be very diverse and various. It is not one by virtue of its population, which as such is only a heap or quantity of different units, or again of its occupations, which are in themselves variegated and manifold. It is one, and has a character of its own, by virtue of the unity of its tradition, which is the deposit and crystallization, in an objective form, of the seething and moving thought of human minds. That is a matter to which we shall necessarily return. For the moment we may turn to consider the implications of two words which have just been used—the word " made " and the word " modifiable."

NATIONAL CHARACTER MADE AND MODIFIABLE

If national character is, on the whole and in the main, something which is made, it follows that there is no such thing as a given and ineluctable national character, which stamps and makes the members of a nation, and is their individual and collective destiny. Character is not a destiny to each nation. Each nation makes its character and its destiny. We cannot therefore draw up an indictment against a whole nation as eternally cursed, or sing pæans in its praise as eternally blessed, by the destiny of an inevitable character suspended above it for ever. Let us rather believe (for we shall be nearer the truth) that a nation is engaged in an eternal turbulence of generation and regeneration, and let us assign to it, in each age, the burden of responsibility for what it makes of itself—in each age, and most of all in our own, in which, through a national franchise and a national system of education, we have a greater power than ever we had before of making ourselves more nearly into what we would have ourselves be.

Not only is national character made; it continues to be made and re-made. It is not made once and for all: it always remains, in its measure, modifiable. A nation may alter its character in the course of its history to suit new conditions or to fit new purposes. The change may be gradual, like that from " the English people of merry England, full of mirth and game," in the fourteenth century, to the stern, struggling Samson of Milton's day; or it may be sudden, and almost of the nature of a conversion, like the change in Scottish national character under the influence of Calvinism. Writers of different periods will give you very different pictures of a nation's character. Pope Eugenius III, about 1140, said that " the English nation was fit to be set to anything it would handle, and one to be preferred to others, were it not for the impediment of levity." Wycliffe, in the time of Richard II, wrote that " the English have properly the moon for their planet, by reason of their inconstancy "; and Torcy, about the time of Charles II, could still celebrate their fickle nature. A writer of the Napoleonic period, or of the days of the Great War, would more naturally speak of fixed ideas and bulldog tenacity. The North Germans of the days of the Hanseatic League were full of a spirit of voluntary enterprise and free association ; the North Germans under the rule of the later Hohenzollerns ran into a pattern of rigorous discipline and State-regimentation. Remembering these things, we may learn not to judge the present of a nation by the characteristics of its past : we may be ready to see and to forecast change in a nation, and even to give it our sympathy, if it brings the nation nearer to our own ideals ; above all, we may beware of facile generalizations about immutable national traits. Yet it remains true that there are profound and abiding permanences in a nation's character ; and the heaving of the surface must not blind us to the stillness of the depths. Puritanism, for example, was nothing absolutely new in English life. There is a settled and reflective melancholy in much of Anglo-Saxon literature. It might go underground for a time : it emerged again in its season. What seems a modification may only be the coming again into light of a facet which was always there ; and even if the modification be something entirely new, it may be but a little thing, however it may dazzle us at the moment, in comparison with the accumulated fund of general disposition. Just because national character is tradition—socially created and socially transmitted tradition—we must believe that it is something which our minds have made and may change. But just for the same reason, because it is tradition, we must also believe that what has been made through the centuries is strong and endures, and that the weight of the past is heavier in the balance than that of the present.

PAST AND PRESENT

It is easy to distinguish past and present ; but there is a point of view from which the distinction seems almost to vanish. The past that matters is still alive in the present, and makes us, in very large measure, what we now are. It is a living past, walking among us, and part of our life. All real history, Croce has said, is contemporary history ; it is a history of the present regarded as containing the past, or, if you will, of the past regarded as constituting the present. Eduard Meyer has said much the same, in very similar words. " History selects for its study, as really historic, those events of the past which did not exhaust their activity in the moment of their happening, but continued to operate and were productive of new events in succeeding ages " ; and therefore, he adds, it " seeks to comprehend the being of the present by regarding it as a becoming out of the past." [1]

It is in that sense that the argument of this book is conceived. It is a study of the process of " becoming " of national character intended to elucidate its present nature, and thereby to make it, so far as may be, more readily controllable in its future growth. And here it is important to appreciate fully the volume and the extent of the past which lives in the present. We must beware of any narrowness of nationalist prepossession ; nor must we regard our creative past as simply the separate past of our own nation. Each national character is a microcosm of humanity at large, presented from a particular angle ; each national tradition is a deposit containing not only indigenous stuff, but also the contributions of general humanity. We are what we are in our country not only because of what happened in London and Edinburgh, but also because of what happened

[1] E. Meyer, *Geschichte des Altertums*, I. i. pp. 188–189.

in Jerusalem and Athens and Rome. Rome influenced the organization of the Church in England, the shaping of English law—and, still more, that of the law of Scotland—and the very vocabulary of our language. We cannot forget Jerusalem so long as we read and recite the Psalms ; we are the heirs of Greece so long as we love ordered beauty in art and literature. It is not merely that these things entered into our beginnings. There is something deeper. In each age they may enter again and anew ; and some element of a distant past, acquiring a new vitality from a new congruity with our present life, may become once more a creative force. It is almost as if the past swung in an elliptical orbit, and at some point in its orbit, coming into closer juxtaposition, warmed us, vivified us, regenerated us. The Greek past came into such juxtaposition in the days of the Renaissance in England ; and we know the fruits of its working. The Jewish past came into such juxtaposition in the Puritan age of the seventeenth century ; and again we know the fruits of its working. The past, as it affects the present, is not a constant or static thing. It waxes and wanes, approaches and recedes. But it is a constant force, if it is not a constant quantity ; and in the development of our theme we must do obeisance to its majesty, remembering that there lives, moves, and has its being among us a past which is not only the past of ourselves, but also that of other peoples—a past which does not die, but, if it sometimes wanes, may also sometimes wax, and shining with a new lustre exercise a new and deep influence on our life.

II

An attempt has been made, in these preliminary observations, to explain the theme, to indicate the nature of the approach, and to state some of the presuppositions on which the argument will proceed. In the rest of this chapter we have to consider the conception of nation in its various implications, and to define it in relation to a number of conceptions—those of race, of language, of religion, of territory, and of State—with which it is, in its nature, closely connected.

NATION AND RACE

A nation is not a race or single stock. Etymologically, it is true, the word nation, connected as it is with words such as "cognate," suggests the idea of birth, and seems to indicate a group of kinsmen. In mediæval records you may find the phrase *natio villæ*—the kin-group of the village—a phrase reminiscent of the old Teutonic village which was a family as well as a village ; and it seems a natural extension of such

language when the Barons at Oxford, in 1258, begin to speak of
the *natio regni Angliæ*—the kin-group of the kingdom of England
—in contradistinction to the foreign following of Henry III.
Men readily thought of greater groups in terms of the smaller
group of the family, and regarded them as the same in kind, if
greater in degree. It was in this way, indeed, that the patriarchal theory of the origin of the State arose, as you find it in
Sir Robert Filmer or Sir Henry Maine : the family begets the
clan, the clan the tribe, and the tribe the nation or State. But
difficulties confront such a theory of the nation, nor can nations
readily be regarded as enlarged but homogeneous and inter-
related groups of kinsmen. In the first place, you will find that
the greater group—the people or nation, generally organized
as a State—historically precedes and begets the family, the
clan, and the tribe. Each of these lesser groups is a juridical
unit—a complex of rights and duties ; and you cannot have a
juridical unit, which is a vehicle of rights and duties, unless you
postulate, as a prior condition, the existence of a larger law-
making group which creates and sustains such units. You
cannot explain the nation by the family, because you have to
explain the family by the nation. In the second place, it is
universally true—at any rate in Europe—that every nation
contains different racial elements, and is therefore mixed of
different kins or breeds or stocks. You know a race—and this
is its essence—by the common physical attributes of its
members. It is a physical fact determined by physical factors
of height and shape and colouring. If you adopt this zoological
conception of race, you must recognize that each nation contains
different races—long-heads as well as round-heads ; and, again,
tall and fair long-heads as well as long-heads who are short and
dark. The soil of each country has been washed over again and
again by different human species, which have left their representatives in its living population. France is the most homogeneous of nations ; but in point of race, as we shall see, France
is perhaps more composite than any other. It is indeed arguable, and it has been argued by Professor MacDougall,[1] that
the cross-breeding and blending of the different races of a given
nation in the course of history may possibly produce a new " sub-
race," fertile in reproduction and full of the fresh variations
which the blending of different races makes possible. To admit
such a possibility is, however, to open the door to confusion ;
and we shall only darken counsel by talk of a French or English
sub-race. A race is a physical fact marked by physical
features ; and we cannot find any physical features which mark
the French as a single and united sub-race distinct from the
English. On the contrary, the persistence of several different

[1] *The Group Mind*, pp. 241–245.

races alike in France and in England is an obvious fact ; and the length of time that would be necessary to blend the different races of either country into a new unity which abolished the old diversities (even if we assume for the moment that such a thing is now possible) is far beyond the period during which cross-breeding has been at work in any of the nations of Europe. We must abandon, therefore, any conception of the nation as a physical unity. The conception of the nation as " an ideal unit founded on the race " is ascribed by Acton, in a profound essay on Nationality,[1] to the French Revolution, and criticized by him as not only fictitious, but subversive of traditional rights, local autonomies, and religious liberties. The sovereign people which professes to be a race as well as a people may well be a dangerous monster of centralizing tyranny, so sternly resolved on the unity inculcated in its new gospel that it defies both the history of the past and the local feelings and religious associations of the present ; but whatever the origin, and whatever the results, of such a conception, we may be content with dismissing it as a fiction. A nation is not the physical fact of one blood, but the mental fact of one tradition. A gulf is fixed between the race and the nation. The one is a common physical type : the other is a common mental content. The one is a natural fact which is already given at the dawn of history : the other is an artificial structure acquired by the thinking, feeling, and willing of human minds in the course of history. That it is artificial is no condemnation of its quality. It is artificial just because it is spiritual, and because men are not born with the spiritual in their blood, but win it through effort in the slow course of time.[2] This spiritual fact of national unity may be dramatized, or mythically expressed, in the fiction of common blood ; the result is only a drama, even though the drama may become, as Acton feared, a tragedy of pity and terror. A nation remains in its essence a fund of common thoughts and common sentiments, acquired by historic effort, and backed by a common will to live resolutely in their strength. " A nation," said Renan, " is a spiritual principle, made by two things — the one in the present, the other in the past : the one the possession in common of a rich bequest of memories ; the other a present sense of agreement, a desire to live together, a will to continue to make effective the heritage received as an undivided unity." [3]

---

[1] *History of Freedom*, p. 288.
[2] Stammler, *Wirtschaft und Recht*, p. 303.
[3] For other definitions see Jellinek, *Allgemeine Staatslehre*, p. 119.

NATION AND LANGUAGE

A nation is not a race ; but we should naturally expect that it would be co-extensive with a language. Common feelings and common thoughts would seem to imply a common and single language, in which they can be expressed and by which they can be communicated. Yet we have to note two things which seem to show the contrary. On the one hand, a group may form a nation without possessing a common language. Switzerland is a nation : but there are three, if not four, languages in Switzerland. There is, too, a British nation ; but there are three languages spoken in Great Britain. Again, and on the other hand, a group may speak one language and yet form several nations. The group which speaks the English language now constitutes separate nations in various continents. Movements may indeed arise, like the Pan-German or the Pan-Slav, which would fain make language and nation co-extensive. They beat in vain against the dikes and embankments of a national tradition which defies linguistic claims. None the less, and just because a nation is a tradition of thought and sentiment, and thought and sentiment have deep congruities with speech, there is the closest of affinities between nation and language. Language is not mere words. Each word is charged with associations that touch feelings and evoke thoughts. You cannot share these feelings and thoughts unless you can unlock their associations by having the key of language. You cannot enter the heart and know the mind of a nation unless you know its speech. Conversely, once you have learned that speech, you find that with it and by it you imbibe a deep and pervasive spiritual force. The fact that Christianity was expressed and preached in Greek carried much of the content of Greek thought into Christianity. The fact that the vocabulary of our own language is so largely Latin has carried into our own thought more than we readily recognize of the Latin tradition and quality. The close and subtle ties which connect language with thought and feeling explain the importance of language in the history of national development. On the one hand, national movements begin with an effort to resuscitate an old national language, and to make it a literary vehicle. Hence the revival of Czech in Bohemia during the first half of the nineteenth century ; hence the cultivation of Erse in Ireland from the days of the Gaelic League onwards. It is not mere perversity : it is an effort to recapture, as it were, an old soul or spiritual principle which lies deep down in speech. On the other hand, a nation sown with minorities which speak another language will often be found attempting to enforce the general use of its own. This was the policy followed before the war by the Germans in

Schleswig, Prussian Poland, and Alsace-Lorraine, and again by the Magyars in Transylvania : it is the policy adopted since the war by some of the new nations in Central Europe.   This again is not mere perversity, though it is not exactly wisdom : it is an effort to impose a new and uniform spiritual principle by the stamp and the suggestion of language.   All in all, and with due allowance for instances which seem to show the contrary, we may say that, as it was common speech which, as we shall see, went mainly to make the earliest nations of history, so it is common speech which is still a main cohesive bond of nations and a generally necessary basis for the formation of an homogeneous national character.   All who speak the same language do not necessarily tend to form a single nation, and policies based on a supposition of that tendency achieve no success ; but all who belong to one nation tend to speak the same language, and a common language becomes the more necessary to the spiritual unity of a nation, as the spirit of a nation plumbs greater depths.

Nation and Religion

Is a common religion also a necessary basis of a common national character ?   It was long a common opinion ; and Queen Elizabeth still held in her day that citizenship involved churchmanship, and that men could not be full members of the nation unless they also belonged to the national church.   It is true that to-day there are nations—for example, Germany—which partly belong to the Roman and partly to Protestant churches.   Where this is the case, it is *pro tanto* a division of the nation ; but even where it is the case, such division may still be compatible with a large common basis of Christian thought and feeling.   Yet we cannot but admit that in our days the policy of a whole nation may be set towards secularism ; and we must confess that Burke's philosophy of the consecration and dedication of the nation by the State-establishment of a church is passing or past.   None the less, if we take any large view of history, we must also recognize that nations long drew for their national unity on some common fund of religious ideas ; and even to-day we may felicitate those nations which still can draw on such a fund.   These are the fundamental ideas which affect conduct and social life, and thereby determine national character in noble ways and to noble issues.   The tradition even of a secularist nation can never entirely lack the presence of such ideas, which have largely shaped its character in the past, and are not entirely gone from it in its present.   And in a nation which still makes religious instruction a part of its national system of education, the shaping force of those ideas may still remain largely intact, and in their measure they may still be agents in the formation of national character. May we not say, on a general view, that a nation is no longer a church, but at the best a number of cognate churches ; that it may even, in its public life, be purely secular ; but that nations were cradled in religious unity in the past, and owe much of their common character in the present to religious influence ?

NATION AND TERRITORY

A nation needs a territory as much as a man needs a home. The Jews, indeed, as a whole, have no common territory ; but the Jews are not a nation, any more than they are a race : they are a church and a culture. The true nation has a home ; and it is by their possession of such a home, and in its shelter, that all true nations have developed tradition and character. If I had to invent a formula for the making of a nation, I should say : " Take first a territory : add some form of organization (or State) to hold its inhabitants together ; let one language, if it was not there in the beginning, gradually prevail by its weight ; let some community of belief and worship unite the spirits of men—and then from the crucible of time and the fermentation of the centuries a nation will emerge." A terri-tory comes first for a nation, just as a home comes first for a man. And as you judge a man by his home, or identify him with it, so you may do with a nation and its territory. An epigrammatic French writer, of the monarchist school, makes " Germany as a race ; Egypt a river ; Judæa a religion ; Great Britain an island ; Austria-Hungary a policy ; Italy a language ; France a dynasty, a tradition, a territory." [1] " Egypt a river . . . Great Britain an island . . . France a territory." There are nations so linked with their home that it colours and almost makes men's ideas of those nations. This is perhaps specially true of France. The unity of the French nation has its roots in the unity, the harmony, the symphony of French territory. " France is a person," said Michelet. " Dear soil of France "— so French writers have said and Frenchmen have always felt, clinging to that dear soil with invincible tenacity.

NATION AND STATE

A nation, then, is not a race : it is not always, if it is gener-ally, a language : it is not generally now, if once it generally was, a church ; but it is always a territory. Is it always also a State ? Must a nation be a State, and conversely a State a nation ? Historically, the State precedes the nation. It is not nations which make States ; it is States which make nations.

[1] R. Johannet, *Principe des Nationalités*, p. 400.

At some nucleus in a territory there arises a person or body of persons possessed of standing and authority—or, in other words, vested with *status*—who gradually organize the territory and come to be called "the State," which is as much as to say, "the person or persons of standing and authority which are prerogative and unique." This "State," or government, by making and administering law, by spreading the language of its court and chancery, by co-operating (or it may be competing) with the clergy, and by waging wars to extend or defend its territory, is the principal agent in the accumulation of that tradition which ultimately constitutes a nation. So it was with the Plantagenets : so it was with the Capetians. In this sense, and from this point of view, there were States which existed before nations, but which in their nature, and by their work, could not but beget nations. Where, as in France, States begat nations that were co-extensive with themselves, so that the State was a nation and the nation a State, we may say that history seems justified of its works. It was not always so. States in their wars of extension might seek to incorporate populations of inveterately separate speech, different faiths, and independent traditions. Where this happened, you might have a nation, like the Polish nation in the nineteenth century, which ceased to be a State, and was dismembered and divided among three other States ; and you might have a State, like the Austro-Hungarian State, which was not a nation, but a congeries of nations. Here history left us with no justification of its works, but rather as it were with a note of interrogation and a baffling riddle of the Sphinx. What is there to be said of the nation that is not a State, and the State that is not a nation ?

Lord Acton, in the essay on "Nationality" which has already been mentioned, defended the ideal value of the multi-national State. The State which is also a single nation (he thought) may be a tyrant exalting its will as the supreme and absolute law of life : the State which is multi-national may be limited and checked by the play and interplay of its contained nations. Lord Acton's argument is abstract, and it is contradicted by facts. He advanced it over sixty years ago ; but even in 1860 it might have been perceived that in a multi-national State the government either pits each nation against the rest to secure its own absolutism, or allows itself to become the organ of one of the nations for the suppression or oppression of others. Apart from considerations such as these, there is a further difficulty in Lord Acton's arguments. He assumed that the quality of nationality might exist in two degrees. In the first, nationality is only a social fact. It expresses itself in common thoughts and feelings, customs and dress, language and possibly literature ;

but it has no political expression, and at the best it only serves in the sphere of politics to constitute a social group which intervenes between the government and its subjects, and limits and checks the State by its intervention. In the second degree, nationality is a political as well as a social fact : it issues in a common organization, possessed of authority, which expresses a common and independent will. There is indeed a truth in this distinction of the two degrees of nationality—a truth which has been emphasized in Mr. Zimmern's essays on *Nationality and Government*. There is a sense in which the Scottish and the Welsh peoples are nations of the first degree, content with the social expression of their quality. On the other hand, the members of these peoples are also members of a nation—the British nation—which is a nation of the second degree ; they are heirs of its past traditions and masters by their voice and vote of its future destinies; nor would they be content with nationhood in the first degree unless, in another form, they also possessed it in the second. The history of the century since 1815, and of the decade since 1914, will teach us that in some form a nation must be a State, and a State a nation. And after all, if a nation be thought, sentiment, will—thought vivified by sentiment and backed by will—we must expect a nation to issue in a State, which in our democratic days is simply an organization for the free play and expression of will. That word " democratic " is perhaps a key to the whole question. An autocratic State might in the past be multi-national, uniting by the one will of the autocrat a number of nations that were merely social groups. A democratic State which is multi-national will fall asunder into as many democracies as there are nationalities, dissolved by the very fact of will which should be the basis of its life—unless, indeed, as we have somehow managed in our island, such a State can be both multi-national and a single nation, and teach its citizens at one and the same time to glory both in the name of Scotsmen or Welshmen or Englishmen and in the name of Britons.

We may end by attempting a definition of a nation in the light of the previous argument. Shall we say that a nation is a body of men, inhabiting a definite territory, who normally are drawn from different races, but possess a common stock of thoughts and feelings acquired and transmitted during the course of a common history ; who on the whole and in the main, though more in the past than the present, include in that common stock a common religious belief ; who generally and as a rule use a common language as the vehicle of their thoughts and feelings ; and who, besides common thoughts and feelings, also cherish a common will, and accordingly form, or tend to form, a separate State for the expression and realization of that will ?

2

If we so define a nation, we may further define national character as the sum of acquired tendencies which a national society has built on the native basis of its racial blend, its territory, and the mass and social variety of its population—the house of thought which men have made that their minds may dwell there together.

LIST OF BOOKS

ACTON, LORD.—*History of Freedom* (essay on " Nationality "), 1909.
CHENEVIX, R.—*An Essay upon National Character*, 1832.
FOUILLÉE, A.—*Esquisse psychologique des peuples Européens*, 1903.
JOHANNET, R.—*Principe des nationalités*, 1916.
NEUMANN, F. J.—*Volk und Nation*, 1888.
PEARSON, C. H.—*National Life and Character*, 1893.
RENAN, E.—*Qu'est-ce qu'une nation ?* 1882.
ZIMMERN, A. E.—*Nationality and Government*, 1918.

PART I

THE MATERIAL FACTORS

CHAPTER II

THE GENETIC FACTOR: RACE

THERE are many words which are made to suffer a constant misuse; but there is none which suffers more abundantly, or with sadder consequences, than the word Race. There are some who speak of the Latin race, or even, upon occasion, of the Latin races; and in the same sense we may often find mention made of the Celtic race (or races), the Slavonic, and the Teutonic. Using a broader sweep, other writers have referred to an original Aryan or Indo-European race, of which the Latins, the Celts, the Slavs, and the Teutons then become offshoots and branches; and others again, moving in a narrower compass, have spoken of a British—or even an English—race, which thus parts company with the Teutonic or Aryan stock to become a race, or a "sub-race," by itself. Publicists as well as scholars have now begun to make play with the "Nordic" race; and Zionists and others have long debated whether the term "race" can properly be applied to the Jews. A usage so large and indiscriminate is an excess which provokes its own Nemesis. It is impossible to think clearly with Protean terms; and the first necessity of argument is the use of clean words, which are always used to denote the same things and connote the same attributes. To use a single word when three or four different ideas are in question, and to use it now for one and now for another of those ideas, is a confusion of ideas and of argument. Such a confusion not only darkens scholarship. When a word is so charged with electric power as is the word "race," it may also disturb the counsels of statesmanship. It is a matter of practical and public importance to distinguish the various ideas which "race" has been made to cover; to assign to each its separate style; and to use each word regularly, and only, for the idea to which it belongs.

There are four ideas which we may distinguish. One is a biological idea; another is linguistic; a third is cultural; and a fourth may be called historical or political. The first is an idea with which the anthropologist works ; the second belongs to the philologist ; the third is in the sphere of the ethnologist ; the fourth belongs to the historian or political thinker. Anthropology [1] is a branch of zoology, which in turn, along with botany, is a branch or division of the general science of biology. Just as the zoologist and the botanist seek to distinguish animals and plants into various kinds or stocks by the use of physical and visible marks of difference, so the anthropologist seeks to distinguish men (regarded as an animal kind or stock) into different branches or breeds by the use of similar marks. The marks which he uses are not merely visible features of shape, such as those which Linnæus used in the classification of plants. They are also facts of human stature and of the dimensions of the human head, which are measurable as well as visible, and can be exactly expressed as quantities in terms of number. The procedure is scientific, and the results can be scientifically verified. It is all a matter of natural science ; and the data used are entirely physical. What is in question is bodily colour, shape, and size : there is no consideration of language, or of culture, or of any other mental attribute. The branches or breeds of men which have been distinguished from one another by means of this procedure have been called by the name of races. To the anthropologist, therefore, a race is a physical or zoological breed ; and it is in this sense, and in this sense only (though it must be admitted that anthropologists are apt to predicate mental attributes of the different breeds), that we should properly speak of the various races—Nordic and Alpine and Mediterranean—which the progress of anthropology has enabled us to distinguish. The word " race " may accordingly be used, as indeed it is generally coming to be used, to denote—and to denote only—a zoological variety of human beings distinguished from other varieties by physical attributes.

The other three ideas—the linguistic, the cultural, and the historical or political—all belong to the mental sphere. If the anthropologist is concerned with the outside of men's heads, the philologist, the ethnologist, and the historian are all concerned with the busy world which lives and moves and has its being inside. The philologist, concerned with language, seeks to classify men on the basis of the languages which they speak. Unlike the anthropologist, who proceeds from above downwards, dividing and subdividing, he seeks to move, as it were, from the bottom upwards, and to integrate in larger groups the smaller units of language from which he begins. He unites the various

---

[1] In the narrower sense of that word, in which it is used to designate the study of the physical attributes of men. In an older and broader sense it denotes the study of " human " things as distinct from things " physical."

peoples who speak languages derived from Latin—the French, the Spanish, the Italians, and the rest—in a larger language-group which he calls by the name Romance ; and by the same procedure he arrives at the parallel language-groups which are called by the names of Celtic, Teutonic, and Slavonic. Taking a broader sweep, he achieves a wider unity ; and he unites the Romance, the Celtic, the Teutonic, and the Slavonic language-groups (along with others which may be found in India and Western Asia) in the inclusive and original language-group which goes by the name of Aryan or Indo-European. From the early years of the nineteenth century philology had a great vogue ; and its concepts and its terms, popularized by Max Müller and other writers, attained a general use. There was much speech of Aryans and Semites and Celts and Teutons ; and it was an easy leap to assume that each of these groups was united by blood as well as by language, and that a common kinship lay behind a common vocabulary. When, towards the end of the nineteenth century, anthropologists began to propound their different ideas, and to claim their own terminology, a confused war of cross-purposes naturally ensued. The dust of the war is disappearing ; and we can now readily recognize that language and race are separate conceptions belonging to different spheres.[1] A language-group is a language-group—but it is not also a race : a race is a race—but language has nothing to do with its nature. The same language is spoken by different races, and the same race speaks different languages. The philologist who deals with languages has no quarrel with the anthropologist who deals with races—provided that he recognizes that a common language is no argument of a common blood. It is likely, indeed, that those who speak the same language will often belong to a common stock ; but a conquering tribe has often imposed its speech on an alien people, and a common language may cloak large racial differences.

A culture or civilization, whether it be only material or more than material, is something distinct both from race and from language. It may be diffused over an area, and practised by a group, in which different languages are spoken and different races are mixed. It is an error to connect the diffusion of culture (which is almost like the diffusion of impalpable seeds in the air) with the spread of a race, or to argue that the appearance of a new culture in a country involves a conquest or settlement by

[1] Max Müller himself remarked (in a passage quoted in Ripley's *Races of Europe*, p. 455) that an anthropologist " who speaks of an Aryan race, Aryan blood, Aryan eyes and hair, is as great a sinner as a linguist who speaks of a dolichocephalic dictionary or a brachycephalic grammar." In the same sense M. Havet (quoted by Pittard, *Les Races et l'Histoire*, p. 55) has said that " language and race are two entirely distinct notions, between which one must not for a single instant admit the shadow of a rapprochement."

a new stock.   It is less of an error, perhaps, to connect the vogue of a culture with the dissemination of a language, and to argue that a common civilization has been a cause—or, it may be, a result—of a common language.   It is possible, for example, that there was some early Aryan community, originally knit by a common material civilization, which gradually formed a common language upon that basis.[1]   A culture, like a language, is a mental construction ; and either has an affinity with the other, which neither has with the physical fact of race.   But the early cultures of which we learn from the discoveries of archæology— the neolithic, in its various forms ; the Bronze ; the early iron of Hallstatt, and the later iron of La Tène—even if they began with, or were spread by, a particular group which spoke a particular language (as, for example, the spread of La Tène culture is associated with the later or Brythonic Celts), nevertheless attained a separate and independent sphere of diffusion ; and the human groups among which they were spread were essentially distinct alike from language-groups and from races. The units of the archæologist are not those of the anthropologist or even the philologist.   Even in historical times we may trace the formation of culture-groups which have an independent existence of their own.   We may say of Greece and Rome and Judæa that, however they began, they all ended in cultures— cultures, it is true, sustained by a common " classical " language, from which, however, the actual usage of living speech became more and more divergent ; cultures, again, which, unlike those of prehistoric times, were more than material, and belong to the sphere of the mind.   To Isocrates, writing early in the fourth century B.C., Hellas has already become a culture ($\pi\alpha\iota\delta\epsilon\iota\alpha$) ; [2] and his phrase attained a deeper and a far wider truth when, a little more than a century later, a common Hellenistic culture (of which the Byzantine Empire ultimately became the outward symbol) united the whole of the Eastern Mediterranean and included in its scope both Egypt and Western Asia.   Rome became first an empire, and then a culture ; and it was as a culture-group, under the inspiration of Latin Christianity, that the single Catholic society of Western Europe was held together

---

[1] We may even speak (according to French writers such as Camille Julian and Meillet) of an Aryan " nation," marked by a common religion (as the identical names of the gods in the different Aryan languages show), as well as by a common culture.   We hardly know where or when it existed (it may have been during the third millennium B.C., and on the fertile plains around the Ukraine) ; but its existence at some time and in some place seems to be implied by the similarity of religion, of culture, and even of institutions, attested by the similarity of the vocabularies of the different Aryan languages. " To create linguistic unity, there must be a nation which feels its unity. Nothing authorizes us to speak of an Indo-European race ; but there must have been an Indo-European nation " (Meillet, cited by L. Febvre, *La Terre et l'Évolution humaine*, p. 186).

[2] *Panegyricus*, § 50.

during the Middle Ages. In the same way it may be said of the Jews that they became, and still remain, a group united by a common culture and way of life. Judaism is neither a language nor a race ; and those who profess it—scattered throughout the world, from New York to Salonica, from Warsaw to Bokhara, from Fez to Jerusalem, speaking here a form of Spanish, and there a variety of German, belonging here to one physical type and there to another [1]—are essentially and peculiarly a culture-group.

There is a fourth idea, besides those of breed and language and culture, which has sometimes been designated by the word "race." This is the idea of the nation, which belongs to the sphere of the historian. A nation, as we have already remarked, is not a race, but a blend of races ; it generally speaks a common language, but it sometimes speaks several ; it has a culture of its own, though it may also be included in some wider circle of culture ; it always lives (unlike a race or a language-group) in a common territory ; and it generally possesses its own political organization. To speak of a nation as a race is to exaggerate one aspect of its unity at the cost of forgetting the rest ; it is to confuse it with something much larger—and much less important. A race is a physical classification, and a nation a spiritual fact. There *may* be a sense in which we may speak of a British "sub-race" (though even that diluted term is hardly justified by science) ; but there is no legitimate sense in which we can speak of a British race. British is an adjective not of race, but of nationality. Yet it must be confessed that it is difficult to apply the term "nation" to a commonwealth composed of nations ; and it is probably some sense of this difficulty which has led to the annexation of a wider and more embracing term. Perhaps we should speak more discerningly, though we should certainly be speaking more clumsily, if we called the British commonwealth of nations by the name of a culture-group. When we think of the diffusion of the Commonwealth, we cannot but reflect that there is a sense in which Great Britain is becoming in her turn what Greece and Rome and Judæa became before. The reflection may seem half melancholy. Our forerunners, if they be our forerunners, perished politically in order to be reborn in a new and more extended form. But history does not necessarily repeat itself ; and the British Commonwealth, if it be a culture-group, is in some respects unlike any previous group of the kind. It maintains a measure of political unity ; and though the unity is loose, and may become looser, there seems no reason for believing that it will entirely disappear. It maintains, again, a single system of common law : it maintains a single living language. If Greece

---

[1] E. Pittard, *Les Races et l'Histoire*, iii. ch. iv.

and Judæa became purely culture-groups, and Rome became a culture-group which was also for long centuries a Church, the fertility of historical development is not exhausted, and Great Britain may grow into a culture-group without ceasing to be also a commonwealth.

II

It is particularly important, in dealing with the origins and the racial character of the British nation, to keep the distinction between races and language-groups always before us. The question has often been debated whether we are purely Teutonic or a mixture of Teutonic and Celtic ; and it has generally been debated as though it were a question of race. Dr. Hodgkin, for example, in writing the first volume of a *Political History of England*, inquires, " Are the Englishmen of to-day pure Saxons and Angles, or partly Celts ? " and he comes to the conclusion that " when we review the circumstances of the Saxon conquest, and especially when we remember the immense influx of Celtic blood which we have received in later centuries from the Gael and the Erse folk, we may perhaps conclude that we should accept and glory in the term Anglo-Celt, rather than Anglo-Saxon, as the fitting designation of our race." [1] We are not a race ; and not one of the terms used in this passage—Teutonic, Angle and Saxon ; Celtic, Gael and Erse—has any bearing on race in the proper sense of that term. Teutonic and Celtic are terms of language : Angle and Saxon, like Gael and Erse, are terms of tribal organization. It is the term " Celtic" which above all others is a stumbling-block and a pitfall. It is a great misfortune that it should have come to be used in a double sense. It is used by a number of French anthropologists (for example, Broca) to designate a race—that of the Alpine round-heads of Central France, Southern Germany, and the Carpathians—which speaks here a Romance, there a Teutonic, and there a Slavonic language, but hardly anywhere speaks any form or variety of Celtic.[2] It is also used, at the same time, by the philologists of all countries, and in popular speech, to denote the various peoples who speak a Celtic language—peoples among whom, at the present time (though, as we shall see, it was otherwise in the past), there is hardly—except in Brittany— a single vestige of the *race Celtique* of French anthropologists, and who belong, almost without exception, to two other entirely different races. In the argument of this chapter it is the latter use which will always be followed. The British Isles contain

[1] *Op. cit.* pp. 109–111.
[2] The *race Celtique* is sometimes called by French philologists Celto-Slav. The term Celto-Slav is less misleading, because it is less liable to suggest any linguistic connotation.

the great majority of Celtic-speaking peoples ; and it is of primary importance that we should be clear that the term Celtic relates—and only relates—to their speech. It is only the slightest of exaggerations to say that the " Celtic race " contains no Celts, as we understand the word Celts, and that the language-group of Celtic-speaking peoples contains no members of the " Celtic race."

We are here concerned with race, and not with language-groups ; and we must leave for a further inquiry any investigation of their significance and influence.[1] But two things may perhaps be said which will serve to illustrate their importance, and to show that considerations of race, which are greatly in vogue to-day, and may readily be pushed too far, are not the only considerations which count. In the first place, language is the storehouse of historic thought. If race counts for the anthropologist, the language-group must count for the historian, who may find in its original language—so far as it can be recovered or reconstructed—a treasury of the thoughts which once were common to a group of peoples now speaking different tongues, and still may unite them to-day by the memories they have bequeathed and the sympathies they have engendered. In the second place, the scholar's conception of language-groups may enter political life and become a practical force. Movements such as the Pan-German or the Pan-Slav attest the possibility. Three stages may be traced in the development of such movements. In the first, the philologist forms a conception, based upon simple facts, of the community existing between the different Teutonic or Slavonic languages. In the second, the publicist misinterprets the conception into the entirely different and unfounded idea of community of blood or race. In the third, the politician adopts the misinterpretation ; and using propaganda to kindle a sense of mutual sympathy between the different members of this or that group, he seeks to translate a supposed unity of blood into the actual unity of a great State. The conception of the scholar, perverted by the publicist, and then harnessed to practical objects by the politician, may thus become dynamite for the explosion of an existing system of States. There is all the more reason that the scholar should " stick to his guns " and his ammunition ; that he should keep his conception pure and undefiled ; that he should watch its use and rebuke its abuse. The scholar who gives birth to an idea can never divest himself of responsibility for its career.

It is curious that the conception of race should have suffered a similar misuse to that of the language-group. Here again the scholar has formed a conception, based upon simple and measur-

[1] See below, Chapter VII. pp. 214–216.

able facts, which should properly be used in the same dispassionate spirit as that of a botanical species or a zoological breed ; and here again the conception has been turned into dynamite. When the anthropologist classifies races on the basis of physical data, he simply adds to the store of human knowledge. It is a very different matter when, not content with a simple classification, men proceed to grade races in terms of quality, and to claim that this or that race is " better " than others. On this basis it is easy to go further still, and to claim that your own nation, or it may be your own social class, belongs to the " better " race, and should accordingly enjoy the political superiority or the social deference which its quality deserves. There are not a few crimes which have been committed in the name of the Nordic race ; and what should be simply a scientific conception has been used, even by anthropologists, to exacerbate national or social conflicts. It was the sad fate of the scholarship of the nineteenth century that it invented two conceptions— that of the race and that of the language-group—which proved as explosive as any invention of the laboratory. Races and language-groups existed before anthropology and philology ; but when men were hardly aware of their existence they did not feel racial or linguistic antipathies, and they were little influenced by differences which were still unknown or unfelt. Science detected the differences : those who had imbibed the little science which is a very dangerous thing exaggerated them greatly ; and it would almost seem as if a new apple of discord had thus been thrown into a world which was already richly supplied. But no discovery is condemned by the use to which it is put ; and the best cure for a little science is an increase of science. The misuse of anthropology is not the fault of anthropologists ; but it is the duty of anthropologists to watch and to criticize the uses to which their discoveries are put. " Ideas have hands and feet." They are restless and moving things ; and they persist in walking with their feet and grasping with their hands. It is difficult to guess how far they will travel or how much they will seek to annex ; but in the days of their heady novelty they need the watchful guidance of their parents.

III

The methods used by the anthropologist in the determination and classification of races are mainly three. One is the measurement of the skull, and, more especially, the determination of the proportion between its length and its width ; another is the measurement of stature ; and a third is concerned with the colour of hair and skin and eyes, or, in a word, with the general character of the complexion.[1] By the use of these methods it has been possible to classify with some degree of accuracy the different races of man ; and in particular a large measure of success has been attained in the determination of the main races of Europe. Anthropologists are now generally agreed in distinguishing the same three European stocks—the Nordic, the Alpine, and the Mediterranean ; and even an anthropologist such as Deniker, who adds three others (the Dinaric in Illyria, the Eastern in Russia, and the Atlanto-Mediterranean along the coasts of Western Europe), none the less incorporates these in his classification. The Nordic race, which is chiefly to be found in Scandinavia, Holland, North Germany, and Great Britain, but also occurs in the west of Belgium, the north of France, and elsewhere, is a race of " long-heads " (dolichocephalic), tall of stature and fair of complexion. The Alpine race, which has its home in the mountainous massif of Central Europe and the adjacent plains, and appears in Central France, Switzerland, Northern Italy, Southern Germany, and the region of the Carpathians, is a race of " round-heads " (brachycephalic), of a shorter stature, a sturdy build, and a darker colouring. The Mediterranean race, indigenous to Southern Europe (and also to Northern Africa), but appearing on the western side of the British Isles as well as in Southern France, the Iberian peninsula, and the south of Italy, is like the Nordic a race of long-heads, but its members are much shorter in stature and far darker in their complexion.

It is the Nordic and Mediterranean races which constitute the racial blend which in turn, along with territory, climate, and similar factors, is the material basis of our national life. The Mediterranean race was the first to make its entry. Settling along the open spaces of hilltops and downland, and avoiding the woods and the marsh of the valleys below, it was already domiciled in Great Britain during the Neolithic stage of culture, five thousand years or more before the Christian era. Successive waves of invasion have washed it towards the west ; and apart from a curious " Mediterranean " island to the north of London, it is in Cornwall and Wales, parts of the Highlands, and Ireland, that it chiefly survives to-day. But it remains the original basis of our racial composition, and it has been said with some justice that " in this primitive dark population, with successive layers of blond Nordics imposed upon it, each one more purely Nordic, and in the relative absence of round-heads, lie the secret and the solution of the anthropology of the British Isles." [2]

Before we turn to the entry of the Nordic race, in its " suc-

---

[1] The shape of the face, the formation of the nostrils, and the form of the jaw, may also be used as criteria.
[2] Madison Grant, *The Passing of the Great Race*, p. 249.

cessive layers," it is important to notice and to explain the relative absence of round-heads." In Europe at large it was the Alpine race of round-heads which was the first to supervene on the earlier Mediterranean stock ; and the appearance of the Alpine round-heads, which coincided with the use of metals and other developments of culture, was a fact of the first importance in the growth of European civilization. There *was* an entry of the Alpine race into the British Isles ; but it was later than it was on the Continent ; the number of those who entered was small ; and they have left few traces among the existing population. The cause of this difference—and it is a very fundamental difference—between Great Britain and the Continent was perhaps geographical. The Straits of Dover is a recent formation. The Mediterranean race had probably entered England by land, and entered with ease : the Alpine race was stopped by the barrier of the sea, and it only entered at last, and then in small numbers, during the age of bronze. It has left its relics : the archæologist detects its passage by the " round barrows " which he discovers, and the anthropologist traces its survival in scattered pockets of round-headed groups, to which he assigns the name of the " Old Black Breed " and the Borreby or " Beaker-maker " type.[1] But it is the relative absence of the Alpine race which, as we shall see, is far more important than the few surviving traces of its presence. Ours is " the only important State in Europe in which the round skulls play no part, and the only nation of any rank composed solely of Nordic and Mediterranean races in approximately equal numbers." [2]

The first element of the Nordic race to settle in the British Isles was a Celtic-speaking body of conquerors who came towards the end of the second or at the beginning of the first millennium B.C. ; and the entry of the Nordic stock into England is thus not very far removed in date (as it is also not greatly dissimilar in its effects) from its entry into Greece and Italy. The Celtic-speaking invaders who first crossed into Britain are

[1] There have been many speculations about this latter type—which was round-headed, and yet tall and " brown to fair in colouring." (See Fleure and James, " Anthropological Types in Wales," in vol. xlvi. of the *Journal of the Royal Anthropological Institute*.) Rice Holmes, in *Ancient Britain*, suggested that it came from Denmark. Pittard, *op. cit.* pp. 271-272, tentatively suggests a somewhat similar theory. Assuming a Dinaric race, indigenous to the eastern side of the Adriatic, he supposes that it may have been diffused across Germany into Norway and Sweden, and thence have penetrated by sea to Eastern England and the north-east of Scotland. The Dinaric race is tall but round-headed ; and it may be this race (rather than the Alpine) which is represented by the Borreby or Beaker-maker type.

[2] Madison Grant, *op. cit.* p. 137. He adds, " To this fact are undoubtedly due many of the individualities and much of the greatness of the English people." Without subscribing to this large conclusion, we must certainly ascribe some influence to the fact on which it is based. On the fact see also Pittard, *Les Races et l'Histoire*, ii. ch. viii., esp. pp. 231-232.

generally regarded as a Nordic strain which had been mixed, in the centre of Europe, with conquered elements of the Alpine race, on which it had imposed its language, and from which it may have borrowed some of the features of its civilization. But if the invaders were of mixed origin, the Nordic strain was dominant in the mixture, and the strain becomes clearer and purer in the later waves of Celtic invasion. The earlier Celts, who are often called by the name of Goidels, and sometimes (from a peculiarity in the form of the Celtic speech which they used) by that of the Q Celts, were succeeded, about the fourth century B.C.,[1] by a later body of invaders who are called the Brythonic or P Celts ; and these were in turn succeeded, about the middle of the second century B.C., by the Belgæ, who are said to belong to the Brythonic type, but were apparently of a purer Nordic stock than their predecessors. The earlier Goidelic or Q Celts were pushed far to the west, or up into the mountains, by later invasions, and they have left traces of their language in the Erse of Ireland, the Gaelic of the Highlands, and the Manx of the Isle of Man. The later Brythonic or P Celts were also pushed to the west in the days of the Teutonic conquest of England ; but they kept a footing in England and Wales, and it is in the old Cornish speech (now dead), and in the language of Wales, that their traces survive. The successive Celtic invasions were probably made by small bodies of men (it would have been impossible for any large numbers to cross the seas in the small vessels of that early period) ; and while the invaders washed over the earlier Mediterranean stock, they left it largely intact. They mixed their blood with it ; they gave it their language ; and the parts of the British Isles in which Celtic languages are still spoken to-day are also those in which the Mediterranean race is strongest. One of the reasons which makes it difficult to speak of a " Celtic genius " or a " Celtic character " is the fact that the attributes of which we speak may as well be due to the presence of the Mediterranean race as to the presence of a Celtic language and literature.

The entry of the Nordic race into England was a long and enduring process. It may have begun a thousand years before the Christian era : it was not completed until the Scandinavian Normans, more than a thousand years after that era, defeated Harold at Hastings ; and it occupied a period of two thousand years. The three Celtic invasions of the first thousand years were succeeded by three Teutonic invasions which fill the latter part of the second, from 406 A.D. (the year in which the German

[1] The dates are all conjectural. Madison Grant puts the first coming of the Celts about 800 B.C. (*op. cit.* p. 199). Sir Charles Oman (*England before the Norman Conquest*, p. 16) dates it about 600 B.C. A. C. Haddon suggests 1200 B.C.

tribes finally burst the barrier of the Rhine-frontier) to 1066. There was the Low German invasion of the Angles and Saxons and Jutes in the fifth and sixth centuries ; there was the Scandinavian invasion from Denmark and the south of Norway and Sweden in the ninth ; there was the Norman Conquest of the eleventh. The Teutonic invaders were purely Nordic : they became more and more numerous with the passage of time and the improvement of seamanship ; and, added to the previous Nordic entries during the Celtic period, their influx made the country predominantly Nordic. The records of stature and colouring attest the fact. The tallest men in the world are to be found in Galloway ; and if our complexion is not what it was, it still remains fair. But the old Mediterranean race, even when Teutonic invasions had been added to Celtic, was only submerged, and not overwhelmed. It is still to-day a large part of our population ; and if, as the records of the past suggest, English complexions were fairer, and English eyes more blue, in the sixteenth century than they are to-day, it would even seem to be a growing part, which is imposing its own dark " dominant " upon our physique. Our racial blend is thus essentially a blend of Nordic and Mediterranean—without any but the slightest mixture of Alpine. It is the same blend which produced the ancient Greeks ; and in so far as we are made by race, we owe what we are to the fusion of these two strains.

These are the facts ; and we have now to examine their significance for our national life and their bearing on our national character. To what extent does the nature of its racial elements, and, more especially, the proportions in which they are mixed, affect the life of a nation ? Pittard has remarked that the different proportions of the various racial factors may possibly serve to explain the variations of French history, the divisions of France, and the particular place which the French people holds among the peoples of Europe.[1] The French are blended in more or less equal proportions from all of the three main European races. The Germans are Nordic towards the Baltic, and Alpine in Bavaria and other parts of Southern Germany ; the Italians are Alpine in the north and Mediterranean in the south, with a slight Nordic tincture due to the passage of successive northern invaders. Like the Germans and the Italians, we are a mixture of two races (with the peculiarity, due to our geographical position and the natural entry of invaders from the eastern side, that the races with us are distributed between the east and the west, and not between the north and the south) ; but unlike the Germans and the Italians—and also unlike the French—we have little or no element of Alpine blood in our mixture. In the light of these likenesses, and these differ-

[1] *Op. cit.* p. 165.

ences, we may now seek to trace, first the characteristics and the results of the several ingredients of our own nation, and secondly the nature and the influence of the peculiar compound they form.

A race, as a race, is a physical fact. Is it possible to predicate of it any mental or moral attributes, or to assign to it any particular spiritual qualities ? The question raises grave difficulties ; and the easiest answer is that of the sceptic. What are the fruits by which we shall know the spiritual qualities of races ? Races, as such, have no language and literature from which we may guess *l'esprit de la race*: they produce no culture or civilization—for the diffusion of culture, as we have already seen, ignores the boundaries of races and even of languages. But provided that they are separate enough to be observed apart, we can conjecture something from the observed qualities of those parts of a modern nation which belong predominantly to a particular race : we can test our conjectures by comparing our observations of the different parts of different nations which go to constitute the whole of that race ; and we can corroborate or check our conjectures by the discoveries of archæologists, who have found the relics of such and such a civilization by the side of skulls which belong to the particular racial type. We can learn something, for example, about the Alpine race from a study of Central France and Northern Italy and Southern Germany ; and we may add to the sum of our knowledge from a study of barrows and *tumuli*. In this way we may begin to see an obstinately agricultural peasantry, and we may even respect its tenacious attachment to old and ancestral soil. It was perhaps the Alpine race which first introduced into Europe, from some original Asiatic home, both the domestication of animals and the cultivation of cereals ; and if this be so, it made possible that permanent settlement on the soil which agriculture at once permits and demands, and, along with it, the growth of arts such as pottery which can only be practised by a settled community. It was also perhaps the Alpine race which, contributing to the arts both of war and of peace (but especially, at first, of war), disseminated the general use of metals through Europe. But the agricultural trend of the Alpine race is its most permanent characteristic, and it still affects, in its measure, the life of modern nations. France has a large proportion of the dark and round-headed Alpine stock, alike in the central plateau and in Savoy and a great part of Burgundy ; and France is still marked by the pertinacious agricultural habits of its peasantry. " When we attempt to find the causes of the tendencies and inveterate aptitudes of a population," M. Vidal de la Blache has said, " prudence counsels us not to confine ourselves to the study of their present environment, but to consider also their antecedents. It is perhaps by imported habits, as well as by the direct influence of the soil, that the obstinately agricultural temperament of the majority of our population is to be explained." [1]   Agriculture has always been far less rooted in England than it is in France ; and while we must take into account, in seeking to explain the difference, the more variable nature of our climate and the operation of our system of land-tenure, which has always discouraged small proprietors, we must also reckon the absence of any but the slightest fraction of an Alpine strain as one of its causes.

But what matters for us is much less the characteristics of the round-headed stock, which is almost altogether absent from our composition, than those of the two long-headed stocks, the Mediterranean and the Nordic, of which our nation is blended. The Mediterranean race, as we have seen, had been settled in the British Isles for centuries, and indeed for millennia, before the Nordic race appeared ; and it is thus the original basis of the British people.   Physiologically, it has found itself forced to struggle against the rigours of a northern climate.   Diseases of the lungs have taken their toll : acclimatization has been slow ; and Nordic invaders, who in part of the south and the west of Britain have been partly submerged in the denser mass of the dark Mediterranean stock, have elsewhere been able, in virtue of their physique, to establish themselves readily as the predominant strain in our population.   Mentally, so far as the scanty evidence goes, the Mediterranean race may be credited with the possession of peculiar artistic gifts. Possibly they were descended, at any rate in part, from the great artists of the Magdalenian period of the later Palæolithic age,[2] who executed the remarkable paintings and carvings which have recently been discovered in caves in Southern France and Spain.   What is more certain is the fact that the earliest areas of historic art coincide with areas of Mediterranean population.   It was in the Eastern Mediterranean, and particularly around Crete, that an art which transcends the simple arts of the Alpine stock can first be traced.   The speculation may be hazarded, even if it is no more than a speculation, that the element of the Mediterranean race in our island has contributed to the development of our art and our literature.   It is curious, in this connection, to remember that, as we have already had occasion to observe, the parts of Great Britain in which many anthropologists detect the clearest traces of the Mediterranean race—the extreme south-west of England, the south of Wales, and the Highlands of Scotland [3]—are also the parts

---

[1] In Lavisse's *Histoire de France*, i. pp. 38–39.
[2] E. Pittard, *Les Races et l'Histoire*, p. 79.
[3] Madison Grant, *op. cit.* p. 203 : " The Mediterranean strain is marked in the Highlands."

in which, if we speak in terms of the language-group, the population is Celtic. For once we may trace a correspondence between the language-group and the race ; and we are confronted with the paradox that the Celtic-speaking group in the British Isles—originally a cross between Nordic and Alpine—has become in the process of time, by the transmission of its language to another stock, predominantly Mediterranean. Now it has been a commonplace of literary criticism since the days of Matthew Arnold [1]—a commonplace, it is true, more honoured by criticism than by acceptance—that there is a Celtic strain in English poetry which has given it "its turn for style, its turn for melancholy, and its turn for natural magic." So far as there is any justice in the commonplace, and so far as any of these features in our literature are derivative, it may be suggested that the strain from which they are derived is more properly called by the racial name of Mediterranean than by the linguistic name of Celtic. A " turn for style " can hardly be said to distinguish the Nordic stock, though it is by no means destitute of artistic gifts ; but it can be vindicated with some justice for the race which has produced the greatest triumphs of European art. And a " turn for natural magic "—an open eye for the divinities of woods and waters, and a secret awe before darker powers—may be ascribed without any great play of fancy to that dark and ancient European strain which has always shown a certain δεισιδαιμονία, and has cherished primitive traditions of a time when man was closer to nature and her hidden ways and processes. Curious survivals may be found among lonely hills ; and the lore of fairies and leprechauns may sometimes give a glimpse into that dark background and abysm of time, when man was still young upon the earth. [2] There are things new and old in the composition of any nation ; and an age of glittering material civilization may conceal in its recesses primitive beliefs and even primitive rites.

The " turn for melancholy," of which Matthew Arnold also spoke, and which he described as Celtic, is certainly inherent in English literature, as it is also inherent in Celtic ; but it exists independently and unconnectedly in the two, and its origin—if we attempt to trace its origin—may be ascribed not to race, but to climatic and historic causes. Let us first observe that the melancholy which we find in English literature—a melancholy

[1] See Arnold's lectures on *The Study of Celtic Literature*, esp. p. 113.

[2] It is possible that there are elements of population in the British Isles which are prior even to the Mediterranean. Some anthropologists believe that Neanderthal man has left his traces in Ireland, and that the receding jaw, low forehead, and heavy eyebrows, to be seen on the west coast, are of this type (Madison Grant, *op. cit.* pp. 108, 202–203). Others, again, have detected primitive strata of population in the more mountainous districts of Central Wales (Fleure and James, *Journal of the Royal Anthropological Institute*, vol. xlvi. pp. 119 *sqq.*).

3

already apparent in Anglo-Saxon poetry—is something different from that of Celtic literature. The one is a grave sadness, mixed with endurance and steeled for resistance ; [1] the other is rather a pensive sentiment of wailing regret, which may pass into resignation or flare into wild defiance. The melancholy of Anglo-Saxon poetry is akin to that which we may find in Icelandic and other early Teutonic literature : it seems the product of the nature of northern countries (like Caledonia, " stern and wild ") ; and it is perhaps less inherent in the Nordic race than it is in northern skies and the experience of northern life. The melancholy of Celtic literature is a melancholy springing from a long historic process of defeat. Celtic literature, as the centuries go, is comparatively recent ; and it belongs to the long period of the recession of Celtic-speaking peoples (mainly of Mediterranean blood) before the advancing Teutons. These peoples have been driven into the peninsulas of Brittany and Cornwall, the mountains of Wales and Scotland, or the westernmost island of Ireland ; and the tradition of the constant thrust, the spasmodic resistance, the ultimate defeat, has been burned into their minds. What we call traits of a Celtic " genius " or " temperament " are perhaps the result of a sad historic tradition, and independent both of the Mediterranean race to which the Celtic-speaking peoples belong and the Celtic language-group in which they are included. Reinforcing the melancholy of tradition, there is the melancholy of the landscapes in which they found refuge—the brooding desolation of parts of Brittany ; the haunted granite of Cornwall ; the lonely mountains of Wales and the Highlands ; the sad, illimitable green pastures of Ireland. Defeated stocks, ·pent among barrenness, they sat down and wept : drawing themselves into septs and clans for comfort, they developed a clannish habit and an awe of " the chieftain " (which may still be traced in the career of Parnell) ; and only too often, after the manner of clans, they fell into feuds—tearing, as it were, at themselves when they were not being torn by the invader. All in all, and by way of summary, we may say that there is no temperament which belongs to Celtic peoples in virtue of Celtic blood or race [2] (since there is no such blood, or

[1] See below, Chapter VII. p. 229.

[2] I am very ready to admit that the line which I have followed perhaps does imperfect justice both to the content and to the continuance of a Celtic tradition. French historians in particular, who have largely " Celticized " French history (in order to prove a pure and native origin), as German historians have " Teutonized " German history, assign a large scope to Celtic influence. The civilization of Gaul in the days before Cæsar's conquest had certainly attained a high level ; and it presents a number of traits which may remind us of Ireland and Wales at a later date. The art, the scholarship, and the literature of Ireland, from the seventh to the ninth century, were hardly rivalled elsewhere. Irish learning passed, by way of Jarrow and York, to the court of Charlemagne ; and Irish models, it is said, affected the form of the sagas of Iceland. But

any such race), but they may possess traits which are common to them all in virtue of the Mediterranean race in which they are mainly included, or, again, in virtue of the historic process to which they have been generally subjected.

From the Mediterranean race, and from the Celtic question into which we have been led to digress in the course of its consideration, we may now turn to the Nordic stock, which first entered the British Isles some three thousand years ago. Comparatively recent in its entry, and settling in our country, for the most part, within the period of historic records and ascertained facts, it might be thought that the Nordic stock would present a clear outline and a definite character. But if there is a haze surrounding our knowledge of the Mediterranean strain in our composition, there is also a cloud diffused around the Nordic— a cloud which was intended as a nimbus, and has deepened into a fog. Some seventy years ago a French writer, Count Gobineau, in an *Essay on the Inequality of Human Races*, invented what may be called the Nordic myth. He assigned to the Nordic race a superiority over all others alike in thought and action : he painted it as naturally dominant, the master of the world, at its best " sweet, just, and boyish " (as a later writer has all too generously said of the English), but always nomadic, martial, and adventurous. Such a theory naturally spread to Germany, which was readily, if falsely, assumed to be a purely Nordic country—actually there is a large amount of the Alpine race in the south—and it spread quickly after 1870. The operas of Wagner, with their old Teutonic themes, helped to fan racial pride ; the writings of Nietzsche, whose Superman, it is true, was a symbol of biological evolution and a goal of human education rather than a racial figure, were interpreted in the same sense ; and Stewart Chamberlain's work on *The Foundations of the Nineteenth Century* openly disclosed the gigantic outline of the Nordic man bestriding the narrow world. The Nordic myth was a basis of Pan-Germanism, ready to ally itself to race no less than to language ; and it must thus be counted in any study of the spiritual origins of the Great War. It is a curious paradox that the myth was also current in France, and flourished for a time in the subdued atmosphere which affected French thought from the close of the Franco-Prussian War to the end of the nineteenth century. There was a tendency in French writers—a tendency so current that it inspires the commonplaces of Le Bon's writings—to lament the inferiority of the Latin, to admit and to exaggerate " the superiority of the Anglo-Saxon," and to explain the decadence of the one and the triumph of the other by the inevitable operation of the dis-

I should still ask leave to doubt whether there is a Celtic " genius," inherited in the blood, which has been continuously transmitted through the centuries.

criminating factor of race. There were even writers, such as Lapouge,[1] who attempted an internal application of the Nordic theory. The upper classes, because they were upper, were assumed to be Nordic; and the towns, because under modern conditions they tend to dominate the country, were equally assumed to be peopled, at any rate in their higher strata, by the dominant Nordic stock. Thus the chosen nation, the chosen class, the chosen town, have all been vested with a Nordic halo; and it has even been possible for a lively imagination to turn the supposed class-war of the Socialist into a race-war between the Nordic and the residuary stocks.

The study of eugenics has latterly spread the cult of the Nordic race in England and the United States. The eugenist, anxious to promote the breeding of the best and fittest stock, is naturally attracted to a cult which also professes an ardent regard for all that is best and fittest. His lamentations about the dysgenic tendencies of modern civilization readily convert themselves into elegies " on the near prospect of the extinction of the Nordic race." War, we are told, selects for its victims the members of a race which is " the first to enlist, the foremost in battle, and the first to fall." [2] Town life, again, is said to be inimical to the tall fair stock, which needs abundant air and the touch of country soil; and a *petite bourgeoisie* of a darker stock, fitter for survival in crowded streets, is argued to be hindering by its rapid spread the survival of the really fittest. Nowhere has " the passing of the great race " caused a livelier apprehension than in the United States of America; and here apprehension has been a mother of action. Concerned for its racial blend, the United States has directed its laws of immigration according to a policy at once eugenic and Nordic; it has restricted the entry of the Alpine and the Mediterranean stocks of Eastern and Southern Europe, and it has sought to secure a large proportion of immigrants of Nordic origin. It would ill become any English writer who realizes the problems and the difficulties of the United States to criticize a deliberate policy intended to preserve an Anglo-Saxon type of civilization. But a type of civilization is one thing, and a racial type is another. One is in the spiritual sphere, and the other in the material. It is a mistake to confuse the two; and the mixture of sad apprehension and passionate panegyric, with which Madison Grant (for example) approaches the consideration of the Nordic race,[3] does not conduce either to sound scholarship or to the advancement of civilization. There is some justice in the argument of

[1] *Les Sélections sociales*, 1896; *L'Aryan, son rôle sociale*, 1899.
[2] W. R. Inge, *England*, p. 26. As a matter of fact, Bavarian regiments of Alpine stock, and French regiments of the same breed, served, fought, and died abundantly during the war.
[3] Madison Grant, *The Passing of the Great Race*, 4th ed. 1925.

the French publicist, Jean Finot, against the prejudices of race ; [1] and it may well be contended that the most harmonious, and certainly not the least civilized, of the nations of Europe is one in which equality has long been the foremost ideal, the distinction of race has been least regarded, and, incidentally, the Nordic stock is by no means predominant.

Is it possible to rescue the Nordic race from its mythical halo, and to discover what it really was and is ?   One thing is clear— that the forefathers of the race had the physique which enabled them to settle in high latitudes, and that their successors were continuously hardened and invigorated by rigours which they had to face without the artificial means of protection invented by a later age.   Another thing may be readily guessed—that, scattered round the North Sea and the Baltic (in Great Britain and the north-west of France, in the west of Belgium and Holland, in Scandinavia and Germany), they were driven to take to the sea.   We can hardly say that they had a passion for seafaring, or that they were originally and essentially a maritime stock.   The earliest monuments of northern literature celebrate the terrors rather than the attractions of the sea ; and the Anglo-Saxons had no sooner crossed to England than they became a people of inland tillage.   Even in an earlier age it was the Veneti of the Bay of Biscay (probably a Mediterranean stock [2]), and not the Nordic Celts of south-eastern Britain, who opposed a navy to Cæsar.   But the Nordic race, pent in a narrow and comparatively inhospitable territory along the coasts of the northern seas, was ultimately compelled to a life of maritime action and expansion.   In its earlier movements it might make forays and attempt invasions by land, towards Constantinople and Rome, or through Gaul into Spain ; but when the land was exhausted, it was driven to attempt the ways of the sea.   It found, as an Anglo-Saxon poet wrote, that " strong is the test to him who long explores the deep sea-road " ; [3] and it rose to the measure of the test.   Apart from the activities of the Arabs in the Mediterranean and the Indian Ocean, the great navigations of modern history are those of the Northmen after the eighth century, and those of the Anglo-Saxons after the sixteenth.

With its hardy physique, and its maritime trend or compulsion, the Nordic race has shown a restlessness of activity, and an adventurous spirit of exploration and colonization, which may help to explain, if they do not serve to justify, the myth

[1] J. Finot, Les Prejugés de Race, 4th ed. 1921.
[2] The French anthropologist, Deniker, supposes a maritime Atlanto-Mediterranean race, distinct from the Nordic and the Mediterranean, on the northern shores of the Mediterranean Sea and the Atlantic coast of Europe.
[3] Andreas, 313, quoted in Dale, National Life in Early English Literature, p. 14.

of Nordic superiority. " The Nordics," it has been said, " are all over the world a race of soldiers, sailors, adventurers, and explorers, but above all of rulers, organizers, and aristocrats, in sharp contrast to the essentially peasant and democratic character of the Alpines." [1] More than this it is difficult to say ; and to say even this is perhaps to say too much. Some would allege that the Nordic peoples have an individualistic temper, adducing in evidence the spread of Protestantism among them ; and it may be allowed that the activities of exploration and colonization are calculated to encourage a spirit of self-reliance. Others again may claim for the Nordic, as well as for the Mediterranean race, the possession of artistic power. There is a rough nobility in early northern mythology ; there is vigour, and even grandeur, in the Eddas and the old heroic poetry ; and the metal-work of ancient Scandinavia has a native quality of design. It would certainly seem to be true that the greatest art arises when, as in ancient Greece, a Nordic stock comes into contact with Mediterranean culture, and adds some austere quality of its own to the rich but unrestrained growth which it finds.

We are thus led to inquire, after considering the Mediterranean and the Nordic races separately, what are the results of a blend between the two. It is certainly one of the most fruitful of human blends. The Alpine race has entered into various combinations ; but it is a silent, industrious race, which, if it does much of the world's work, makes but little stir in the world's affairs. The blend of Nordic and Mediterranean is a blend of two historic and expressive races, which have served as complements to one another. The one can bring to the union physical strength and a certain direct moral vigour, which sometimes falls into rough cruelty, or even a baresark barbarism : the other perhaps has subtler perceptions and a greater wealth of artistic faculty. It may be fanciful, and yet it is tempting, to discover in the art of Greece an example of the value of such a blend. The Hellenes of the north entered into a Mediterranean region which had already an old civilization and an ancient tradition of art. They brought an astringent and austere sense which more and more penetrated the art which they found. It suggests the confluence of clear mountain waters with a warmer and more turbid stream. A quality of chastity and clarity is mixed with the old luxuriance ; and the further we trace the course of Greek art, the more we find that its development runs towards a finer simplicity. The elements which were mixed in Greece have also been mixed in England ; and our civilization, like that of Hellas, has its racial basis in a blend of Nordic and

[1] Madison Grant, *op. cit.* p. 228. Some discount may be taken from the statement, and especially from the words " rulers, organizers, and aristocrats."

Mediterranean elements.[1]   With us the fusion has been slower :
the blend has been more imperfect ; nor has there been the
clear stage, or the comparative absence of external influence,
which enabled the union of the two stocks on the soil of Greece
to develop its fruits in a purity of isolation.   But we are none
the less a blend of the same elements ; and though every country
will desire to boast itself " the Greece of the modern world,"
there is perhaps some particular justice, on anthropological
grounds, in the application of such a title to a country which
calls itself Anglo-Saxon, but may also be called, like ancient
Greece, by the name of Nordo-Mediterranean.

But there is a value in any blend—if only the blended
elements are not too dissimilar—and not merely in the blend of
Nordic and Mediterranean.   Nations pride themselves on racial
purity.   If they were more discerning, they might pride themselves with a greater propriety on racial impurity.   There are,
it is true, elements which it is better not to mix, because they
are so unlike that their offspring, with its ill-assorted mixture
of discrepant qualities, will be ill-balanced and unharmonious.
Miscegenation of East and West, or of white and black, has its
perils.   But inter-breeding of the different varieties or races of
Europe, which unite a fund of similarity to all their differences,
is an entirely different matter.   If it is true that *fortes creantur
fortibus et bonis*, it is also true that there is a eugenic quality in
the mating of different stocks.   The children of such a union
inherit the possibilities of both sides : the range of variation is
wide ; and new combinations of inherited qualities may produce
new mental power and a richer civilization.   It is difficult to
explain the origin of genius.   But it is possible that there is a
greater probability of its occurrence in a blended strain ; and,
to take one example, it may be seen in the record of many
families that the union of Huguenot blood with a native English
stock has been singularly fertile of ability.[2]   On a larger scale
it may well be argued that a nation of blended race may develop
further, and attain to greater heights, than a nation bred from
a single stock.   On the other hand, a nation of a mixed ancestry
may suffer from problems and divisions which will not beset a
nation of less varied pattern.   Races are remarkably persistent ;
and though there will always be blending between the different
races of a single territory, pure and unblended elements of the

---

[1] Madison Grant, *op. cit.* p. 153, remarks that the Mediterranean race
" gave us, when mixed and invigorated with Nordic elements, . . . the most
splendid of all civilizations, that of Hellas, and the most enduring of political
organizations, the Roman State."

[2] If a man could choose his ancestors on the female side, he might well
desire a Huguenot great-grandmother for grace and ability, a Scottish grand-
mother for prudence, and an Irish mother for wit and charm.   He would
probably be less concerned about the male side ; but he might prefer the persistence of a solid and unexciting English stock as the basis of grafting.

races will also remain, and the opposition between their different qualities may translate itself into terms of political conflict. The history of the British Isles is a history of blending ; but it is also a history of the survival, and sometimes of the opposition, of different and unblended stocks. This is particularly evident in Irish history. Ireland long maintained an original racial fund, and was but little affected for many centuries by Nordic settlement, whether of the Celts or the Scandinavians or the Normans. The first large accession came with the settlement of Ulster, at the beginning of the seventeenth century ; and with that settlement an old antinomy received a new edge and a sharper accentuation. The Irish question has been explained in terms of many factors : some have emphasized its religious aspect, and some the economic ("it is the Pope one day, and potatoes the next ") ; but one of the factors which has always been operative is the factor of racial division, separating an ancient Mediterranean stock (perhaps containing still earlier elements) from a Nordic stock which entered Ireland so late in its history, and at so late a period in its own development, that any fusion between the two has been unusually difficult.

The Nordic stock itself has its own divisions in the history of the British Isles. The branches which have entered at different periods have brought their own diversities ; and the union of those diversities has produced a pattern at once original in its blend and firm in the texture of its complementary elements. Not to speak of the Nordic Celts, and their different strains, we have to distinguish the Low German stock of the Angles, Saxons, and Jutes [1] from the later Scandinavian stock of the Danes and the Latinized Normans. The Angles and Jutes belonged originally to a stem or amphictyony settled round Schleswig, with its holy place on an island in the quiet waters of the south-western corner of the Baltic.[2] They gradually moved south-westwards, along the sandy flats of the North Sea coast, settling on the delta of the Rhine, and in Flanders and the Pas de Calais, until they were carried by the current of their movement over to England. The Saxons first appear in history towards the end of the third century A.D. ; they are a confederacy of stocks from the lower course of the Elbe ; they are also a maritime power, " far superior in nautical knowledge, and in the rapidity of their movements, to any other." [3] They were Vikings before

---

[1] H. M. Chadwick, in his work on *The Origin of the English Nation*, has pressed the view that Angle and Saxon are simply two different names for a people which was fundamentally one. The traditional view which I have followed distinguishes the Angles from the Saxons. On this view the Angles were perhaps more nearly akin to the Danes and the other Scandinavians, and thus formed a natural bridge for their entry and settlement.

[2] L. Schmidt, *Geschichte der Germanischen Völker*, pp. 148 *sqq.*

[3] *Ibid.* p. 154.

the Vikings, plundering the coasts of Britain and Gaul by a series of forays; and when they turned from forays to settlement, as they had already done by 441–2 A.D., it was this martial stock of the Saxons which played the most vigorous part in Anglo-Saxon England, and gradually acquired a dominance over the other tribes from its basis in Winchester.

The Scandinavians who made their forays upon England from the end of the eighth century, and began to settle there in the last quarter of the ninth, were of an origin not greatly different from their immediate predecessors; but the process of history in the intervening centuries had differentiated stocks which may once have been similar. The Scandinavian stock of Denmark, Southern Norway, and the south of Sweden was a Germanic stock which had entered from the south; and though there were other elements (Alpine or possibly Dinaric), which can still be traced, they were always inconsiderable. The Germanic settlers in Scandinavia had early developed an art of metal-work; and in the course of time they sharpened in other ways the edge of their ability. Travelling the watery ways of the Sound and their native fiords, they became a people of far adventurous voyages; they carried their trade to Greenland and Novgorod; they learned to face danger with a gay laughter; and they added ruse and diplomacy to a taut and eager courage. They had the dash of Algerian corsairs, mingled with something of the youthful ardour and the poetic vision of the heroic age of early Greece; and in their own heroic age they fell like a thunderbolt on the older and more settled branches of their stock, alike in France and in England. Receptive of the older culture which they found, they absorbed in Normandy, when they settled there in the tenth century, the older Latin tradition of the West which survived among the Franks; and the Scandinavian corsair of one century thus became the Norman knight of the next, an adept in all the graces and the refinements of his age.

There is a curious difference between the heavier and more Flemish qualities of the Anglo-Saxons and the lighter but finer temper of the Scandinavian invaders who were superimposed upon them from the end of the ninth to the end of the eleventh century. The one is a people of sand-dunes and marshes; the other of long sea-inlets and lofty encompassing mountains. The Anglo-Saxons, a Low German stock, were a rural people, with a melancholy strain (abundantly exemplified in their poetic literature), and with a ready propensity for heavy carousing.[1] At one end of the scale there is the profound sad-

[1] Angli sua solummodo rura colunt, conviviis et potationibus non praeliis intendunt. Ordericus Vitalis, iv. 13 (quoted in Stubbs, *Constitutional History*, I. vii. *ad finem*).

ness of Bede's apologue of the life of man, "like the sparrow
that flies out of the night into the lighted hall at a feast, and
then back into the night "; at the other there is the story of
the drinking-cups devised by Dunstan to lure his countrymen
into the ways of moderate potations.　The Scandinavians, and
especially the Normans, were at once gayer by nature and more
temperate by habit.　In their legal pleadings, for which they
had a natural propensity, they developed a vein of legal acumen; [1]
their far-flung trade gave them commercial aptitudes; and
when, during their period of expansion, they entered into foreign
relations and negotiations, these aptitudes were refined into a
diplomatic ability which made men such as William the Conqueror or Robert Guiscard foreign statesmen of the first order.
They showed in particular a gift of assimilation, which enabled
them at once to unite themselves to others and others to themselves.　As William of Apulia wrote of the Normans in South
Italy :

> "Moribus et lingua, quoscunque venire videbant,
> Informant propria, gens efficiatur ut una." [2]

Gens efficiatur ut una was indeed the consequence, if it was
not the intention, of the Norman conquest of England.　The
Normans made England a nation by the drill they imposed, the
discipline they gave, and the polish of Latin civilization which
they transmitted as readily to the untutored English as they
had received it themselves in their own raw beginnings.
"Without them," wrote Carlyle, "what had it ever been?
A gluttonous race of Jutes and Angles, capable of no grand
combinations; lumbering about in pot-bellied equanimity; not
dreaming of heroic toil, and silence, and endurance, such as
leads to the high places of this universe and the golden mountain-
tops where dwell the spirits of the dawn. . . . Nothing but
collision, intolerable interpressure (as of men not perpendicular),
and consequent battle often supervening, could have been
appointed those undrilled Anglo-Saxons; their pot-bellied
equanimity itself continuing liable to perpetual interruption, as
in the heptarchy times."
　　Carlyle, with his vehemence, his zeal for heroes and his

---

[1] See below, p. 153.

[2] The description which Geoffrey Maleterra gives of the Normans in South
Italy deserves to be quoted (Book I. *ad initium*, and II. 38) : " They are great
hunters, loving horses and arms : they like to dress well : they are excellent
dissimulators : they can one and all flatter, and they are all eloquent : each
thinks little of his home, if he can get a greater gain elsewhere : their princes
are seekers of reputation, and they themselves, unless sternly governed, the
most lawless of men."　William of Malmesbury (*Ant. Lib.*, iii. p. 230) describes
them as " proudly apparelled " (Anna Comnena, who saw them at Byzantium
about 1096, remarks with a woman's eye on their pointed and curved shoes—
πεδίλων προσλήματα), " delicate in their food . . . inured to war . . . and where
strength fails of success, ready to use stratagem."

passion for drill, was an undiscriminating admirer of the Norman type. We may well admire the Normans for the ease and the rapidity of their fusion with the English. (At the siege of Lisbon in 1147 the English contingent is already conscious that all its members are sons of one mother ; and by 1176 an official of the Exchequer can confess that Normans and English have intermarried so much that you cannot now tell which is which, and the exaction of the " murder-fine " for the assassination of a " Norman " has become an administrative problem—or rather would have become such, if it were not that the Exchequer, concerned as always for the profit of the revenue, had ruled that the " murder-fine " should henceforth be paid for *any* assassination.[1]) We may admire the Normans, again, for their polish and gaiety. But we must also admire the Saxons for a gravity which, if it is sometimes heavy, is sometimes also profound ; and we can continue to detect the Saxon strain in English life for many centuries. The contrast between the two has been traced in *The Flyting of the Owl and the Nightingale* : " the one is sober and severe, more ready to weep than to sing . . . ; while the other makes of life a merry song, a time of rejoicing, a season of gallantry." [2] The owl may still be heard in *Piers Plowman* ; but the fourteenth century is also the century of Merry England—*Anglia plena jocis, gens libera et apta jocari.*[3] The alternation and the interplay of the two elements remains an essence of our national history. In the Elizabethan age there is not only the nightingale, but a nest of singing birds ; but in the Elizabethan age there is also the note of Puritanism, which grows dominant for a time under the Stuarts. The note was not new, and Puritanism was not a sudden mutation. It was the revival, in a new form, of an old element of the national life, which appeared again in Wesleyanism and in some of the aspects of the Victorian age. The " flyting " of the owl and the nightingale may perhaps always be heard in every nation, as the contention of sun and cloud may be traced in every sky. But no nation is more clearly chequered than ours, and nowhere is the interplay of gay and grave marked more distinctly.

[1] See the Expugnatio Lyxobonensis in the volume of the Rolls series entitled *Itinerarium Regis Ricardi*, p. clviii. : " Cum nos omnes unius matris filii simus." (Incidentally the writer remarks : " Quis enim Scottos barbaros esse neget ? "— but he adds that even they have never overstepped the laws of a proper amity.) See also the Dialogus de Scaccario (edited by Crump and Johnson), pp. 99–100. The picture of the division of Saxon and Norman in *Ivanhoe* is pure romance.
[2] R. C. Dale, *National Life in Early English Literature*, p. 195.
[3] Two centuries before Trevisa thus celebrated Merrie England, the author of the Dialogue on the Exchequer had already praised " our island," rightly called
" Divitiisque sinum deliciisque larem."
Op. cit. p. 101.

IV

The course of the argument leads to a final consideration. What is the actual and practical importance, as a matter of civic duty and political obligation, of an understanding of the racial fund on which the life of a nation is based ? Is it a point of theoretical interest ? Or does it ramify and radiate into issues which cannot but engage the attention of statesmen and citizens ?

The understanding of the present is a necessary condition of any shaping of the future. But we can only understand the present by understanding the past which is so large a part of all our present life. If all true history is contemporary history— a statement and explanation of the present which takes the form of a statement and explanation of the elements of the past which are still alive in the present and largely determine its nature—it follows that the history of racial origins is a matter of deep contemporary interest. They are not only origins ; they are also living factors, which move to and fro in relations and combinations incessantly renewed : they are threads of the roaring loom on which the living cloth of a nation is constantly being woven. Races matter to us, because we are born of their substance, and because they are in our blood. We do not know what we now are unless we know whence we have come ; and unless we know what we now are we cannot determine what we shall be. It is true that the importance of race has been greatly exaggerated by speculative writers who have made it the factor of factors in international politics, in the struggle of classes, and in the relations between the town and the rural community. Race is not destiny ; nor does the racial composition of any nation determine its history and character. On the contrary, as we have already had reason to observe, race is a material substratum or stuff which has to be shaped by the mind ; and the mental shaping is a greater thing than that which has to be shaped. But every artificer and craftsman must know the qualities of the material on which he works. Just as each individual man must analyse and understand what is in him, in order to shape and mould it into a character, so too must a nation ; and in that sense it is a civic duty, incumbent upon us all, to know the pit from which we are dug and the rock from which we are hewn. More especially, it is the duty of all statesmen not to play with false "isms," whether of race, or of language, or of any other species. Perhaps statesmen can never be philosophers—as it would seem to be certain that philosophers cannot be statesmen ; but at any rate they can refrain from adopting and seeking to realize false philosophies of race and racial superiority ; and they can set themselves to understand, with a sober mind, the blend which makes their nation, and to discover the bearing of what they have learned on the national polity.

But race is something more than a passive stuff or substratum. If it is matter, it is also, as has just been said, a moving matter ; and the combinations of different stocks are restlessly at work in producing new mutations and variations which modify the substance by which they are produced. Nor is this all. The racial blend of a nation may serve as a selective agency, which chooses for survival this or that mental structure —a form of law, or a variety of religious belief—because it is most congenial to its own hidden inner character. If we take this ground we may say that race is not only important for what it is, as a material basis of national life, but also for what it does, as a discriminating force which operates among the beliefs and institutions presented to national choice. There is perhaps a dangerous determinism in such a doctrine—a determinism all the more dangerous, because the determining factor invoked is itself more nebulous than its own alleged results.[1] Yet it has always been a fascinating inquiry to investigate the diffusion of human beliefs, and to seek to explain why some advancing tide has been stayed at its boundary. Macaulay has remarked that Protestantism is coterminous with " the nations of Teutonic blood." It is not exactly coterminous, and " Teutonic " is an adjective of language rather than blood ; but if the term Nordic be substituted (and, after all, it is only a change of terminology to suit a more modern vogue), Macaulay's remark has a measure of truth. But history is a field of rich multiplicity ; and many forms of historic causation were united, along with the vicissitudes and accidents which play their part by the side of larger causes (pygmies among giants, but far more numerous than the giants), to determine the course and the extent of the Reformation. No more can be said of the course and the consequences of the Reformation in our own country than that the abiding permanence of race was an operative factor, and that a population predominantly Nordic was ready to accept a religious revolution which, if it affected Alpine Switzerland, was more particularly at home among the Nordic populations of Holland, Northern Germany, and Scandinavia. What is possible in religion is also possible in other spheres. The racial basis of a nation, acting as a continuous force, and serving as a selective agency, may promote not only the form of religion, but also the system of economics, or the variety of political organization, which is most congenial to itself ; and a unity may thus be infused into all the manifestations of national life, in its various fields, which makes them not only congruous

[1] See below, Chapter VII. *ad initium.*

with their basis, but also harmonious with one another. But it is also possible that such a harmony may be the result of the interaction of the different manifestations upon one another ; and the religion, the politics, and the economics of a nation may all be in tune, not so much because a common basis of race produces similar effects in different fields, as because a common sympathy naturally unites, and even assimilates, the different products of a nation's thought.[1] There is a process of *reductio ad unum* in the life of every nation ; but it is an immanent logic, rather than the external influence of the material factor of race, which mainly determines its course.

If it is of practical importance, and a matter of civic duty, to understand the racial basis of national life, alike in its origins and its subsequent motion and influence, it may also be no less important, and no less a matter of duty, to control that composition by deliberate policy. There are many countries in which every citizen has to face the question whether the maintenance of a definite type of racial composition should not be made part of national policy in the interests of national welfare. It is a question which particularly arises in new countries which are still in the process of colonization. It affects Australia ; it affects South Africa ; it affects, to some extent, the Dominion of Canada ; it affects, in obvious ways, the United States of America. The old Greek colonies regulated immigration ; and while some consented to be mixed, others preferred to be purely of Dorian or, again, of Ionian stock. The United States is turning towards the same policy : it is beginning to pick and choose among the immigrants whom it admits ; and just as Syracuse preferred to be Dorian, it is showing a preference for what may be called the Dorian elements of the European continent. In old and settled countries there can be but little question of any control of immigration, and such control as is attempted will be based less upon racial than upon economic considerations. But even in old and settled countries the maintenance of a type of racial composition, by methods other than the regulation of immigration, may conceivably become a matter of policy. If, for example, the conditions of urban life are inimical to the survival of elements in the national amalgam which it is vitally necessary to preserve, we must more than ever promote measures of public health (necessary in any case) to improve those conditions and ensure the survival of those elements. We cannot indeed be sure, until anthropology is a more established science, what are the selective effects which urban life exercises on the different strains of our population ; but we can at any rate recognize that the problem deserves investigation, and that the results of investigation may in turn suggest the need of remedial

[1] See below, p. 235.

measures. A cognate problem is that of the different rates of increase of different strains. It may be contrary to public policy that a strain should so diminish, or increase, its birth-rate as to disturb the existing proportion of the different strains— provided, of course, that there is sufficient reason for regarding that proportion as satisfactory. It may accordingly be necessary that a sound opinion should be fostered, among the different strains, about the life of the family and the replenishing of national population. The problem of the birth-rate is one which is often discussed in regard to classes ; and the study of eugenics has been more particularly directed to that aspect.[1] But it is a problem which may also arise in regard to racial strains. We do not know why empires fall and states decay ; but we can at any rate conjecture, with no little justice, that a disturbance of the racial composition of the effective core of the Roman Empire was one great cause of its fall.[2] Right laws and sound morals form the strongest safeguard of every national State ; but a sound racial basis is also necessary. A nation may be enriched by the varied contributions of foreign immigration ; but if the stream of immigration grows unchecked into the volume of a great river, a nation may lose the integrity of the solid core which is the basis of its tradition. And the nation which loses its tradition has lost its very self.

[1] See below, pp. 113–114.
[2] See Rostovtzeff, *Social and Economic History of the Roman Empire*, ch. xii. and esp. pp. 478–487.

LIST OF BOOKS

BRYCE, VISCOUNT.—*Race Sentiment as a Factor in History*, 1916.
CHAMBERLAIN, H. STEWART.—*Foundations of the Nineteenth Century* (Eng. trans.), 1911.
DENDY, A.—*Biological Foundations of Society*, 1924.
FINOT, J.—*Les Préjugés de Race* (4th edition), 1921.
FLEURE, H. J.—*The Peoples of Europe*, 1922.
GRANT, MADISON.—*The Passing of the Great Race* (4th edition), 1925.
HADDON, A. C.—*The Races of Man and their Distribution*, 1924.
KEANE, A. H.—*Man Past and Present* (new edition), 1920.
KEITH, A.—*The Antiquity of Man* (new edition), 1925.
    ,,   ,, *Nationality and Race*, 1919.
PITTARD, E.—*Les Races et l'Histoire* (in *L'Évolution de l'Humanité*), 1924.
RIPLEY, W. Z.—*The Races of Europe*, 1899.

CHAPTER III

THE GEOGRAPHICAL FACTOR: TERRITORY AND CLIMATE

I

HISTORY, we may say, is a time-line; geography a space-circle.[1] The elements of the racial blend which constitutes a nation enter into history at successive points along the time-line; but the generations proceeding from each of those elements, or from their mixture, move steadily, and have their constant being, within the space-circle of a geographical environment. The form and the frontiers of that environment, its soil and its general sum of resources, its climatic play—all these are physical factors, more or less constant, to which human beings, in a greater or less degree, must adapt their movements, their habits, and their lives. Man is, in a sense, a part of the fauna of the territory in which he lives; and some degree of adaptation to the environment of that territory is a necessary law of his life. We must beware, indeed, of regarding the physical environment of man as a steadily constant or identical quantity. His environment changes— changes because he modifies its nature by his own action (when he clears the forest or drains the marsh); changes, again, because he alters the direction of his attention—allowing himself to be influenced now by this factor, and now by that—according to his needs, or his policies, or his inventions, at any given moment of time. We must beware, too, of believing too readily in the direct influence of his environment upon man's growth and action. Unlike the flora, and unlike the other fauna, man has a mind and ideas. The physical factors of his environment exert their influence not by affecting his body, but by entering into his mind and becoming motives of action; and the ideas which he forms may modify, or even contravene, the influence which we might expect any given factor to exercise. He may refuse an obvious food or a "natural" way of life from some notion of taboo, or some obstinate adherence to a previous tradition; and far from being the servant of environment, he either may pit himself against its suggestions, or, at

[1] Jean Brunhes, *Human Geography* (Eng. trans.), p. 592.

48

the most, condescend to an independent co-operation.   We cannot escape the ineluctable mind of man in any investigation, however physical its subject may seem to be, which touches human growth and development.

Neither race nor environment—neither the genetic factor nor the geographical—is a skeleton key to the doors which hide the secrets of the formation of nations and the development of national types of character.   If we may use a simple metaphor [1] (with the caution that a metaphor is not an argument, and a simple metaphor may be all the more misleading for its simplicity), we may compare the planting of a racial blend in a given territory, and its development in that territory through the general influence of what we may call by the name of " culture," to the planting of a stock of trees in a given soil and the development of it in that soil by a system of forestry.   Race, territory, and culture all count in the one case ; stock, soil, and forestry all count in the other.   It would be foolish to ascribe the thriving of the trees to stock alone, or to soil alone, or to claim it exclusively for forestry ; and it would equally be a folly to ascribe the peculiar development of a nation only to its racial blend, or solely to its environment, or exclusively to its " culture "—that is to say, to the sum of the spiritual influences generated within itself or adopted from other nations. But it is easier to commit the folly of believing in " a singularity of causes " when man is in question, than it is when the question is one of trees.   Men are infinitely less simple than trees.   You can distinguish a stock of trees precisely.   It is much more difficult to distinguish a racial blend, or to assess the proportions of each of its elements.   You can readily analyse the soil in which a stock of trees is set ; but the environment of a nation is a subtle and complicated thing.   Silviculture is a single study ; but the study of human culture is the study of law and government, of art and literature, of religion, of education. Where a theme is complicated, an artificial simplification is especially tempting.   When the subtle shades of spiritual influence have to be distinguished and weighed, a timid spirit may readily fly to what seems to be the plain and obvious " matter " of race or environment.   One school will be composed of votaries of race, and will explain civilizations and nations by conjuring with a supposed " matter " (which is really an anthropological hypothesis) of Nordic and Alpine skulls.   Another school will be composed of votaries of climate, and will explain why civilizations rise and fall, and nations are what they are, by the aid of a conception (for it *is* a conception)

---

[1] The metaphor is used in the opening chapter of Ellsworth Huntington's *Civilisation and Climate* ; but the use made of the metaphor in the third edition (1924) differs from that in the earlier editions.

4

which itself needs explanation. We do not really simplify the history of the past or the civic life of the present if we seek to reduce it to a function of " matter." The matter—whether it be race or whether it be climate—proves itself to be immaterial. It is an hypothesis of anthropologists, or a conception of geographers. We do not damn it when we reduce it to that category. Hypotheses and conceptions, when they are understood as such, are the tools of science. When they masquerade as matter, they only mislead.

What are the geographical conceptions which we may properly entertain, and profitably use as tools, in seeking to understand the formation of nations and national types of character? There is one conception, at any rate, which we shall do well to avoid, and that is the conception of geographical determinism. On such a conception the territory of a nation becomes its destiny, and the climate of a given territory, in particular, becomes the special genius which presides over the formation and development of national character. A modern form of this conception appears in the writings of Ratzel and his followers.[1] A territory, Ratzel taught, was always the same and situated at the same point of space ; it served as a rigid support of the humours and changing aspirations of men, ruling the destinies of peoples with a blind brutality ; and a people must accordingly live—and die—on the territory which it had received from fortune, undergoing the yoke of its law.[2] The steppe, the island, the desert — each regarded abstractly as a regular geographical form, and each considered apart from the general or regional milieu in which every particular form must necessarily be set—were held to show uniform attributes and to exercise uniform effects. To Ratzel, therefore, the territory, and the form and character of the territory, was a solid and immutable channel which served to determine the course and the current of national life. He was not the first to hold such views, though he was perhaps the first to give them a fully scientific form and a large inductive basis. Among the ancient Greeks we find a writer of the school of Hippocrates, and Aristotle himself, ascribing varieties of national character to geographical differences, and especially to differences of climate. In modern times a similar tendency has for a long time marked the history of French thought. Just as it was a French thinker—Gobineau— who first gave vogue to a theory of the racial determination of national life and character, so it is French writers who have given vogue, for centuries past, to the idea of geographical

[1] The first volume of F. Ratzel's *Anthropo-geographie* was published in 1882; the second in 1891. Miss Semple's *Influences of Geographic Environment* (1913) is a statement of Ratzel's main principles.

[2] These theses are quoted in L. Febvre's *La Terre et l'Évolution humaine* (1922), pp. 22, 436.

determinism. In the sixteenth century Bodin, at the beginning of one of his " Six Books on the Republic," following and expanding the hints of Aristotle, argued that constitutions must be adjusted to human characters, as these were in turn adjusted to climate, and particularly to temperature.[1] In the middle of the eighteenth century Montesquieu devoted one of the books of the *Esprit des Lois* to a study " of the influence of the nature of territory upon laws," and four others to a consideration of the connection between laws and climate.[2] Montesquieu was especially fascinated by the English climate—not indeed in itself, or for its own sake (who would be—except an Englishman ?), but because of the influence which he supposed it to exercise on English manners and politics ; and he found it easy to explain the virtues of the English constitution by the vices of the English climate, arguing that a climate which made everything—and a fortiori any tyranny—intolerable must inevitably result in liberty. The same fascination of the English climate, and the same facility of geographical explanation, may be found in Émile Boutmy's *Study of the Political Psychology of the English People* and in the introduction to Taine's *History of English Literature*. In England itself we have been generally oblivious alike of our climate and of climatic influence on politics or literature ; and almost the only Englishman to invoke the influence of geography has been Buckle, who, in the second chapter of his *History of Civilisation in England*, examining the influence of the physical aspects of Nature on imagination and understanding, sought to prove that where, as in India, Nature was terrible, imagination ran riot, and where, as in Greece, she was simple and modest, the understanding achieved its highest triumphs.

A modern writer has remarked that " the French inclination to materialism has offered a favourable opportunity for the propagation of environmental doctrines."[3] The remark has some justice ; but it is only fair to add that it is from modern French geographers, and especially Vidal de la Blache, that the most searching criticisms and the best correctives of any doctrine of geographical determinism have come. The theory which they propound (as it is enunciated in L. Febvre's *La Terre et l'Évolution de l'Humanité*) is a theory of what may be called by the name of " regional possibilities." A region is a natural complex—a complex of mountains, plateaux, valleys, rivers, and it may be coasts—which by our observations (meteorological, botanical, and geological) is shown to be a unit and to possess uniformity. Such a region, as it confronts the society of men

[1] *De Republica*, v. I.
[2] *Esprit des Lois*, Book XVIII. and Books XIV.–XVII.
[3] Ripley, *Races of Europe*, p. 4.

who are its inhabitants, is a sum of possibilities—not a destiny which determines, but an area of choice which, by the selection it makes, the society itself determines. We must conceive, therefore, the racial blend which inhabits a given region as selecting, more or less freely, among its possibilities—as choosing this rather than that, or again choosing this at one time, and that at another. The name " region " is generally used by French geographers for smaller areas (Vidal de la Blache, for example, enumerates some seventeen regions in France) ; but there seems to be no reason why we should not apply the theory of " possibilities " to a larger area. If we do so, and if we take the territory of England for our example, we can see that this territory offers, and has always offered, possibilities by land and possibilities by sea ; that on land it offers, and has always offered, the possibility of agriculture (itself double, and embracing the pasturage of sheep and cattle as well as the cultivation of crops), as well as that of coal and iron and industry ; and, again, that on the seas it offers, and has always offered, the possibility of fisheries as well as that of transport and commerce. Among all these possibilities the society of Englishmen has chosen—not once and for all, but again and again (with different choices and different results), at different epochs of history. From this point of view it follows that it is for the geographer to state the sum of possibilities ; it is for the historian to show the use which societies have made of those possibilities by the choice which they have made. It is in this sense that Eduard Meyer has written : " Nature and geography are only the substratum of the historic life of mankind ; they offer only possibilities of development, and not necessities. History is in no way prescribed or foreshadowed in the nature of any territory, though a territory is undoubtedly one of the given conditions of history. In human life the decision always rests with spiritual and individual factors, which use or neglect the given substratum, as disposition and will determine in each case." [1]

In the light of these considerations we can see the poverty, and the error, of the geographical conceptions of those historians who write a preliminary chapter on geography—at the beginning, for example, of a history of Greece—and then bid geography good-bye for the rest of their voyage through time. They are postulating (perhaps unconsciously, but none the less erroneously) a fixed environment, always and uniformly present, and *determining* human history in a constant way—the same (as it were) yesterday, to-day, and for ever ; they are forgetting that geography is a record of *possibilities*, which themselves (as we shall see) are by no means fixed or free from change, and among which man is constantly choosing from age to age. The record

[1] E. Meyer, *Geschichte des Altertums*, i. i. (3rd edition), p. 66.

of geography must therefore be considered in every chapter, and not only in an isolated chapter ; and it must be considered not as a uniform sum of determining forces, but as a variable area of possible choices. We must start from the assumption that again and again men make new possibilities for themselves. Man in his measure makes the earth and its geography, even if the earth and its geography also make him in their measure ; just as a nation makes its law, and the other spiritual factors of its life, even if that law and those spiritual factors in turn make the nation. " Fashioned, modified, adapted by man, the ' humanized ' earth without doubt reacts in turn upon him. But it is he who, in the beginning, has exercised upon it his power of transformation and adaptation." [1]   A territory is not simply a given natural datum : it is also in part a created and artificial thing. The territory of Italy contained one set of possibilities in the second millennium B.C., when it was still largely covered by primeval forests : it contained another set of possibilities in the second century B.C., when men had cleared the forest, had created the culture of the vine and the olive, and had introduced into their environment a new geographical possibility of their own making—when, again, they had realized their military and commercial needs, had built (or, as it runs in Latin, " fortified ") great roads that ran through marshes or over hills in defiance of natural obstacles, and had thereby once more introduced into their environment a new geographical possibility which once more was their own creation.

Human selection of possibilities, and human creation of possibilities—these are the essential things. It is true that the number of possibilities offered, and the volume or weight of each possibility in proportion to the rest, must necessarily limit or influence choice. But it is also true that man's choice determines his environment more than his environment determines his choice. And here a further consideration comes into view. As choice changes, it changes the environment ; and environment, therefore, is not always the same, or fixed and simple, but a shifting and complex thing. It is not merely that man makes or adds new features to the environment by his culture of crops, his roads, or his other creations : it is rather that, by his selection and preference of one set of possibilities (which may all be given and natural) at any given period of time, he fixes for himself the environment by which he will be influenced during that period, and that, when in another period he alters his selection and preference, he alters also the environment (as he may do without adding any new features or factors) by which his life will henceforth be affected. It is a matter of the direction of

[1] L. Febvre, *op. cit.* pp. 10–11. The passage is based upon the writings of Buffon.

attention and interest. A conclusion follows which may seem paradoxical. Just as the past, in the form in which it appears to the present, is not always the same, but varies from generation to generation ; just as the past shifts and veers according to the direction of attention and interest, and according as each generation emphasizes this or that part, or this or that aspect— so, and in just the same way, the spatial environment of men may change its character with the changing generations. A shifting past ; a veering environment—these seem difficult conceptions. But since the past lives in our minds, and our environment lives in our minds, and since our minds have their changes, the past and our environment are both at the mercy of change. So far as either is an active force (and not merely dead time or dead space), it is active in the form and to the extent of its residence in our minds ; and it must alter with the alteration of that form or that extent.

On the basis of these conceptions we may proceed to consider the bearing of geographical factors and possibilities on the growth of national character, particularly in Great Britain. Three inquiries naturally suggest themselves. The first relates to the external shape or outline of our territory, and it raises particularly the question of the possibilities implicit in an insular position and maritime frontiers. The second relates to the internal content of our territory and the general sum of its inner resources—its hills and its plateaux ; its plains and its valleys ; the geology of its rocks, the chemistry of its soil, and the bearing of both on the development of its agriculture and industry. The third relates to climate ; it is a matter of the barometer and the thermometer ; it leads us to questions of sunlight and temperature, humidity and storms, and the effects which they produce on the bodies and minds of men. In each inquiry, and whether we are dealing with external outline, internal content, or general climatic conditions, we shall be concerned with the study not of the action of nature on individuals, but of the interaction between a complex of natural possibilities, with all its hints and suggestions, and a society of men with its general will and purposes. We do not ask how Englishmen severally have been affected by seas or rocks or mists : we ask how the general society of Englishmen has reacted upon the geographical possibilities which it has found or created—how it has imposed its purposes on them, or adapted its purposes to them—in a word, what a group of men has made of a group of resources.

II

THE EXTERNAL OUTLINE

The mere size of a given territory, apart from its form or outline, may often be of importance. Jellinek has remarked that England was early and easily centralized, because it was small, and less than double the size of Bavaria.[1] But it is the insular form of our territory which is obviously of supreme importance. Great Britain was not always an island. There was once a connection with the Continent ; and even now " the Straits of Dover is so shallow, that were St. Paul's Cathedral sunk in it, the dome would rise above the water even in the deepest part." [2] There was once a connection also with Ireland, and a man might fare on foot from Norfolk to Donegal. The two breaks, and the formation of the two channels, are comparatively recent happenings. The first may help to explain why the round-heads from the Alpine regions (stopped, perhaps, by a new-formed sea) were so late in entering Great Britain and entered in such small numbers. The second may similarly help to explain why Ireland is more limited in the range and more primitive in the character of its human stocks (and also of its flora), and why, again, there was but little entry of the Nordic races into Ireland, and that little was mainly late. Once established, the insular form of Great Britain was full of new possibilities. We can hardly subscribe to the judgment of Bodin, who laid down the rule *insulani infidi*, citing the example of Odysseus of Ithaca, and anticipating the later taunt of *perfide Albion*. A natural partiality may incline us more readily to the dictum of Montesquieu, that " islanders tend more to liberty than the peoples of a continent," and we may remember that one of our own poets also has said that one of the voices of liberty is " of the sea." But these are at the best mere *obiter dicta* ; and if we place ourselves on the ground of science, we shall only remark that, owing to its isolation, the human stock of an island (like the human stock of peninsulas such as the Iberian or the Scandinavian) will be less mixed than a stock which is set in the crucible of a continent traversed by continual migrations, and again, for the same reason, more archaic in its character, unless, as in our own case, a recent immigration by sea has added new elements. In much the same sense biologists have observed that island fauna and flora are less in amount and more archaic in character, and often show a tendency towards dwarf formation, such as we may note, for example, in Shetland ponies. Vidal de la Blache has summarized admirably, in words

[1] Jellinek, *Allgemeine Staatslehre*, p. 76.
[2] H. J. Mackinder, *Britain and the British Seas*, p. 25.

which may well be quoted, the general tendencies of an insular territory: " Les îles . . . puisent dans un fond ethnique moins riche que les continents. Elles offrent le spectacle de développements autonomes, interrompus de temps en temps par des révolutions radicales. . . . Le cadre où elles sont contenues est pour elles une sollicitation permanente d'autonomie. . . . Cette autonomie, plus facilement réalisée qu'ailleurs, s'étend aux habitudes, au caractère, parfois jusqu' à l'histoire. . . . Mais nulle part non plus on n'a observé de changements plus radicales. N'est-ce pas dans les îles . . . que se sont produites, et là seulement que se pouvaient se produire, des ruptures telles que la substitution d'une Angleterre saxonne à une Bretagne celtique ? " [1] One may add that a perfect example of the breaches of continuity from which an island may suffer is Sicily—by turns Greek, Carthaginian, Roman, Byzantine, Arab, Norman, Angevin, Spanish, and Italian.

From considering an island as a form, marked by isolation, we may turn to regard it as an extent of coast, and a gateway to the sea. Regarded as an extent of coast, an island may afford a rich area of economic possibilities. If and provided that it is frequented by sufficient shoals of fish, and if and provided that the eating of fish (to which man seems less naturally inclined than he is to the eating of meat) has a certain vogue or encouragement, the long coast of an island may draw its people to fishing and the building of fishing-fleets for the sake of food. From that they may be drawn—if they have goods to export and goods which they would like to import—to trading and the building of merchant-fleets for the sake of wealth ; and from that again it is an easy step to maritime expansion and the building of battle-fleets for the sake of power. It is a process which moves from the herring-smack to the East Indiaman, and from the East Indiaman to the three-decker and the Dreadnought. It is the process which has actually marked our history ; and we may readily pronounce it inevitable. Is not a councillor of Henry VIII reported to have said, in 1512 : " When we would enlarge ourselves, let it be that way we can, and to which eternal Providence hath destined us, which is by the sea " ? But there is a whole millennium between the Teutonic settlement of Britain and the beginnings of any manner of fleet or enlargement by the sea ; and during all that millennium the possibility of the sea was dormant—dormant because men's minds were not directed in that way—and England lived an inland life of pasturage and agriculture. The sea is primeval ; but it is a recent factor in our history. Natural events and human inventions and policies had to co-operate before we became a seafaring people. It was a natural event of the first

[1] Lavisse's *Histoire de France*, I. i. p. 26.

order—an event which made history—when about 1416 the herrings left the Sound, and migrated to the coasts of Britain and Holland. That gave us a fishing-fleet. The inventions of the shipbuilders of Rye and other ports helped us to sail the seas farther and farther ; the policy of English traders, directed in the sixteenth century (and especially at its close) to the capture of the transport of cloth and other commodities from the Hanse, turned the possibility of the sea into an apprehended fact. In a word, we took to the sea by choice and not by destiny ; and we chose the way of the sea because we apprehended freshly a number of possibilities, some of which were old (if unnoticed before), one of which, at least, was new, and some of which were of our own making.

It is the apprehension of the possibility, and action on that apprehension, which matter. Ireland is an island—an island with a long coast and an open gateway into the Atlantic. She has fared differently from Great Britain in history (though it must be confessed that she has not been altogether free to determine how she should fare), and she has chosen the life of the land. The sea, after all, can act in different and indeed in almost opposite ways—just because it can be apprehended differently by different peoples or at different times. It may be a motive towards isolation ; it may be a spur to navigation and multiple contacts. Corsica and Sardinia are examples of the first ; Sicily is an example of the second. The same island may at one time be isolated, and at another a centre of busy relations. This is true of Japan ; it is also true of Great Britain —isolated from the Continent in Anglo-Saxon times, but rich in contact with it from the Norman Conquest onwards. In-sularity is certainly not the necessary temper of islanders, as the history of the islands of the Ægean long ago proved. On the other hand, an island cannot enjoy those " zones " of contact and influence which may extend for many miles on either side of a land-frontier, and may blend the inhabitants on both sides together. It has necessarily and inevitably a sharp frontier-line. Its people will feel the existence of this line, and they may cling to their local peculiarities, and feel themselves sharply distinct, when they cross to the mainland. Conversely, the people of the mainland will feel an immediate contrast as soon as they enter the island, and they may emphasize, and even over-emphasize, the difference which they feel. At the same time, the history of our own island is not really a history of division from the Continent. The *prima facie* and superficial impressions of difference begin to fade, or at any rate to dwindle, upon inquiry. Spiritually we are still, and always have been (what we once were physically), a part of the Continent. It is impossible nowadays to admit the distinction, once emphasized by historians, between English and continental feudalism. There was only one feudalism. The problem of municipal origins is fundamentally the same in England as in Western Europe ; and the manor was much the same thing in France as in England. We cannot isolate or insularize the process of our national history.

Yet there are some respects in which our island-frontier has affected our national life to special issues. Our constitution, for example, still bears the mark and attests the influence of our island-frontier. The influence of the character of its frontier on the life of a nation is always profound. Peoples with a long and exposed land-frontier (the people of France, for example, and still more the people of Germany) must inevitably feel a lively sense of the danger of a thrust against any point in the long line. Feeling that sense, they realize that the Executive must be strong ; its officers respected ; and their acts, as far as possible, unquestioned. If the Executive is to be a strong man armed, it must not be amenable to the ordinary courts (with all their cavils, inquiries, and delays) for its own executive acts or the impersonal acts of its officers. In this way there has arisen the Droit administratif of France and the Verwaltungsrecht of Germany. Both are based on a strong sense of *raison d'État*, which itself is based, in the last resort, on the problem of frontiers ; and both issue in the rule that executive acts, if they are questioned, should be questioned before special executive courts. In England we have gone along a different line—just because we could afford to do so. We have island-frontiers, and around us is the " moat defensive " of the seas. Upon occasion we have known alarms and the pangs of peril ; but we have not felt a constant sense of danger. We have not been driven to arm our Executive with any special powers ; we have not been led to institute any special system of administrative law ; and our Executive, with all its officers, has always been amenable to the ordinary courts and under the cognizance of the ordinary judges of the common law. This has been a great feature in our public life and an essential factor in our constitutional law ; and it has distinguished our life and our law from those of neighbouring nations. It is true that impulses of internal development have co-operated with the influence of external frontiers to produce this result. England, as we have already remarked, was early centralized ; and we may add that its centralization began in the domain of law, when, as early as the reign of Henry II, all persons and all cases were made subject to the common law administered by the king's judges. France (and still more Germany) achieved any measure of centralization at a later date ; and when centralization came, it came in the form of an extension of the powers of executive officials to new territories and fresh spheres of action.[1] An early centralization in the sphere of law necessarily affected national life and character in a different way from a late centralization achieved in the sphere of administration ; and here we may already see in advance the effects upon national character of an influence (that of the national system of law and government) which we shall have to consider more fully in a later chapter. But it is the influence of frontiers which, in the last resort, has permitted or controlled the development of law and government in this respect. We owe a large debt to that influence. The fact that the public official as well as the private citizen is subject to the law of the land has prevented the growth of officialism ;[2] it has helped to secure that " Rule of Law " which is the quintessence of our constitution ; and in that way it has aided in creating a spirit of law-abidingness (issuing in a firm imperative, " Keep firmly the laws you make, and make no laws that you cannot or will not keep "), which has been a very core of our national character. In the light of these considerations we may see a point in the dictum of Montesquieu, and we may admit that islanders have an advantage over the peoples of a continent in finding the road to a secure and guaranteed liberty.

If frontiers may affect the constitution, and thereby the internal life of a nation, it is obvious that they may also affect its foreign policy, and thereby the character which it shows to its neighbours. Our own peculiar insular position has certainly affected our policy and ourselves. On the one hand, our island, which was once part of the Continent, is still in close and immediate proximity ; and it has been drawn into constant contacts which have increased with every increase in the methods and rapidity of communication. On the other hand, we are not actually and physically part of the Continent, nor are we directly drawn into the fiery crucible of all its inter-actions and inter-relations. We have necessarily sought to influence the Continent ; but we have, no less necessarily, sought to influence it *ab extra*, and from a position of independence. The more thickly our sea-borne commerce and our maritime relations have ramified, the more keenly have we felt the need of protecting our interests, by some system of " understandings," against any threat of interference or interruption from the Continent ; and yet we have always feared any system of entangling alliances or any engagements which grappled us permanently, as it were, to the

---

[1] See A. L. Lowell, in the chapters on France in his *Governments and Parties in Continental Europe* ; and see also his *Government of England*, ii. ch. lxii.

[2] " It prevents every policeman or tax-collector from feeling himself an incarnation of the idea of the State ; and thus . . . the individualism of the people is preserved " (Hatschek, *Englisches Staatsrecht*, i. p. 93, quoted in Lowell's *Government of England*, ii. ch. lxii.).

shores of the Continent. Our interest has lain in a system of
Europe in which equal powers, or equal concerts of powers,
lived peaceably with one another ; and our method of securing
that interest has been that *justum potentiæ æquilibrium* (as it is
styled in one of the articles of the Treaty of Utrecht) which our
statesmen, and sometimes also the statesmen of the Continent,
have (wisely or unwisely) sought to secure. " A nation whose
strength depends upon the flourishing state of trade and credit
. . . whose commerce extends to all parts of the world . . .
must have a more extensive and particular interest to foresee
and obviate those troubles which, if not prevented in time,
might place so large a share of dominion in the hands of one
prince as to endanger the liberties of the rest, and consequently
interrupt her trade." [1] The policy of a balance of power, as it
has been pursued by English statesmen, has hardly made us
turn an attractive or engaging side to our continental neighbours. Its postulate has been a position of independence and
isolation, which could not but be annoying, because it could
not but suggest something of an attitude of superiority, to
those who felt themselves immediately and vitally engaged. Its
method was necessarily a method of changing alliances which
—constant as it was in opposing us to the designs of any power
(whether the Spain of Philip II, or the France of Louis XIV
and Napoleon I, or the Germany of William II) that seemed
set on too large " a share of dominion "—could not but appear
inconstant ; and the fruit of that method was a reputation not
only for inconstancy, but also for hypocrisy and perfidy—a
reputation which is not dead. The rise of a system of government by cabinets composed of the leaders of a dominant party,
coupled as it was with the vicissitudes of parties according to
the fate of elections, contributed to produce the same result ;
and when Harley and Bolingbroke supplanted the Whigs in
1710, and turned a war against France into the treaty of Utrecht
and an attempt at commercial alliance with France, they set
a precedent which was followed, and a memory which endured.
There is thus a sense in which we may subscribe to Bodin's rule
of *insulani infidi*, just as there is a sense in which we may accept
the dictum of Montesquieu that islanders tend to liberty.

· There are other operations of a frontier upon national
character or national reputation. (Reputation is by no means
always the same as character ; and a reputation for perfidy need
not always denote a perfidious character.) By its frontiers a
nation marches with another nation ; and as a man's character
may be affected by the company which he keeps, so the character
of a nation may be affected by the neighbours with which it

---

[1] Coxe's *Memoirs of Sir R. Walpole*, ii. pp. 137–138, quoted in Egerton's
British Foreign Policy in Europe, pp. 55–56.

comes into contact. England has been formed, in no small measure, ever since the days of the Norman Conquest, by contact with the genius, the policies, and the arts of France. France, more multiple in her relations by reason of her geographical position, has been largely formed by her contacts not only with the maritime aspirations and foreign policy of England, but also with the force of Germany, the culture of Italy, and the chivalry or the ambitions of Spain. England has tended to be a land of one contact, and if she has drawn on the Continent for her spiritual resources, she has tended to acquire her gains through the mediation of France : France, set in a far more central position, has drawn more directly, and has become a centre and a clearing-house of ideas which she has interpreted and diffused among her neighbours. There is another respect in which the difference of frontiers has contributed to differentiate France and England. The one has the given and obvious line of a maritime frontier ; the other, at any rate on the north and the east, fades away (as it were) into the indeterminate. The French have accordingly been led to cherish dreams of an ideal frontier, whether that dream took the form of insistence on the historic frontiers of ancient Gaul, or that of a belief in the natural frontiers assigned by nature herself to the people of France when regarded as one of her products.[1] The *ancien régime* might cherish the one conception, and the Revolution the other ; but the historic frontier agreed with the natural when both were translated into concrete terms, and in either form the dream of a frontier other than the actual has haunted the imagination of Frenchmen, and contributed with other factors (such as racial inheritance and the ambitions of absolute rulers) to create a military character zealous for expansion and avid of the glory of battle.[2]

III

THE INTERNAL CONTENT

Great Britain was once glacial ; and the Scottish glaciers covered the country as far to the south as a line drawn from the lower Severn along the course of the Thames. The south was thus the earliest centre of life ; and it continued to be the chief centre until very recent times. The general operation of geological factors on the course of our development may be seen

---

[1] A. Sorel, *L'Europe et la Révolution Française*, vol. i. book ii. ch. ii. and esp. § xi.
[2] L. Febvre, *op. cit.* pp. 366–371, deals with the conception of frontiers, and shows that any given frontier is a free human choice among a number of given possibilities. See also C. B. Fawcett's *Frontiers*, and Lord Curzon's Romanes lecture on the subject.

most clearly if we confine our attention to England and Wales and examine the distribution of its different strata and soils. England and Wales form an inclined plane, which rises from the south-east to the hilly regions of the north-west. Level and well-watered, and in close proximity to the Continent, the south-east has readily attracted invaders and immigrants. In this quarter the Celts and the Saxons entered from Gaul : in this quarter the Anglo-Saxons and the Danes entered from Low Germany and Southern Scandinavia. But though peoples have entered and settled readily in the south-east, they have seldom pushed far up the inclined plane ; and they have rarely crossed the Severn on the west or the Pennines in the north. It is not merely a matter of the difference between hill and plain : it is also a matter of a deeper difference. There is a line of geological division which runs across England and Wales from the Humber to the mouth of the Severn—or from Cleveland to the Cotswolds. It coincides with the trend of the Jurassic belt or escarpment. On the south-eastern side of the line are recent formations of chalk, oolite, and sands ; on the northwestern side are the more ancient formations of mountain limestone, millstone grit, and carboniferous measures. Geologically, the line of the Jurassic escarpment divides two Englands. Racially, economically, and for many centuries also politically, the same line marks a deep and important division.

" Old rocks, old stocks." The words are a natural jingle, and they express something of a natural tendency. The peoples of an older entry into a country tend to be pressed by the later comers into the older parts of that country. The older stocks of our country mainly reside on the older formations of Cornwall, Wales, and the Highlands of Scotland. The more recent invaders took the more recent formations, which in an agricultural age were the better, and drove the older peoples into the older rocks. One may trace the same tendency in France, where the old stock of the Bretons inhabits the archaic massif of Brittany. This co-existence of old stocks with old rocks is a co-existence of racial and geographical factors. We have to take both factors into account when we study the characteristics of an ancient people living on an ancient formation ; and we shall hardly be wise in assigning those characteristics exclusively to either factor. There is, for example, a distinction between the " nucleated villages " of Eastern England and the " scattered hamlets " of the west. Meitzen, in his work on *Siedelung und Agrarwesen*, would explain the distinction by considerations of race, making the nucleated village Teutonic and ascribing the scattered hamlet to Celtic origin. But geography as well as race affects the modes of men's habitations ; and a rocky and mountainous country, with scattered valleys, is a natural home of scattered hamlets, whatever may be the stock of its inhabitants, and even though inherited tradition may help to reinforce the suggestions of natural environment.[1]   Another, and a more crucial, example of the same tendency is furnished by descriptions of " Celtic temperament," which ascribe to the Celtic " race " a brooding melancholy over a past which is too often a past of defeat.   " They went to the battle and they always fell." Here again we have to remark that a defeated and evicted people, living under the shadow of ancient rocks, may readily develop a mood and temper of melancholy from the *genius loci*, whatever its original stock, and may even establish a tradition which is none the less due to history and environment rather than race. And we have to add that in any case the Celtic " race " is a myth, and that among the members of the Celtic language-group (for the Celts, as we have seen, are a language and not a race) there are included a variety of races.

Economically, the distinction between the north-west and the south-east was a distinction which for long centuries of our history was favourable to the south-east.   It was better adapted to agriculture ; and in days in which wool and wool-fells were our main export, and corn was our chief product, it was the home of our " greatest industry " and all its appurtenant industries. Again it was turned to the Continent, with which, in the times before the discovery of America, all our trade was conducted ; and it was therefore also the home of transport and general commerce.   The south-east was thus a place of industry and commerce, towns and cathedrals ; the north-west was the abode of fighting, marcher lordships, and castles.   This was the posture of the two till the end of the Middle Ages.   Commerce then began to flow westwards ; and England turned over as it were to its western side when the " Oceanic Revolution "—the discovery of America, and the opening of a maritime route to India—disclosed new and more lucrative prospects in the course of the sixteenth century.   Industry in its turn moved west and north two centuries later, and the Industrial Revolution set men to the mining of coal and the smelting of iron among the ancient formations.   The capital remained, and grew, in the south-east ; but with the exception of Norwich in the east, and Portsmouth and Southampton in the south, all the independent industrial towns with over 100,000 inhabitants now lie to the north and west of the Jurassic escarpment.   We have used the possibilities of our territory according to the different conjunctures of

---

[1] Conversely a French journalist, Jean Finot, in a work on *Les Préjugés de Race*, is willing to emphasize geography (in order to minimize race) to the extent of saying that according as men live on chalk or on other soils their teeth, their morals, and their pronunciation differ.   But teeth and morals and pronunciation may all be affected by racial inheritance as well as, or more than, by geological factors.

different centuries; and we have used them with different results to its different parts.

If we turn from considerations of race and of economics to the consideration of general politics, we shall find the distinction between the two Englands equally operative. The south-east was the area of the effective occupation of the Romans: they held in civil possession the land on and under a contour line of 500 feet, and left to military rule the higher ground in the north-west. The south-east was equally the area of Anglo-Saxon settlement and mediæval development. It became the home of government and literature, as well as of industry and commerce; and the English we speak to-day is sprung from the dialect of the East Midlands. The north-west was feudal and turbulent—traditional and sometimes reactionary; and the civil struggles of our history may be interpreted as the struggles in which it engaged with the more advanced south-east. In the Barons' War of the reign of Henry III the towns of the south-east fight for that "buccaneering old Gladstone," [1] Simon de Montfort: the West and the Marches stand for the king. The Wars of the Roses were wars between the Yorkists, representing the cause of "law and order," dear to the business men of the south-east, and the turbulent Lancastrians of the north-west. The Pilgrimage of Grace in 1536, the rebellion of Devon in 1549, and the rising of the Northern Earls in 1569, were reactions of the north and west against the Reformation of the south-east. The Civil War of the seventeenth century was roughly a struggle between a Royalist north and west and a Parliamentarian south and east.

Except in its racial expression (and even there the exception can only be made within limits), the geographical division of the two Englands is a matter of the past, and of economic and political history. But the geographical influences, or possibilities, which serve in their measure to affect the life and the character of a nation, are not only the influences or possibilities which are now in action: they are also, and even more, those which have acted during the past, and have acted (it may be) in different ways at different periods. The struggle of the two Englands has been an incentive to growth; and the very change which shifted the balance from the south-east to the north-west has meant that both have been fully enlisted (either in its own proper hour) for the whole of their contribution to the general national life. It is in this sense that the geographical factors operative in the past have helped to make us what we are in the present.

If we now turn from the parts to the whole, and from a consideration of division to a consideration of union, we may

[1] The phrase occurs in a letter of Bishop Stubbs.

say of our country, regarded as a single unit, first that it offers a wide range of possibilities, and next, that these possibilities are well spread over its surface. Of the possibility offered by our long and indented coast and its wide surrounding seas something has already been said. It is a possibility which leads to fisheries, commercial transport, and maritime expansion. The possibility was always there, and a good deal of our stock, from an early date, was of the roving Nordic strain which knew the ways of the sea. The possibility long lay dormant, as we have seen, because it was not focused by human attention or exploited by human choice ; and it was not till the close of the Middle Ages that we began to take to the sea, and a new and powerful factor was thus added to the influences which shaped our national character—a factor of audacity and adventure, of endurance mixed with a new gaiety, of chivalry that could sink to piracy and buccaneering, of inquisitive exploration which was based only too often on anxious greed. It was the solid if more pedestrian possibilities of the land which engaged men's attentions for the ten centuries between the Teutonic settlement of Great Britain and the close of the Middle Ages. Here it was a matter partly of pasturage, particularly of sheep, and partly of the cultivation of corn. The peculiar English use of the land has tended towards pasturage. The green grasses of England—that product of our moist skies which is so vivid, and so wonderful, when one returns home from a foreign country in the spring—are a very essential part of the internal content of our country, and they naturally incline us to the rearing of cattle and sheep. It was the rearing of sheep, and the production of wool for export, which was for many centuries the staple English activity. It may be that our rolling downs and gentle hills and moorland slopes invite the rearing of sheep : it may be that we have been fortunate or prudent in the strains we have bred. It is certainly true that wool was one of our chief exports in Anglo-Saxon times, and our staple export during the Middle Ages. Our general life for many centuries seemed pivoted mainly on wool.[1] Cistercian monasteries kept their flocks : one of our chief taxes was " the great and ancient custom " on wool ; many of our churches were built from the profits of its sale. It was on the stepping-stones, as it were, of wool that we climbed from a purely rural life to a life which included seafaring and industry. The desire to wrest the lucrative transport and marketing of wool from foreign shippers was a main incentive to the development of a mercantile marine. The desire to weave the wool which we had grown, instead of sending our crop to the Flemish looms, was equally

[1] Even now we breed one-sixth of the sheep of Europe, and our Empire produces one-third of the wool of the world.

5

a chief incentive to the development of our first great
industry

The cultivation of corn has always been with us. More
than once it has seemed to be threatened by an overgrowth of
pasturage. The enclosures of the sixteenth century, mainly
intended to secure fresh ground for the raising of sheep, were
a serious threat. The see-saw between pasturage and arable
cultivation, and the tendency of the former to overbalance the
latter, have constantly attracted the attention of Government.
Anxious for an independent supply of food in time of war, and
concerned to maintain on the land a large population from which
the army could readily be recruited, the Government long
directed its policy to the support of arable cultivation ; and a
crop of corn laws, from the fourteenth century to the nineteenth, attest its anxiety and prove its concern. It would
almost seem as if arable cultivation, under our geographical
conditions, and with the instincts embedded in our population,
was somehow against the grain. It is a possibility—a possibility to which attention has always been directed, and which
has been steadily emphasized by the State ; but it has always
been engaged in a fight, and sometimes a losing fight, with other
possibilities. If those who follow the plough are the backbone
of a country ; if they give steadiness, solidity, and virility to a
nation—we may well lament the fight and grieve for the losses.
Some will add criticism to their laments, and urge that the
system of great estates, with which arable cultivation has long
been connected in England, has been, if not its enemy, at any rate
an obstacle to its success. It may be so ; but it is only fair to
say that it was the great landlords who found out agricultural
inventions, made drains, and erected farm buildings. Perhaps
they profited by their labours ; but they also served the State
without pay (if not always without perquisite) as a matter of
duty incumbent on their estates ; and they were a factor in the
national life which we can hardly condemn. If arable cultivation has long been engaged in a struggle, we have to remember
that there are not only such things as landlords, but also uncertain skies—possibly, too, a lack of that racial strain which is
strong in the French peasantry—and certainly the distraction
of rival possibilities.

Of all other possibilities, that which for the last two centuries
has been the greatest is the possibility of mining—mining in its
widest sense, and mining with its connected industries. Mining
is at once comparatively recent and of a primitive antiquity.
The tin mines of Cornwall are mentioned in the most ancient
records of our island. Iron has been smelted in the Forest of
Dean continuously since Roman times. Lead was being mined
for export within six years of the Claudian conquest of Britain :

" Domesday Book" records the *plumbariæ* of Derbyshire manors, and the lead mines of the Peak may still be seen to-day. To the ancients Britain was a country of minerals : " It produces," writes Strabo, " corn and cattle and gold and silver and iron." In the eighteenth century it returned to its ancient character : it became again a country of minerals—not, indeed, of " gold and silver and iron," but primarily of coal and iron, and secondarily and consequentially of engineering, and of cotton and woollen factories using machines of iron and operated by the power generated from coal.[1] A possibility which had always been present in the older formations of the north and west now became dominant : England shifted to the other side of the Jurassic escarpment ; and mining, smelting, engineering, spinning, and weaving became the dominant activities of the nation. The profound social results of that change, in the way of specialization of work and urbanization of life, belong to a later chapter. It is sufficient to notice here the general national apprehension and use of an old possibility, in a new form, and on a vastly greater scale, and to reflect that, in some future age, other dormant possibilities may find their use, or new possibilities may be explored and exploited.

Seafaring, sheep-rearing, corn-growing, and mining—these are some of the main possibilities contained in that treasure-house of internal resources, from which our nation, like a prudent housewife, has brought forth in the appropriate day things new and old. We have seen how at different periods different choices have been made ; we have seen how, in the same period, different possibilities have competed with one another, and a choice has had to be made by deliberate policy between their rival claims. The wisdom (and the education) of a nation consists in the exploration and appreciation of the possibilities inherent in the content of its territory, and in the adjustment of its use of those possibilities at once to the needs of the hour and the circumstances of contemporary environment, and to the demands of a sound long-time development. In each age a balance has to be struck by thought, and a choice made by will. There is nothing constant in a territory, which entails constant and permanent consequences ; nor again can any decision be taken once and for all. There is a flux of possibilities ; and new decisions are always demanded to meet new situations. Our ancestors chose in their generation : their choice has been, in its measure, our destiny ; and we also have to choose in ours. We have reason to be grateful alike to our ancestors and to the wealth of the possibilities among which

---

[1] The machines of the earlier part of the Industrial Revolution were made of wood, and they were operated by water-power. But the iron machine and the use of steam were soon established.

they chose. That wealth of possibilities, which gave us the chance of seafaring and sheep-rearing, of corn-growing and mining, has been a stirring and provocative force in our development. We have not rested in any traditional way : from time to time we have chosen afresh, and struck out anew on a different line. There has been a dynamic quality in the rich sum of our possibilities ; and the formation of a type of national character which, if it is not marked by forethought and the planning of long policies, shows none the less both ready initiative of sudden design and prompt energy of execution, owes something to the nature of a territory which has been mobile in its resources, rich in its provocation, and exacting in the demands it has made on the will and the choice of the nation.

It remains to examine the nature of the distribution of the different possibilities which have just been indicated. Is one set here, and another there ? Is one part of our territory specialized in one direction, and another in another ? In a sense, as we have already seen, there is a division. Agriculture has flourished in the south and east ; coal and iron are set in the north and west. In another sense, the different parts of our country and its different possibilities are knit and dovetailed into a unity. The natural centres of each activity are multiple enough, and in each region (not to say county) the different activities are sufficiently intermixed, to make an homogeneous national life possible. North may differ from south, and east may differ from west. But Northumberland is a county not only of mining, but also (along the mouth of the Tyne) of seafaring and shipbuilding ; and it also breeds more than eight hundred sheep to each 1000 acres, which is as high a percentage as any in the country. At the other end, Kent has ships and sheep (as numerous as in Northumberland), and Kent is also developing coalfields. " Let us imagine that coal and iron had been confined to Scotland. Would there now be the same harmony . . . as actually obtains ? "[1] We have not, perhaps, that natural harmony and symphony of territory which makes France so wonderful a country, and has made her soil so strong a magnet to its inhabitants that they will hardly, or rarely, emigrate. We can hardly apply to England what Michelet (thinking of her soil) said of France: " La France est une personne."[2] On the other hand, if we have not the harmony and the self-sufficiency of France—if we have a certain top-heaviness (as of predominant coal and iron), and a large dependence

[1] W. MacDougall, *The Group Mind*, p. 129.
[2] Cf. Vidal de la Blache in Lavisse's *Histoire de France*, i. p. 50 : " L'Allemagne représente surtout pour l'Allemand une idée ethnique. Ce que le Français distingue dans la France, comme le prouvent ses regrets quand il s'en éloigne, c'est le bonté du sol. . . . Elle est pour lui le pays par excellence." We may almost say France is a soil, England an island, and Germany neither, but a folk.

on other countries for our food-supply—we have in most parts of our country that mixed life of various activities which makes each part responsive to a number of interests ; and we have that ease of general intercommunication which, added to the mixed life of the parts, makes possible the formation of an homogeneous public opinion. Lancashire has its peculiarities : it may sometimes think to-day what England will think to-morrow, and sometimes be thinking to-day what England was thinking the day before yesterday ; but with all its peculiarities it is not a Fronde, or a " cave," but an incorporate member in a single national life. On the whole, we may say of ourselves that we have enough to make something of, and that enough so distributed that we cannot readily fall into a clash of con-flicting local interests ; and yet not enough to make us inde-pendent of others, or so much contented with what we have that we cannot readily leave our country, for our country's eventual good, at the beckoning of either interest or adventure.

IV

THE CLIMATE

The effects of climate, as a *causa causans* of national life and character, have often been emphasized, and especially perhaps by French writers (such as Montesquieu and Boutmy), who have added to the study of English institutions and char-acter a period of residence under English skies and in English fogs, and have readily been led to explain their observations of the one by their experience of the other. Strabo (who was himself interested in the connection between the character of a country and that of its people) remarked nearly two thousand years ago that " the airs of Britain incline to rain rather than to snow, and in the atmosphere mist lasts long, so that, in a whole day, the sun is only seen for the three or four hours about midday." Our climate is indeed old and indigenous ; and it is a pity that Strabo was not sufficiently versed in the habits and literature of the Britons of his day to explain them by its effects. Strabo was not the first to be interested in climate and its effects.[1] The first discussion of the influence of climatic factors on social character (and even to-day it is still, in many respects, the most arresting) appears in a treatise on *Airs, Waters, and Places*, composed by a medical author of the school of Hippo-crates, who also wrote a treatise on *Epilepsy*, during the second half of the fifth century B.C. He was the founder of climatology ; and he attempted a comparative study, based on

[1] On Strabo and the author of *Airs, Waters, and Places*, see Wilamowitz-Möllendorff, *Griechisches Lesebuch*, pp. 184, 199–207.

his own original experience, of the climates of " Europe " and
" Asia "—that is to say, of the Greek mainland and islands and
of the western and northern coasts of Asia Minor. He takes
four factors into account—the character and contour of the
soil ; its rainfall and general humidity ; its temperature ; and its
changes of weather and frequency of storms. He is particularly
clear on the disadvantages of climatic uniformity and the value
of change (alike in temperature, rainfall, and wind) ; for " change
stimulates the spirit of man and prevents its stagnation " (§ 16),
and it thus explains the more martial and stirring spirit of
Europeans in comparison with the peoples of Asia (§ 16, § 23).
He notes that " the inhabitants of a country which is mountainous, rough, well-watered, and visited by great changes of weather,
are big and fit for endurance and courage, if they are at the
same time wild and savage ; the inhabitants of a valley-country,
which is moist and oppressive, with hot winds and warm water,
will hardly be big or well-made, but will incline to breadth and
be fleshy and dark ; they will be phlegmatic rather than choleric,
and of less native courage and endurance (*though law, if it were
applied, might produce these qualities*) . . .; the inhabitants of
high ground which is level, windy, and well-watered, will be big.
in body, but less courageous and of softer temper ; and where
the soil is bare, waterless, and rough, pinched by winter and
parched by the sun, you will find men hard, thin, well-built,
sinewy, and hairy, with diligence and alertness strongly marked
in their natures, self-willed and self-opinionated in temper and
passions, with an inclination to be savage rather than gentle,
quicker and of better judgment in the arts, and superior in
martial pursuits " (§ 24). It shows the writer's scientific
attitude, that he is no one-sided votary of natural causes.
Climate is indeed a cause, and a cause which deserves scientific
investigation ; but law—the product of the human spirit—is
also a cause. Asiatics are what they are owing to climate—
" and also owing to laws ; for most of Asia is under the rule of
kings, and where men do not govern themselves, but are under
masters," they behave accordingly (§ 16, § 23). Bodin was
only repeating this caution when he wrote, in 1570 A.D. (*De
Republica*, v. i.), that he dissented from the view (which he
ascribed to Polybius and Galen) that " the nature of sky and soil
changed the character of men by a certain necessary force,"
and when in opposition he argued that nurture, laws, and customs
had power to change nature. Possibly Plato, and certainly
Aristotle (the son of a doctor, and profoundly interested in
biology), were influenced by the writer of this treatise. Both
Plato and Aristotle are concerned with the description of ideal
States and the discovery of their proper geographical basis.
Soil and atmosphere, according to a passage in Plato's *Laws*,

influence the human mind and temper.[1] It is, however, the influence of the sea which he particularly discusses and particularly dreads. " It makes a people of shopkeepers ; it breeds double-dealing and perfidy ; it spreads a spirit which is faithless and friendless over the inner life of a State and over its relations with neighbouring States " (*Laws*, 705 A). This is a large accusation, which is repeated (if with less force) by Aristotle. But Aristotle is more concerned than Plato with the definite influences of climate, and he seeks to discover the climate best suited to produce the population best fitted for an ideal State. In the seventh chapter of the seventh book of the *Politics* he describes the peoples living " in cold places and round Europe " (by which he would appear to mean Thrace and the Balkans) as full of spirit but deficient in skill and intelligence, and therefore as free but without proper government of their own or power of ruling others. The peoples of " Asia " (to the climate of which he does not specifically refer, though by implication he suggests its heat) have intelligence and skill, but are deficient in spirit, and are therefore in subjection and slavery. The Greek stock, intermediate in the " places " which it inhabits, possesses the qualities of both the others : it exhibits both spirit and intelligence : it is therefore free, possessed of the best government, and capable of ruling all the rest if only (in place of its many city-states) it were united under a single government.

There is little depth in Aristotle's remarks, which are indeed singularly exiguous and are simply an obvious and unchecked application of the formula of " the mean." But Aristotle was Aristotle ; and his remarks made long voyages and had strange fortunes. They recur, and are curiously expanded, in a chapter at the beginning of the fifth book of Bodin's *De Republica*. Between the time of Aristotle and that of Bodin there had been a long reign of astrology. The notion of climatic influence had been confused with that of the " influence " of the planets on human fortunes ; and when men thought or wrote about the effects of climate on peoples and nations, they were moving in the circle of ideas which still survives in descriptions of " saturnine " or " jovial " or " martial " or " mercurial " temperaments. Bodin still moved in this circle. He argued, admirably enough, and with some novelty, that constitutions must be accommodated to the characters of peoples, as these were in turn accommodated to differences of climate. When, however, he came to distinguish climates, he followed Aristotle (though

---

[1] *Laws*, 747 D–E. To quote the paraphrase in E. B. England's edition : " Differences in the prevailing *winds*, and in the amount of *sunshine*, are either prejudicial or the reverse, just as the *drinking-water* and the *crops* impart benefits or evils to souls as well as to bodies."

he went into greater detail of geographical factors and historical examples) in dividing climates into north, middle, and south and giving the prize to the middle ; and he hardly improved upon Aristotle when he added that the three zones corresponded to three planets, and that Mars ruled the north, Jupiter the middle, and Saturn the south. There is wisdom, indeed, in his remark that law and government affect the characters of peoples, and that an absolute government may enfeeble the strong or a free government ennoble the weak ; but the wisdom, as we have seen, is as old as the author of *Airs, Waters, and Places.* Nor did Montesquieu greatly advance the cause of knowledge when, nearly two centuries after Bodin, he investigated the relations between laws and climate. Like Bodin, indeed, he taught the useful lesson of " relativity," and suggested that a uniform " law of nature " was contrary to nature itself, which varied climates as climates in turn varied laws. In scientific equipment he went beyond Bodin. He was a student of natural science, with an interest in anatomy and physiology ; and he had escaped from the astrology which trammelled Bodin, if he had perhaps fallen into Cartesian notions of mechanical determination. The science of his day was physical rather than biological ; and it did not help him either to envisage the problem of the relations of climate and society in terms of life and living interaction, or to illustrate the problem by any new body of knowledge. He moved in the traditional terms of Bodin, Aristotle, and the author of *Airs, Waters, and Places.* Climate is for him mainly a matter of temperature : he simply sees the antinomy of the hot and the cold, with its corollary of the dry and the damp. He has therefore no full apprehension of the cause he investigates ; and he gives no full account either of the modes of its operation or of the sum of its results. The hot and the dry, he believes, affect men's bodies, men's minds, and men's laws and institutions in one way ; and the cold and the damp produce opposite effects. Indolence is the product of the former, and energy of the latter ; with the one are conjoined slavery, the subjection of women under a system of polygamy, and absolutism ; with the other are conjoined their opposites. His remarks on the cold and the damp of England as the parents of English liberty are famous ; and when he adds the irritability which he thinks they engender to the energy which he believes they encourage in order to explain our impatience of control and our free institutions, he makes a suggestion which is new. When he treats of the attributes of soil, as distinct from climate, he simply uses the antinomy of sterility and fertility—the one productive of struggle, achievement, and liberty, and the other of contentment, stagnation, and servility ; and if he also distinguishes mountain and plain, we find that these are aspects of the sterile and the fertile, as the dry and the damp are corollaries of the hot and the cold. He assigns to islanders, as we have seen, the same trend to liberty which he attributes to mountaineers and the peoples of cold and damp regions ; and here his theory ends. It is all an artificial simplification ; and in its results the *Esprit des Lois* hardly goes beyond the treatise on *Airs, Waters, and Places* (which it resembles in the contrast drawn in its pages between Europe and Asia), while in original observation and genuine scientific poise it hardly goes so far.

It was natural, in the days in which men were simply regarded as all the descendants of a single historical progenitor, to explain the differences which, none the less, very obviously existed between their different varieties by a recourse to differences of climate. We have less to explain by climate than our forefathers thought they had ; and it is easier for us to approach more critically both the definition of climate and the consideration of its results. We have a far larger body of knowledge ; we can analyse what was before left indeterminate ; we can resolve climate into its elements, recognize the variety and the complexity of their combinations, and study their effects scientifically with a due regard to the operation of other causes (such as, for example, race or occupation) which may have produced, in whole or in part, the effects too readily assigned to climate.

Climate includes more elements than simple temperature. Temperature is one of its elements, and that in *two* forms : the form of the annual average, and the form of the range of fluctuations. Such fluctuation is a powerful influence, as the author of *Airs, Waters, and Places* again and again remarks : the same average temperature (let us say of 50 degrees) will produce very different results according as it is produced by a range which is only from 45 to 55, or by a range which runs from 15 to 85 degrees. In addition to temperature, in both its forms, climate includes also humidity, not as a function of temperature, but as an independent factor ; it includes light, again as an independent factor, the influence of which on our bodies and our minds we are more and more recognizing ; and it includes winds and storms and all disturbances of the atmosphere. These various factors, of which it is obvious that a number of different combinations are possible in different regions, and which must therefore be studied in regional combination rather than in abstract isolation, may operate in at least three ways. They may possibly affect physical form ; they may certainly, as observation shows, affect the energy of the human body and mind ; they may conceivably affect not only energy, but also the direction and attitude of thought and will.

Of the first of these ways of operation there is little which need be said here. The physical changes which have been remarked among the descendants of immigrants into the United States have been invoked as a proof of the effect of climate upon physique. They are taller than their fathers ; their faces, it is said, assume a square formation ; their feet and hands, it is reported, need special " American " shoes and gloves. Anthropologists are sceptical about these assumed effects of climate.[1] There are at least three other factors to be taken into account. One of these is racial crossing. A second, which is perhaps even more important, is change of occupation. The hard manual labour of an East European peasant in his native home may have affected physique and stature in one way ; the different methods even of agricultural work, and more especially the different demands of industry on the body, may affect the physique and stature of his descendants in the United States differently. Still another factor is change of diet and (it may be) of the hours of sleep and the possibilities of leisure. If we take into account these various factors, we shall hardly assign to climate the sole, or even the main, responsibility for changes in human physique in changed environments.

The influence of climate upon the energy of body and mind deserves a fuller consideration. The relation of climate to civilization, and of climatic changes (or " pulsations ") to the changes and cycles of civilization, has recently been investigated, in a number of works, by Professor Ellsworth Huntington. Under what conditions, he inquires, and in virtue of what factors, does climate affect that output of human energy, both mental and physical, which in turn affects and determines the course of civilization ? In order to answer the question he has compiled statistics, and constructed tables, to show the correlation between human energy and the various climatic factors of average and fluctuating temperature, of light and humidity, of wind and storms.[2] He comes to the conclusion that the English climate, at which Englishmen delight to grumble, is in many respects the best which they could possibly desire, alike in its advantages for health, its stimulation of energy, and its encouragement of work. In virtue of its climate England is a

---

[1] Cf. Pittard, *Les Races et l'Histoire*, pp. 16–17. His scepticism is shared by Febvre, *op. cit.* pp. 116 *sqq.*

[2] See his *Civilisation and Climate*. In measuring physical energy, he uses the records of production in different works and factories in different climates. In measuring mental energy, he is on more difficult ground ; and his measurements, partly based on school records and partly on the estimates of their own and of other countries made by scholars and men of affairs, are largely conjectural. It is indeed obviously difficult to assess the degree of the mental energy shown by Englishmen ; and even if it can be assessed, it has to be correlated not only with climate, but also with other factors—such as, for example, the freedom of English institutions.

natural home for a large population, living healthily, working energetically, and amassing a vigorous and growing national inheritance. We have in London an optimum average temperature through the year of some 50 degrees: we have an admirable seasonal range of fluctuations, from 64 degrees in summer to 38 degrees in winter ; and we have besides an invigorating range of weekly—and indeed of daily—changes of temperature. These are matters of the thermometer. The instability of the barometer, which makes our " weather " incalculable, is exactly what also makes it invaluable. Change, as the old Greek observer long ago noted, is a source of vitality. Body and mind both flag under uniformity ; quick movements of the air beget nimble spirits. We may accordingly thank the variable ocean winds which blow on us from the west ; we may thank the gentle but constant variations of our temperature, and even the swinging of the index of our barometers from " stormy," through " wind " and " rain," to sparse and infrequent periods of " set fair " ; and if we reflect sadly on the humidity, and even more sadly on the dull grey skies of our atmosphere, we may hug the comfort that while we are " sometimes unduly damp for long periods," we none the less " enjoy a relative humidity of not far from 70 per cent much of the time." [1] All in all, " England apparently comes nearer to the ideal than almost any other place. The climate is stimulating at all times, both by reason of abundant storms and because of a moderate seasonal range. It never, however, reaches such extremes as to induce the nervous tension which prevails so largely in the United States." [2] Charles II remarked even more tersely of England that " it invited men abroad more days in the year, and more hours in the day, than any other country." The moral of the observations of Professor Huntington and of Charles II is simple. If health and energy may be taken as the criteria of goodness, we have perhaps the best climate in the world.

Whether climatic changes have affected civilization, and changed the history and character of nations, we cannot here attempt to consider. There is perhaps some evidence for long-time cycles of climatic variation—not, indeed, in the matter of temperature, but rather in that of rainfall and storms. Periods of bad weather, here resulting in the growth of malaria, and there in famine and pestilence, may explain in some measure both slow movements of history, such as the decline of the Greeks and the Romans, and sudden violences, such as the popular risings (the Peasants' Revolt, the Jacquerie, and the upheavals

[1] *Civilisation and Climate* (3rd edition), p. 222. A relative humidity of 80 per cent appears to be best (*ibid.* p. 161).
[2] *Ibid.* p. 226.

in Florence and Ghent) which mark the latter half of the fourteenth century in Western Europe.[1] The decline of peoples is one of the mysteries of history. We see a general lowering of fibre and character ; we cannot trace its hidden springs. Some may blame a declining birth-rate and speak of " social suicide " ; some may accuse an excessive miscegenation (such as seems to have befallen the Romans) which swamped the native quality of an original stock by an admixture of discrepant and inferior elements. It is natural to plead climate also in aid ; but the evidence is far from sufficient to warrant a verdict of guilty. History is a tissue of many factors, and a web of many threads ; and though a prudent historian will do well to keep his weather-eye open, and to allow for the possible influence of climatic change when it is historically certain, he will also be wise to consult meteorological records, and he will probably find that, where they are available, they suggest a large measure of uniformity over any broad period of time. Jevons' theory of the eleven-year cycle of sunspots and its influence on economic crises may have its truth in the sphere of economics. In the sphere of general history, and still more in the large sphere of the making and modification of national character, we can hardly allow any weight to the influence of climatic cycles.

On the other hand, we may admit that the same conditions of climate may have produced different effects at different times, and that in days in which men lay more openly exposed to the rigours or the stimulus of climate they were more readily amenable to its effects. Without supposing changes in climate, we may thus suppose changes in climatic influence. Civilization is, in this matter, a great umbrella held over our heads. It enables us to defy the weather. We are less at its mercy than our forefathers were a hundred years ago, as they were less at its mercy than their predecessors a thousand years before ; and both again were less affected than the earliest men who inhabited our island. In this sense, and so far as climate is concerned, geographical influence diminishes with time. In another sense, and if we take a broad view of all its factors and do not restrict ourselves merely to climate, that influence may well appear to be constant, and may even seem to increase. The man of to-day has a livelier sense of all the possibilities of his environment, and a livelier disposition to adapt himself to them more closely in order to exploit them more fully, than ever his primitive ancestors possessed. The savage might obstin-

[1] Huntington, *op. cit.* pp. 325–326, deals with climatic conditions about 1350 A.D., which, he suggests, were bad from China to California. On the other hand, the number of severe winters from 1200 to 1450 A.D. seems steady at the rate of thirteen in every fifty years. See Sir R. A. Gregory's Presidential Address to the Geographical Assocation (1924) on " British Climate in Historical Times."

ately maintain some way of life, which he had preserved by tradition, in the teeth of a new environment and with a flat disregard for its suggestions. Modern man stoops far more ; but he stoops to conquer. The one might defy his environment—and be bent by it : the other obeys his environment—and controls it.[1]

We have finally to inquire whether the climate of a country affects the general direction and attitude of thought and will in a people—or, in other words, whether it influences national temper. Here we enter a region of conjecture, and we begin to walk through an unknown country in the dark.

" Ibant obscuri sola sub nocte per umbram."

To speak of the influence of climate on the character of peoples, says a French writer, *c'est vouloir expliquer le vide par l'arbitraire*.[2] National character is not *le vide* ; but the explanation of it by climatic influence may well become *l'arbitraire*. Science proceeds by measurement. You can measure physique, and you can correlate your measurement with measurable factors of climate. You can even measure energy (though the criteria by which you measure are not very certain) ; and here again you can correlate your measurement with the figures of the thermometer and the barometer. You can hardly measure the temper of a nation ; and the factors of climate by which national character may be held to be moulded are themselves impatient of measurement. The result of any attempt to correlate national temper with some selected element of climate may well be an airy speculation, such as appears, for example, in Émile Boutmy's work on the political psychology of the English people. The humidity of our atmosphere, he supposes, is such that we are driven into an activity of work or exercise to counteract its effects ; and hence we must always be doing, and are for ever consumed by a passion of action. Again our grey skies (on which Strabo remarked many centuries ago) prevent us from seeing objects in definite outline or warm colouring. Debarred in this way from a clear perception of objects themselves, we are also debarred from making pictures in our minds, on the basis of our perceptions, by the use of creative imagination, or from making generalizations in our minds by reflection on what we have seen ; and thus, with the gates of imagination and generalization barred against us, and artistic and philosophic gifts denied to us, we seek and we find a compensation for realms we cannot enter and gifts we cannot attain by the feverish activity of an indomitable will.[3] We are, in a word, to

---

[1] See Miss Semple, *Influences of Geographic Environment*, pp. 69–71 ; L. Febvre, *op. cit.* pp. 428–434.
[2] L. Febvre, *op. cit.* p. 130.   [3] É. Boutmy, *op. cit.* (Eng. trans.), pp. 1–20.

use a latter-day term, a people of " introverts," who can only escape from the prison of self by the aid of some artificial stimulus : we stand opposed to the " extrovert " nations whose members gaily flow outwards, in the effervescence of their own natural spirits, into harmony with a surrounding world which stands obvious and comprehensible, in a laughing sunshine, before their eyes.

Such speculations, dear to French writers, are another form of that astrology which appears in Bodin. They rest on the assumption of an " influence " assumed to be exercised, not indeed by planets, but by mist and cloud and rain, on disposition and temper. It is no longer a matter of Saturn and Mercury : it is a question of Brumaire and Pluviose. We are not dealing here with a matter of science : we are hardly dealing even with a matter of speculation, in the stricter sense of the word. Speculation may one day be verified ; but a guess which remains a guess admits of no verification. There is, it is true, a way in which these guesses may be to some extent tested. Englishmen live in climates other than that of England. We have grown into an Empire ; and within that Empire, under other skies and in other climates, our countrymen have built societies, which are already of the dignity and dimensions of nations. Have we become something different in each place—in Canada and in Australia, in South Africa and in New Zealand—or have we, along with some measure of difference, retained a fundamental unity ? And if we are different, or in so far as we are different, is the difference due to differences of climate, or to the development, on new lines, in new surroundings, and under new conditions of life, of a cutting which initially may have had some slight variety of its own from the mass of the parent stock ? [1] On the whole, it would appear that there is the fundamental unity of a common English temper behind the differences, and that the differences which exist are due not to new skies or a new climate, but to the new conditions of colonial life, which engender a more restless and enterprising temper—that " colonial " temper which, from the days of the colonies of the ancient Greek city-states in Asia Minor and South Italy, has always distinguished the colony from the mother-country. We may therefore conclude that, so far as the test of our Empire goes, it leads us to discount the influence of climate on national character. The Australian has his differences from his kinsmen in England—differences alike of physique and temper ; but in both respects the differences are compatible with a basic unity, and in both respects they may be explained, so far as they exist,

[1] The Puritan settlement in New England, for example, early in the seventeenth century, was a " variety " or " mutation " from the general English stock of the time.

by the influence of new occupations and a new way of life rather than by the influence of a new climate.

But we cannot yet dismiss, as a *res judicata*, the question of the effect of climate on national temper. Climate certainly does not explain everything; but it may explain something. We have to remember, in the first place, that climate works slowly, if it works at all, and that its effects are long-time effects. We in this island have been weathered for many centuries by the play of wind and rain and sun and cloud; and we may well have been affected more than the Australian, in his far shorter national life, has yet been affected. We have to remember, in the second place, that the effects of our climate may seem one thing to the foreigner, who notes only its strange peculiarities, and another to us, who know rather its established intimacies. We may reflect accordingly that in our own experience the mark of our climate is its uncertainty (*varium et mutabile semper*); and we may ask whether this quality of uncertainty—favourable, as we have seen, to physical energy—may not also produce, or at any rate encourage, certain qualities of the mind. For long centuries we were an agricultural people. To practise agriculture in uncertain weather is to learn not to make plans ahead, but to seize the occasion with a ready initiative, and to improvise for the emergency the measures which it demands. To distrust foresight (perhaps unduly) and to cultivate insight (perhaps with too large a temerity)—this will be a natural tendency. A people prone to such a tendency may seize opportunity by the forelock with a prompt response to the need of the hour

("Fronte capillata, post est occasio calva"):

it may show a rich individuality in design and execution; but it may readily fall into opportunism—being afraid, and almost incapable, of making plans for to-morrow—and it will rely on a genius of improvisation, having for its hero (if altogether unconsciously) the Greek statesman of whom Thucydides wrote that he was "the best, by force of nature but with the minimum of preparation, in improvising whatever was necessary."[1]

Initiative and individuality are the obverse of the character of such a nation: an opportunist habit of "muddling through," and a capacity for seeing to-day's small symptoms rather than last year's general tendencies or next year's general necessities—these are the reverse. We have, indeed, in an unpremeditated way, built a great constitution and a wide empire; but the outbreak of a European war, or the coming of a social crisis, may find us groping with our lamps untrimmed, and we love

[1] Thucydides, i. 138.

the easy way of tinkering with difficulties far more than the effort of a real solution. And yet, in the sphere of practical affairs, we are perhaps wiser than we know. Who knows to-morrow, or what it will bring ? The conduct of practical affairs is like tacking before an uncertain wind towards an uncertain harbour. It may be that we tack too obviously. Our goings look like uncertainty; they may be interpreted as a Machiavellian duplicity; and a charge of perfidy is also readily brought against a people of so baffling a motion. And yet we arrive.

These may seem to be large conclusions hung on a little peg. " Even if we are like this," some may say, " and even if we do these things, what has it to do with the weather ? We are not all farmers ; and even if we were, the English farmer, for all his exposure to the stimulus of a variable climate, hardly resembles the Greek statesman who was ' best in improvising whatever was necessary.' " The objection has its force ; but no more has been urged than that the mutability of our climate, if it has not produced, may at any rate through the long centuries have helped to encourage some national characteristics which are now so engrained that we carry them with us wherever we go. There is another characteristic, often noted by observers, which may also have grown under a similar encouragement. We have a steady national habit of grumbling at ourselves and everything which is ours ; but there is a smile behind the grumble, and it is a sense of humour which really inspires what is only a mock indignation. It is not irony—though it has something of the quality of an inverted irony, which exaggerates what is not really felt to be serious. It is not satire or sarcasm—for there is no intention to chastise or to wound. It is rather a matter of good-humoured self-caricature. It has been called by the name of " humorous grousing." Perhaps it began with the weather : it has certainly sharpened its edge on the vagaries and inclemencies of the weather ; but it readily exercises itself, by a ready transference, on other themes—the conduct of Government, the course of trade, or the speed of the trains of a particular railway. It is a habit particularly affected by soldiers ; [1] it lightened the miseries of the trenches in the war ; it is a safety-valve for the feelings, and it may serve as an armour against despondency and a very nerve of endurance. " What we cannot alter," wrote Horace, " is made lighter for us by patience." An Englishman makes what he cannot alter more tolerable by a grumble. He takes the rough with the smooth ; but he has his revenge by making the rough into a mountain—and laughing at the mountain. The origins of this idiosyncrasy may well

[1] The word " grousing," of which the etymology is unknown, is drawn from army slang.

transcend the scope of English climate. It remains a happy idiosyncrasy—so long as a laugh goes with the grumble, and the grumble ends in a laugh. If the two are divorced, the grumble may become a boring iteration—or it may grow into a dangerous snarl.

V

The general consideration of territory and climate, which, in its various aspects, has been the theme of this chapter, not only throws light on our past development : it has also a practical and civic importance in the immediate present. If it helps to explain the past, which is still in us, and therefore still with us as part of our present, it also suggests questions about the present when we regard it, in another of its aspects, as issuing into the future. Here we recur to that theory of possibilities on which we have already dwelt. In each age, we have seen, a nation is forced, under the urgency of its development, to find the possibilities in its environment which are most opportune to its needs ; and by its use of those possibilities, and the consequences of that use, it affects its own temper and character. We have seen, too, that national action and character, so far as they are influenced by any geographical factor or complex of factors, are not influenced in a constant and uniform way. It is true that the shape and outline of a territory are permanent in themselves (except in so far as frontiers may change) and permanent in their effects ; it is true again that climate (though it may have its variations, and may exercise a diminishing influence as civilization interposes a thicker veil between man and its impact) is uniform both in itself and the effects which it tends to produce. But the internal content and resources of a country vary with the variations of human attention and exploitation ; and these variations affect in their measure the growth and the changes of national character. In our country, for example, after the early part of the eighteenth century, we saw and we used the possibilities of the carboniferous measures of the northwest for the production of coal, and the possibilities of the humidity of Lancashire for the production of cotton. Exporting our coal and our cotton in return for food, we increased our population vastly (with results upon national temper which fall to be considered in the next chapter), and we turned a community which had been largely agricultural into a great industrial and commercial State. To-day the world is changing before our eyes. The countries which grow raw cotton are beginning to manufacture for themselves the cotton which they grow ; our coal has rivals in Germany and the United States (not to speak of the resources which may yet be discovered in China) ; and at the same time, under that law of economics by which

6

the older and dearer article is constantly being ousted by the newer and cheaper

> ("The priest who slew the slayer
> And shall himself be slain"),

it is being threatened in its present markets by the growth of hydro-electric power and the increasing use of oil. What possibilities, inherent in our territory, are we to seize, if coal and cotton go, and we still desire to maintain at its old or an even higher standard of comfort the great population which has hitherto rested on foundations that are now insecure? That is the riddle of the present ; and it is here that the idea of changing possibilities has its comfort. A sane and vigorous people will not be defeated even by the exhaustion (and we have not yet reached the point of exhaustion) of its old possibilities. It will seek new possibilities, and it will not cease from seeking until it finds. We have still coal supplies for some hundreds of years ; and we have not yet properly explored all the possible uses of coal. We may make more of our agriculture than we have ever done ; and even in the way of manufacture we may yet, with cheaper power, produce a greater store of commodities by methods of specialization which we have still to discover. We have to think not only of our island and its resources : we have also to think of the many parts of the earth to which we are linked, and of the possibilities which they have still to reveal. The Empire is not a name ; and " this realm of England is an Empire" to-day in a broader and deeper sense than Henry VIII ever dreamed. There are resources still to be found and used ; and we may make ourselves a new people by their discovery and development. Our danger is not a failure of natural resources : it is rather that we should let the ardour of our energy and the curiosity of our initiative be dulled, and that we should permit the appetite for work, which was once our native quality, to drain itself away in a round of amusement, or to sink into the repetition and routine of a mechanical industry, uninspired by a free spirit of co-operation, and only disturbed by industrial struggles and "crises."

LIST OF BOOKS

BODIN, J.—*De Republica*, v. i.
BOUTMY, É.—*The Political Psychology of the English People* (Eng. trans.), 1904.
BRUNHES, J.—*La Géographie humaine*, 1910.
BUCKLE, H. T.—*History of Civilisation in England* (vol. i. ch. ii.), 1867.
DEMOLINS, E.—*Les Grandes Routes des peuples : comment la route crée le type social*, 1901–1903.
FAWCETT, C. B.—*Frontiers*, 1918.

FEBVRE, L.—*La Terre et l'Évolution humaine* (in *L'Évolution de l'Humanité*), 1922.

HUNTINGTON, E.—*Civilisation and Climate*, 1915 (3rd edition, 1924).

MACKINDER, H. J.—*Britain and the British Seas*, 1904.

MEYER, E.—*Geschichte des Altertums (Einleitung)*, 1910.

MONTESQUIEU.—*De l'esprit des Lois*, Books XIV.–XVIII.

RATZEL, F.—*Anthropogeographie*, 1882, 1891.

RIDGEWAY, W.—"Influence of Environment on Man," *Journ. Roy. Anthr. Inst.*, xi., 1910.

SEMPLE, Miss E.—*Influences of Geographic Environment*, 1913.

TAINE, H.—*History of English Literature*, vol. i., Introduction.

VIDAL DE LA BLACHE, P.—*Tableau de la géographie de la France* (in Lavisse's *Histoire de la France*, 1905).

CHAPTER IV

THE ECONOMIC FACTOR: POPULATION AND
OCCUPATION

I

FROM the physical factors of race and climate, which
have been considered in preceding chapters, we now turn
to two others, so closely related that they may readily
be regarded as functions of one another—the factors of volume
of population and the nature and variety of social occupation.
Both of these factors lie in the economic sphere : they are
mutually dependent—different sets of occupations requiring for
their prosecution different volumes of population, and different
volumes of population demanding for their maintenance
different sets of occupations ; and they may accordingly be
grouped together under the single designation of the economic
factor. Like the similar factors of race and climate, and along
with them, the economic factor serves to constitute the material
basis of national life and character. Population is a material or
physical fact ; and occupations which are directed to the production of material commodities are from that point of view a
part of the physical order of nature. Both of these physical
facts, like the physical facts of race and climate, affect the nature
and the development of the inner life of a nation. A tightly
packed population has one effect upon national character ; a
thinly spread population has another ; and industrial occupation (which is generally a concomitant of a dense population)
has a different effect from agricultural. But if, in its nature and
its effects, the economic factor, composed of these two elements
of volume of population and nature of occupation, is similar to
the factors of race and climate, it has none the less its own
characteristics ; and it differs from the other two in one important respect. Race and climate are almost entirely physical
data ; and although in some degree they are subject to human
control, and may be altered by human agency, they remain on
the whole the material constants of national evolution. The
growth of population has indeed its physical aspect, and it is
subject to the physical control alike of the soil and its crops and
of disease and its ravages ; but it has also and equally been

regulated, throughout recorded history, by the control of social purpose and social institutions. Occupations also have their physical aspect ; they are, in their measure, dictated by nature and the resources which she provides ; but they are also, in an even larger measure, the inventions of man, and they may be varied, as we have seen, by the choice which he makes among the resources and the rich " possibilities " of nature. It follows that the economic factor, in its influence on national character, is an intervening ground, or half-way house, which lies between the more purely material and conditioning factors of race and climate, and the more purely spiritual and determining factors of law and government, of language and literature, of religion and education. Combining as it does both matter and spirit, it is a factor of double influence, serving at once as a natural power and an expression of human purpose. The great economic development of the last century and a half, since the beginning of the Industrial Revolution, with all its vast changes, has added a new momentum to the inherent weight of this factor. We are now in danger of falling into an almost exclusively economic interpretation of national history and national destiny ; and when, as is too often the case, the economic interpreter falls in his turn into one-sided economics, directed only to the material woof, and oblivious of the spiritual warp with which that woof is threaded, an economic interpretation, falsifying the double nature inherent in economic facts, may become a purely materialistic interpretation. We have to remember that the economic is only one aspect of human life, and only one factor in national development ; that political and religious ideas and institutions, as well as literature and the general forces of education, are also creative agencies in the growth of all civilizations. We have no less to remember that economics must reckon with human purposes and values, no less than with material objects and forces, and that any account of the economic factor in the formation of national life and character will be halt and maimed if it fails to include the action of social ideas and the play of social choice.

Population, regarded in terms of quantity, and as consisting of this or that mass, is something different from population when it is considered in terms of race, and as consisting of such and such stocks settled side by side in such and such proportions. It is a matter not of the shapes of different heads, but of the quantity of all heads counted indifferently. The only question is that of density. The degree of the density of its population affects a nation in two different ways. In the first place, it helps to determine the national standard of life. The wealth of a nation, and the amount of a nation's income which is available for distribution among its members, are quantities which vary with the quantity of its population. A given addition to the population may produce a much more than proportionate addition to wealth and income ; and a growing population may thus increase (if in different degrees) the prosperity of all its members. More important, alike in itself and for the purposes of this inquiry, is the effect of different degrees of density of population on the national standard of conduct. The welfare of a nation, as well as its wealth—its character, no less than its comfort—are affected by any large movement in the mass of its population. A crowded and urbanized society is different from a society which still remains spacious and rural. A difference in quantity produces a difference in quality ; and there are virtues and vices inherent, or apparently inherent, in numbers, which compel us to regard an increase of population as not merely a material but also a moral fact

We cannot isolate density of population from the nature of national occupations. The one is mainly, if not entirely, relative to the other. The same soil supports one density of population if the occupations followed are those of hunting and fishing ; another if they are mainly pastoral ; another still, if they are a combination of arable culture with pasturage ; and still another if industry is added, and added as the predominant partner, to agriculture. It is the last of these stages which is marked by the greatest and the most sudden change. The population of England and Wales, at the time of the Norman Conquest, may just have exceeded 2 millions. It multiplied itself by three in the seven succeeding centuries ; and it was estimated at 6¾ millions in the year 1760, in which George III came to the throne, and the Industrial Revolution began to create an industrial England. In the century and a half from the accession of George III to that of George V, it multiplied itself by more than five, and rose from 6¾ millions to 36. There could be no more striking proof of the relation of density of population to the nature of national occupation.

Modes of occupation not only affect the national standard of conduct indirectly, through the effects which they tend to produce on the density and the volume of national population : they also exercise a direct and immediate influence. Men are like the dyer's hand, subdued to what they work in. Each profession produces a certain temper or habit ; and each has, in a sense, its own code of honour. Aristotle long ago remarked, in the first book of the Politics, that the modes of men's lives differ according to the ways in which they get their food. He distinguished the fisherman and the hunter (with whom he curiously linked the pirate) ; the shepherd, who follows the laziest of occupations, "and leads an idle life, getting subsistence without trouble from tame animals, wandering with flocks, and cultivating a sort of living farm "; the husbandman; and what he regarded as the more dubious vocations of the retailer and the usurer. Each of us to-day, in the range of his daily observation, can still trace the effect of occupation on outlook and behaviour, as well as on face or physique. The profession of the law refines the judgment, as it chisels the face. If we know a miner by his gait and his carriage, we know him also by the dogged perseverance with which he fights his battles. If the textile worker is stunted by his work, he has also an ingenuity worthy of the ingenious machines which he controls; and a Lancashire man may even dream that the towns of his county in which the " finer counts " are particularly handled have even greater liveliness than those which deal more specially with the coarser.

A nation is a sum of occupations; and though it may seem at first sight as if different nations, each composed of the same sum of different occupations, were in this respect identical, reflection will readily lead us to other conclusions. There may be the same sum of elements; but the proportions in which these elements are mixed will always differ. The amalgam of occupations which constitutes a nation in the economic aspect of its life will therefore vary, in its quality and composition, from nation to nation; and the peculiar quality of the amalgam will tend to impart a peculiar temper and a peculiar habit of life to the whole of a nation. The predominant occupation, or group of occupations, of a given nation will affect its outlook and way of life; and a nation based, in the main, on an agricultural peasantry will differ from one which is predominantly based on an artisan body of miners and weavers. Not only does each occupation affect the lives of its members; the national amalgam of occupations which marks and distinguishes a nation affects the general national life.

We may test these hypotheses by a cursory review of English development in so far as it has been affected by the general nature of national occupation and the general volume of national population. In the first beginning of such a review we cannot but note that there is a great divide about the middle of the eighteenth century. It is called by the name of the Industrial Revolution. The coming of the revolution had been heralded and prepared during the century which succeeded the Revolution of 1688, partly by a development of natural science (more particularly in the field of physics) which smoothed the way for invention, and partly by the growth of an acquisitive temper and accumulation of private funds, which made a system of large-scale industry at once congenial and possible. Whatever its preparation, the revolution was a revolution indeed; and it changed profoundly both the material framework and the general habit of men's lives. It is comparable, in its profundity, to the prehistoric revolutions of culture, such as that which substituted the age of bronze for the age of stone. Before 1760 men had lived for millennia a daily life—in ploughing and harvesting, in spinning and weaving, in their methods of communication and modes of transport—which had varied but little from that of Sumer and Akkad about 5000 B.C. After 1760 it might seem as if a voice had said, " Behold, I make all things new." It was the age of the machine. The machine, applied to production, altered the houses in which men lived, the places in which they worked, the clothes they wore, the food they ate. Applied to transport, it made human movement far more free and far more speedy ; it drew men together in larger groups ; it undermined the old little local societies and habits and dialects. In both of its applications, the machine revolutionized human relations ; it created a new economic society, in which men were differently grouped, worked differently, felt differently, and developed a different temper and disposition.

In the period which lies on the further side of the great divide, England had been for centuries an agricultural country. She had grown corn ; she had also bred sheep for the sake of their fleeces on her many pastures. The breeding of sheep had made possible a large export of raw wool to the Continent. During the Middle Ages that export, as we have seen,[1] was the pivot and the peculiarity of our national system of economics. The profits of the wool trade furnished a large part of the national revenue : they produced and enriched new classes of society ; and they were the incentive of social movements—enclosures and re- bellions against enclosures—as late as the sixteenth and seven- teenth centuries. At an early date, and by the end of the thirteenth century, it had already become an object of national policy that wool should be handled and manufactured at home, instead of being manufactured abroad ; a cloth industry—the first, as it was long the greatest, of our industries—was gradually established ; and the export of manufactured cloth began to take the place of that of raw wool. In addition we resolved— and by the end of the sixteenth century we had managed to secure—that the shipping of our exports, whether of raw wool or of manufactured cloth, should belong to ourselves and our own merchant vessels, and should no longer be handled by the Hanseatic merchants of the North German ports. The develop- ment of fisheries, and specially of the herring fishery, had already begun : a fishing-fleet was the natural precursor of a mercantile marine, and fishermen prepared the way for master mariners and " navigators." Starting with agriculture, and with agri- culture which was mainly pastoral, we had thus added, by the end of the reign of Elizabeth, three other things—a cloth in-

---

[1] See above, p. 65.

dustry, a transport trade, and a certain amount of fishery.   In the whole development the sheep and the herring had been of peculiar importance ; it was the combination of the two (the sheep providing the material for transport, and the herring impelling men to frequent the seas) which led to the growth of sea-borne commerce ; and our arms, if we had followed a " canting " heraldry and sought to show our foundations, might well have displayed a couchant sheep by the side of a herring regardant.[1]   But though our economic system had become more complex, and though new occupations had been added, agriculture long remained the predominant occupation which coloured the national life.   Down to 1757 we regularly exported more wheat than we imported ; and it is only in 1759 that we may be said to have ceased to be an exporting country.[2]   The density of our population was naturally adjusted to our economic system.   With a slight tendency to increase, the population was on the whole stationary until 1760.   It had been estimated about 1688 that there were 5,500,000 persons in England and Wales ; and it was estimated in 1760 that there were 6,750,000. England and Wales were thus comparable with France, which was also (as, unlike England and Wales, it has continued to remain) an agricultural country.   If they, with 58,300 square miles and a population of 6,750,000, counted 115 to the square mile, France, with about 200,000 square miles and a population of about 25,000,000,[3] counted some 125.   We shall only realize the significance of these figures if we remember that there are now 649 persons to the square mile in England and Wales— and in France 187.

We shall have to consider presently the general bearing on national character of what has just been said in regard to the occupations, and the density of population, in England and Wales before 1760.   For the moment we may cross to the other side, over the great watershed of the latter half of the eighteenth century, and seek to observe the fundamental changes which have made themselves clear by the end of the nineteenth century. It is like crossing from an agricultural valley, over the hills, to

[1] The token peculiar to our coins was neither, but a ship.   It first appeared on the gold noble struck by Edward III after the capture of Calais in 1347.   By the fifteenth century the author of the *Libel of English Policy* is already suggesting that a sheep would be more appropriate than a ship.   But the ship continued to figure on our coins for many centuries ; and it was only about the time of the Diamond Jubilee of 1897 that the ship (with the lighthouse) disappeared from our pennies, and left Britannia sitting, trident in hand, on the solitary waves.

[2] Curtler, *Short History of English Agriculture*, p. 349.   In 1750 we exported nearly 1,000,000 quarters of wheat, and imported 279.   By the beginning of the reign of Victoria our export of wheat sinks to a figure of under 50,000 quarters, and our imports rise to over 3,000,000.

[3] The population of France in 1801 was 27,000,000.   It may be conjecturally estimated at 25,000,000 in 1760.

look down on a country of chimneys and factories ; as if one climbed from the valley of the Usk, over the shoulder of the Brecknock Beacons, to look upon Merthyr Tydfil. The woollen industry has grown to still greater dimensions in the West Riding. A great cotton industry has been established in Lancashire. There are busy collieries in the north, the Midlands, and Southern Wales. There are foundries and forges and engineering works, with their fire and vapour of smoke, from Swansea to Newcastle. There is a shining network of railways all over the land. There is still a countryside, and there is still agriculture ; there are still over 25,000,000 sheep, and nearly 12,000,000 cattle. But if there are over 1¼ million of persons employed in agriculture and fishery, there are over 1,000,000 in mines and quarries, over 3 millions in commerce and transport, and over 7½ millions who are engaged in some form of industry. The national amalgam of occupations has changed its character entirely. Miners and engineers, transport-workers, and factory-workers, predominate. The population has shifted its place of habitation. In 1688 it was calculated by Gregory King that of a population of 5½ millions, 1¼ million lived in towns—or less than 20 per cent. It is estimated to-day that nearly 80 per cent of the population is urban. But above all, the population has altered its mass and its volume. A predominantly industrial system of economics needs for its working a much denser population than a predominantly agricultural system. Specialization of function and division of labour, which enable industry to achieve its triumphs and exemplify its law of increasing returns, are only possible when there is a great supply of labour which can be detailed to various tasks. Not only so, but large-scale industry, with its recurrent crises and booms, needs a " reservoir " of workers on which it can draw in a boom and into which it can discharge what it does not need in a period of crisis. And industry gets what it needs. There is room for a far greater population in an industrial community. In agriculture each man requires a large space of soil to occupy his labour, and to support his existence by its product. Thousands may work in a mine of which the pithead covers only a few acres ; hundreds may work in a factory which covers but two or three ; and the products of their labours will readily support them all. If the birth-rate and the death-rate co-operate with the needs and the possibilities of a nation which turns to industry, there will thus be an increase of population which may attain amazing dimensions.

Such an increase may be traced in England after the accession of George III. During his reign the population of England and Wales increased from the 6¾ millions which had been estimated in 1760 to the 12,000,000 which were recorded by the census of 1821. It had, in a word, nearly doubled itself in sixty years. It continued to grow. In the ninety years from the death of George III to the accession of George V (1820–1911) it tripled itself, and rose from 12 to 36 millions. A density which in 1760 had been probably less than that of France was in 1921 nearly four times as great, and greater than that of any other country in Europe. At the beginning of the nineteenth century the population of England and Wales was a little short of 9 millions, and that of France was about 27 ; in 1921 the population of England and Wales was nearly 38 millions, and that of France just over 39. The comparison with France becomes the more striking when one remembers that during the whole of the nineteenth century England and Wales were losing a steady flow of emigrants, who were populating the British Empire and helping to populate the United States, and that during the same period France was keeping her population at home. The growth of our population in the nineteenth century is indeed one of the most remarkable facts, and one of the greatest revolutions, in all our history. What were the immediate causes of a change so remarkable ? What were its main concomitants ? And what were its chief results ?

II

The immediate causes of a change of population are changes in the rates of births and deaths. Of the two it is the change in the death-rate which is the more important.[1] There may have been some increase in the birth-rate in the latter half of the eighteenth century and the early part of the nineteenth. There are no regular returns before 1837 ; and we do not know. Probably the birth-rate was about 34 for each thousand living persons in England and Wales at the beginning of the nineteenth century, and possibly it had been less than that amount about 1750, and had increased between 1750 and 1800. What we certainly know is that the birth-rate remained constant at about 35 from the beginning of our records until 1875, that it has decreased since 1875 until it has fallen to 23, and that it is decreasing still.[2] An increase of the birth-rate may therefore perhaps explain some of the increase of population between 1760 and 1800. There may have been earlier marriages, and larger families, owing to the earlier age at which incomes could be earned under an industrial system. But an increase of the birth-rate does not explain the increase of population from the beginning down to the middle of the reign of Queen Victoria ; and after 1875 we are faced by the parallel facts of a declining birth-rate and an increasing population. The cause of the

---

[1] This section is based on Professor Carr-Saunders' work on Population, to which I desire to record my indebtedness. [2] In 1926 the rate was 18.

increase of population must therefore be mainly sought in the decline of the death-rate. We became a more numerous people, not because more children were born, but because fewer died. Here again we can only guess what were the figures before the accession of Queen Victoria. Possibly the death-rate had been as high as 30 in each 1000 during the eighteenth century ; probably it had sunk to 25 in the early years of the nineteenth. In the middle of the nineteenth century it was as low as 22 ; it is now less than 14. It is thus the death-rate which has altered most notably ; and it is the alteration of the death-rate which principally explains the movement of population.[1] It is a matter of the discoveries of physicians, such as Jenner and Lister : it is a matter of measures of public health, and especially of measures designed to protect the lives of children.

We may pause at this point to notice a fact of importance. The " devastating torrent of children " which dismayed some Victorian writers has now become a more placid stream, flowing along a more level surface. In the last fifty years the birth-rate has sunk from 35 to 23. It is true that the death-rate has also declined, during the same period, from nearly 21 to under 14 ; and a falling birth-rate is thus still accompanied by a rising tide of population. But on any statistical computation it would appear that we are now approaching the stationary stage of our population. Professor Bowley has calculated that, assuming a birth-rate and a death-rate of the present dimensions, and ignoring the effects of emigration, we may expect the population of Great Britain, which was 42¾ millions in 1921, to reach the amount of 48¼ millions in thirty years, and thereafter, for the next sixty years (that is to say, until 2011) to remain nearly constant at that amount. The assumptions made by Professor Bowley are obviously favourable to increase. In practice the birth-rate is likely to shrink further, and if the death-rate also decreases, we can hardly expect it to decrease proportionately ; and again there is likely to be an annual emigration which may possibly increase in volume. A stationary stage of population may therefore be reached even before 1951 ; and after that date there may even be some decline.[2] It

---

[1] This is a fact to be remembered in any comparison of the populations of England and France. The difference between the two is due less to differences of the birth-rate, which are often emphasized, and more to differences of the death-rate, which are too often neglected. It is the amount of infant mortality in France which is serious. In 1923, according to a table in Professor Carr-Saunders' book, the number of children born in France was the same as in England and Wales. Two populations which were practically equal to one another produced an equal number of children. But the number of children who died under the age of one year in France was over 20,000 more than it was in England and Wales.

[2] Professor Bowley's calculations, which appeared in the *Economic Journal* (vol. xxxiv.), are quoted by Carr-Saunders, *op. cit.* pp. 50–51.

follows that the future may differ but little from the present, so far as the volume and density of our population are concerned. At the same time, the conditions of the present may very well give us pause ; and before we indulge in any vein of optimism we have to consider what have been the concomitants and the results of the great growth of the population which has already taken place.

It was industrial production, on a great scale, which (as we have seen) at once made possible the increase of population and was itself made possible by that increase. Large-scale industry has two concomitants. One of these is specialization. Industry on the great scale means the articulation and the division of any branch of production into single constituent processes, each of which is simplified and standardized until it can be reduced to terms of machinery. The human material of industry is drawn into the same development ; work becomes a matter of the single process, and often of attendance upon machines ; a great accuracy may be required, but it may be the accuracy of a single faculty engaged in a single movement. The other concomitant of large-scale industry is urbanization. An industrial society naturally precipitates itself in great towns. Just as process must be linked in contiguity with process within the single factory, so factory tends to be linked in contiguity with factory in some single urban area. It is partly that factories are drawn together on the same ground by the magnet of adjacent water, or coal, or iron, which they all in common need for their operations. It is partly that works engaged in one branch of production may be the necessary complement to others engaged in related branches, and that all may be drawn together by a mutual interdependence or a common convenience. But the main reason for urbanization is seated in human nature. Men will flock together for company and comfort, and have done so through the ages, unless they are necessarily scattered in space by the scattering of the substance on which they work and from which they get their subsistence. It is not so much that great industry created the great town : it is rather that it releases an old and inveterate instinct, and removes the obstacles to its satisfaction. Men praise the country, but they dwell, if they can, in the town. In England the natural process of urbanization was all the more rapid during the eighteenth century, as an agrarian revolution was proceeding side by side with the revolution in industry. A movement for enclosures was bringing the land still more into the hands of large landed proprietors, and taking from the country folk their rights in the commons and their attachment to the soil. It was not only the captains of industry who drew men into the towns : it was also the owners of land who sent them into the towns by depriving them of their interest in the country.

It was these concomitants of specialization and urbanization which largely determined the nature of the results which flowed from the change of national occupations and the growth of national population. The wealth of the nation was certainly increased and the standard of life improved. It has been calculated that, if the population increased more than fourfold between 1800 and 1914, the national income increased about tenfold ; and down to the end of the nineteenth century there was a steady rise of real wages. What is not clear is whether the national income might not have been increased to almost the same extent, and the standard of life have been more permanently and more greatly improved, if the increase of the population had been at a slower rate. Industry needed a great increase, but perhaps it received an increase which was even more than it needed. Over-population is not, in itself, the cause of unemployment, which is rather due to industrial depressions that in turn may be due to the state of distant markets or a variety of external causes ; but the question still remains whether our population has not outrun our resources for production and the markets open for our products, and whether, if that be so, our national economy and standard of life are not already feeling the effects. It is not, however, with wealth, or the economics of its production and distribution, that we are concerned. The problem we have to discuss is that of welfare ; and the questions before us are questions of the national standard of conduct and the temper of national character. What have been the moral effects of the new life of specialized function and urban agglomeration ? Our nation has now largely become a nation of men from whom only some single aptitude or faculty is required by the demands of their daily life and occupation, and who are cantoned in towns and changed by their cantonment. What has the change meant, and how has the character of the nation been modified ?

We may begin by considering the effects of industrial specialization. In the days before it came, which were days of a far less degree of professionalism for the mass of the population, the dwellers in the country—and they were a large majority— might often follow a double occupation. They were generally engaged in agriculture, partly as labourers on the land of others, partly as members of the village community, using its common pasture for cows and pigs and poultry, and partly as occupiers of a plot, attached to their cottages, which they could cultivate for produce.[1] They were also, in many parts of the country,

---

[1] A law of the reign of Elizabeth had required (which is very different from saying that it had secured) a plot of 4 acres for each cottage.

engaged in domestic industry : the members of their families might spin or weave ; and though (particularly in the south) such industry was often controlled by " undertakers " who supplied the instruments and the raw materials of industry on harsh conditions, and though it too often meant overwork and under-pay, it also meant a new interest and a further development of powers. A life lived under such conditions might be in itself, and without any school, a general education of general faculty. It was full (perhaps, indeed, too full), and it was varied ; it produced handiness, and escaped monotony ; it might satisfy and stretch the faculties of the mind. The specialized worker naturally tends to a single-faculty development ; and he may fall into a tedium of uniformity which is only relieved—and is accentuated even when it is relieved—by the distraction of mass amusements. The rest of his faculties may suffer from the atrophy of disuse ; and unless society comes to the rescue, and provides a chance and a scope for their exercise, they may become as withered hands and as palsied limbs. A national society of men organized on a basis of specialization will be a society of men over-developed on one side, and under-developed on others, unless some general scheme of education, which includes not only the education of the young but also that of the adult, provides for the general development of the whole man. The supreme reason for a national system of education in an industrial society is less that it improves the efficiency of work, than that it corrects the effects of work ; less that it prepares men for their vocation, than that it trains them to know, and to love, something other than their vocation, and helps them to fill the times, and to use the faculties, which are outside the area of work and belong to the spaces of leisure. The word school is derived from a Greek word which signifies leisure ; and to provide some training for the right use of leisure is still a necessary purpose of all education. It was the tragedy of our Industrial Revolution that the educational revolution which should have been its concomitant was postponed for a whole century, and that, while the great industrial inventions were made about 1778, the first effective Education Act only came in 1870.

Specialization not only produces single-faculty development : it also encourages and accentuates a spirit which we may call the spirit of occupationalism—a habit of turning away from the commonwealth to the interests and the claims of the profession, and of paying devotion and offering loyalty before the shrine of vocation. Such a spirit and such a habit are nothing new in history. They may be seen in the mediæval guilds ; they can be traced alike in the rivalries between guild and guild, and in the division between " journeymen " and their employers which distracted the guilds in their later history. But they appear on a greater scale, and with far larger consequences, when an industrial society emerges in which the bulk of the members are engaged in occupations, each anxious to establish a monopoly for itself, and each, at the same time, moving more and more towards an internal cleavage between the directing staff and the operative units. In the old pre-Revolutionary society occupations had faded into one another: one man might follow more than one ; the worker might rise to be a master, and the small master still remained a worker. In the new post-Revolutionary society specialization is far more profound and demarcation much more in evidence ; occupation is distinct from occupation, and in each occupation management and operation are separate and even opposed. On the one hand, there emerges an antithesis—new not in itself, but in its dimensions and the precision with which it is enunciated —between the " Two Nations " of " capitalism " and the " proletariate " ; on the other hand, and side by side with this dualism, we may see an analysis and resolution of the nation into constitutive cells of occupation, which under the name of " syndicates " or " national guilds " pretend to an independent life and lay claim to independent action. From this latter point of view, the national unity which has been formed by a long historic process would seem to be returning to the crucible. The autonomy now vindicated, in a greater or a less degree, by each occupation, may come to verge upon sovereignty ; and the solidarity which rallies men to their fellow-workers in the same industry may rise to the height of an absorbing loyalty. Such results, if ever they came to pass, would obviously entail profound changes in national character ; and indeed, on the logic of a *reductio ad extremum*, they might end in its disappearance. But it would be folly to expect any development so drastic. The engrained character of a nation is far more likely to affect and control the growth of occupationalism than to be controlled or expunged by it. There have always been guilds, but there are still nations ; and the spirit of a nation still rises readily (perhaps only too readily) to meet even a fancied challenge, whether from without or from within, which menaces the sanctities of its tradition. It is true that a new and qualifying factor has been added to the national temper by the growth of occupationalism. But if it is new in itself, it is perhaps the same in its operation as other factors which have been active in the past. It seemed at one time, in the course of the seventeenth century, as if religious confessionalism might permanently divide the nation, and as if the play and the wars of sects might split the body politic. Actually we managed to reconcile confessions and sects with national unity. If occupationalism has now taken the place of the old confessionalism, it may in the end, like confessionalism, prove more of a friend than an enemy. The sects, as we shall see later when we come to consider the religious factor, reinvigorated an old strain of individualism and self-reliance in our national character by the claims which they made in the name of religious liberty. Occupations may act as a similar leaven, and beginning in the threat of disruption they may in the issue only raise and stimulate the national substance.

When industrial growth is common to a number of contiguous nations, a form of internationalism is a natural accompaniment of such growth. Nations may be divided into occupations ; but the occupations of one nation are united to those of another by a common sympathy. Here again we may be reminded of the confessions of the seventeenth century, and of the sympathy which united the Calvinists of different countries. But it would not appear that internationalism, whether of confessions or of occupations, is a very potent force. Certainly the international federations of miners and textile workers and the members of other occupations, which have been established in modern times, have played a modest part. The international bonds between the miners of two different countries can do but little, either to prevent hostilities between the governments of those countries, or to determine the issue of an internal conflict between miners and mine owners in one of the two. But there is another form of international development—or, to speak more correctly, of cosmopolitanism—which has more assured foundations and a deeper influence. As industrialism and its consequences (specialization ; single faculty development ; occupational feeling) become more and more common to the nations of Europe, the peculiarities of each nation tend to be overlaid by the common phenomena of industrial life. Whether or no there is reciprocal feeling and mutual alliance between the same interests in different countries, there are certainly common traits, and very similar trends, in the development of national character among all industrialized nations. The touch of common nature may yet help to make the whole world kin.

III

Not the least of the common traits which produce a certain assimilation between different countries is the growth of urban life and habits. Something has already been said about the causes of urbanization. Nowhere has it gone further, or produced profounder consequences, than in England and Wales. The density of our population is not exceeded, or indeed equalled, by that of any other European country. And this dense population is peculiarly and particularly centred in towns. Here we differ from Belgium, which has also a dense population, but distributes it over the countryside, through a system of small owners and *petite culture*, as well as among the towns. With us the rural population is already thin, and tends to become thinner ; our system of farming is not calculated to maintain any large population in the country, and the attractions and prospects of the town outweigh all the possibilities of rural prosperity. Nearly 80 per cent of our population is urban. That is not all. There is a difference between town and town. There are some towns which are definitely urban—with urban congestion ; with the countryside far removed from the bulk of their inhabitants ; with urban smells, urban sights, and the round of urban happenings. There are other towns which have, as it were, a rural bias. The country flows readily into them, for business or pleasure, during the day, and they can readily flow into the country, on summer evenings or on half holidays, to " take the air." Here there is a circulation of the blood, and an ebbing and flowing of the tide ; here there is *rus in urbe*, or, again, here is *urbs in rure*.[1] So far as a dividing line can be drawn between the town which is definitely urban and that which has a rural flavour, it is fixed by a population of 50,000 inhabitants. Most observers would agree that a town with a larger population is definitely urban ; most observers would allow that a town with that population, or less than that population, can still preserve rural contacts. If this be so, it is a fact of great importance that 48 per cent of our population resides in towns with a population of over 50,000. If we add that over a third of the population (38 per cent) resides in towns with a population of over 100,000, and exactly a quarter in towns with a population of over a quarter of a million, we shall realize still more clearly the definitely urban life of a great part of our population.[2]

It is a speculation of some French anthropologists that urban centres primarily select for their inhabitants, by some process of natural selection, the members of the fair and long-headed Nordic race—only, however, to eliminate them under unhealthy conditions of life, and thus to establish in a final preponderance the members of the dark and round-headed Alpine stock. The

[1] Cf. Thomas Hardy's description of Casterbridge (Dorchester), in *The Mayor of Casterbridge*, ch. ix. : " Casterbridge was in most respects but the pole, focus, or nerve-knot of the surrounding country-life ; differing from the many manufacturing towns which are as foreign bodies set down, like boulders on a plain, in a green world with which they have nothing in common. Casterbridge lived by agriculture at one remove further from the fountain-head than the adjoining villages—no more. The townsfolk understood every fluctuation in the rustic's condition. . . ."

[2] These are the figures for England and Wales according to the census of 1921.

speculation is airy; and even if it were a matter of ascertained fact, we could not condemn the influence of towns unless we were certain that the race which was selected for elimination was better than that which was selected for survival. There is perhaps but little profit in any study of the racial aspects of urban life. The serious problems which are raised by urbanization are intellectual and moral rather than racial. In these respects towns have their advantages as well as their defects. Because they are centres of population, they are also homes of organization. It is not an accident that the Latin word for a city is the origin of " civics," or again that the Greek word for city is the source of " politics." In the same way, and for the same reason, towns are also the homes of taste and of tact in human intercourse. The greater the number of men living in contiguity, the greater the need for measure and grace in their relations with one another; and the Romans (like the Greeks, in their use of the word ἀστεῖος) connected " urbanity " of manners with the fact of urban residence. Towns are the whetstones of wit, which they sometimes polish into a smart facility, more urban than urbane, of cockney repartee : they are permeable by new ideas—of which they are not necessarily retentive. The countryman may seem, in comparison, unorganized and unmannered ; slow-witted in speech, slow-moving in apprehension. These are simple observations, which were made long ago by the Greeks. But it was one of the Greeks—Euripides—who also observed and painted the sober countryman of sane and steady judgment, " who rarely frequents the city and the market-place—a worker with his own hands, of the sort that alone preserves the land—shrewd, and ready to come to close quarters in debate, but unsophisticated, and a man of blameless life." [1] There is a talent which builds itself best in stillness ; and those who draw the quiet night into their blood may gain a poise and a harmony which are otherwise denied. A nation which is not supported, as equally as may be, on the double basis of town and country may be a nation such as an ancient Athenian said that Greece would be without Sparta—" lame of one leg." It loses a necessary ingredient in its national character. What the proper amount of the rural ingredient in our own country should be is a question not readily answered. But when the rural population has dwindled to 20 per cent of the whole, it may well be argued that the amount which actually exists is below the minimum which ought to exist in the national interest. There are powers and feelings, just as there are problems and difficulties, which are specifically rural ; and an over-urbanized country at once loses those powers and feelings, and neglects those problems and difficulties. It is curious to notice

[1] *Orestes*, 917–922.

how often the vexed questions of our national life slew round, as it were, towards the industrial quarter. A statesman may raise, for example, the issue of Protection, and he may even raise it with a primary regard to agriculture; but his policy, drawn from its course by a powerful if invisible current, veers rapidly towards urban industry. Another may be concerned with problems of education, and may desire to frame new methods for the training of teachers, or to plan new developments of elementary education for the whole country; but he will find that he is insensibly led to treat the industrial majority as the whole, and to prepare schemes which, professing to be general, are really adapted only to that majority. As we unconsciously neglect the problems, so we may insensibly lose the powers and faculties which belong to the country—the love of rooted tradition; the feeling for old sanctities; sympathy with living things; congruity with the unhastening and unresting processes of nature; the patriotism which loves the very scent and surface of the soil; the sense of the presence of God in the beauty of gardens and fields. It is easy to idealize the country; and it is foolish to forget its monotonies and its pettinesses, its parochial bickerings and its personal backbitings. None the less, a nation loses vitality when it loses contact with the soil—just as an individual loses the fullness of life when he is barred from outlet into the country. " Country life influences the physical as well as the mental side of human nature. We are apt to forget that our bodies were slowly evolved by a series of changes through millions of years which adapted our forefathers to meet what we may sum up as country conditions. Our senses are adapted to seize upon country sights, country sounds, and country smells, and, far-fetched as the suggestion may seem to many people, there is good reason to believe that, when our senses do not receive the stimuli which alone can satisfy them, we are discontented. Our bodies are adapted to perform a certain amount of work in the open air, and failing suitable opportunities we cannot experience the sense of physical well-being that does so much to drive away discontent. Much deeper than that goes the influence of the country upon the other side of human nature. The countryside is a continuous revelation of beauty—" the self-revelation of the creative spirit in its own works." There can on this account alone be no compensation for the loss of effective contact with the country." [1]

Life in a great modern city is a great artifice. A river may flow through its length; but if it does, it becomes " a trough between banked warehouses." It has its roads; but what moves along them is the mechanism of grinding trams. There

[1] Professor Carr-Saunders, *Population*, pp. 101–102.

may be municipal trees along the streets—and each will be set in its grating. There may be municipal parks—but they will be regular and uniform, and their flowers will be protected by iron bars and warning notices. You will see thousands of men swarming to and fro on their regular occasions ; but of other living things you will see, at most, only a few horses, and, it may be, some pigeons and sparrows. This is the daily environment of that part of our population which lives in towns with a population of 100,000 and upwards. Their houses are close-set : thousands live packed together on each square mile ; each street is a cage, and none the less a cage because there may be bursts of gaiety and flutterings of excitement from time to time among its captives. One element in the temper which is engendered in such an environment is nervousness—a nervousness which one may almost call by the name of feverishness. When men live in overcrowded houses, without sufficient air, and when their food is itself mechanical preparations (only relieved by the piquancy of fried fish or the satisfying sweetness of jams—the necessary stimulants of jaded appetites), it is difficult for their bodies to acquire the firm tone which will foster a quiet temper. They may work in bursts for short periods : they cannot readily exert a continuous effort. On this physical basis, itself ill-balanced and insecure, the conditions of industry erect an edifice which tends to exaggerate its defects. To get to work is a rush ; the work itself may be timed and speeded ; it is surrounded by noise and bustle. A body prone to nervousness works under conditions which accentuate nervousness. When the physical conditions of life are of this nature, we may expect to find them accompanied by their mental and moral corollaries —a lively and impressionable receptivity, which readily sheds what it has quickly imbibed ; an instantaneous zest for some new purpose or mode of life, coupled with a rapid cooling and evaporation of the interest and the energy necessary for its permanent maintenance. The dweller in the great town is always receiving fresh impressions ; and he may readily fall into a longing for a constant renewal of his sensations. A kaleidoscope is constantly revolving before his eyes ; and he may make his own life kaleidoscopic. Meanwhile there are powerful agencies ready to provide sensations (such provision being the most lucrative of trades), and to minister alike to the appetite for news, or the excitement of gambling, or the passion for new amusement. In such conditions steady purpose and sustained effort labour, as it were, in sand. There is, indeed, a multiplication of contacts between man and man ; and the multiplication of contacts, if they are enduring enough to go deep, is an enrichment of interests and of personality. But such multiplication may also mean a frittering of the self in a constant series of little attritions, too numerous to produce any real relation of persons and too superficial to produce any lasting effect on personality. Personality, it is true, can only be formed in society ; and it is a wise saying of Goethe that if talent is built in stillness, character can only be built in the stream of the world. But a society may be too large, and too much engaged in flux, to stimulate the growth of personality or to aid the growth of character. Everything depends on two things—the fixity of the station which a man occupies, and the permanence of the relations which he establishes with other persons. If he has a fixed station in a community, with definite duties ; if again, in virtue of that station, he is brought into permanent relations with others which elicit lasting powers and establish modes of steady behaviour—he gains in every way from society and its contacts. But a fixed station and a system of regular relations are hardly possible in our great towns under modern industrial conditions. Employment, which determines station, is not a steady thing. A man may have a short term of employment here and another there ; and from time to time he may fall into the pool of unemployment. Sometimes he may be to blame for his instability ; often he is the passive victim of a social order which he cannot control. In any case he loses the permanent basis of permanent habits ; and it would need a giant of self-discipline to maintain, under such conditions, any of the characteristics—whether of solid common sense, or of bull-dog tenacity, or whatever they may be—which are ascribed to the imaginary Englishman living a settled life in calm placidity. We are not the dregs of our ancestors or the *fæx Romuli* : we simply live in other times which involve other manners ; and we have been changed with the changing times.[1]

There is another feature of urban life, which runs parallel to its feverishness. This may be called by the name of gregariousness. The inevitable congestion of a great town, and particularly the conditions of residence under which the mass of its population spend their lives, impose a constant keeping of company. There is a gregarious instinct in all human nature which draws men together—just as, when once they are drawn together, there is also an imitative instinct which tends to their

[1] " A quick if superficial observation of human characteristics and a ready wit are the natural products of a type of life where things and persons move quickly—a fire, a fight, a quarrel develops suddenly, claims attention for a few minutes, and is as rapidly succeeded by something else. . . . The very rapidity of the habit of observation makes against the power of that slower and more connected train of thought which pieces together observations more fragmentary and more slowly acquired, and issues in some attempt at rational conclusion. This mental characteristic has its reactions on character. Where principles are not easily grasped, action is apt to be dictated by the circumstances of the moment." (Extract from a memorandum on the conditions of life " across the bridges " in South London.)

assimilation. It is easy to exaggerate the influence of both instincts. Under normal conditions they are balanced by complementary and corrective instincts. If men desire company, they also, and especially in moods of reaction, desire solitude ; and Hobbes, whose view of human nature combines shrewd observation with an exaggerated cynicism, can at one and the same time write of " men's natural aptness for society " and remark that they " have no pleasure, but on the contrary a great deal of grief, in keeping company." If, again, men are imitative, they have also a longing to show initiative, and a desire (which may readily pass into heresy) to be somehow different from others. The great industrial town, alike by the pressure of its congestion and by the uniformity of its mechanism, leaves little chance for the play of forces which tend to correct the gregarious and the imitative instincts. Boys and girls begin their life as members of a crowd. They readily form themselves into groups or gangs, and " go with " one another in pursuit of amusements which may sometimes sink into street feuds, and sometimes rise to the power of a fine club spirit. Such associations are natural in adolescence ; but the great town perpetuates an impulse which the adult may elsewhere outgrow, and maintains a gregarious habit of life through manhood and middle age. There is the crowded street and its lights by night ; week-end by week-end there are the crowds of spectators at organized games, drawn together partly by a taste for excitement and a love for the fluctuations of the game, and partly, too, by the pleasure of standing together in one great assembly. The habit of the crowd becomes a second nature. The fruits of that habit are a follow-my-leader temper : a way of swimming with the stream in a general company ; the formation of mass-opinion which is not based on thought or discussion. Catch-words float readily from lip to lip ; advertisement, with its magic suggestion of " Everybody's doing it," is a potent suggestion ; the last cry and the newest fashion readily sweep the field.

These things are tendencies rather than rules ; and there will always be counteracting forces which impede their actual operation. They are, too, tendencies which can be traced elsewhere than in great towns ; and the life of a great public school may be swayed by a similar tide of conformity. But even if they are only tendencies, and though they have their parallels in other spheres, the tendencies of urban life may none the less give the observer concern, and their strength may suggest the need which exists for securing freedom of play for other and opposite tendencies. We may feel this need the more if we reflect on the growth of organized occupations, mainly centred in towns, with their rules of group action, the strength of their group opinion, and their spirit of solidarity. A group is not an ogre, or a great industrial town a prison-house ; but neither of them is favourable in its nature to individual thought or individual responsibility. Urbanization accentuates and strengthens a force which, on its finer side, and in due combination with other forces, is necessary for human progress—the force of social cohesion, the force of social opinion, the force of social drill and discipline. It depresses and weakens, unless social policy is directed to their protection, the force of original thought and original enterprise which is the peculiar dignity of human nature and the primary condition of human development. The protection of this force is the essential purpose of education. For education, if in its early stages it is directed to the purpose of training the young to think alike about the elementary and indisputable truths of language or mathematics, is essentially, and in its higher stages, a training of the mind to think for itself—to form opinions on the basis of evidence, and not by hearsay—to follow the truth, and not the crowd. If the specialization of modern industry makes the spread of general education more than ever imperative, the urbanization of modern life has just the same consequence. The great market-places of human congregation have many *idola* ; and the truth which will make men free from their influence is a truth which has to be taught " line upon line, line upon line," by a steady process of continued instruction. Education can refine social opinion until no man need fear its pressure. It can ground social opinion on the individual thought, and the free discussion, which are its only sure basis and its only safe origin. Solitude ceases to be a terror, when it becomes the solitude of the study. Initiative ceases to be a rarity, when the mind is trained to discovery. The balance of human faculties and instincts is adjusted, when men have learned to unite hours of solitude with seasons of company, and to blend the free play of initiative with the reasonable demands of conformity.

It may seem paradoxical to associate homelessness with the gregarious habit of the great town ; and yet the association is a simple fact of ordinary observation. A great urban community, for all its sociability, is too great to be a home. It is not a centre of human affections, as a village or small town can be. It does not give men a status or position in its life, as a village or small town can do. Great civic communities find it difficult to develop a common spirit. There is such a thing as " the multitudinous desolation of a great city." It is one of the sad results of such desolation that the communities in which men live are not intimate enough to create those lesser local loyalties which are the nursing mothers of larger loyalties. The man who does not feel himself rooted in local life will hardly feel himself grounded in national tradition. But the homelessness of great cities is not only a want of local, and thereby of national feeling. It may also be homelessness in the simpler and more primitive sense of the want of family life. It is true that the intimacies of the family may flourish in the most unpromising conditions. But when a tenement, or lodgings, or a single room, is the only shelter which thousands can ever provide for these intimacies, they may wither away because they have fallen on stony ground. Some sort of home, which can be recognized and felt as " home," is a necessary condition of the primary loyalty of the family— which in turn is a root of civic feeling, as civic feeling is a root of national sentiment. The city cannot be a home until men have homes in the city ; and housing is a matter which affects men's minds as well as their bodies.

We have said that cities are in their nature places of organization. They draw men together in sociable life ; and by the problems which they present they necessarily invite the control of some organizing power. The life of a village or small town may adjust itself easily on customary lines : the great urban community must live a regulated life, in which the element of regulation grows with the growth of the community. The supply of water, of light, of means of transit, has to be secured ; public health has to be guarded ; means of education have to be provided. It was in the mediæval city that the methods of modern governments were first developed. It is in the modern city that new methods of government, which are often called socialistic, have been elaborated. The name does not greatly matter : the civic governments which develop schemes of civic regulation are not necessarily socialistic in creed ; and men move irrespective of party towards municipal enterprises which would be denounced if they were projected upon a national scale. The simple fact is that density of population, with all the multiplication of contacts which it entails (so that each man inevitably affects the health and well-being of others, in more ways than he knows, by all that he does), is bound to invite and receive regulation. The Liberal creed of non-interference was built before the days of great industrialized cities. The urbanization of England has not only added new traits to national character. It has necessarily changed our concepts and methods of government. Politics have to alter with the body politic. A body politic which has quadrupled in population during a century, and has altered fundamentally the methods of its distribution on the soil, is a different body politic.

IV

We have sought to trace the ways in which a great increase of population, produced by a new system of industry (which in turn it has helped to produce), and accompanied by the growth of specialization and urbanization, has affected national temper and character. On the one hand, and in virtue of the growth of specialization, it has fostered, if our argument is true, what we have called single-faculty development and the growth of occupationalism ; on the other hand, and in virtue of urbanization, it has produced a type at once more nervous in disposition and more gregarious in habit. This is the darker side of the picture ; and there is much which might be set on the other side. The special ability fostered by industrialism is often ability of a very high order. Occupationalism, if it has its selfish side, shows also the nobler aspect of solidarity. Urban life has its lights as well as its shadows ; and if it tends to a more feverish and a more crowded life, it quickens intelligence, encourages a good-humoured sociability, and produces a high degree of social organization. None the less, we have to admit that under modern conditions it is more difficult for men to attain a general development of faculty, and to shape and maintain a steady individuality. And if we make that admission we are naturally led to inquire whether there is any line of policy which will diminish or remove that difficulty, and help to solve the problems of a dense, industrialized, urbanized population.

Some will conduct a frontal attack on the problem, and urge a reduction in numbers, by means of birth-control and large-scale emigration. Such a policy seems simple and direct, and as if it went to the roots of the matter. In its essence, however, it is a policy of pruning ; and the health of a tree does not depend only on pruning. Even if methods of birth-control were universally adopted, they would not alter the present position in any fundamental way. With a birth-rate which has been steadily declining for the last fifty years, we have still an increasing population ; and though, as we have seen, the increase is likely to diminish, and a stationary population may well be established in the course of the next generation, there is no reason to anticipate any decrease. There will be fewer children born, but fewer will die ; and the natural tendency of population towards stability—a tendency to which the last century and a half, in England and Wales, has been so remarkable an exception —will again reassert itself. Birth-control, if it becomes generally prevalent, may alter the proportion between the rate of increase in one class, in which it is now hardly practised, and that in another, in which it is already used ; but it is not likely to affect the total aggregate to any very great extent. Nor is it certain that any large reduction of the population would be economically prudent. It is difficult to determine what amount of population will produce the maximum of wealth for all its members. But it is certainly not always the case that, the fewer there are, the more there is to go round. On the contrary, it is sometimes true that the more there are, the more (in virtue of the law of increasing returns) there is to be distributed. It is possible that we have now a greater population than is economically desirable ; that we might produce almost the same amount of wealth with fewer persons ; and that, with a reduction of numbers, we might each have a larger share. It is possible ; but it is far from certain. It follows that birth-control is not likely to produce any great alteration ; nor can we be certain that it is economically desirable that it should. Large-scale emigration might be an advantage, if it would relieve the congestion of great towns without diminishing the volume of national production, and if it spread the British stock more evenly over the British Empire. But we can hardly anticipate any volume of emigration which will in any degree affect the density of our population. If there are a hundred thousand emigrants from England and Wales in each year, it is the maximum which we can expect for many years to come ; and it is difficult to draw from our great cities, even to that extent, the men whom the Dominions need and whom they will readily accept. Yet it is from the cities that the tide of emigration must set. The country, already evacuated by the drain of the city, cannot be further evacuated by the drain of emigration.

Another policy which has its advocates is that of breaking up urban centres and substituting garden cities. It is a policy which has its attractions. The cities which we have are units (if they can be called units) as accidental in development as they are enormous in size ; and the city which is deliberately planned and kept within a limit of size, and which sets factories in gardens and gardens among factories, is a city of a new type. In practice, however, the garden city often becomes either a dormitory of the great city or a residential retreat. The great urban centres remain unaffected ; their industries and their workshops are so interconnected that they cannot be separated ; railway communications have been adjusted to them ; and they are fixed by the communications on which they have come to depend. It is difficult to see how Birmingham or Manchester (not to mention London) can undergo any fundamental change. At the most we may anticipate an increase of open spaces and a proper provision of playing-grounds for children ; the improvement of facilities for transport into the country ; and, above all, the disappearance of those crowded tenements (however " modern " they may be in their plan and equipment) which encourage and enhance the gregarious temper natural to great centres of population.

If we are to have large towns, with a density of population which may perhaps be slightly relieved by emigration, and conditions of life which we may hope to see ameliorated (but not radically altered) by some system of town-planning, we must seek a solution of the problems which they present, not so much in a reduction of population, or, again, in a break-up of urban centres, as in the fuller development of civic education. The physical environment, it would seem, is likely to remain in large measure what it is. It is left for us, therefore, to apply the methods of the mind in order to modify, and if need be to correct, the effects produced on the mind by physical environment. Education is meant to form and strengthen character as well as to awaken intelligence. Both in the public school and in the public elementary school it produces moral as well as mental results. The teachers of a country cannot achieve a revolution. But they can help in liquidating the effects of a revolution—the revolution of the last hundred and fifty years— which has altered our numbers and our dwellings, our occupations, our habits, and our outlook. If the education of the young is spread over a long enough period, and lasts (let us say), at the least, to the age of fifteen ; if it is continued by part-time, and supplemented by adult education—may it not produce a development of general faculty, even in a day of specialization ; stability, even in an age of excitement ; self-confidence, even in a time of collective organization and sentiment ? These are perhaps large hopes. But, after all, the industrialization of our country has made education the paramount necessity of our times. If our minds have been subdued to what they work in, and to the conditions under which they work, we have to reconquer our freedom—and to reconquer it in the field of the mind. Those who labour in that field will not think of pruning. They have to go deeper. It is their business to dig about the roots of the tree, and to ensure for it healthy growth by giving it healthy nurture.

V

In any attempt to estimate the influence of the economic factor on national character, it is not only density of population, or the distribution of population between town and country, that counts. We have also to consider the distribution of population between nation and nation ; between sex and sex ; between age and age ; and between class and class.

The attitude of nations towards one another depends upon many factors. One of these factors is volume of population. In an age of universal military service, when each army is a whole nation in arms, the force of a nation depends on its population. A nation with a greater population will be more insistent in its demands and more peremptory in its negotiations, because it knows that, if matters should come to the arbitrament of war, it has the weight of battalions on its side. The increase of one nation over another in the mere mass of numbers may thus affect its feelings, stimulate its pride, and determine its policy on lines of aggression. The temper and character of Germany before the war, more particularly in her relations to France, were affected to no small extent by the fact that her population exceeded 60,000,000, and was still increasing ; while the population of France was under 40,000,000, and was stationary at that amount. In the same way the suggestion of Home Rule for Ireland raised one set of feelings about 1841, when the population of Ireland was over 8,000,000, and that of England and Wales was under 16,000,000 :[1] it raised other feelings about 1921, when the population of Ireland (apart from the six northern counties) was something over 3,000,000, and that of England and Wales was nearly 38,000,000. The relative weight of numbers will always count in determining political estimates. Generally such calculations will only affect variations of policy ; but a conscious sense of size and increase may sometimes give a permanent bias, which only a great shock can correct, to the general temper of a nation.

The position of women, and the estimation in which they are held, are important elements in the character of any nation. While they rest fundamentally on spiritual factors, such as the conception of marriage and the general standard of morals, they are also determined in part by the material factor of numbers. The excess of women over men has often been remarked in our own country ; but the same or an even greater excess may be found in France and Germany. In England and Wales there are about $1\frac{3}{4}$ million more women than men, in a population of 38,000,000 ;[2] in France about $2\frac{1}{2}$ millions, in a population of under 40,000,000 ; in Germany about $2\frac{1}{4}$ millions, in a population of over 60,000,000. It would almost seem as if old and settled countries tended towards a condition in which women were normally in a majority. A majority generally commands respect ; and while many other causes are

[1] In 1801, at the time at which the Union was carried (because England thought it vital for her security in time of war), the population of England and Wales was nearly 9,000,000 ; that of Ireland was nearly 6,000,000.

[2] In Ireland at large, out of a population of over 4,000,000, the excess of women is about 6000.

contributing to alter the position of women, the fact of their numerical majority has to be counted. But it cannot be said that it produces any uniform results in the different countries in which it can be uniformly traced. France has a greater preponderance of women than England or Germany ; but women have not the same political position in France (whatever may be said of their social influence) as they have in either of the other countries. Where women have both a numerical majority and the suffrage, they may contribute particular elements to the determination of national temper and character. They may introduce changes of policy in matters such as the sale of alcohol and the law of the family (especially as regards divorce) ; and changes of policy in such vital matters will have large effects. Even where there is simply a numerical majority of women, without the right of the suffrage, new elements are obviously introduced into the national life. Women enter the employment market : working side by side with men, they also follow the same pursuits in their leisure ; and entering the same avocations, they prepare themselves for their entry by the same methods of education. Of old it might be said that a nation drew into its public life only its male population, and left its women to find their fulfilment in a multitude of family circles. To-day the nation is a nation not of men only, but of men and women ; it draws both alike into many ranges of its economic activity, and more and more includes both in its political life. It cannot be said that the result is any feminization of national character. There is an alteration in social habits, which the old-fashioned deplore, as they deplore all alterations ; but there is no more general change. Nations are, indeed, the better for having enlisted a far larger interest in the service of their public life ; but they are no less bellicose, and no more sentimental. The truth is that women readily accept the standards and ideas which they find in existence when they enter into public life. Those standards and ideas are old and inveterate ; women, in the mass, have no different point of view, or any new set of standards and ideas to oppose to the old. They accept what they find ; and in some ways the paradox is true that the growth of feminism leads to a greater masculinity, as women, shedding the old habits of their own sex, embrace the habits and the fashions of men. Nothing, however, is very signally changed. Men are indeed in a minority, but neither men nor women are consciously affected to any extent by that fact. The sexes are not organized groups ; they do not count their numbers with the anxiety of nations ; and they are not, like nations, swayed in their feelings or attitude by the numbers which they can " put into the field." The numerical preponderance of women may to some extent soften national manners, and it may help to command a greater respect for women's work and women's claims ; but it is hardly likely to lead to any further or more far-reaching results.

The movement of our population, at the present time, tends towards an increase of age over youth. This is the effect of a period of transition. The birth-rate has been steadily shrinking during the last fifty years. The result is that, if we take the population at the present time in year groups from the age of 50 downwards, we shall find, on allowing for the greater toll taken by death in the older groups, that there is a tendency towards a progressively diminishing number of people in each group. On the other hand, the death-rate has also been steadily shrinking. The result of that is that more and more people have survived in each year group above 50, as well as in each year group under 50—or in other words that, while fewer and fewer of the young come into the world, more and more of the old continue to stay in the world for a longer period. A falling birth-rate accompanied by a falling death-rate inevitably produces such a result. It gives an abnormal weight to the older members of the population in comparison with the younger.[1] A comparison of the census of 1911 with that of 1921 will illustrate the position. In 1911 there were about 12½ millions over the age of 35, and 23½ millions under that age. In 1921 there were nearly 15 millions over the age of 35, and a little short of 23 millions under that age. In the one year the older group was nearly 35 per cent of the total population ; in the other it was nearly 40. In the one year the older group was 53 per cent of the younger ; in the other it was 65. The population had increased by nearly 2 millions in the ten years ; but while the older group had increased by nearly 2½ millions, the younger group had decreased by over half a million. The ravages of the war have to be taken into account ; but when we reflect that persons who were 35 in 1921 were only 28 at the beginning of the war, and that the age of military service at that time was between 18 and 39, we shall realize that the war must have affected the older as well as the younger group, even if it affected it less. The facts are in themselves striking ; but the question which is important for us is their bearing on national life.

There is always a tendency to gerontocracy in any community. Sparta had its γερουσία, and Rome its Senate ; and both were assemblies of the aged (γέροντες ; senes). Our own community, with its ingrained habit of respecting experi-

[1] Another result may be mentioned. Women are stronger, or at any rate survive more, than men. In the age-groups under 15, males preponderate. In the age-groups over 15, women preponderate more and more. It follows that, if the older groups of the population gain for a time on the younger, the numerical preponderance of women is for that time abnormally accentuated.

ence and established prestige, has always paid a large deference to age. The more there is of age in the community, the greater its weight and its influence. It is an old observation that age is conservative and youth radical; it is an old lamentation, " si jeunesse savait, si viellesse pouvait." Plato had made the observation and echoed the lamentation long ago; and in the *Laws* he proposed that the older members of his Nocturnal Council should each be associated with a young colleague, in order that age and youth might correct and supplement one another. It is not a fanciful proposal. One of the problems of society at large (as, on occasion, it is a problem of family life) is to reconcile the aspirations of the young with the traditions of the old. If all posts of importance are vested in the old, the young men may become revolutionaries (in the world of trade unions, as elsewhere, it is often the baulked ability of the young which breeds extremist views), or at any rate, losing any chance of early responsibility, they may protract to a later date the age of irresponsibility. We who are over fifty cannot readily blame the young men of our day if they are more extreme, or if they are less grave and sober, than we were—or imagine that we were—at their age. The conditions are different; and the growing longevity of men entails new habits and raises new questions. How are we to give youth a chance without disfranchising age? Should the age of retirement be altered; or should it remain the same, and are we to see a larger and larger part of our population living in leisure, engaged in contemplation of the mysteries of number, or, it may be, the cultivation of gardens? Should men wait longer before they attain their majority, or at any rate before they marry? If they may expect greater length of days, should they give more time in their youth to securing a more adequate education; and should boys and girls enter work before the age of 15 or even 16? We must not exaggerate the importance of the issue by the multiplication of questions. Some of the factors, as we have said, are peculiar to a period of transition, in which the birth-rate and the death-rate are falling together; and in more stationary conditions we shall not have such marked changes as those which distinguish the census of 1911 from that of 1921. But the growth of human longevity, even when the peculiar conditions of the present time have disappeared, will remain an influence upon national character. We may become, as it were, a little more Chinese in our characteristics—unless, indeed, the young set the fashion, and the old, resolved to protract their youth, continue youthful habits, and study to continue a youthful temper, into a green old age.

It is on the distribution of population between class and class that the attention of observers has mainly been fastened;

and it is the theme on which eugenists have chiefly thought and written. It is obvious that the increase of one class at a greater rate than another alters the proportion of classes in the national body, and that it may thereby affect its composition and character. In the middle of the reign of Queen Victoria the different classes were still increasing at about the same rate. At the accession of George V, in 1911, the position was very different. The decrease of the birth-rate, which began shortly after the middle of the reign of Queen Victoria, was far from uniform among the different classes. It was most marked in the wealthier and professional classes; it had hardly made itself felt among the poorer and unskilled classes. It is calculated that, in the year 1911, 181 children were born, and survived during their first year, for every 1000 married men under the age of 55 among unskilled workers; 136 among skilled workers; and 110 in the upper and middle classes. The change in this respect during the last fifty years is great in itself, and it may produce great effects upon national character. If we assume the inheritance of ability, and of the concomitant qualities which crown ability with success, we must conclude that ability and its attendant qualities are being reproduced at a rate which is less than two-thirds of that of the reproduction of unskilled power. The top of the pyramid is being denuded; the base grows thicker and thicker. It is not clear, however, that society should be likened to a pyramid, or that ability cannot be produced among unskilled workers. It is perhaps arguable that the same distribution of pure and innate ability will be found among the children of any 1000 married men in the class of unskilled workers as among the children of any 1000 married men in the upper and middle classes. Pure and innate ability is not everything; and it does not at all follow that, even if the same degree of such ability is present at birth, the same results will follow. The children of one class have different environments from those of another; they have different educations; they have different opportunities, at the age of maturity, of entering into active life and following a definite career. It is still an unsolved question how much depends on pure and innate ability, and how much on environment, education, and opportunity; and though men speculate freely, the nature of their speculations is biased by the nature of their own training and the history of their own lives.[1] If we assume (and it is very much of an assumption) that pure and innate ability is not unevenly distributed among the children of different classes,[2] we may conclude that, if favourable environ-

[1] See above, p. 7.
[2] Some experience of university life and of the achievements of different students suggests that such an assumption is not unreasonable.

ment and education, and some amount of opportunity, are ensured, many of the 181 children in the one class may contribute to the welfare of the community in the same way as the 110 children in the other. Our social system, through the development of secondary education, with its scholarships and its allowances in aid of maintenance, is providing more and more for the children of the poor both facilities of education and opportunities for development. There is no great reason for fearing the " barbarization " of our society by the disproportionate increase of its " lower " strata. The remedy is largely in our own hands. We can always, if we take the necessary means, encourage the drafting of new supplies into the ranks of the skilled and professional classes. It was what Plato contemplated in his Republic ; but he was logical, and he proposed that if the golden children of iron parents should be drafted upwards, the iron children of golden parents should equally be drafted downwards. It is not easy to encourage the process of sinking (though it will often take place of itself, without encouragement) ; but at any rate we can encourage the process of rising. Some will lament such encouragement, and urge that it deprives the working classes of their natural leaders. Some will welcome it, but they will none the less fear that when new recruits have been encouraged to join the upper and professional classes, they will in their turn produce fewer children, and the danger of exhaustion of those classes will therefore recur. We may respect the fear ; but we may hope that the fertility of nature is not exhausted, and we may say to ourselves *uno avulso non deficit alter aureus.* We may listen with respect to the lamentation ; we may admit that the educational " ladder " leads men to climb away from their origins ; we may allow, and allow gladly, that a broad " highway " should be built, on which the workers can move freely, by the aid of their own associations, towards a workers' education which, while it leaves them still workers, will give them a new vision and outlook. But the interest of the nation at large demands the ladder ; and the harmony of the whole can only be increased by free movement between the parts. There is no bounden duty on any man to remain in his class. But there is a bounden duty on those who leave their class to retain a sympathy with it ; to seek to interpret its needs ; and, so far as they can, to become mediators in that clash of interests which will perhaps last as long as classes endure.

LIST OF BOOKS

BRUNHES, J.—*La Géographie humaine*, 1910.
CARR-SAUNDERS, A. M.—*Population*, 1924.
DOBBS, A. E.—*Education and Social Movements*, 1919.
FEBVRE, L.—*La Terre et l'Evolution humaine*, 1922.
MACDOUGALL, W.—*Social Psychology*, 1908.
    ,,   ,,   *The Group Mind*, 1920.
PEARSON, C. H.—*National Life and Character*, 1893.
LE PLAY, P. G.—*L'Organisation de la famille*, 1871.
    ,,   ,,   *L'Organisation du travail*, 1870.
    ,,   ,,   *Les Ouvriers Européens*, 1877–1879.
DE TOURVILLE, H.—*L'Origine des grands peuples actuels : histoire de la formation particulariste*, 1905.
WALLAS, G.—*Human Nature in Politics*, 1908.
    ,,   ,,   *The Great Society*, 1921.

PART II

THE SPIRITUAL FACTORS

CHAPTER V

THE GROWTH AND SIGNIFICANCE OF A NATIONAL SPIRIT

I

THE theme of the last chapter was a half-way house in the middle of the way of our argument. The factors of population and occupation are a mixture of given natural data and creative human purposes. On the one hand, population is a matter of the natural process of reproduction, and occupation a way of using natural resources to satisfy natural instincts for comfort and livelihood ; on the other, the growth of population, even in the most primitive communities, has always been regulated by human control, and the occupations of all human groups have always been determined less by natural resources than by the free choice which men have made among the variety of nature's gifts. From the intervening ground which lies between the material basis and the spiritual superstructure of national life, we have now to turn to a consideration of the latter, first in its general nature, and then in its various manifestations.

The spiritual essence of a national life may exist without the members of a nation being aware of its presence. Men can talk grammatically without grammatical consciousness : they can belong to a race without consciousness of race : they can be members of a language-group without feeling a sense of their linguistic affinities. National consciousness is a spark more readily kindled by the intimacies and the contacts of daily life than the consciousness either of racial or of linguistic groups. But it is possible for nations to exist, and even to exist for centuries, in unreflective silence. This is true in a double sense. You may have a nation without its members being aware of their peculiar nationality as a fact or a feeling which distinguishes them from other nations. Here there is an absence of the sense of nationality. Again, and still more, you may have a nation without its members being seized by the idea of nationality as the one cardinal principle on which their life, and that of other nations, ought to be organized and developed. Here there is an absence of the passion of nationalism. A sense of nationality and a passion of nationalism are different things. The one may be realized, and is likely to be realized, before the other. But both may be posterior to the fact of nationality.

If this be so, it follows that we may possibly find nations already existing in early history, even if we find no sense of nationality and still less any idea of nationalism. We have already seen that it is an inversion of the facts to start with the family, and to regard it as developing, through a series of wider and wider concentric circles, into the national State. On the contrary, the State is prior to the family ; and it must first be there, as a sovereign law-making group, to determine the legal nature of the family, which always appears in history as a legal unit—organized on patriarchal or matriarchal lines, and guided by this or that law of succession—and which can only appear in such a form, and be organized in such a way, if there is a superior law-making and organizing body to give it the fact and the right of legal existence. This larger body may have been, in very early times, something of the nature of what we should now call a nation.[1] It may have been more than a political unit : it may have been united not only in law, but also in culture, in language, and in religion. The discoveries of archæology have revealed the diffusion of homogeneous cultures in Central Europe before the days of recorded history. The researches of philologists suggest—and indeed we may say that they prove—the descent of different languages, such as those of the Indo-European group, from a single original ancestor ; and we cannot understand the diffusion of that single original language unless we suppose some form of society as the cadre of its growth and the channel of its dissemination. From this point of view some have spoken of an early Indo-European " nation " (a nation which was not a race, and whose unity was compatible with racial differences) ; and their speech is corroborated by the study of comparative religion, which reveals the common deities of the different branches of the Indo-European group, and attests the existence of an original society united by common religious beliefs. Unity of language and religion, coupled with some unity of law (for the same law of the family may be traced in the different branches), and with a probable unity of culture, may well be held, without any great licence of speculation, to warrant us in ascribing the title of nation to societies which existed many centuries before the days of Greece and Rome.

But if there were large societies, of the quality and dimension

---

[1] See above, p. 22 n. 1.

of nations, in very early times, they had already been disin-
tegrated when we see the first dawn of history.   We may connect
the process of disintegration with the spread of arable agriculture.   Agriculture settles men on the soil in separate colonies,
each in its clearing, and all divided from one another by intervening tracts.   The old societies, which may have been connected
with a free and wandering pastoral economy, disseminated over
wide spaces, would naturally dissolve into smaller units when a
new economy altered the conditions of social life.   A type of
the smaller unit, which was general in antiquity, was the ancient
city-state.   Such states were common in early Babylonia, where
they took the form of city-kingdoms, administered by *patesis*,
or priest-kings, who ruled the central temple and regulated
the irrigation of all the surrounding land.   They were the units
of ancient Greece, where the *polis* was ubiquitous ;   they were
widespread in ancient Italy ;   and alike in Greece and in Italy
they were agricultural units.   The city, in which men lived
together while they farmed the country round, was a golden
discovery in the day of its prime.   It reconciled the human need
for general society with the system of separate settlements
which agriculture necessarily demanded.   But the city, in spite
of all its promise and all its actual achievement, was something
far short of a nation, alike in the strength of its arms and in the
general resources of its life.   The Greeks, who might have been
a nation if they had not preferred to be a number of cities, paid
the price of their preference when they succumbed to Philip and
Alexander.

The first units of size and consistency which arose out of the
multiplicity of city-states were generally Empires.   Force and
military power, combined with economic advantages, created
political aggregates round Egypt, Babylonia, Assyria, Persia,
Macedonia, and ultimately Rome.   Each of these successive
aggregates might contain within its boundaries a number of
different languages, a variety of different cultures, and a mixture
of different religions.   Each of them, so far as it possessed
coherence, was united less by any internal sympathy of its units
than by the pressure of an external bond of control ;   and in this,
as also in the absence of community of language or religion or
culture, they differed fundamentally from nations, which are
units of common sympathy as well as of common control.   But
in the Macedonian and the Roman Empires we may trace a
curious phenomenon.   In order to create an inner sympathy and
to form some bond of internal cohesion, the Emperors, either
in their lifetime or after their death, were deified ;   and a common
adoration from all his subjects was vindicated for the ruler under
the title of " a manifest god."   The policy was initiated in the
lifetime of Alexander the Great :   it was continued and developed

during the reigns of his various successors in the Hellenistic age ; it was adopted and perpetuated, along with other bequests from that age, by the Roman Emperors. The deification of the Emperor serves as the cement of the Empire : [1] it unites rural tribes with city-states in a single society which finds its spiritual bond in the common worship of " a god among men."   In a sense it may thus be said that imperial unity, in the form which it took from 300 B.C. to 300 A.D., was a unity of religion.   But the unity of a formal imperial religion always coexisted with a large variety of purely religious beliefs which seethed under its surface ; and the next phase in the development of human society is the product of the deepest of those beliefs—the unique belief which we call by the name of Christianity.

Christianity adopted and consecrated the Empire which it found.   But it altered, and altered radically, the Empire of the past.   It made two fundamental changes.   It deepened and intensified religious unity, which it turned from a common form of emperor-worship into a common faith in the Christian creed and Christian principles.   It broadened and extended, in idea if not in fact, the scope of the Empire.   Universal itself, it vindicated universality for the Empire in which it was enshrined ; and seeing the world as a kingdom of God, it desired that the Kingdom of God should embrace the world.   So there arose, before the eyes of faith, the glittering fabric of the Holy Roman Empire of the Middle Ages.   It was an Empire which was united in virtue of religious belief—a religious society rather than a structure of law and government : it was an Empire, again, which was universal in virtue of the universality of its belief.   But the unity and the universality of the Holy Roman Empire were both the fabric of a vision.   In a sense, indeed, there was the unity of a common language ; but the single Latin of ancient Rome had already become a variety of different Romance languages, and the inclusion of Germany as a part (and indeed the central part) of the Empire added a language which was not even a derivative from the Latin stock.   In a sense, again, there was the unity of a common law ; but there were large tracts of the Empire in which the law of Rome never ran, and it was by a multiplicity of customary laws of Teutonic origin that the lives of the great majority of men were actually regulated.   In a sense which was far more real there was the unity of a common Christian culture, pervading the market-place and the study as well as the castle and the abbey ; [2] but it was the clergy—who came more and more to form a separate corporation—in whose keeping its traditions were vested and by

[1] Cf. W. B. Ferguson's *Greek Imperialism*, and the chapter on the " Conception of Empire " in *The Legacy of Rome*, edited by Cyril Bailey.
[2] See below, Chapter VII. pp. 185–186.

whose sanctions they were, for a time, enforced. A common Christian culture clerically controlled, could not, however, prevail against the existence of many languages, many laws, and many local and vernacular cultures ; and the supreme infirmity of the Empire was the absence of any effective imperial government to act as the secular arm of the imperial idea. There was indeed an Emperor ; but he could not control the local magnates of his own immediate dominions in Germany, and he was overshadowed by the growth of the Papacy, which more and more became the sovereign power over all the clergy, and, through the clergy, over all the area of life which lay within their control.

It is towards the middle of the Middle Ages, and about the year 1000 A.D.,[1] that we may begin to see the first stirrings of the movement which issued in the growth of the nations of modern Europe. Slowly, and without apparent design, the pattern of life is changed ; the universal religious society, which had always mainly lived in the world of ideas, begins to fade ; and the lineaments are discernible of a new society, particular and territorial in its range, and mainly secular in its objects and character. The germ or embryo of the new society is some unit of government—a " State " in the original sense of the word, as it is used in our language till the seventeenth century [2]—a person or group of " standing," vested as such with prestige, and able in virtue of prestige to exert authority. From this point of view, as we have already seen,[3] the State may be said to precede and mould the nation : it is States which make nations (rather than nations States) until the beginning of the nineteenth century. From the same point of view we can readily understand the alliance which was struck for long centuries between the cause of monarchism and that of nationality. The monarch was the necessary symbol and core of nationality, because he was " the State," and because the State was the maker of the nation. The fidelity of a nation to the cause of monarchism was the fidelity of a child to its parent.

The State starts its work of nation-making (not that it is concerned about nation-making : it is simply hungry for power) at some convenient geographical point which serves as a natural nucleus for its expansion.[4] Around this point it slowly groups some circle of homogeneous territory. The basis of the

---

[1] Germany began something of an independent life under the Saxon Dynasty in 919. The Capetian monarchy started on its long career in France in 987. William I began to make a new England after 1066.

[2] See the *Oxford Dictionary* under the word " State," vol. ix. pt. i. pp. 851–852 (headings iii.–iv. and sub-headings 21–23). Even the magnates of a town are called " States," and a civic governing body is " the State of this town " or " the State of this city."

[3] See above, Chapter I. p. 16.

[4] See Febvre, *op. cit.* pp. 376 *sqq.*

French State, for example, was Paris and the Isle de France (a "natural hydrographic centre," as it has been termed by Sir Halford Mackinder) : from this basis it extended its power down the river valleys to the North Sea, the Bay of Biscay, and the Mediterranean ; and, the work once done, it radiated roads and routes of communication to maintain the unity which it had made.   Spiritual bonds are then gradually added to the material. In England—though not in France, or at any rate very imperfectly in France—a uniform law is created which runs through all the gathered territory, and unites men's minds in acknowledgment of common standards of conduct.   Everywhere a single language tends to be formed by the triumph, among a variety of dialects, of the standard use of the central court and chancery.   The State does not create the national language, but it can make a local dialect into a national possession, as it did in England, in France, and in Germany ; and when a national speech is formed, and a national literature is developed, the bonds of a common written tradition and a common culture of the mind are added to those of political allegiance and geographical communication.

The new State was necessarily compelled to determine its relations to the religious society in which it found itself included. No great question arose between the various European " States " and the Emperor ; and the theory soon triumphed which was expressed by a fourteenth-century jurist in the words, *Rex est in regno suo imperator regni sui.*   It was otherwise with the relations between the lay rulers of secular societies and the Roman pontiff who stood at the head of the great clerical corporation of the Middle Ages.   In the struggles by which those relations were vexed two different solutions were achieved or attempted.   The State, as in France, might establish a form of concordat, limiting the power of the Papacy, and asserting its general control of the clergy within its sphere.   Or it might, as in England, provoke (or at any rate encourage) the growth of a national church; and a majestic lord, breaking the bonds of Rome, might sever his country entirely from the " foreign " corporation which governed the Church of the West.   In either case the struggles of the State against the clergy form the great epochs in the genesis of modern nations ; and the monarchs who wage these struggles (Philip IV in France or Henry VIII in England) become the great figures and symbols of national history.

Such, in the most general of outlines, were the early stages in the building of the spiritual superstructure of modern nations. In all this development, as it pursued its course to the end of the Middle Ages, England was in some respects exceptional and even precocious.   The Anglo-Norman State was the earliest of organized States in the West ; and the English sense of nationality, which was already aroused against the foreign " favourites " who invaded Church and State during the reign of Henry III, is both early and lasting.   In part, the fact of a sudden and sweeping Conquest had made the State uniquely strong, and it was able to establish an organized government and a system of law which effectively covered and closely united the whole of the country : in part, again, there was an homogeneous insular territory which, almost immune from the disturbance of war and unvexed by frontier-problems, could readily be gathered together in peace on a basis of national unity.   For these and for other reasons, not least among which may be counted a wealth of economic possibilities, England had already developed a vigorous and self-contained national life, enriched by a national system of law and a body of national literature, before the beginnings of modern history.

It is customary to date the beginning of modern history, and with it the definite entry of nations into the system of Europe, at the end of the fifteenth century.[1]   History begins at this point, it is often said, to be the history of nations, and when it begins to be the history of nations, it becomes modern history. We may admit at once that the Reformation, which started its course early in the sixteenth century, was a great landmark, and a great factor, in the development of national life alike in England and Scotland, in Germany and Holland, in Scandinavia and Switzerland.   A national Church was a new and striking expression and a new and powerful organ of nationality.   We may equally admit that the wars between France and Spain in the sixteenth century, though they were really wars between the two dynasties of Bourbon and Hapsburg rather than national wars, nevertheless stirred national pride and inflamed some measure of national feeling.   But it is easy to exaggerate the influence of nationality in the sixteenth and the two succeeding centuries ; and there are other and contrary factors which have to be taken into account.   There was far more of confessionalism than there was of patriotism or national feeling in the tumults by which Europe was vexed between the Diet of Worms (1521) and the Treaty of Westphalia (1648).   The French wars of Religion did not aid the development of France, or the Thirty Years War the growth of a united Germany.   The power of the confessions was partly contemporary with, and was partly succeeded by, the power of the dynasties ; and the dynasties, like the confessions, were not altogether the friends of the

---

[1] There are various dates which may be selected—in general European history, the fall of Constantinople in 1453 : in English history, the accession of Henry VII in 1485 : in the history of Spain, the conquest of Granada and the voyage of Columbus in 1492 : in French history, the invasion of Italy in 1494 : in the history of Germany, the meeting of the Diet of Worms in 1521.

nations. If France owed much to the Bourbons, and Germany
something to the Hohenzollerns, it still remains true that the
feuds of Bourbons and Hohenzollerns and Hapsburgs—not to
mention the Romanoffs—were waged over the heads, and sometimes over the prostrate bodies, of the nations within their area.
The State which had made the nation was not always tender to
its child ; and a reigning house might be more concerned with
family politics than it was with national interests. Austria-
Hungary remained a State which could never evolve a nation
from its discrepant mass of materials ; [1] Germany had some
stirrings of a national life, but at the end of the eighteenth
century it was still some three hundred separate States or
dynasties. It is hardly surprising that, in these conditions, the
political theory of the times was not a theory of nations.
Thinkers regarded the State as simply a juristic society of individuals, with the one common factor of a single government,
which had to be explained by the invocation of a social contract.
Even Bodin and Montesquieu, though they recognize the influence of climate and soil on the characters of peoples and the
nature of their constitutions, have nothing to say of the spirit
which makes a nation or the significance of nationality. It is
not until we reach the stirrings of a new breath of life in the
writings of Rousseau, and in the theories of Hegel and Fichte,
who were both affected by him, that we find any appreciation of
that " moral collective being " which we call by the name of a
nation. Nor is it until the days of Mazzini that nationality
as such, and under that name, comes by a philosophy of its own,
or that a theory is definitely built to explain its place and its
function in human life.

The self-consciousness of nations is a product of the nineteenth century. This is a matter of the first importance.
Nations were already there ; they had indeed been there for
centuries. But it is not the things which are simply " there "
that matter in human life. What really and finally matters is
the thing which is apprehended as an idea, and, as an idea, is
vested with emotion until it becomes a cause and a spring of
action. In the world of action apprehended ideas are alone
electrical ; and a nation must be an idea as well as a fact before
it can become a dynamic force.

There were three things which conspired to make nationality
an apprehended idea. The first was the partition of Poland,

[1] The Hapsburgs had state and authority, and they started from an admirable geographical centre at Vienna—the natural pivot of the Danubian lands.
Unfortunately they tried to unite a territory which, if one may use a geological
term, was full of " faults " ; and they inevitably failed. A nation can only be
made by a State if the population on which it works already possesses some
homogeneity. The mixture of Magyar, German, and Slav was too rebellious
to the potter's hand.

during the last quarter of the eighteenth century, by the three dynasties of the Hohenzollerns, the Hapsburgs, and the Romanoffs. This was the first destruction of a nation : in it the dynastic regime committed a crime which was eventually to prove its own undoing ; and by it was kindled a passion of nationality, and an undying hope of resurrection, which not only burned in Poland, but ran like a fire through Europe at every moment of crisis. The nations became aware of nationality ; and nationalism became the apprehended idea of their lives. The cataclysm of the French Revolution was a second force which made for the growth of national consciousness. The greatest nation of the day asserted its claim to mould its internal life, and demanded a form of government congenial to its own nature. After the French Revolution it is the nation which makes the State, and not the State the nation ; and the principle of nationality, no longer championed by monarchism, espouses the cause of democracy. There were excesses in the Revolution : nationality, inebriated by its own heady gospel, was ruthless within and revolutionary without ;[1] and the eventual product of a theory of national self-determination was the Napoleonic Empire, which sought to impose the will of a new and greater dynast on the whole of the Continent. But even Napoleon himself aided the growth of nationalism, and his career was the third of the forces which combined to give it vogue. It was partly that he lent it, in Italy and in Poland, a voluntary but calculated support ; but he aided it even more by the nationalist reaction which he involuntarily provoked. National self-consciousness arose in Germany under the pressure of French garrisons and French levies ; and the theory of Fichte and Hegel was inspired not only by Rousseau's teaching, but also by Napoleon's action.

While the French Revolution was an internal and spontaneous expression of the principle of nationality, the career of Napoleon thus produced, by the influence of external pressure, a new expression which took the form of a challenge to the system of Empire masquerading under the guise of a would-be emancipator. Henceforward, instead of the fact of a national existence being slowly formed and precipitated before the idea is consciously realized, the opposite process seems to become an established law. The idea is prior to the fact ; and the idea seeks to create the fact by a revolutionary challenge to the existing order. The teaching of Mazzini precedes, and with the aid of Cavour and Garibaldi produces, the unification of Italy ; the teaching of Palacký, and later of Masaryk, precedes and helps to produce the united Republic of Czecho-Slovakia.

---

[1] See Acton's essay on " Nationality," in the volume entitled *The History of Freedom*, and *supra*, pp. 16–17.

Beneath the process, and explaining its vigour and its vogue, there lies a fact which has already been noticed in passing, but which must now be brought into definite relief. The idea of nationality, in pursuing its revolutionary path, has, for more than a century past, gone hand in hand with the idea of democracy. The French Revolution, as we have seen, combined the two ideas. They were combined in the teaching of Mazzini ; they were combined in the teaching of Masaryk. And if the unification of Germany seemed to be an exception, and appeared to be achieved by a resolute will which was ready to act by the way of " blood and iron," the process of subsequent history has shown that, in Germany as elsewhere, nationality and democracy are natural bed-fellows. The passion of nationality is reinforced by the passion of civic freedom ; and the cause of liberty finds its surest basis when it is rooted and grounded in the autonomy of a national group.

We may summarize in four propositions the conclusions to which we have been led by the course of our argument :

1. Under the conditions of modern life, and since the beginning of the nineteenth century, the idea of the nation precedes, and tends to produce, the fact of a national existence.

2. Under the same conditions, and since the same date, it is the nation which makes the State, and not the State which makes the nation. The creation of the State by the nation was an achievement of the French Revolution ; it was the secret of the unification of Germany and Italy ; it is the basis of the " succession " States which have issued from the Great War.

3. The nation, in seeking to make the State, allies itself with democracy ; and nationality, which had been associated with monarchism when States were the makers of nations, associates itself with the cause of representative government as soon as nations become the makers of States. The alliance and association were not accidental ; and the two causes were joined together by something more than the fact that they enjoyed a simultaneous vogue. There was an inner logic of sympathy. Negatively, the cause of nationality was forced to assert itself against monarchs, who had made themselves dynasts and turned their States into Empires, by attacking the claims of dynasties and attempting the division of Empires. Positively (and this is a deeper reason), the nation which had found its being, and had learned to elevate the apprehended idea of its own existence into a general will for the maintenance of its own highest life, had already become by that very fact a self-governing group (whatever the claims of its rulers), and was committed by its very nature to the cause of democracy.

4. Finally, it would seem that we are moving towards a scheme of political organization in which each nation is also a

State, and each State is also a nation ; in which there are no longer nations included in alien States, or States composed of different nations.   But here we touch on a large issue, which deserves a separate investigation.

II

It may help us to elucidate the problem which has just been raised if we ask, and attempt to answer, three questions.   What was the nature of the philosophy of nationality which Mazzini preached, and how did he seek to prove that a nation must be also a State ?   On what grounds, and with what degree of success, has the thesis been criticized by thinkers such as Lord Acton and Mr. Zimmern ?   How far can we apply any theory of the relation between nationality and the State to Great Britain and the British Commonwealth ?

It was the general assumption of English Liberals during the reign of Victoria that the State should naturally be co-extensive with the nation.   The assumption was clearly expressed by John Stuart Mill in his essay on *Representative Government*.   " It is in general a necessary condition of free institutions," he wrote, " that the boundaries of governments should coincide in the main with those of nationalities."   In this philosophy liberty, or " free institutions," is the end or goal ; and the national State is regarded as a means or " necessary condition."   It is democracy which creates, or at any rate postulates, the national State, rather than the national State which creates or postulates democracy.   The emphasis may be inverted ; and it may be argued that democracy is simply a necessary condition or means for the free unfolding of the spirit and the general will of a nation.   But the form in which Mill stated the assumption was natural to political thinkers who were more interested in abstract principles of government than they were in the concrete tradition and the moving life of nations ; and we need not greatly concern ourselves with the precise degree of emphasis to be attached to either side.   To many the concrete fact of the nation will seem to be more important than any principle of government ; but we may content ourselves with the proposition that as soon as will, and not force, comes to be recognized as the basis of States, the group in which, through force of tradition and association, men naturally and instinctively form their will and seek to realize their purposes, will determine the boundaries of governments.[1] . . . And that group is the nation.

The assumption of Mill was also that of Mazzini.   **But in**

[1] See above, p. 17.

the theory of Mazzini it is coloured, as it is not in that of Mill, by a religious consecration which may remind us of Burke's conception of the hallowing of the State by the establishment of the Church. The watchword of Mazzini was " God and the People " ; and by the People he meant the self-governing nation, regarded as a necessary agent for the realization of God's plan in the world of men. The theory which lay behind his watchword was a theory based on the fundamental conception of the free man. The free man was not a mere individual : he was not the bare unit supposed as the basis of juristic constructions such as that of the Social Contract : he was engaged, by his very being, in a double communion. He was united to God by a communion which issued in duty to Him : he was also, and in consequence, united to his fellow-men (because they also were united in communion with God) by associations, especially the associations of the family and the nation, which were units divinely appointed for the discharge of men's duty to God. The zeal of the nation was upon Mazzini, and he regarded the family as a thing to be loved, and yet, at need, to be sacrificed— an antetype of the nation, preparing men by its lesser loyalties for love of the greater duty. " Between the mother's kiss and the father's caress the child learns the first lesson of citizenship." [1] The nation is the absorbing unit : Italia is the magic name. In the nation and by the nation, associated with their fellows as free partners in its life, men rise to the height of their duty to God. It follows that the essence of a nation is mission. It is appointed and sent for the realization of a divine plan. It must realize that plan within its own borders by the riches of its own development ; but it has also a larger and broader obligation. No nation can live for itself alone ; and each owes a duty to others, to the general system of Europe, and to humanity at large. A generous initiative of intervention should proceed from a nation which has won its freedom ; and it should help to realize God's plan for the world by aiding other nations to order their lives as free States and to shoulder the burden— the divinely appointed burden—of responsibility. In Mazzini's conception the nation was thus a consecrated society of free men, intended for the discharge of a national duty alike in its internal life and in its external action. In form it would be democratic, or even republican ; in spirit it would be at unity with itself and in collaboration with others. Its unity would prevent it from falling into the ideas of the French Socialists of Mazzini's day, who, blind to the life of nations, sought to split them into communistic phalanstères (just as a later generation of French thinkers has sought to vindicate the separate autonomy

[1] I have borrowed the quotation from an essay on " Mazzini," in Professor MacCunn's *Six Radical Thinkers*, which has always been a delight to me.

of syndicalistic guilds) ; and its genius of collaboration would be poles asunder from the theories of those German Socialists who, no less blind, were anxious to merge the independence of nations in a ghostly Internationale.

Lord Acton, writing in 1862, espoused a different theory ; and his theory has been adopted and expanded by Mr. Zimmern in his essays on *Nationality and Government.* Nationality, the argument runs, is a social fact : it is a form of dress, a set of customs, a way of living, a vernacular language and culture. It belongs to the independent life of the mind, which goes its way in the spaces which lie outside the scheme of politics : it may be defined as an educational principle. The State, on the other hand, is an impartial and impersonal structure : it is a scheme of organization : it is a political and legal fact. The nation and the State belong to separate departments. The nation, as a social fact or form of existence, may content itself with the social expression of its peculiar attributes. The State, as a political scheme, may safely embrace a variety of national cultures, if only it is wise enough to practise the virtue of toleration. Lord Acton, writing (we have to remember) over sixty years ago, was prepared to believe that a multi-national State, containing nations which were contented to pursue a social form of existence, was the best of political arrangements. It might attain a broader and richer culture ; for its different nations would not pursue an exclusive ideal of self-sufficiency, and each would contribute to the life of a whole on which each in its turn could draw. Above all, it might achieve a greater liberty ; the various natural groups, sheltered by a corporate social life, might check the pressure of the State ; and each of the groups might learn to recognize, and to respect, the social rights of the rest.

There is a dichotomy in this argument which may give us pause ; and the distinction which it postulates between the form of political structure and the substance of national tradition can hardly be maintained. An appeal may indeed be made to precedents or examples—the Austria-Hungary of the past ; the United States ; the British Commonwealth. Of Austria-Hungary enough has been said in the introductory chapter ; [1] and in any case it is sufficient to say that it has been tried and found wanting. The United States, which resolved to be a single State at the end of the war of North and South, is no less resolved to-day to be also a single nation. It is regulating the influx of immigrants with a view to national homogeneity ; it maintains a uniform system of education ; it speaks a single language ; it preserves—we may even say that by the pressure of public opinion it imposes—a single culture from the Atlantic

<hr>
[1] See above, p. 16.

to the Pacific.   The British Commonwealth raises an abundance of questions ; but as it can hardly be called either a nation or a State, it cannot be called in evidence on either side.   There is little comfort to be found in precedents or examples ; and the argument of Lord Acton can be more readily contradicted than it can be corroborated by an appeal to facts.   We have seen with our eyes that nations refuse to be contented with a social expression of the fact of their national life.   The waters of social life cannot be checked and diverted from political channels : they spill over and run into politics ; [1] and the people of Southern and Western Ireland, never deprived of their social rights by the British State, have none the less vindicated for themselves the political right of being an Irish Free State. Conversely, just as the nation readily passes from the area of social expression into the political form of a State, so a State which is based on will must necessarily seek to make itself co-extensive with a nation if it is to be true to its basis.   To say this is not to confuse nationality with democracy, as Mr. Zimmern would urge.[2]   It is to recognize the inner connection which, as we have seen, unites them together ; it is to admit that when once the State is based on the democratic principle of government by the will of its members, it must logically and necessarily be co-extensive with the group in which men cherish a common tradition, develop common ideas, and attain a common will.

We may thus follow Mill and Mazzini, and assume that, under the conditions of modern life, the nation will tend, as a rule, to be also a State.   But every rule has its exceptions ; and just as there were States in the past which never issued into nations, there may also be nations in our own and in future times which do not and will not issue, or desire to issue, into separate States. It is possible to conceive a nation possessing its own social customs, its own form of religion, its own system of education, and it may be its own body of law, which is contented with what it possesses, and finds enough liberty in some larger scheme of political organization to acquiesce in the absence of an independent State.   The example of Scotland is one which readily occurs to the mind ; and the example of Wales is similar.   We are thus led to the last of the questions propounded at the beginning of this section.   What is to be said of the relation between State and nationality in Great Britain ?   Can the facts of the British Commonwealth be fitted into any theory ?

The British Commonwealth may be compared to a system of zones, which fit concentrically into one another.   There is the

[1] See an article on " Nationality " in the issue of *History* for October 1919.
[2] *Nationality and Government*, p. 50.

broad and general zone of the whole Commonwealth, which includes the United Kingdom of Great Britain and Northern Ireland, the Irish Free State, and the British Dominions beyond the Seas. There is the narrower zone of the United Kingdom. Within that again is a zone in which move the separate bodies of England, Scotland, Wales, and Northern Ireland—with England and Wales peculiarly united, and yet again (both in education and in form of religion) divided from one another. Finally there is the innermost zone of the counties or shires, of which many have ancient traditions and local peculiarities, and all have a large and growing power of local self-government. It is a system which, if we speak in terms of the State and of political organization, is more than difficult to define ; and there can be little wonder if, when we seek to speak in terms of the nation and of national life, the difficulty still remains.

Two observations may be made. In the first place, we have a curious genius for combining local self-government and local loyalties with central attachment and central control. In virtue of that genius the Yorkshireman can combine shire-feeling with a feeling for the national life of England ; and in the same strength the English, the Welsh, and the Scottish can unite their national loyalty for England or Wales or Scotland with a larger British loyalty for the national life of Great Britain. In just the same way, in the Commonwealth at large, the British, the Australian, the Canadian, and the South African can all wed their different nationalities to a pride in a common culture [1]—a common inheritance of law and language and loyalty—to which they all pay allegiance. It would seem that there may be a double (if not a triple) nationality. A Scotsman, for example, has his own national fund ; but he is also a partner in the broader fund of British nationality. He has the two homes of the Scottish and the British nation. If he is satisfied with his double domicile, no question arises. If he should ever resolve to prefer a single home, and to stay there, he will have his way.

In the second place, we may observe that there is a range of possibilities in the relations between the nation and the State. If at one end of the scale there are nations which are content to exist as social groups, and at another there are nations which are both social groups and political societies, there may also be intervening grades. It is possible to conceive a nation which, if it is not also a State, may at any rate be called a quasi-State. It would at any rate be difficult to deny that Scotland, which possesses not only its own religious establishment and its own educational system, but also its own body of law, has some of the

[1] On the conception of the Commonwealth as a culture, see above, Chapter II. pp. 23–24.

attributes of a State ; [1] and if such attributes are less numerous in Wales, they cannot be said to be absent. The multiplicity of our system (if it can be called a system) may remind us of the multiplicity of the old Austria-Hungary ; but there is a fundamental difference. Austria-Hungary had no common national fund which could contain, without abolishing, the separate national funds of the Austrians, the Czechs, the Poles, the Magyars, and the Southern Slavs. It was a congeries of separate languages, separate cultures, and separate traditions, for which it could not provide either a common basis or even a *modus vivendi* ; nor did it ever concede any system of autonomy under which the various nations could have enjoyed the position of quasi-States.[2] We have been more fortunate, and perhaps more prudent. We have combined separate national funds with a common national substance : we have given to some of our nations the dignity of quasi-States. We have drawn no line of division between the " social fact " of nationality and the " political scheme " of the State. Our common State has a fund of common nationality : our separate nations are separate quasi-States. Definitions are dangerous, and epigrams are edged tools. But we may say, with some measure of truth, that Scotland is a nation which is a quasi-State ; Great Britain is a State which at the least is a quasi-nation ; and the Commonwealth is a common system of culture which is also a quasi-State and something of a quasi-nation.

The life and action of the modern State becomes more and more complicated. Theorists speak of its " plurality," and abjure the notion of any single centre of sovereignty. It is certainly a place of many loyalties. Besides the national groups with which we are concerned, there is also a range of professional groups, or occupations, which advance their claims and profess their solidarity. Any theory which attempts to fit the modern State must be like " the leaden rule of Lesbian architecture," which bends to fit the contours of the material. Meanwhile it is curious to notice how an acute French observer, nourished, it is true, in the tradition of a highly unified national State, has misconstrued the multiplicity of our State and nation. Émile Boutmy, in the work on the political psychology of the English people to which reference has already been made, has occasion to refer to the other nations of Great Britain. " Neither the Scotch," he writes, " nor the Irish nor the Welsh have borrowed anything from the English. . . . The absence of all sympathy with the English and their customs is apparent in every word and deed of Scotch, Irish, and Welsh. . . . The enmity of

[1] On Scotland, see below, Chapter VII. pp. 189–194.
[2] Such a system was projected in 1849 (under the Kremsier Constitution), but the projecture was abortive. See L. Eisenmann's *Le Compromis.*

Ireland, Scotland, and Wales towards their conquerors is particularly marked in questions of government." But the English,
he adds, have on their side accepted the Scotch, who (and here
he makes a just remark) " are by no means insensible to the
conveniences of residence which England offers them " ; while
the Scotch, "who are like the Germans . . . have inoculated
England with learned political economy and philosophy," and
supplied her "with the exalted experimentalism which has
become superimposed upon her flat empiricism." [1]

III

We may now seek to analyse the idea of the nation and to
discover its philosophical implications. We have termed the
nation a spiritual superstructure upon a material basis ; and
we have said that in the nineteenth century the nation became
an apprehended idea. Are we also to say that the fact that
men consciously entertain an idea of the nation means that they
have now discovered a being or person ? Can we ascribe personality to a nation, or hold that it has a character in the sense
in which persons have characters ? Is there a national soul—
an *âme du peuple* ?

Each of us forms some picture or physical image of an idea
such as that of a nation. That picture tends to be personal.
The picture of England is the figure of John Bull ; that of the
United States is the figure of Uncle Sam ; and we know the
pictures of la belle France and Germania. If we interrogate
ourselves, we shall at once admit that the picture is a composite
photograph, which may represent, as it were, a blur of many
persons, but is not a picture of any. If, however, we are ardent
nationalists, who not only entertain an idea of a nation, but
have coloured it by our emotion and made it throb with our
feeling, we shall go further. We may think of " holy Ireland " [2]
as a being who demands devotion—tragic and beautiful, wronged
and suffering ; and one even of our English poets has written :

> "All too late we love who wronged thee,
> Ireland, Ireland, green and sad."

There is a passage in a book written by an Indian missionary
which admirably shows how the compelling vision of a personified
country can seize the imagination and dominate the will. A
young Hindu student, stimulated by the news of a Japanese

---

[1] Émile Boutmy, *op. cit.* (Eng. trans.), pp. 98–99.
[2] "It is not merely," said an Irish leader in 1916, "the love of country . . .
the love of the sod of Ireland. . . . It is the knowledge that there still lives in
this country, in this race, a holy cause."

victory in the war against Russia some twenty years ago, and unable to sleep in the exaltation of his national feeling, dreamed a waking dream. " The vision of his own country came to him in an almost objective form. She seemed to rise in front of him like a sad and desolate mother, claiming his love. The face which he saw was very beautiful, but indescribably sorrowful. It was so real to him that for months afterwards he could shut his eyes and recall it. . . . What happened to him, as far as one could judge from his story, was something analogous to the experience described in religious language as conversion. With overwhelming force he heard the call to give himself up for his motherland. He could think of nothing else. Night and day the vision was before him." [1]

But the personification of nations has run far beyond both popular pictures and the imaginative visions of nationalist exaltation. The tendency to endow a nation with being and personality may be traced in reflective thought as well as in moods of sentiment. German thinkers about 1800, in days before the Germans had become a nation, but when, under the influence of the Romantic movement, they were already beginning to regard themselves as a people, assigned a transcendent existence, and even a power of creation, to what they called the " Folk." Wolf's *Prolegomena to Homer*, published in 1795, discovered a series of popular lays behind the Homeric epics ; Jacob Grimm and his brother found in the Folk-Saga the earliest history of every people ; Herder carried the folk-soul into the study of literature ; and Savigny taught that law was an ex- pression of the life of the people, and that lawyers only developed and refined what folk-life had originally created. The folk thus became the maker of song and story, music and dance ; it became, in the theory of Hegel, the maker of constitutions, " the self-conscious ethical substance " ; [2] it became, in juristic theory, the author and begetter of law ; and had not Rousseau, the precursor of this romanticism, already defined the State (which lies behind the Folk, and into which the Folk is always tending to pass) as a " moral collective being " which possessed a " general will," and was vested with the cardinal quality of personality ?

New forces of thought which also encouraged the personifica- tion of groups appeared at the close of the nineteenth century. Gierke, in his great legal work on *Das deutsche Genossenschaftsrecht*, vindicated the real existence of corporations, which he refused to regard as fictitious persons that could only be fabricated by

---

[1] C. F. Andrews, *The Renaissance in India* (1914), pp. 20–21.

[2] *Philosophy of Mind* (Wallace's translation), § 535. To Hegel the spirit of a nation, as a manifestation of objective mind, and as itself objective mind, reconciles " ought " with " is " in its system of social ethics (*Sittlichkeit*), which transcends alike the mere morality of conscience and the mere legality of law.

an act of the State, and preferred to conceive as actual persons, which might grow as well as be made, and were capable of forming their own " group-will " in the strength of their own " group-personality." The theory of Gierke was expounded by Maitland, in a preface to a translation of one of the chapters of his book ; [1] it was adopted by Dr. Figgis (more particularly in his work on *Churches in the Modern State*), and used to support the claims of religious groups ; it was called in aid of the rights of Trade Unions by Mr. and Mrs. Sidney Webb, in the preface to the 1911 edition of their *History of Trade Unionism*. The doctrine of the real personality of groups which was thus given currency has generally been used in what may be termed a syndicalistic sense. It has served to limit the State ; it has been made an ally alike of religious confessions and economic professions, and used to support the claim of " inherent rights " which has been advanced on behalf of ecclesiastical and social groups. But the doctrine which challenges the State may also be cited, without any great paradox, to appear on the side of the nation. If a trade union or a church is a person, may not a nation, with its old and established intimacies, be also conceived as a person ? In France, at any rate, where a nationalist party has established a peculiar cult of the nation, a theory of national personality has had its vogue. The theory, it is true, is independent of Gierke and of jurisprudence ; and it finds its foundations in the study of collective or social psychology. Le Bon has argued that there is a Soul of a People, which dominates and makes its history. Durkheim, a psychologist of far greater power, propounds the view that mind is a social entity—a single unit conducting the intellectual processes of a society—which thinks, it is true, in and by the convolutions of the brains of individuals, but uses them only as the physical organs of its own transcendent existence. " Not I, but the social mind thinking in and through me—and through others," will on this basis become the confession of every thinker. This psychological realism, which may almost remind us of the Realism of the mediæval schoolmen, has not found a following ; but the work of Professor MacDougall on *The Group Mind* attests the influence which a somewhat similar theory may exert on a student of social psychology.

In the study of human relationships, and in the sphere of secular life, there is no room for any postulate of a soul, or mind, except in the individual human person. The interplay of minds in a society is full of creative fertility ; but it remains an interplay of individual minds. The seeds of thought may be blown over a wide territory ; they may germinate in new places or form new combinations ; but each originally came from one

[1] *Political Theories of the Middle Ages* (1900).

particular plant. Personality is a more complex conception; and it raises more difficult issues. If will be regarded as its essential attribute, we may distinguish between two different forms, in both of which that attribute is present, but present in different ways. One of these forms we may call by the name of moral, and the other by that of juristic personality. Moral personality, which is expressed in a moral will, and issues in moral responsibility, can only be predicated of individual persons. No moral indictment can be drawn against a nation—though it may very well be drawn against a person, or a number of persons, who have willed and acted in its name, and have incurred by their act and deed a moral responsibility. Juristic personality, which is expressed in a power of legal action and issues in legal responsibility, can be predicated not only of individual persons, but also of any group of persons which, in virtue of either express law or of generally recognized custom, has the power of action and the burden of responsibility. Such a group can formulate a will, by the vote of a majority or by some other method prescribed in its constitution; and it can accordingly carry what the Roman lawyers called a *persona* of rights and duties—rights which it legitimately expects to enjoy, and may legally claim; duties which it is legitimately expected to recognize, and may be legally forced to discharge. A nation, if it is legally organized in the form of a State, will have a juristic personality; it will exercise rights, or be subject to claims, under international law or custom. But a nation does not possess a moral personality; and it has no moral will of its own distinct from that of its members. Apart from law, and apart from the legal position of nations which are legally organized in the form of juristic societies or States, there is no national " person " over and above the persons of the individual members of the nation. In a nation of forty millions there will not be any forty million and first personality which is that of " the nation itself."

The unity of a nation, therefore, is not that of a person which transcends the persons of which the nation is composed; and there is no separate national mind or will or personality apart from the minds and wills and personalities of its members. National unity is not that of a mind, but that of a mental substance. It consists in a common structure or content of ideas—ideas made electric by feeling, and therefore issuing in will and effort and action—which are resident in the minds of the members of a nation, and, except in so far as they are apprehended by the minds of the members of other nations, are resident only in them. There is no single vessel or vehicle: there are as many vessels or vehicles as there are persons; but they hold and carry—some more and some less, according to their several powers of comprehension—a common substance or content. It is true that a number of persons, when they are habitually acting together under the influence of common ideas and the feelings related to those ideas, will act in a new and different way. Whatever they will, whatever they do, whatever they pour from themselves into the outer world of fact and act, will be something different from what it would be if they were only acting as individuals in the strength of their separate ideas and feelings. It is this which may lead us to think of some transcendent unity ; but to think in that way is to misinterpret the unity which actually exists. A nation is nothing more, and nothing less, than a body of men who are united and made one body in virtue of having in their minds, and in so far as they have in their minds, a common substance or content of ideas, which has been in the minds of men now dead and gone, as it will be in the minds of men unborn and still to come. If on this basis we seek to make a picture of a nation, we shall not delineate a person. Our image will be more delicate : it may even seem tenuous and airy ; but it will not be any the less real —for an image of men's minds must follow the subtlety of what it copies. We shall see a multitude of persons, each as it were a dot (like the stars in the heavens at night), united to one another—as they are also united with their ancestors and successors—by the finest of connecting filaments. You may call the sum of these filaments by the name of social heritage ; you may call it, if you will, by the name of national tradition. It is spun of the threads of language and literature ; the threads of law and government ; the threads of religious belief and educational policy. It is made by men's minds, and it is transmitted by mind to mind, from one generation to another. It is a structure of the mind, at once made by the mind and constituting a large part of its substance, which serves as a dwelling-house in which men's minds find a habitation together, assume a position or station, and enter into regular relations on the basis of such a position.[1]

It is perhaps more to the national State than to the nation in itself that the fullness of such a conception is relevant. But the nation is the sustaining force and the spiritual foundation of modern States ; and it is natural to speak of the nation at its highest power. The nation which is also a State is an organized body of individual wills controlled by a common fund of organizing ideas. It is these " organizing ideas " which group men in a society, giving them position in themselves and a

---

[1] I am indebted here, as in almost everything that I have written on social matters, to the late Dr. Bosanquet's *Philosophical Theory of the State*. I would also refer to an article, entitled " The Discredited State," in the *Political Quarterly* for February 1915.

fixed relation to others ; or rather, to speak more exactly, men group themselves, and themselves assume position and a system of fixed relations, in the light of these ideas. They have been made by individual men in the past (though they are always receiving new additions from age to age) ; and it is by individual men that they are apprehended, vested with feeling, and accepted as motives for action, in each successive present. All are concerned in their making and apprehension ; but all do not equally make or apprehend, just as all do not equally feel or act. Those who have clarity of vision and energy of volition—who see ideas clearly, and will them strongly—are the makers of nations. The rest accept and follow their guidance, some with a ready conviction, and some for reasons which we have still to study.

IV

The description of national life in the terms we have sought to use may perhaps be described as intellectualist. It is a statement in terms of reason ; it is a statement in terms of ideas, rationally formed, rationally adopted, and rationally willed. But psychologists have been criticizing of late the theory of the State (and by implication that of the nation) for its excessive rationalism ; and we have to reckon with their criticism. Do men always, or mainly, act consciously in the light of reason ? Do they not often, and perhaps mainly, act subconsciously in the strength of instincts ? And must we not therefore allow for the operation of those instinctive modes of action which were developed in primitive times by primeval men, have come to be inherited in our blood, and are automatically adopted, as the stimuli of reflex action, in what may be called the submerged area of our minds ?

Before we discuss these questions we may begin by observing—as we have had reason to observe already and shall have reason to observe again in a later chapter [1]—that men may act without a full consciousness of the ultimate reasons or ends of their action. They may do a thing for one reason, and as purpose is heaped on purpose, and insight added to insight, the thing may come to serve another and higher end. The State began for the sake of mere life, Aristotle said, but it exists for the sake of moral life. Marriage began for the sake of the reproduction of our kind : it exists for the moral purposes of married love and family life. This growing sublimation of purpose which can be traced in the development of human institutions may have roots in the processes of instinct ; but it transcends its origins. We cannot judge the end of an institution from its first beginnings ; and it would be a fallacy to

[1] See above, Chapter I. pp. 5–6, and below, Chapter VI. p. 143.

assume that the instincts which may have helped to produce, and may still serve to maintain, a given institution are the secret of its interpretation.   Rational purpose is the essence of human action ; and it is present in all men's doings.   It is true that they may act originally on a basis of instinct ; it is true that they may still continue to act with the support of instinctive tendencies.   In any group there is a basis of instinct which is a necessary aid to rational and purposive thought and will, just as in each individual there is a basis of reflex action which is a necessary aid to conscious life.   But the conscious life of each individual lies beyond his reflex action ; and in any group there is similarly present a fund of thought and will which lies beyond the region of instinct.

Instincts have been defined by Professor MacDougall as " innate specific tendencies of the mind that are common to all members of any one species," and as " slowly evolved in the process of adaptation of species to their environment." [1]   One of these innate specific tendencies is the gregarious instinct, which is common to animals and men, and unites the former in herds as it helps to unite the latter in a variety of social groups. It draws like to like, both for security and for company ; and it may do more.   It may issue in a demand for likeness—a demand directed against the uncomfortable fact of difference. In a herd of animals the demand may take the negative form of expulsion ; in a human society the positive method of compulsion may be followed.   Fraternity and conformity may thus become watchwords ; and the observer may notice in the United States the vogue which, under the influence of a common fund of Puritan tradition and stimulus of a flow of foreign immigrants, these watchwords have attained.   In Great Britain an intimate national life has long been combined with a respect for peculiarities and even for eccentricities (the one, it may be, serving as the corollary to the other) ; but here too the gregarious passion has profited, as we have seen, by the growth of urbanization, and an old instinct, long dormant, has acquired a new strength.   It may even seem, as Professor MacDougall remarks, that an instinct which helped to build the nation has become a danger to its life.[2]

The instinct of imitation, strong in most men, with its corollary of suggestion, strong in some, is an instinct closely allied to the gregarious.   Tarde has emphasized and elucidated its working in his treatise on the *Laws of Imitation*.   It explains, in his view, the process by which ideas spread downwards from originating minds, which have a general prestige, through a whole community ; and it therefore aids in the formation of that common content of many minds which we call a national

---

[1] *Social Psychology*, p. 22.   [2] *Ibid.* p. 301.

tradition. It has been said that it may be called "a prime condition of all collective mental life."[1] We may admit the description, but only with the proviso that a prime condition remains a condition, and is not a cause. We may add, following Tarde, that imitation serves the ends of collective mental life in two different ways. On the one hand it is a stabilizing and conservative agency which deposits and preserves tradition ; on the other hand, by providing a channel for the flow of new ideas, it may be a progressive, and even a revolutionary force. We may see from its general operation how a sub-rational element can help to secure the acceptance of ideas which deserve to be accepted on rational grounds by a mind which is conscious of their value. Masses of men may be led by its force to embrace a belief or a practice not for its own intrinsic worth, but because it has been expressed or exemplified by men who carry prestige. This may explain how the influence of great men has been intensified. They not only count for what they are, or were, in themselves : they also count for the infinite suggestion of even their simplest doings and sayings to a multitude of minds. In this way Washington and Lincoln have become, as it were, the *divi Cæsares* of a great nation. In this way, again, the figure of Cromwell has gradually imposed itself upon English imagination, and become a symbol of England. "Like him," wrote S. R. Gardiner, "modern Britain has waged wars, annexed territory, extended trade, and raised her head among the nations. Like him, her sons have been unable to find satisfaction in their achievements unless they could persuade themselves that the general result was beneficial to others besides themselves. It is inevitable that now as then such an attitude should draw upon itself the charge of hypocrisy."[2]

But whatever weight we allow to the play of instincts in human society, we are bound to conclude that they do not go far to explain the facts of national life and tradition. They belong to our species at large, and not to the nation. There are general instincts of the human race : there are no special national instincts. The general human instincts help the formation and the spread of a common national tradition : they underlie every form of society. But each nation makes its own tradition, in its own way, on the common human basis ; each forms by a rational process, and transmits by the rational process of social instruction and discipline, the ideas on which it is based. It is particularly in the process of transmission that

[1] *Social Psychology*, p. 326.

[2] See also C. H. Pearson, *National Life and Character*, p. 238 : "The countrymen of Chatham and Wellington, of Washington and Lincoln, of Joan of Arc and Gambetta . . . are richer by great deeds that have formed the national character, by winged words that have passed into current speech, by the example of lives and labours consecrated to the service of the Commonwealth."

we may note the gulf which is fixed between instinct and tradition. Instincts are biologically inherited : they are innate and flow in the blood. The tradition which constitutes a nation is socially transmitted from mind to mind : it is not innate, but implanted from generation to generation : it is kept alive by a process of teaching, in the widest sense of that word—the teaching of law and its sanctions ; the teaching of religion and its exaltations ; the teaching of all the suggestions embedded in language and literature ; the teaching of all the precepts and methods of a system of education. Instincts which are supernational and inherited by a natural process cannot explain the existence of traditions which are purely national and are transmitted by human action and discipline. But they play an ancillary part ; and without the gregarious instinct which helps to hold nations together, and the instinct of imitation which aids in maintaining the community of their ideas, the achievement of national unity and a national character would be an impossibly arduous process.

We may end by recurring to the analogy between the growth of individual and the growth of national character which has already been mentioned in the introductory chapter. In the growth of individual character, Professor MacDougall has taught us, we may distinguish three different factors. There is the factor of temperament, which is a matter of bodily constitution, and depends upon physical elements such as the endocrine glands.[1] There is the factor of disposition, which may be defined as the particular sum of instincts and their correlated emotions which distinguishes, and in its measure determines, a personality. Finally there is the factor which is particularly and essentially the character—" the sum of acquired tendencies built up on the native basis of disposition and temperament." Similar factors may be distinguished in the growth of national character. A nation too has the temperament of its racial blend, acting under the influence of its physical environment. A nation too has a disposition or sum of instincts which may be varied from time to time by the density of its population and the nature of its occupations. A nation too has a character, which is the sum of acquired tendencies built up by its leaders, in every sphere of its activity, with the consent and the co-operation—active in some, but more or less passive in others—of the general community. To that process of building, which creates the spiritual superstructure and the essential tradition of a nation, we have now to turn.

[1] The relation of the glands to personality has been examined, and perhaps exaggerated, by L. Berman in a work on *The Glands and Personality*. Sir Arthur Keith, in a presidential address on the differentiation of mankind into racial types, delivered before the British Association in 1919, has dealt with the effect of the glands on the development of human races.

LIST OF BOOKS

ACTON, Lord.—*History of Freedom* (essay on " Nationality "), 1909.
LE BON, G.—*Lois psychologiques de l'Évolution des Peuples* (17th edition), 1922.
BOSANQUET, B.—*Philosophical Theory of the State*, 1899.
DURKHEIM, E.—*De la division du travail social*, 1893.
   „   „   *Les Règles de la méthode sociologique* (6th ed.), 1912.
JELLINEK, G.—*Allgemeine Staatslehre* (3rd ed.), 1914.
MACDOUGALL, W.—*Social Psychology*, 1908.
   „   „   *The Group Mind*, 1920.
MACIVER, R.—*Community*, 1917.
MAZZINI, G.—*Scritti scelti* (Florence), 1916.
MUIR, J. R. B.—*Nationalism and Internationalism*, 1916.
ROSE, J. H.—*Nationality as a Factor in Modern History*, 1916.
TARDE, H.—*Les Lois de l'Imitation* (7th edition), 1921.
WALLAS, G.—*Our Social Heritage*, 1921.
ZIMMERN, A. E.—*Nationality and Government*, 1918.

CHAPTER VI

THE POLITICAL FACTOR: LAW AND GOVERNMENT

I

THERE is an area of human life which is, as it were, built over by a series of buildings at once unseen and real—words and language and thoughts; customs and beliefs; laws, practices, and institutions. Men are visible bodies, inhabiting a visible territory; but they are also invisible minds, dwelling in invisible buildings which their minds have made. Constructed by the mind for its habitation, these buildings (like visible historic buildings) affect the mind which inhabits them. The language, the beliefs, and the laws of a nation determine, or at any rate influence, the nation from which they proceed. Men project the ideas of their minds into an outer world in which, escaping like fugitive birds from their creators, they acquire their own habitation, and from which they return to control or limit their originators. This is the universal experience of all creative minds—to originate an idea; to seek to realize it externally; and to find, as soon as it is realized, that it has escaped and is lost to its originator. You cannot recall and remould what you have once projected into the world outside you. It makes its own combinations with other elements, and assumes its own settled form; it will confront you henceforth as something which has its own separate being, and it will exercise, even upon you, its own particular effect. It is the tragedy of action, that men lose control over what they create; but it may also be the power and the triumph of action that the thing created transcends the ideas and intention of the creator.

If we thus believe that the law and the constitution under which a nation lives are a creation of mind—but a creation which acquires a substantive existence of its own, and may in turn affect its creators—we shall have a clue which may guide us in approaching a vexed question of political theory. Are laws and institutions made, or do they grow? Savigny defined law as " the organ of folk-right," by which he intended to convey the idea that it naturally grew from a sense of right inherent in

a community. Hegel, in a resonant dictum, proclaimed that
constitutions were never made. " What is called making a
constitution is a thing that has never happened in history. A
constitution only develops from the national spirit identically
with that spirit's own development." [1] If this were entirely
and absolutely true, and if the law and the constitution of a
nation simply developed from its sense of right and its national
spirit, we should have to hold that national character issues in a
system of law and institutions which it inevitably precipitates,
rather than that law and institutions issue in a type of national
character which they help, along with other forces, to mould.
But it is not entirely and absolutely true. Men—individual
men ; judges, administrators, and legislators—make laws and
constitutions. It is true that what they create undergoes a
change, and suffers a process of alchemy, when it enters into
composition with other existing elements ; it is also true that
the process of making is sometimes so slow and so gradual (here
a little and there a little), and each stage is often so innocent of
any intention to produce the next, that growth may seem a more
natural category than creation. But law and institutions are,
in their ultimate nature, ideas ; and ideas do not grow—they
are made by human minds. The ideas which we call by the
names of laws and institutions can seldom be traced directly
to their original springs, but they always proceed from the
initiative of single and personal minds. To ascribe them to the
national spirit or the soul of the people is to use a short-hand
expression (which may sadly confuse those who do not realize
that it is only short-hand) for a complicated process—the process
by which the initiative of an individual mind gradually infects
others, is modified as it is transmitted to other minds, is altered
as it blends with other initiatives, and finally emerges into the
light, as a visible stream, in what seems a collective and impersonal form. In the earlier and more unconscious stages of
history the slow percolation of initiatives, of an unknown and
unknowable origin, was the natural and inevitable form of legal
and constitutional development. The nearer we come to
modern times, the more we are able to trace direct and deliberate
creation. The constitution of the United States, for example,
was framed and made by the conscious thought of a few creative
minds reflecting on the experience of the past and the theories of
contemporary writers, and building, in the light of such reflection,
a system of institutions. In the last century and a half the
sphere of deliberate creation has grown and grown : it has prevailed in France ; it has made codes and constitutions in Germany ; it has created unions and commonwealths in Canada,
Australia, and South Africa ; it has captured the world.

[1] Hegel, *Philosophy of Mind*, § 540 (Wallace's translation).

Even where percolation is the process by which laws and institutions are made, the laws and institutions of a country are less the product of a national spirit than they are the producers of national character. They are not something which flows inevitably from a national genius : on the contrary, they might have been otherwise than they are ; and a " happy accident " (or it may be an unhappy accident), the ingenuity and the resource of a great conqueror (like William I), the acumen of a body of lawyers (such as those who surrounded Henry II), or, it may be, the influence of a neighbouring country, may all have helped to make them what they actually became. But once they are established, they become, as it were, encompassing banks—like the banks of the Po or the Hoang-ho—in which the stream of national life must henceforth flow. They are given and determining facts ; and they affect the direction of national movement. In the process of their own becoming they were themselves subject to contingency ; but when once they were fixed in their outline, they made the process of national develop-ment contingent upon their own nature. The character of English feudalism, the genius of English common law, the nature of the English parliament—none of them inevitable expressions of an English national spirit—all became moulds in which the English nation was set and in which it acquired its character. Where deliberate creation has been the parent of institutions, it is even more obvious that institutions exercise a greater influence on national character than national character exercises upon institutions. The rules of the American constitution have been the mould of the development of American life. The rule which forbids interference with freedom of contract has prevented any legislation, and any action by the courts, which might tend to regulate wage-contracts ; it has determined the relations of employer and employed and encouraged the free hustle of business. The division of powers between executive and legislative has diminished the importance of the legislature : it has made its debates, as Bagehot remarked, much less of an interest, and much less of an education to the community, than the debates of the English parliament ; it has made discussion less of a passion, and the formation of public opinion more of a problem. The electivity of magistrates, and particularly of the bulk of the judicature, has diminished their prestige and their influence : it has prevented leadership from becoming a national force, and hindered the growth of a law-abiding habit. The uncalculated results of deliberately adopted rules have affected the general life of the whole community ; and the example of the United States goes far to prove both the freedom of the initiative with which institutions may be framed, and the inevitability of the consequences which they produce as soon as they have become a frame-work of national life.

It has been suggested, in an earlier chapter, that the State makes the nation, and not the nation the State ; it has been indicated that the State, in its original and etymological sense, is a " standing " (*status*) or " position," and that it comes, by a natural transference, to be identified with the man or body of men who hold such standing or position ; and it has been shown that a nation is brought into being when such a man or body of men, starting from an original nucleus or hearth, extend a system of law and institutions over an ever-widening territory which becomes the national home. The action of the State upon national character, in the course of this process of nation making, is generally neither direct nor conscious. The State is concerned with powers, prerogatives, jurisdiction, and taxation ; it pursues immediate and material objects of authority and revenue ; it does not seek to spread a temper or to inculcate a tone. It commands, in its nature, only external means of compulsion ; and it has generally been content with the external results which such means can secure. It is not, indeed, impossible that the State should consciously attempt to use direct methods of giving a bias to national feeling, especially in preparation for war or during the course of hostilities. There is a modern invention which goes by the name of propaganda. Psychologists are beginning to teach—what statesmen and business men had long treasured among the *arcana imperii et negotii*—that there is a power in suggestion, a use in advertisement, an efficacy in symbols and catchwords, and a value in iteration. With the development of national systems of education, the State may use schools to inculcate a materialistic form of patriotism. History may be taught with a view to inflaming national pride or stimulating national resentment ; and the presentation of a nation's past from a particular angle may deflect its character, for the time being, in the direction of that angle. But these are the discoveries of the present ; and even in the present their influence is perhaps less than is often thought. They have a short-time value in moments of excitement, but they do not create any permanent and universal disposition : you cannot fool all the people all the time. If there is such a thing as suggestibility, there is also what psychologists call contra-suggestion, which drives the obstinate in an opposite direction ; and in the modern State the play of parties may be trusted to correct excesses which will probably always be the result of some party's enthusiasm. Even to-day the influence of the State on the temper of national life is due less to what the State does than to what, in its nature, it is.

That influence, flowing unconsciously and by indirect

10

channels, may pour its waters through many tracts of the national life. The speech of the government, for example, may become the speech of the governed ; the use of the court and the chancery may become the use of society and of men of letters ; and the State may give to the nation the unity of a common and uniform language. It was in this way that the East Midland dialect became the general standard of English ; that the *langue d'oil* became the language of France ; and that the High German used by the Hohenstaufen chancery became the German of Luther and the whole of Germany. In a larger way, and on a greater scale, the policy of a government, if it is steadily pursued through a period sufficiently long, may be a primary factor in determining the habits of a people and the disposition of a nation. The action of the French Government through the centuries vitally affected the character of France. The *ancien régime*, by depressing the nobility and levelling classes, produced that " equalitarianism " which produced the French Revolution, and is still the main characteristic of France at the present time.[1] The influence of the State, exerted in other ways and to other ends, has been no less operative in England ; and indeed we cannot illustrate better the part which the State may play in determining national life, than by comparing the national temper of England with that of France, and by seeking to trace the extent to which differences in the form and action of the State have produced the difference between the tempers of the two countries.

Professor MacDougall, in a passage in his work on the *Group Mind*,[2] has addressed himself to this question. How, he asks, are we to explain the difference between the sociability, the centralization, and the officialism of France, and the individualism, the local self-government, and the passion for the liberty of the subject which we find in England ? His own explanation, which can hardly be accepted, is grounded on reasons of race and the abiding influence of primitive occupations. He assumes that the French are the descendants of the Alpine Gauls—an assumption which leaves out of count the large element of the Nordic and Mediterranean races to be found in France ; and in the same way he assumes that the English are the descendants of the Nordic Teutons—not taking into account

---

[1] There is a fable, which I remember hearing in New York, that liberty, equality, and fraternity had once to be distributed among England, France, and the United States. England came first, took liberty for its portion, and has continued to show a passion for political and civil liberty. France came next, and took equality ; and France has always remained constant to the cause of social equality, refusing to recognize inequalities of colour, creed, or class. The United States came last, and taking the remaining gift of fraternity, has always cherished a brotherhood which issues in a general demand of conformity to type.

[2] W. MacDougall, *op. cit.* pp. 223–241.

the Mediterranean strain with which the Nordic is crossed in our composition. Borrowing from Demolins and de Tourville, two speculative writers of the school of Le Play, a theory of the influence of primitive occupations in producing acquired characteristics, and assuming that such characteristics are naturally inherited (which is perhaps a dubious assumption), he suggests that the Alpine Gauls were nomadic in occupation; that they were therefore (as nomads tend to be) patriarchal in organization; and that they were accordingly (in virtue of the influence of the patriarchally organized family) sociable, ready to accept a centralized authority, and disposed to respect official power—characteristics which they handed down to their descendants. The Nordic Teutons, originating in Scandinavia, lived the life of fishermen in long narrow fiords, with little strips of plough land (one here, one there), on the narrow coast between the sea and the mountains, to give a subsidiary occupation. Fiord was separated from fiord and plough land from plough land; each man was on his own, and each was compelled to manage for himself; and all developed a temper of individualism, all tended to local self-government, and all were lovers of liberty. We may readily admit, as we have done in a previous chapter, that racial bias counts for something; we may equally admit, and we have already sought to show, that the nature of occupation and the distribution of population— not only as they occur in the past, but also (and even more) as they are to be found in the present—are potent influences. But Professor MacDougall's argument, even if its assumptions were correct, is too great a simplification of the problem. To explain the difference between France and England we must not only take into account the racial factor (the only difference in this respect is that there is in France an Alpine element which is not present, or present only to a very slight degree, in England); we must not only weigh the factor of occupation—which only suggests the reflection that France has always been predominantly engaged in arable agriculture, and England, as we have seen, has pursued a variety of occupations; we must also consider the difference between the territory of France and that of England, and especially the gulf which separates a small island country, with no serious frontier problem, from a continental country which has a long and exposed frontier;[1] but above all, we must turn our attention to the action of the historic State, which weighs more heavily in the balance than all other factors. The Roman State romanized Gaul far more than it did Britain; it left in Gaul its language, and the inheritance and the implications of its language; it left the tradition of its sociable town life; it left the spirit of a clear-cut law and a

[1] See above, pp. 58–59.

centralized imperial government. There was another historic difference between the action of the State in France and its action in England. The Capetian Government after 987 A.D. was unlike the Norman and Angevin Government after 1066 A.D. It had to deal with a large country, in which any centralization could only be slowly achieved. The feudatories, further removed from the centre than they were in England, were more firmly entrenched. The government, annexing one feudal province after another, by a process which lasted all through the Middle Ages, could only connect them with Paris by a system of executive officials and the methods of administrative centralization. The Norman and Angevin Government was concerned with a far smaller country. It started with the fact of a conquest ; it could count, from its first beginnings, upon a measure of unity. The feudatories, less protected by distance, were less powerful ; and the kings, absorbed in continental interests, were able to devote their attention to securing a revenue which would enable them to promote those interests. They founded a central treasury ; they founded a system of judges, who went on circuit to gather the fines which would replenish the treasury, but who also—as it seemed at first, incidentally ; but as it proved in the long run, essentially—administered a single law and a single system of civil rights in every shire and every locality. Unity in France was late, and achieved by a struggle which issued in a centralized form of administration and a hierarchy of powerful officials. Unity in England was early ; and it took the form of a single system of jurisdiction, which gave power to judges rather than officials, ensured civil rights rather than State authority, and (being administered locally, and in co-operation, as we shall see, with local juries) encouraged the growth of local responsibility. It is this difference in the action and the history of the State which fundamentally explains, if not the difference between the sociability of France and the individualism of England, at any rate that between the centralization and the officialism of the one country and the localism and civil liberty of the other.

In the light of these considerations we may turn to the English State and the system of government and body of law through which it has worked, and we may seek to study its action in some of the main spheres of its operation. It is the more instructive an instance, because the State in England was of a particularly early growth and a peculiarly long and un-interrupted continuity. The continuity of the English State is the most remarkable of its features. The work of Henry II and Edward I, of Henry VIII and Queen Elizabeth—common law and parliament ; church establishment and local government—is still with us ; and we can the more readily trace the fruits because the tree has so long a growth, and is still alive to-day. Even if we go back beyond the reign of Henry II, and start with the system of feudatories which attained its final form after the Conquest of 1066, we shall be dealing with something which—perhaps in its last surviving traces—*spirat adhuc vivitque*.

II

Feudalism was a general European system—the product of an agricultural age and a regime of " kind," in which the rent of land was paid, not in money (which had largely disappeared from circulation), but in commodities or in labour ; the product, again, of an amateur and non-professional society, in which an army had to be raised, and other functions of government discharged, by the obligation of all landowners both to do military service and to pay " suit " to their lord for the purpose of forming a court of justice and a council of deliberation.   There was no distinction in nature, such as has sometimes been alleged, between English and continental feudalism.   Alike in England and on the Continent, the sovereignty of the king co-existed with the right of the feudal lord over his vassals ; alike in England and on the Continent, it was a generally acknowledged principle that a superior and " liege " fealty was due to the king.   But if there was no difference in nature, or in theory, there was yet a difference in practice and in the actual working of the system ; and it was only in England that the king was actually able, as early as the end of the eleventh century, to make the doctrine of liege fealty an accomplished fact, and to exact from the vassals of his feudal lords an overriding allegiance to his own sovereign " State."   The power of the Crown was effective in England by virtue of the fact of conquest, and because the king was able to ally with the English—conquered, it is true, but still organized as a local militia on which he could call in his hour of need—against his feudatories.   The effective action of the king's power produced two results in the English feudal system.   In the first place, it stopped the feudatories from achieving their natural ambition of forming local sovereignties. They had not sufficient control over their own vassals ; and they were compelled, if they desired to exercise political influence, to seek it centrally, in a national co-operation with other elements (the church, the boroughs, and the communities of the shires) designed to check a king, such as John, who sought to turn his royal supremacy into a royal autocracy.   This was the origin of Magna Charta ; it was one of the bases of a national Parliament ; it helped to prevent the baronage from becoming a class apart, and associated them with the general " community of all England."   In the second place, it was the power of the

Crown which prevented the feudatories from becoming a special blood or "sangre azul." Anxious that the eldest son, as a single definite person who might easily be subjected to process of law, should succeed to the whole body of duty of an undivided fief, the king enforced the principle of primogeniture, which prevented the division of estates and thereby the division of duty among a number of successors. That principle, whatever might be its effect on the life of the family, proved advantageous to the nation. The younger sons of the feudatories dropped into the ranks of the commoners; and since at the same time the king could always elevate commoners, on the ground of service and by way of reward, to the ranks of the feudatories, the result was a ready transposition of ranks, and the establishment of a ladder—at once of descent and ascent—between different classes. This led to a process of social movement, and helped to establish a degree of social homogeneity, which distinguished the English nobility from the exclusive French *noblesse* and the equally exclusive *Adel* of Germany. It is significant that our Parliament (in spite of talk of "the three estates of the realm "—the clergy, baronage, and commons) was never actually organized on the basis of social classes, like the French États or the German Diet. It was a Parliament of *houses*; and in the lower house the knights, who belonged to the feudal class, attended as representatives of the communities and commoners of the shires, and sat side by side with the townsmen who represented the boroughs. The contrast with the États Généraux of France, in which the *noblesse* sat apart as a class, and the *tiers état* consisted only of representatives of the towns, is clear and striking. Whatever the practical division of classes in the actual play of social life in our own country, there was little recognition of such division in the formal organization of our State; and the absence of political recognition of social cleavage [1] was itself a force which tended to attenuate social distinctions. On a long view of our national history, it is the absence of class distinction, or at any rate of the formal recognition of class distinction, which is more striking than its presence. The Marxian conception and terminology of opposed and warring classes was perhaps natural in Germany: it wears something of a strange and exotic appearance in England. Yet it must be admitted, as we shall have reason to observe when we come to treat of religion and education,[2] that the period of our history which followed on the Restoration of

---

[1] The House of Lords was always in a sense a class assembly. But it included bishops as well as feudatories; and the point of importance is that it did *not* include a large number of feudatories, but only those who were specially summoned. It was thus based less on the principle of social class than on the fact of official summons.

[2] See below, p. 209 and p. 249.

1660 saw the emergence of a deeper gulf between the poor and the upper classes, and that England—socially if not politically —was more and more divided into two nations by the process of national development between 1660 and 1832.

That division was a fact of profound significance ; and it must never be forgotten by those who are concerned with the state of England. But we have also to remember that it was something comparatively new, and that it was a new class based on plutocratic principles—a class recruited from those who had speculated in landed property after the Reformation, or had thriven by commercial enterprise at a later date—which now stood opposed to the class of the labouring poor. The older nobility, based on the aristocratic principle of inherited estates and inherited responsibility, was something different ; and it has left a different tradition, which is not yet dead. It has not stood apart or aloof in an isolation which would eventually have led to a violent overthrow in the days of democratic principles and industrial organization. If they have sought to lead, its members have marched side by side with those whose leaders they sought to be. They lived on their own estates among their people—fortunate in the absence of any Roi Soleil, and free from any attraction to flit round the blazing light of a splendid court. They played their part, as unpaid amateurs, in the local government of their shires ; and they thus continued, in a new form, the old idea of a special service incumbent on landholders. Their very field sports were a source of strength and of popularity ; and by the mansions they built, the estates they managed, and their work and their play in the countryside, they acquired the prestige of an active aristocracy. In virtue of that prestige they were able to render two services to the nation. On the one hand they gave it the ballast of a tradition —a homely tradition rooted in the very soil. On the other hand they could introduce new ideas, and carry them to triumph by the vogue of their backing. This is the rôle which M. Tarde, in his work on the *Laws of Imitation*, would specially assign to all aristocratic classes ; and the English nobility, if it sometimes showed an English imperviousness to new ideas, was sometimes also true to that rôle. It helped to bring the Renaissance from Italy and France to Elizabethan England ; it helped to bring French taste and grace into the England of the later Stuarts ; and it still kept touch with France in the days of Horace Walpole and Charles James Fox. Many of the agricultural improvements of the eighteenth century were also due to the English nobility. The work of Coke of Holkham is justly remembered ; Townshend, whose conversation, said Pope, was of turnips, was the inventor of the Norfolk course of cropping even before the days of Coke ; and before Townshend's day

Jethro Tull, heir to estates in Berkshire and Oxfordshire, made himself "the greatest individual improver agriculture ever knew."

There is another side to the history of the English nobility. They were great engrossers of land ; and if they sought to justify enclosures by their economic gain to the nation, they were not oblivious of their own private profit, and they turned a blind eye not only to the needs, but also to the rights, of the peasantry. If they did not greatly haunt the Court as its satellites, they loved sinecures and pensions ; and though Lord Lyttelton might say in 1738 that " the weight of taxes lies so heavy upon them that those who have nothing from the Court can scarce support their families," it is difficult to applaud the jobbery of eighteenth-century parties. We can hardly say " latifundia perdidere Angliam " ; but the system of great estates was certainly inimical not only to small proprietors, but also to small culti-vators, and it did much to create that rural proletariate which became the reservoir for the supply of urban industry.[1] But these things happened, in the main, after the infusion of a new plutocratic strain into the old aristocracy ; and it still remains true that the part which the nobility has played, from first to last, on the general stage of our history, is not unworthy. It elaborated the ideal, derived from mediæval chivalry and the Italian Renaissance, of " the gentleman " ; it mingled energy with reserve in a type of character which amused the Continent, but helped to build an Empire ; and it guided the nation, so long as the nation was content to be guided, with a solid judg-ment (sometimes mixed, as in Palmerston, with a gay insouci-ance) which, while it was capable of a multitude of mistakes in lesser things, was seldom wrong in the greatest.

III

The greatest product of the English nation in the sphere of social organization is perhaps not Parliament, but the Common Law ; and it has exercised a deeper influence on the behaviour and temper of the nation than any other single force. The common law of England is the only great system of jurisprudence besides the Roman ; and the world is divided to-day between bodies of law which follow the Roman, and those which follow the English system.[2] The civil law of Rome has inspired the law of France and Holland and Germany, and indeed of the Continent generally, and has spread to South Africa and South America : the common law [3] runs not only in the British Isles,

---

[1] See above, pp. 93–94.
[2] W. M. Geldart, in F. S. Marvin's *Unity of Civilization*.
[3] Common Law is used in three senses (of which it is only the first which is here in question) according to the other body of law to which it is regarded as

but in the British Dominions and the United States. The nature of its content, and the character of its rules for the treatment of crimes and torts, and of property, contract, and succession, lie beyond the scope of this book and the powers of its writer.[1] Nor can we discuss here the question—which has been debated by students of jurisprudence—whether rules of law are framed to meet, and intended to express, the existing ideas of society, or precede and produce those ideas—whether, in other words (and to take but a single example), social ideas on the nature of property are anterior to the law of property, or the law of property is anterior to and responsible for such ideas.[2] It may be that, just as political institutions issue in national character even more than they issue from it, so legal rules have produced rather than registered, or at any rate have produced even more then they have registered, much of our social framework and many of our social ideas. But we are here concerned less with the substance of legal rules and the nature of their relations to social ideas, than with the methods for the enforcement of such rules which have been devised in the course of our legal development. It is the peculiarity of these methods, and the peculiar and definite results which they have produced, that have peculiarly affected national temper and behaviour.

Our Anglo-Saxon forefathers produced the earliest body of Teutonic law, written in the vernacular language, of all the Teutonic peoples. The Scandinavians who began to settle in England during the ninth century were a legally minded and indeed a litigious people. One of their greatest sagas, the *Saga of Burnt Njal*, finds its climax in the breathless interest of protracted legal pleadings ; and Professor Vinogradoff has shown how the Scandinavian settlers in England contributed both to the development of the jury and to the progress of criminal law.[3] The Normans who entered England in 1066 had the legal-mindedness of their Scandinavian ancestors ; and it is said that Normandy to-day still provides the Parisian bar with lawsuits and barristers. Yet if one were asked to answer the question, " Who made the common law ? " it would perhaps be the part

opposed : 1. In opposition to Roman law, it means the whole body of English law. 2. In opposition to equity and other similar bodies of law, it means the general body of English law except (a) the law of equity administered in the old Court of Chancery, (b) the law (based on ecclesiastical usage) of the old Court of Probate and Divorce, and (c) the law (based on maritime usage) of the old Court of Admiralty. 3. In opposition to Statute law, it is that part of the law of the land which does not rest on Statutes, but is based on old tradition or judicial decisions. See Digby, *History of the Law of Real Property,* p. 65, n. 2.

[1] See O. W. Holmes, *The Common Law.*

[2] See R. Stammler, *Wirthschaft und Recht.*

[3] *English Society in the Eleventh Century*, pp. 4–11. The contribution to criminal law was the idea of *nidingswerk*—conduct unworthy of a soldier and a gentleman.

of wisdom to answer, " Not the genius of Saxons in general, or Scandinavians in general, or Normans in general, but the capacity and the industry of definite men or bodies of men, acting as the king's judges from the reign of Henry I to the reign of Edward I, and steadily finding out legal inventions and the methods of their enforcement in the actual and daily business of their courts." Of some of them—the Clintons, the Bassets, and the Trussebuts of Henry I, the new men " raised from the dust and exalted above consuls and illustrious oppidans "—we know but the names ; but men such as Glanvill, Hubert Walter his kinsman, the famous Bracton, a busy justice of assize, and Edward I's less famous judges, Ralph Hengham and Gilbert Thornton, left their memorials. They were men of excellent good sense and sound legal acumen ; they knew Roman law, and they used its logic and method to introduce system into the old customary law of the land ; but above all they actually enforced the law which they made, and delivered justice throughout the land, by a series of legal institutions. First among these was the institution of Justices on circuit, both for criminal and for civil matters,[1] who went from shire to shire, sitting for the purpose in the shire-court, to administer in the name of the king, and as his vice-gerents, the common law of the land. The second was the institution of the Jury, which associated with the Justices local bodies of men—partly for the presentation of criminals, and partly for the " recognition " or decision of disputed facts—and thus inaugurated that happy co-operation between local initiative and central control which has been so fruitful in our history. The third, which was later in its origin, and only developed to its full powers in the sixteenth century, was the institution of the Justices of the Peace, recruited from the local gentry, and armed with power to hear and determine locally disturbances of the peace—an institution which is peculiarly English, and marks the zenith of the English system of co-operation between local and central government. The Justices on circuit, the Jury, and the Justices of the Peace are the triad of our legal system. Important as was the position of Jury and Justices of the Peace, it is the Justices on circuit who exercised the profoundest influence. Wherever they appeared, they carried the person of the king, and took precedence of all others ; they were the " court of the king," vindicating " the king's peace " (*pacem domini regis*), and asserting his rights to the profits of justice at the expense of all other courts, and especially of the feudal and the ecclesiastical courts. They, and they alone, could use a jury—for the use of a jury was a prerogative of the king, and a

---

[1] Criminal justice was done by Justices on Eyre, and civil by the Justices of Assize. The latter took over all the work towards the end of the fourteenth century.

jury could only be empanelled in the king's court ; but by grant-
ing the use of a jury to settle the cases of subjects which came
before the king's court, they made the prerogative of the king
into the privilege of the people. By the majesty with which
they were clothed and the attraction of the special processes
which only they could employ, by their regular circuits and
their pervasive presence, they made the court of the king a
court of general resort and universal competence ; and the
law of that court became the common law of the land.

There were at least four results which flowed from the
development of our legal institutions. One was a common
spirit of law-abidingness, pervading all classes equally, and
uniting all persons in a common obedience to a common law.
Another was the protection and encouragement of what we call
the liberty of the subject. A third was the supremacy of the
judges of the common law in all cases, whether administrative
or civil—whether they affected the power of the executive, or
only concerned the rights of the ordinary citizen. A fourth and
last was the sovereignty of Parliament—the final author and
maker of law.

The common law was a law for all—for the army and the
administration no less than for civilians and subjects ; for the
noble as much as the commoner. The judges judged all alike
by a single law. The nobles kicked against the pricks, and
demanded a judgment by peers ; their resistance was unavailing,
and silently disappeared. Even the king was conceived to be
legibus alligatus. This is the keynote of Magna Charta ; " for
in brief it means this," wrote Maitland, " that the king is and
shall be below the law." A chief justice of the fourteenth
century could even declare that he had seen a writ addressed
to Henry III, " Præcipe Henrico regi Angliæ," by which he was
summoned to give redress under the law ; and it is certain that
the Song of Lewes (of the year 1264) goes to this length :

" Think not it is the king's goodwill that makes the law to be—
For law is steadfast and the king has no stability—
No I law stands high above the king, for law is that true light
Without whose ray the king would stray, and wander from the
    right.
When a king strays, he ought to be called back into the way
By those he rules, who lawfully his will may disobey
Until he seeks the path ; but when his wandering is o'er,
They ought to help and succour him, and love him as before." [1]

When all are thus bound by law, the nation acquires a fundamental unity, which is a unity of the common framework of
law ; and along with unity it also acquires equality—not indeed
in social position or status, but at any rate in the sense (and it

[1] The translation is that of Professor York Powell.

is a very important sense) of a formally equal legal standing of all its members. Unity and equality, in and before the law, are great things; but they are only sounding brass and a tinkling cymbal unless the law is actually enforced. It was the merit of the judges of the common law that they actually enforced its rules, and so burned law-abidingness into the substance of the nation, that a suspicion of breach of the law can become a momentous force in the very throes of a national dispute.

It is true that a poet of the fifteenth century, living in the lawlessness which preceded and accompanied the wars of the Roses, can sing:

> " Many laws and little right,
> Many Acts of Parliament,
> And few kept with true intent."

Many mediæval statutes were indeed unavailing; and they rather attest the evils which they sought to combat than the remedies which they failed to achieve. But the decisions of the courts were regularly enforced; and on that basis, when the State recovered, under the Tudors, from the weakness of the later Middle Ages, it was possible to proceed to the effective enforcement of statutes. It became the tradition that a law once made will be honoured in the observance; that a law made by one Parliament will not be altered by the next; that a tax imposed by law will be duly and certainly collected.[1] The definite and permanent establishment of such a tradition can only be achieved when the force of a regular administration is added to that of the judicature; and the general rule of law to-day owes no small debt to the Civil Service, which is now so intimately concerned in the execution of so many laws. But the Civil Service is almost entirely the creation of the nineteenth century; and for many centuries of our history it was the judges and the justices of the peace who laboured chiefly (sometimes stimulated, and sometimes thwarted, by the Privy Council) in the regular and daily enforcement of law. They had the reward of their labours. We have escaped in England

---

[1] This was not always so. In the days of imperfect administration the evasion of taxes was too easy not to be attempted. But the courts could always enforce the payment of an authorized tax; and as Parliament acquired the control of finance, it tightened the machinery for the collection of taxes. If kings had failed to collect taxes, and had fallen (like Charles I) into virtual bankruptcy, Parliament was rigorously resolved to pay its way. If, in the emergency of war, it failed (as in 1693) to do so, it contracted a debt, which it fastened for greater security (the king having shown himself capable of repudiating debt in the reign of Charles II) round the neck of a body called " the Public," as a " national " debt. " The Public " has always paid its creditors regularly; and the national debt has thus helped to ensure national stability (see Pearson, *National Life and Character*, ch. iii., and Lecky, *History of England in the Eighteenth Century*, vol. i. pp. 390 *sqq.*).

that distinction, which has established itself in the United States, between the ninety or so per cent of "real law," intended to be obeyed and actually obeyed, and the ten or so per cent of "fancy legislation," in which some would include the laws against the use of alcohol and most would include the eugenic laws of some of the Western States, and which is hardly intended, and certainly fails, to secure any general obedience.[1] Such a distinction is a grave peril to the law-abiding habit; and one of the gravest objections to "progressive" legislation which does not command a large measure of general assent is that it may undermine a habit of mind more vital to social well-being than most of the articles of any progressive programme.

But the law-abiding habit, as it has operated in our history, has seldom shown itself inimical to progress. What it has done is to make progress clothe itself in the disguise of a recovery of some ancient, but forgotten or neglected, law or right. This is conspicuous in the struggles of the seventeenth century. The adherents of the Parliamentary side desired progress, and they even went to war for its sake; but they stood on legal ground, and they called their cause the recovery of the undoubted birth-right and inheritance of Englishmen. They desired, as a member said in 1628, "to see that good old decrepit law of Magna Charta, which hath so long been kept in and bed-rid, as it were, walking abroad again."[2] They sought, in a word, for progress; but they called it precedent. No doubt precedent gets twisted and distorted when it has to be bent to the course of progress; no doubt progress moves tortuously, when it has to go by an imagined way of precedent. There is a certain unreality in a legal revolution; there is a certain frank directness in the pure revolutionary doctrine, embraced in France, of a natural law which transcends the positive law, and of "natural rights of men and citizens" which abrogate legal prescriptions. But compromise is dear to Englishmen; and the compromise between precedent and progress is peculiarly characteristic of their history. Nor is it unfortunate in its results. It leaves the temper of law triumphant, even in the midst of change. It makes change less rapid; but it also makes it more secure. We cannot advance until we feel that we have secured our communications with the past, and are accompanied and guarded by the ghostly artillery of venerable precedents.

A uniform legal system, to which all men can equally go for redress, and on which they can count for the regular

[1] The distinction was suggested to me by my friend, Professor Monroe Smith, of Columbia University.
[2] Gardiner, *History of England*, vi. 264.

enforcement of every decision, is a system which guarantees rights and ensures the liberty of the subject. The citizen can sue the official, and the judges are bound to entertain the suit : Bate or the Five Knights can refuse, on a legal point, to pay an imposition or a forced loan, and a court of common law will decide whether the right of the subject has been invaded, or the officials of the Crown are authorized by law to make the demand which the subject has challenged. If the judges burned law-abidingness into the substance of the nation, they also gave to their country the corollary and the complement of that temper— a passion for civil liberty. To believe in a system for the enforcement of rights, and to obey that system, is also to believe in the vindication of your own rights, and to claim that they shall always be vindicated. This is one aspect of that interdependence of law and liberty which philosophers have always proclaimed. Everything, it is true, depends in this matter on the temper and impartiality of the judge. A servile judge may demand obedience to the law in the same breath that he refuses to guarantee civil liberty. The judges of the days of the early Stuarts were too often " lions under the throne," ready to bend the law in favour of reason of State ; but even in those days there was a Chief Justice Coke, who revered the law which he administered even more than the Crown which he served. Any list of " leading cases in constitutional law " will show the services rendered by our judges, century by century, to the cause of civil liberty. It was a legal judgment, in the case of Pigg *versus* Caley (1617), which ended the status of villeinage : it was another judgment, of the great Mansfield, in the case of Sommersett *versus* Stewart (1771–2), which declared that " the state of slavery . . . is so odious that nothing can be suffered to support it but positive law," and was the forerunner of the abolition of slavery and the slave-trade. The judges have defended freedom of speech and the freedom of the press ; and it was a decision of the judges in Cox's case (1701) which went far to emancipate education from episcopal control.[1] The law of the land thus became the liberty of the subject ; and under the operation of case-law freedom has slowly broadened down from precedent to precedent. It was in this way that " my legal rights " became the Englishman's motto ; and it was this encouragement which created the figure of the Kampflüstige Engländer (admired by the German jurist Ihering), who preferred the hazard of imprisonment in a foreign land to the paying of some small overcharge on his bill.

It is essential to this liberty, and it is cardinal to our constitutional system, that the judges are vested with the interpretation of the whole of the law, and have power to enforce it in all

[1] See below, pp. 241, 252.

cases and upon all persons. We have had no separate body of administrative law, administered by separate administrative courts ; we have not remitted to a special cognizance the cases which affect administrative action or personnel. We have already observed that this principle of our public life prevents the growth of officialism, and differentiates us from continental countries such as France and Germany ; and we have already remarked that while its historical origin is to be found in that early centralization, achieved in the domain of law, which marks our history and has tended to secure for our judges a universal competence in all legal questions, there are also reasons of geography, connected with our insular position and our comparative freedom from frontier problems, which explain the permanence of a tradition originally due to the peculiarities of our constitutional development.[1] It need only be added here that the principle has not gone unassailed in the course of our history. The strength of the monarchy under the Tudors, and the claims which it advanced under the early Stuarts, both tended towards a system of administrative law. The Court of Star Chamber lay outside the common law ; and Lord Bacon himself (being a judge in equity, and not in the common law proper) was prepared to advocate a system under which the judges of the common law, if they were seised of a case which raised some question of State, should not proceed to the cognizance of that case until they had consulted the Crown or its officers.[2] His advocacy, based on a theory that " consideration of State " was conclusive and sovereign, would have established the fundamental principle of administrative law ; and it was fortunate for our constitution that it was unsuccessful. Considerations of a different kind are again in our own day leading to a growth of administrative jurisdiction which needs to be carefully watched. The vast multiplication of legislation, which seems inevitable in a complicated society, is leading Parliament to entrust administrative departments with the settlement of judicial questions—in matters of education, housing, national insurance, and the like—which arise in the course of administration. No one who knows the modern Civil Service would refuse it the honour of a very large measure of confidence ; but those who know best the genius of our constitution and the record of our judges may feel some alarm at a

---

[1] See above, Chapter III. pp. 58–59.
[2] He alleged a writ, " De non procedendo rege inconsulto," the working of which, if he had had his way, " would have been to some extent analogous to that provision which has been found in so many French constitutions, according to which no agent of the government can be summoned before a tribunal, for acts done in the exercise of his office, without preliminary authorization by the Council of State " (Gardiner, *History of England*, iii. pp. 1 *sqq.* and esp. p. 6, n. 2).

development which at first sight seems as necessary as it is modest.[1]

The spirit of law-abidingness ; the guaranteed liberty of the subject ; the absence of administrative law—all these may be regarded as expressions or aspects of a principle which may be called by the name of " the rule of law." The rule of law has for its corollary the sovereignty of the Parliament which, in the last resort, makes the law. Originally, it is true, it was the judges who made the law, or induced the king to issue in the form of " assizes " the rules of action which they had framed. Even in the thirteenth century the judges continued to change and frame the law. " Do not gloss the statute," said the chief justice in 1305 to counsel ; " we understand it better than you do, for we made it." [2] By 1300, however, a Parliament had come into existence, and that Parliament (as it is still expressed in the Book of Common Prayer) was a " High Court," capable of judicial decision which, because it was *the* High Court, must necessarily be regarded as final. It is impossible, in dealing with the history of the Middle Ages (to understand which, as Maitland has said, we must think ourselves back into " a mediæval haze "), to draw any clear line of distinction between judicial decisions and legislative enactments, or between judg-ment-giving and law-making bodies. What we can say is that Parliament, beginning in the main as a judgment-giving body, acting in the sphere of jurisdiction and by way of judicial decisions, became a law-making body or legislature, which acted in the sphere of legislation and expressed itself in statutes. Those statutes, like the judicial decisions of an earlier age, were conclusive and final ; they were accepted and enforced by the judges, just as before the judges accepted and followed the judicial decisions of a Parliament which was primarily a High Court of justice. In all its phases, and whether it be regarded as a court or a legislature, Parliament is sovereign ; and its sovereignty is an integral part of the system of common law.

We are thus led from the common law and its judges to Parliament and the national system of representation. But before we address ourselves to that theme, there is one element in the actual substance of law (apart from the methods of its interpretation and enforcement, with which alone we have hitherto been concerned) which deserves some consideration. That element is the law of trust, which is part of the law of equity. The law of trust means that A, as trustee, without any consideration or in return for a consideration which is only nominal, administers property or otherwise assumes obliga-

[1] See the *Political Quarterly*, No. 2 (May 1914), article on " The Rule of Law," and more especially the last edition of Dicey's *Law of the Constitution*.
[2] See Baldwin's *The King's Council*, p. 314.

tions under the instructions of B, the trustor, for the benefit and in the interest of a third person, C, who goes by the name of the cestui que trust.[1] The trust is often meant for the benefit of a minor, and comes to an end when he comes of age ; and two of the features of an ordinary trust are accordingly, first, that it involves the trustee in gratuitous but highly responsible work, and secondly, that it belongs to a period of tutelage in the life of the beneficiary. The law of trust, originally a part of private law, has gradually entered into our public life and national ideas ; and it has produced a number of consequences of the very first importance, alike in our constitution, our Empire, and the Covenant of the League of Nations. In our own constitution it issued, after 1688, in what may be called the trustee conception of government, expounded in the pages of Locke, which dominated political thought during the eighteenth century. On this conception the king—or rather the legislature, if, as Locke inclines to do, you prefer to call the legislature sovereign—is a trustee appointed for its own benefit by the public, which is thus at once the trustor and the beneficiary of the trust ; and if he mismanages his " fiduciary " power, it is liable to revocation, and he may suffer the determination of his trust. This was the conception on which the Whigs of the eighteenth century sought to base their power, and which appears in the pages of Burke under the name of the " virtual trusteeship " supposed to be exercised in the national interest by a properly constituted party.[2] It was a conception which was readily extended from the constitution of Great Britain to the British Empire at large. Burke definitely regards the Empire as a trust which is exercised by Great Britain for the benefit of its component parts ; and it was the gravamen of his charges against Warren Hastings—charges less justified than he believed—that he had violated the terms of the trust by his treatment of the peoples and princes of India. The same view appears in the speeches of the younger Pitt ;[3] and it inspired his successors in the nineteenth century. It is this view of its nature and purpose which has differentiated the British Empire from the Roman and other Empires, and has determined the course of its evolution. We have sometimes failed of our duty ; but at any rate we have believed it to be our duty to hold our Empire, not as a possession of our own

[1] On the law of trust and its importance see Maitland's Essays, vol. iii., *Trust and Corporation.*

[2] Burke's definition of party is well known : " a body of men united for promoting by their joint endeavours the national interest upon some particular principle on which they are all agreed." A party once placed in power is thus readily regarded as a virtual trustee.

[3] Professor Coupland, Beit Professor of Colonial History in the University of Oxford, cites a number of passages which express this view in his inaugural lecture published by the Clarendon Press.

intended to bring us profit or power, but as a trust-property which was to be administered freely for the sake of the beneficiaries to whom it ultimately belonged. In the strength of that belief, and acting on the conception that the trustee ceases to administer when the beneficiary comes of age, we have gradually conceded the right of self-government to the various Dominions when they have attained political maturity. The theory which has thus shaped and determined the growth of the British Empire has been extended in recent years by the system of "mandates" to the Covenant of the League of Nations. It is an English trust which is concealed under a designation borrowed from French law ; and it is to General Smuts, a statesman from the Dominion of South Africa who had been trained in English law, that the suggestion of the scheme of mandated territories has been generally attributed. A mandate is fundamentally a trust ; and it is recited in the Covenant of the League that mandated territories are to be administered (on principles similar to those which have always been applied to trusts) for the benefit of the inhabitants who are their final owners, and until such time as they are able to administer them for themselves. The conception of trust has thus moved in ever-widening circles ; and the gift of that conception has been not the least valuable of the gifts which have come to us—and to others—from our law.

IV

The English Parliament, in its first beginnings, was a monarchical creation.[1] It was the king who added to the existing feudal body of the House of Lords a number of other elements—representatives of shires, representatives of boroughs, and (for a time) representatives of chapters and dioceses—which ultimately became the House of Commons. His object was twofold. Partly he desired to increase his revenue, and thus the same purpose which determined the judicial growth of the twelfth century determined also the parliamentary growth of the thirteenth : partly, again, he desired, through the attendance of spokesmen who could present petitions and explain grievances on behalf of all sorts and conditions of men, to gain a broader and more exhaustive review of national needs and national defects than the regular system of judicial circuits could give. Whatever the objects which he intended, the results were different from his intention. The creation of the king rapidly became an independent creature ; and from an

[1] The origin of the English Parliament is admirably treated by Stubbs in the second chapter of the second volume of his *Constitutional History*. The main additions to Stubbs' account have been made by Maitland (Preface to the *Memoranda de Parliamento* in the Rolls Series), Pasquet (*L'Evolution de la Chambre des Communes*), and Professor Pollard (*The Evolution of Parliament*).

early date there was a struggle between the Parliament and the King. We must not exaggerate the importance of the House of Commons in the earlier stages of that struggle. It was the baronage, hiding its real power behind the apparent action of a House of Commons which it largely controlled, that inspired, for example, the reforms of the Good Parliament of 1376 and the attempts of the Lancastrian parliaments to control the composition and action of the King's Council. But the Commons had large factors in their favour. They were rooted and grounded in that indestructible element of English life, the English shire, which is a peculiar feature of English history, and has been, in successive stages, the basis of the circuits of the king's judges, the electorate of the " knights " who till the seventeenth century led the Commons, the area of the Quarter Sessions of the Justices of the Peace, and the foundation of the modern County Council and its powers. Why the shire—originally a general Germanic institution, carried by the German invaders of the Roman Empire into all the parts which they conquered—should have survived in England and perished elsewhere is too large a question to treat in this place. It is sufficient to say that the shire was to the House of Commons what the earth is fabled to have been to the giant Antæus—an invigorating and reviving force. Strong in the local opinion and the local support of their shires, the shire representatives, who had themselves been trained in the judicial and general affairs of their shire, were doughty antagonists ; and they rallied round them the more numerous but less powerful members who represented the boroughs. In this way they represented the general body of the nation ; and, as we have already had occasion to remark, the Commons in England were never, what the French Tiers État always was, an assembly representative of a single class.

Rooted and grounded in local life, and representing the nation rather than a class, the House of Commons was early led to challenge the Crown. The first issue was naturally the control of taxation. If the King had created a national Parliament to increase his revenue, the national Parliament equally sought to diminish the incidence of taxation ; and the only way of success was to secure that all taxes should depend on parliamentary vote. Another issue naturally followed on the first. The amount of revenue which the King sought to raise depended on the policy which he followed and the ministers, or members of the Council, by whom he was advised ; and Parliament was thus led to seek control of the membership of the Council and thereby of the policy of the Crown. A struggle was thus engaged between Parliament and the Crown—a struggle in which Parliament appealed to its privilege and the general legal birthrights of Englishmen, and the Crown alleged its prerogative and the general ground of " reason of State." The first phase—or rather the prelude—of that struggle, in which, as we have already observed, the baronage was the dominating influence, fills the history of the later Middle Ages, from the days in which Edward I was forced by his Parliament to grant a " Confirmation of the Charters " (1297) to the days in which the Lancastrians were compelled to concede a measure of parliamentary control over the royal Council (1406–47). For a long interval afterwards the " New Monarchy " of the Yorkists and Tudors (1461–1603), fortified with special powers in order to secure peace after the Wars of the Roses and unity during the breach with Rome, controlled the life of the nation without any serious challenge from Parliament. A new and final battle came, when a new dynasty from Scotland succeeded to the Crown, and a new issue of religion divided an Anglican king from a Puritan Parliament ; and it is the House of Commons (the House of Lords having been decimated by the struggles of the fifteenth, and packed with a new and obedient nobility by the sovereigns of the sixteenth century) which conducts the hostilities. We may speak of " battle " and " hostilities " ; but the words are only a metaphor. The struggle between King and Parliament, which fills our history for so many centuries, and colours our national ideas so largely, was almost entirely a legal struggle. Parliament took its stand on the ground of law ; and the weapons with which the Parliaments of the seventeenth century fought the Crown were the precedents of the Middle Ages, from Magna Charta and the Confirmation of the Charters to the proceedings which had ended in the deposition of Richard II. It was all a matter of discussion and debate, conducted on traditional lines, in which either side discharged a fusillade of precedents, and if the one cited historic privileges, the other quoted no less historical prerogatives. The ground of law was seldom abandoned ; the word was only once (during the Civil War) deserted for the sword ; and even during the Civil War a form of debate still proceeded in the propositions of Parliament and the counter-propositions of the King. It was by way of restoration of precedents of the past, rather than by a revolutionary adventure into the future, that Parliament sought to vindicate liberty ; and the process of debate and discussion sometimes seems to assume the form of legal pleadings in a court of law.

Parliament won. It finally assumed control of taxation after the Revolution of 1688 ; it finally assumed the control of policy, through its control over the appointment of the Ministers of the Crown, when the Cabinet system was gradually evolved in the course of the eighteenth century. The battle seemed ended, and the long discussion brought to a close. It was not so.

Before the old division was ended, a new division was emerging ; before the old debate was concluded, a new debate was being engaged. It was in the reign of Charles II, and while the monarchy was conducting the last operations of its long and losing battle against Parliament, that the system of parties emerged. Parliament, in the very act of the winning of victory, split into two ; and the two divisions of Parliaments henceforth contended with one another for the control of policy and the glory of office. The struggle remains ; the debate and discussion continue ; the Whigs, with their Puritan backing, and their hold on the manufacturing and commercial classes in which Nonconformity was particularly strong, contend against a Tory party rooted in the support of Anglicanism and the landed interest.[1] It became the practice that party should vie with party to gain the verdict of the new and uncrowned king—" the Public," as it was called in the eighteenth century, or, as we call it to-day, " Public Opinion "—and this by means of unending discussion in Parliament, on the Platform, and in the Press. It was once said of Coke that four P's had overthrown and put him down—Pride, Prohibitions, Præmunire, and Prerogative.[2] It might be said of our system of government to-day that five P's have made and built it up—Public Opinion, Party, Parliament, the Platform, and the Press. We call it by the name of democracy or representative government. We might also call it by the name of a gladiatorial game of discussion. Public Opinion sits in the seats, ready to turn down its thumb ; the Parties are the gladiators ; Parliament (particularly and peculiarly Parliament), along with the Platform and the Press, are so many arenas in which the Parties contend. Montesquieu said of England that the mark of its constitution was the separation of the legislature from the executive, and of the judicature from both. His saying has been rejected, and the union of different powers in the hands of a single Cabinet has been proclaimed as the genius of the British constitution. This is true enough ; but it remains none the less true that a certain division or separation, leading to debate and expressed in discussion, has always been characteristic of our political institutions. There *was* a time when it was a division between the executive and the legislature. To-day we unite the two ; but we set an Opposition over against the Cabinet in which they are united. It is the essence of our constitution that a Cabinet *in esse* is confronted, criticized, and not seldom checked by a Cabinet *in posse*. His Majesty's Opposition is as integral a part of the constitution as His Majesty's Government.

[1] On the origin of parties, see below, in the chapter on Religion, pp. 199, 200.
[2] Coke, in the Pride of a masterful man and the common law, opposed the claims of Prerogative in the two cases of Prohibitions and Præmunire.

What has been the effect upon our temper and character of the long process of political discussion which fills our history ? Before we seek to answer the question, we may note two features of this discussion which bear on the answer. It has always been practical discussion, leading to action and determining practical policy. It has not been that theoretical discussion about general principles which we often find in continental assemblies. It has been intended to settle a particular and current question of taxation : to vindicate a disputed right or to remove a pressing grievance : to institute, or to dismiss, a particular ministry. Again it has been organized discussion, which has followed set rules of procedure, whether it has been the discussion between King and Parliament in regular form on the basis of precedents, or the discussion between party and party according to the rules of the House and the conventions of party behaviour. It is analogous to (and indeed it may in some measure have sprung from) the regular pleadings of barristers before a judge according to the rules of the court. From the beginnings of Parliament many of its members were practising lawyers ; from the end of the sixteenth century many more were justices of the peace, with a certain amount of legal experience derived from that office ; and the temper of the proceedings of courts thus affected the temper of political debate.[1]

The general effects of a continuous tradition of practical discussion, regularly conducted according to set rules, may be roughly résuméd in three propositions. It produces a method of compromise ; it ensures a spirit of moderation ; it affords a training in the difficult art of collective mental action. A cynic might define compromise as the finding of a formula which professes to reconcile conflicting views, but really serves as an omnibus in which they ride together in a union of disagreement. It may also be defined as an alias for a makeshift and an excuse for procrastination. But it is something more than any of these definitions. In practical affairs there is perhaps never an absolute truth. " Some see one side of a matter, and others another " ; and both see some aspect of truth. Life again seldom presents us with clear issues between right and wrong ; and the conflicts both of individual and of national life are often conflicts between right and right—between duty and duty, both of which are imperative, but both of which cannot be simultaneously discharged. From the one point of view compromise

---

[1] Parliament may be said to vary in its temper according to the prevalent social ideal expressed in its behaviour. At one time it may be legal—and that ideal always persists. At the end of the eighteenth century it seems smitten by a passion for the stage and the infection of Garrick : Chatham plays the suffering patriot, and Burke throws a dagger on the floor of the House. To-day Parliament approximates to the temper of a meeting of shareholders or a gathering of business men.

may be a setting of jewels in a common frame, so that each throws its light and shows its facets to the rest ; from the other it may be a Solomon's judgment, dividing what seem to be impartible wholes, and assigning to each the " half " which may, in the given case, be " better than the whole." To compromise of this nature, which may be the best we can attain in a world of conflicting aspects of truth and the conflicting demands of rights and duties, discussion is the best of guides. We must talk with others in the gate, if we are to see the side which they see and to incorporate it in the setting of an agreement ; and right must run the ordeal of debate with right before the judgment of the court can be given. The compromise which is the fruit of honest debate, in which " one shrewd thought devours another," may often impress those who have united in its achievement as something of the nature of a revelation ; and any man who has presided at a hot debate, in which sparks have flown, but a light has ultimately dawned, can remember the glow of a sense of discovery with which he has sometimes found himself left. The habit of compromise which the process of our history has infused into our political temper is a habit for which we may be grateful ; and it has been generally where we have failed to compromise that we have failed to succeed.

The habit of compromise has a natural ally in a spirit of moderation. It seems a paradoxical thing that a record of struggle should issue in such a spirit ; but what has been said of the nature of the struggle may serve to explain the paradox. Law has been dominant ; precedents have had a large influence ; set rules of procedure have been observed. It is often said that a national passion for collective games, in which team contends with team in a strict obedience to rules, has engendered among us a national habit of respect for " the rigour of the game " and a national instinct towards " fair play." It may perhaps be said, with greater truth, that such a habit and such an instinct are earlier than the games to which they are ascribed ; that they were born among the real interests of politics rather than on the field of play ; and that it was a habit of obedience to sterner rules which was the cause, rather than the result, of a habit of obedience to the rules of a game. We had certainly learned, before we had acquired a national passion for collective games, to acknowledge the victory of the better side and to recognize the principle of majority rule. Such recognition is a difficult thing to attain. It seems an easy thing to count numbers, and to assign the greater weight to the greater number ; but it is a very hard thing for a minority to learn to confess that the other side " has it " in virtue of a mere array of figures. It was long the custom in Poland that even a single dissident could claim to impose a veto ; and even in the sixteenth century the Diet of the Holy Roman Empire (as the " Protest " of the Lutheran minority against the recess of the Diet of Spires in 1526 attests) had hardly come to recognize that a majority binds the minority. It needs a long training in the methods of discussion before the spirit of moderation can arise, in the strength of which men will be ready to admit that the majority *may* be right, and in any case had better be obeyed. It has been said that the rule of a majority means that "we count heads instead of breaking them." But the counting of heads is more than a cheap substitute for the use of force. Men only begin to count heads when they realize that force is not an effective argument in any process of discussion, and that it is not force, but the weight of opinion, which has to prevail. Majorities are not always right —neither are minorities—but there is generally a cogency in the weight of opinion which is not merely external, or due to the number of those who hold the opinion, but also internal and logical. In this sense we may say that the rule of a majority means that we get inside men's heads instead of hitting the outside.

Discussion is a guide to compromise and the parent of a spirit of moderation ; it is also a trainer of men in collective mental action, and it is because it gives that training that it guides them to compromise and begets in them moderation. Any effective discussion presupposes two organized bodies (it may be more, but ideally it is two) which at once dispose and arrange themselves separately for their work, and combine together to constitute some common organ and procedure for its conduct. The long debate between King and Parliament led to the regular organization of Parliament and aided the formation of a regular royal Council ; and the subsequent struggle of parties has at once promoted the internal discipline of each party and the growth of a series of rules (partly inscribed in the procedure of Parliament, and partly of the nature of understandings about the conduct of constitutional questions) by which all parties alike informally agree to act. The conduct and the methods of collective mental action—the rules of debate, the forms of motion and amendment, the powers of the chairman, the rights of the members, the procedure of voting—have thus been formulated ; and they have become a general national possession, distributed over a multiplicity of public bodies and voluntary societies, and guiding the actions of meetings of every sort and kind. We are ready in any emergency to appoint a committee (or to become a committee without appointment), with understood rules of action which need not be formulated because they are, as it were, in the air. Such committees naturally, and almost inevitably, appeared in the prison camps in Germany during the war wherever Englishmen were prisoners ; such committees grew on the soil of New England, in the be-

ginnings of Puritan colonization, and became colonial legis-
latures which ultimately challenged Parliament and claimed
and secured independence.   There is a French epigram at our
expense which is not altogether unkind: " Un Anglais, c'est un
imbecile ; deux Anglais, c'est un ' match ' ; trois Anglais,
c'est une grande nation."

Discussion is a noble thing ; and even if it has its wounds,
they are wounds that do not fester, and may on the contrary
stimulate, if only there is present the antiseptic power of moderation and compromise.   Carlyle praised famous men—heroes of
incisive intelligence and resolute will, silent and strong, who
gave little heed to speeches or " government by the word "—
and he professed a high contempt for Parliaments, which he
reduced to their etymological level of " talking-shops." [1]   We
must admit that discussion can decline into the exuberance of
an inconclusive verbosity ; but it is best to judge both men
and institutions by the actions of their healthy state more than
by the symptoms of an occasional disease.   Nationalize discussion (and that is what Parliament has done in England by
the interest of its own debates and the process of its own elections), and you elicit and enlist the mental co-operation of all
the nation in the process of the government of its own affairs.
You stimulate and you pool men's minds ; you elevate and
direct to general objects their wills ; in a word, if such a phrase
may be permitted, you make a nation a spiritual " going
concern," in which all the elements have vitality, and a steady
pulsation runs from mind to mind.   The energy of a nation in its
own self-government may be a greater thing than the efficacy
with which a nation is governed.   Archbishop Temple once
contrasted those to whom government was an " ergon," a result
which had to be produced and must be measured by the efficacy
of its production, with those to whom it was an " energy," a
spiritual vitality which had to be elicited and must be measured
by its own intensity and quality.   He was repeating, in an
emphatic form, a distinction which already appears in John
Stuart Mill's Essay on *Representative Government*.   In the light
of that distinction we may say that our nation has trodden the
path of " energy," and that it has been guided by the way of
discussion to that system of government, working by means of
discussion towards the eliciting of a fuller activity of mind and
will, which is called by the name of democracy.   Our national
energy, if that be one of our attributes, has produced its finest
fruit in a system of national self-government ; and that system
in its turn is a constant demand on our energy.

[1] In strict accuracy, *parliamentum* means not a talking-shop, but an act of
talking.   Parliament, that is to say, is not the place of debate, nor the body
engaged in debate, but the act of debate itself.

Here we touch, at any rate by implication, upon an old theme—the effect of different types of political constitutions on the people who live under their influence. It is a theme handled by Plato in the later books of the *Republic*, where he studies "the democratic man" as the corollary and the product of the democratic constitution, and finds him unstable in his ways; inconstant in his purposes; a bizarre museum of contradictions; in his own eyes "versatile," but to impartial eyes a meddlesome busybody. In the same way C. H. Pearson, in his *National Life and Character*, sadly inclines to the fear that democracy may encourage "changes of purpose" and entail an "approval of mutability." [1] But one may equally cite, and ascribe to the influence of democracy, the attributes expressed in a phrase which John Stuart Mill borrowed from Humboldt—"individual vigour and manifold diversity," arising from the play of a society rich in the variety of its members, and fitly joined and knit together by that which every joint supplies. We cannot, however, readily ascribe any definite effects to the influence of an abstract type of constitution, without regard to the country in which it works and the environment in which it is found. The example of Tocqueville may serve as a warning. Devoting himself to the study of democratic institutions in the United States, and inquiring into the nature of their effects, he was led to connect democracy not with variety or mutability, but with a monotony of uniformity which made all men alike, and frowned upon variety as a breach of the constitution. The consideration readily occurs, and it is clearly expressed in Maine's book on *Popular Government*, that there is little profit in discussing the abstract influence of an abstract democracy. Democracy does not work in the same way in different nations: it is one thing among the English, another among the French, and another among the Swiss. In each nation the institutions which we call democratic enter into combination with other elements of the national life; and the results which they produce depend on the combination. In the United States democratic institutions are combined with a spirit of general "fraternity," and a general demand for conformity, which may partly have been the product of an original Puritan temper, and partly, again, may be due to the instinct of the older settlers for imbuing the mass of immigrants with their own ideals and temper; and the sovereignty of the people only adds the new force of an organized public opinion, expressing itself by the regular machinery of the vote, to habits of mind which are in themselves indigenous and independent.

There is another consideration, of a similar order, which will equally suggest that it is unprofitable to seek to study democracy

[1] C. H. Pearson, *op. cit.* p. 115.

in a general and abstract form, or to seek to trace the effects which, in that form, it produces in civic character. The effective working of a democratic system of government by discussion depends on two principal conditions. One of these is the possession of that legal or procedural habit of mind, derived from a long training in the spirit of law, which enables men to debate without fury and to discuss without animosity. Another condition, which was justly emphasized by Gneist in his studies of the English constitution, is the possession of an experience of local affairs, through a system of local self-government, by which men have learned to apply the method of practical discussion to lesser affairs before they attempt the greater. Both of these conditions were present in England ; and both were also present in the United States, which inherited and developed our common law, and practised in its townships an even more democratic form of local government than that of the English parish or shire. They have not been present, or they have been present to a far less extent, in many continental countries which have adopted a democratic form of goverment. Nor, again, have continental countries generally developed that simple form of party organization—tending always (in spite of occasional difficulties) towards two parties, each disciplined, and each directed to the practical object of attaining office and putting its principles into active operation—which would seem to be another condition of the effective working of a democratic system. They have multiplied their parties and theorized their principles ; and discussion has tended to be too subtle to be practical, and too acrimonious to be fruitful of action. In the absence of these conditions, a system of government by discussion may fail to work, as appears from the experience of the three peninsular countries of the Northern Mediterranean ; but a system which fails to work in the absence of its necessary conditions is not condemned as a whole in all its manifestations.

V

We have already touched on the methods of local self-government which appear at an early date in our national history ; we have remarked on the peculiar vitality of the shire ; we have noted, in explaining the institutions by which the common law was practically enforced, the institution of the Justices of the Peace, who gradually became not only the local judicature, but also the administrators of the shire. It was at the end of the twelfth century that the germ of the Justices appeared, in the form of the " knights assigned," in 1195, to take the oath of the peace from all the King's subjects. It was during the fourteenth century that the Justices acquired judicial powers ; it was during the sixteenth that they became administrative officers ; it was during the eighteenth that they attained their zenith, and appeared in the exercise, not only of judicial and administrative powers, but also in the form of something of a local legislature, which sought to make general rules.[1] It was the system of poor relief which mainly led to the acquisition of administrative powers by the Justices. That system has been peculiarly important in our history. In its economic bearing it served, till the nineteenth century, as the one measure of social policy which the Government steadily sought to pursue in the face of social difficulties. In the sphere of education, as we shall see,[2] it was the germ of the first attempts made by the State to promote the education of its members. In the field of politics it was the principal cause of the growth of local self-government.

The problem of pauperism existed before the dissolution of the monasteries, and a number of other causes—for example, the influence of a depreciated currency in reducing real wages, or, again, the effect of enclosures (intended for the purpose of sheep-rearing) in producing unemployment—contributed to increase its urgency. But the dissolution of the monasteries, none the less, accentuated the problem. Hitherto pauperism could be regarded as a matter for the ecclesiastical sphere ; after the dissolution it became more obviously a matter for the secular government. The Government had never instituted any general system of administrative officials ; and if we had an organized judicature as early as the twelfth century, we only acquired an organized civil service many centuries afterwards. Destitute of any local officials to undertake work which was necessarily local in its nature, the Government threw the onus of collecting a local poor rate, and administering a local system of poor relief, upon each locality. From the time of Elizabeth the local gentry, in their capacity of Justices of the Peace, were made to supervise the system, by appointing the overseers of the poor, enforcing their rates and auditing their accounts ; from the time of William III, when it was enacted that no relief could be given to a new applicant without the consent of a Justice of the Peace, they became the responsible administrators of the system. But if the administration of a system of poor relief was their principal charge, they had a large variety of other duties. By the Statute of Artificers of 1563 they were made to supervise the working of the rules of apprenticeship, and ordered to rate and appoint local wages annually in their

---

[1] Cf. Sidney and Beatrice Webb, *English Local Government*, iii., the " Parish and the County," Book II. ch. v.

[2] See below, pp. 247–248.

quarter-sessions ; and indeed they were generally regarded, alike by Parliament and the Privy Council, as the proper local executive for the enforcement of " stacks of statutes." Saving and excepting that they were paid at the rate of five shillings a day for the time they spent in execution of the Statute of Artificers, they worked without fee or reward ; and though they held their office under commissions from the Crown, issued from the Chancery, they were in reality designated by the inevitable logic of their position as the leading gentry of the shire, and it might be said of them :

" Fato Metelli consules Romæ fiunt."

There are two features in this system of local government which demand attention. In the first place, it is a system of government by unpaid amateurs, who by the work which they do " acquit " the landed property which they possess of a burden of public duty which is still conceived to be incumbent on it. This, as we have already remarked, is a survival of feudalism, on its finer side, and in its aspect of obligation ; it gives to a land-owning class, in addition to such economic justification as its management of its estates may provide, a political *raison d'être* ; it extenuates, if it does not excuse, that " engrossing " of land by the gentry which destroyed small properties and prevented the continued existence of a free peasantry. But the system of local government by unpaid and unprofessional service has wider and less disputable merits than these. It also provided, as we have seen, a training in local affairs, and a consequent experience and confidence, which were invaluable to the members of Parliament who had received it when they came to Westminster to deal with the affairs of the nation ; and a body of local opinion which could support and sustain the action of its representatives, and which they, again, could express, was yet another fruit of a system which involved the regular meetings of the Justices in quarter-sessions. Alike by the local experience they gained and the local opinion they were able to form, the Justices of the Peace became—particularly in the crucial period of the reign of Elizabeth and the reigns of the early Stuarts—the stay and strength of the members of Parliament. It must be admitted that it was only a limited circle of landowners which thus received a political education ; but the circle was capable of expansion, and the system of local elected bodies, ranging from boards of guardians to county councils, which was introduced during the nineteenth century, was only a new expression of a principle which had already been conceded and established. It mattered less that the Justices were only drawn from a local aristocracy than that they embodied the idea—an idea of profound importance—that the conduct of government belongs not only to the official, but also to the ordinary citizen. This is the essence of all self-government, whether local or national.

A second and obvious feature of our system of local self-government is the division of powers which it implies, or at any rate may produce, between local authorities and central government—a division which, on its other side, assumes the form of consultation and co-operation. This is an old tradition in our history—older than the Justices of the Peace. It goes back to the shire, and the shire goes back to Anglo-Saxon times. Some of the shires had been independent kingdoms in their day ; all of them still remained, after the Norman Conquest, genuine " communities," which found themselves in the regular meetings of their members in the shire-courts.[1] Devonshire had a seal of its own : Cornwall received a charter from the King : Worcestershire, in 1297, refused to pay a tax voted at Westminster until it had received seisin of the liberties of Magna Charta : Northumberland, attempting a form of legislation, enacted a close time for salmon. It was the shire which made possible the Justices on circuit and our legal development ; for the Justices came round to sit in shire-court. It was the shires which made possible, as we have seen, the members of Parliament and the growth of representative government ; for the knights of the shire who led Parliament were the elected spokesmen of the shire-court. After the fifteenth century, and except as an electorate, the shire-court dwindled and disappeared ; but the shire remained, and it found itself, if not in shire-court, at any rate in other bodies—from the sixteenth to the nineteenth century in quarter-sessions, and from the end of the nineteenth century in the county council. In the shire (and in the great cities which have grown since the Industrial Revolution, and now are vested, under the name of county boroughs, with the powers of shires) there still remains the old tradition of division and co-operation. Nowhere, perhaps, is it more strikingly expressed to-day than it is in the relations between the great Local Education Authorities (which are committees of County and County Borough Councils) and the Board of Education. They divide the control and expense of education—and incidentally dispute with one another about their powers and, more particularly, about the methods to be followed in the sharing of their expenditure ; they co-operate, in what we may almost call a *condominium*, for the advancement of education. There is nothing perhaps in our public life which is more characteristic. The chairman of a great Education Committee will meet the

---

[1] The membership of the shire-court was never clearly defined. But the duty of attendance (for it *was* a duty) was widely distributed, and fell on the possessors even of small plots of land.

President of the Board of Education in the gate; and an Education Authority, taking its stand on the strict letter of statutes, will stubbornly challenge a ruling of the Board in the matter of teachers' salaries.

If we put together the two features of unpaid and unprofessional political work, and of division and co-operation between local and central authorities, and seek to estimate the mental qualities on which they depend and which they elicit, we shall find, as indeed we should naturally expect, that they tend to corroborate the qualities which are connected with the working of representative institutions. The check and counter-check between local and central authorities has its analogies with the old division between King and Parliament, and the more recent division between party and party, of which we have spoken, and it tends to produce the same habit of compromise and the same temper of moderation. The Justices of the Peace, through their long history, were far from being always in the right. They had a social bias; and in the matter of enclosures, for example, they attempted—not unsuccessfully—to thwart the policy of the Crown, which was directed to the maintenance of a large agricultural population with a definite interest in the soil. But they mingled good sense with philanthropy in their administration of poor relief; nor was their general record in social matters unworthy. And whatever the judgment we may pass on their social action, we must admit, with Sydney Smith, that they did, in their day, and in the sphere of politics, " really constitute a bulwark of some value against the supreme power of the State." If we turn to another aspect of local government, and regard it not in its relations to central authority, but in its own nature and operation, we shall recognize that it has given, over an ever-widening field, and to an ever-increasing number, a discipline and a technique of collective mental action which has been valuable both in itself and as a basis of national self-government. From the same point of view we have equally to observe that it has helped to interest the whole nation, through all its limbs and members, in the conduct of its affairs and the government of its life. In a word, we have to thank the vigour of our local life for much of the vitality of our national being; and we may ascribe to local self-government no little share in the making of that general system of government by discussion, which in turn has so largely made us what we are.

All things change; and many may feel, in sadness of heart, that all the features of national organization which have been depicted in this chapter are changing to-day, before our eyes, with the growth of a class-conscious spirit and a tendency to substitute the vocation for the nation. We have inherited a majestic mansion, it may be said, but are the bulk of us willing to dwell in its rooms? Are law and the habit of discussion engrained in the minds of those who believe in a dictatorship in the interest of the proletariate, which is to be achieved by a revolutionary minority? What does the shire matter to men who think in terms of their union, or Parliament to those who prefer the general congress of unions?

It would be idle to deny the existence of new and disturbing currents of opinion, or of new and arresting features of social organization. Their consideration must be reserved for the conclusion of this volume. But two things may be said at the close of this chapter. In the first place, the old and inherited structure of the national State—not only in our own country, but in the world generally—is now confronted by the problems of a new industrial life and new economic creeds, just as centuries ago, in the age of the Reformation, it was confronted by the problems of new ecclesiastical movements and new religious beliefs. Europe was shaken in the age of the Reformation : the world is shaken now. The national States of Europe incorporated the new ecclesiastical movements in their life : the nations of the world may yet make their peace with the new industrial movements. In the second place—and to confine our attention to our own country—it would not appear that those who guide the industrial movement in England have failed to approach or to adopt the legal and political traditions of the national State. The industrial movement is expressed in an organized political party ; and that party includes the vast majority of those who desire industrial change. If it is founded on the basis of working-class organizations, it is not by any means wholly identified with a single class, and it is more and more drawing into its ranks the representatives of other classes. In its action it has followed the old methods of discussion and obeyed the old rules of procedure. The Trade Unions, on which it is mainly based, are legal associations, which have been regulated by law throughout their history ; and save in rare moments of excitement they have always acted within the domain of law. The essence of our national inheritance has pervaded the working-class movement ; and it is imbued with the same respect for law, the same habit of discussion, and the same temper of compromise, which has been shown by the nation at large. If many of its members have strongly expressed the sense of class difference, we have to remember that the same sense was present, and was strongly expressed, on the other side of the line of social division, in the eighteenth century ; and we must equally remember that even a class movement, if it becomes a political party, will be drawn by the natural desire of a party for the increase of its adherents to transcend the limits of class. It would be foolish to deny the existence of revolutionary elements ; it would also be foolish to exaggerate their strength. The long and unbroken course of English history is marked by two movements which may be called Revolutions. The Puritan Revolution, which issued in Civil War, none the less clung to tradition and precedent. The Revolution of 1688, which dethroned the Stuarts, was a revolution by legal process. If there should be a third revolution, we may prophesy two things about its nature. It will be achieved by Parliament ; and it will place itself on the ground of law.

LIST OF BOOKS

ADAMS, G. B.—*The Origin of the English Constitution*, 1912.
BOUTMY, É.—*The Political Psychology of the English People* (Eng. trans.), 1904.
DICEY, A. V.—*The Law of the Constitution* (8th edition), 1915.
    ,,   ,,   *Law and Public Opinion in England*, 1905.
LOWELL, A. L.—*The Government of England*, 1908.
MAITLAND, F. W., and POLLOCK, F.—*The History of English Law* (2nd edition), 1898.
STUBBS, W.—*The Constitutional History of England*, 1873.
WEBB, S. and B.—*English Local Government : The Parish and the County*, 1906.

CHAPTER VII

THE RELIGIOUS FACTOR AND THE INFLUENCE OF CHURCHES

I

IS there any connection between race and religious belief ? It is a question on which speculation is more fascinating than fruitful. It is possible that the racial basis of a people may act as a selective agency, and may help to determine the general form of religious belief by giving the greatest power of survival to those ideas and practices which are most peculiarly congruous with the trend of its own inner essence. The general diffusion of Protestantism among the peoples in whom the Nordic element is strongest has been explained by this hypothesis. But the inner essence of a race is an intangible thing ; and even if we place ourselves on the ground of natural science and evolutionary principle in dealing with the facts of religious experience, we do not greatly aid the advancement of science by referring ascertained facts to the operation of an intangible cause. The spirit blows where it lists. A variety of natural causes may combine to affect the mode of its operation ; but it is impossible to hold that a single natural cause determines the course of its action. The history of a given people, the genius of its law, and the nature of its relations to its neighbours, are all factors which may contribute to explain its adoption of a particular form of religious belief ; but the racial blend of which that people is composed will be only one, and perhaps the most obscure, among such contributing factors. Wales has but little of a Nordic element among its population, but Wales is strongly Protestant ; and if we seek to explain the Calvinistic Methodism of the Welsh people, we shall be wise to turn our attention chiefly to the history of the Welsh evangelists and to the relations of Wales to England—relations which may help to explain, on the one hand, why Wales followed England in the century of the Reformation, and, on the other hand, why Wales eventually adopted a form of Protestantism differing greatly from that of England.

If the connection between religion and race is obscure, the connection between religion and national life is obviously close.

In some cases we may even say that religion is the nation, and the nation is what it is in virtue of its religion. We may take two examples—one from South-Eastern Europe, and one from the far North-West. The modern Greeks largely owe their existence to their religion. They were saved from extinction, and given a new moral fibre, by the Greek Church. It was not in the mould of the Byzantine Empire, but in the arms of the Orthodox Church, that they survived through the Middle Ages and the early centuries of modern history to achieve a new independence a hundred years ago. It was there that they learned, as Dean Church has said,[1] their three great lessons— the lesson of endurance in the face of odds which would have utterly dismayed the Greeks of pre-Christian times ; the lesson of a new fraternity, ennobling that ancient sociability which had always made Greeks love to " talk into the middle " of a circle and to hear or see together " some new thing " ; and the lesson of undying hope in a national resurrection. Even to-day, and in a somewhat unhappy form, religion is still the nation in South-Eastern Europe. You make a Bulgarian citizen by enrolling a new recruit in the Church of the Bulgarian patriarch ; and bishops will distribute rifles to guerilla bands for the purpose of a proselytization which is also a process of nationalization.[2]

At the other end of Europe there is the example of Scotland. The Scotch were much later than the English in attaining national unity and a definite national habit. The process occupied the two centuries from 1550 to 1750—or, more exactly, from Knox's beginning of his mission in the Castle of St. Andrews in 1547 to the abolition of hereditary jurisdictions in the Highlands in 1746. It was the kirk which made Scotland one during those centuries, and it was by the kirk that Scotland was stamped with a permanent national character. Scottish nationality is a church. It finds its satisfaction not in the sphere of politics, but in a religious organization, which is at once established (or, as some would prefer to say, " recognized ") by the State, and at the same time remarkably independent—so independent that, by an act recently passed by the State itself, it can solemnly declare its " inherent " liberties under God ; so independent that (except for the fact that it is built on a national basis) it almost recalls the *respublica Christiana* of the days of Hildebrand, which was also essentially a Church, over- shadowing, and almost obliterating, the State. It is the char- acter and genius of Calvinism—operative also in Holland and Switzerland, in Hungary and among the Huguenots, but no- where so strongly operative as in Scotland—which have made the genius and the character of Scottish nationality. There is

[1] R. W. Church, *Christianity and National Character*, pp. 165 sqq.
[2] A. E. Zimmern, *Nationality and Government*, p. 66.

indeed another factor which must not be forgotten—a system of national education which is a century older than that of any other European country, and two centuries older than that of England. But the Scottish system of education, as we shall see, was itself due to, and sprang from, the Scottish Church.

Even where religion is not the essence of a nation, it is a great constitutive element in its life and disposition. The effects of Mohammedanism on the character of the peoples who have embraced its tenets and imbibed its spirit are as large as they are obvious. The effects of Christianity are larger still, if they are subtler and more moving. Mohammedanism is like a stamp which fixes a permanent pattern. Christianity is a dynamic force, moving itself, and a cause of motion—a spirit which " passeth and goeth through all things by virtue of its pureness . . . the breath of the power of God, and a pure influence flowing from the glory of the Almighty."

The effects of religion in general on the life and character of nations, and more especially on their progress, have been discussed in rationalistic terms by writers such as Buckle, Kidd, and MacDougall. The question, as it has presented itself to these writers, has been a broad question of sociology. Has the progress of nations been due to, and consisted in, a progress of moral ideas—under which, it would seem, religious ideas must be subsumed ; or has it been rather due to the progress of intellect, and more especially of scientific inquiry ? Buckle argued in favour of the former hypothesis ; Kidd, in a somewhat confused way, in favour of the latter. To Buckle, religion was something constant and fixed, which, as it did not move itself, could hardly explain any motion : science, on the other hand, was a growth, and therefore a cause of growth. Kidd was more alive than Buckle to the difference between the content and the power which makes the content—the content, for example, of scientific knowledge, and the innate mental power which creates or discovers that knowledge. He contended accordingly, in his work on *Social Evolution*, that intellectual capacity has not increased, and that the intellectual faculty is in its nature too deeply interested in self and self-development to be a cause of general and social progress ; and on the other hand, that religious tendencies have grown in volume and intensity, especially during and since the age of the Reformation, and have promoted progress by inducing the individual to abandon self and to serve the " social organism "—which, it would appear, is the final object of religious emotion. Why religious tendencies themselves became peculiarly progressive in the age of the Reformation ; why Protestantism should be peculiarly altruistic ; why religion in general should particularly serve the social organism—all these are questions which Kidd's answer to the general question he raises leaves unregarded and unsolved.[1] Nor does Professor MacDougall carry his readers much further by his suggestions. In his *Social Psychology* he suggests, much like Kidd, that Christianity, or the conservative spirit of religion, is necessary as a brake on the progressive spirit of science, which, left to itself, would indeed promote progress, but would also dissolve the bonds of social cohesion (presumably, if the argument is to be followed, non-rational in their nature) by its own rationalizing tendencies. In his work on the *Group Mind* he begins his argument by the thesis that Christianity has encouraged the mental evolution of European peoples through its influence on social organization, and particularly by its antipathy to caste; but in the issue he comes to the conclusion that religious belief was far from being the only force which dissolved the system of caste; and indeed the reader is left in some doubt whether it ever produced any particular effect whatsoever.[2]

The influence of Christianity on the life of nations cannot be measured by these general and nebulous observations. We must " condescend upon particulars." An argument uncircumscribed by any geographical or historical limitations, concerned with religion in general rather than with different varieties of religious belief, and dealing rather with the progress of all nations than with the different characteristics of different nations, is not calculated—nor, indeed, intended—to explain the formation of national character. We can better estimate the actual influence of religion if we study the development of our own country, and examine the part which religion has played, at different periods, in determining the history and character of its national life.

II

The ten centuries which precede the coming of the Reformation at the beginning of the sixteenth century are centuries filled, and largely controlled, by the spirit of a single and undivided system of Latin Christianity. It is not a period of national churches, affecting different nations in different ways; it is the period of a single society, which claimed to be, and in the conception of its members actually was, a universal society,

[1] I may perhaps quote some words from a previous work on *Political Thought in England from Herbert Spencer to To-day* : " Kidd regards societies or social organisms as the products of a law of life that overrides a recalcitrant but selfish reason, and enlists in its service, to secure its victory, a religion which apparently has nothing to do with reason, except, indeed, to keep it in subjection " (p. 142). It is from this point of view that he argues that the evolutionary force of modern society is not intellect, but the immense fund of religious sentiment generated by Christianity.

[2] W. MacDougall, *Social Psychology*, pp. 319–320 ; *The Group Mind*, pp. 274 *seq.* and p. 293.

acting as such uniformly on the nascent nations of Europe. It is true that there is constant speech, during the Middle Ages, of an *ecclesia Anglicana*, or, again, of an *ecclesia Gallicana* ; and under the sanction of such a name the clergy of either country claimed special rights or immunities for the branch of the Catholic Church within its borders. It is true again that there were different liturgical "uses," not so much between country and country, as between one great See and another ; and it is also true that the action of the clergy—and of general religious belief and organization—upon national life might vary from nation to nation according to different conjunctures and circumstances. The Church, which helped to perpetuate the division of mediæval Germany, helped also to consolidate the union of mediæval France ; and its action in Italy, where the Papacy preferred a balance of divided powers, was vastly different from its action in England, whose early unity, as we shall see, owed no small debt to the Church. But we must not exaggerate the element of nationalism in the system of Latin Christianity during the Middle Ages. Even in England, and even in the ages in which England was most isolated from the Continent, the genius of the universal Church was dominant. It has been urged that the Anglo-Saxon Church was peculiarly independent of Rome. Freeman has said that it only needed a vernacular liturgy to become a national Church ;[1] and other writers, citing for example the greeting of St. Anselm in Italy, "*quasi patriarcha et apostolicus alterius orbis*," have held that traces of its independence survived even the Norman Conquest. On the contrary, it has been remarked by Troeltsch,[2] the Anglo-Saxon Church was peculiarly dependent on Rome, from which it had sprung, as a sort of colony, in the days of St. Augustine, and to which it looked, with a peculiar veneration, as its founder and mother-city. There are indeed large traces on the Continent, in the two or three centuries before the age of Hildebrand (750–1050 A.D.), of a system which has been called by the name of the "territorial church" (*Landeskirche*). Rome had not yet asserted her universal primacy ; and great metropolitans, at Rheims or Mainz, could still assert a large measure of independence from the Papacy, and could act in close conjunction with their territorial sovereigns. These territorial churches were not, however, national : even in their heyday they did not affect Anglo-Saxon England ; and after the assertion of papal power in the age of Hildebrand—coupled with the rise of new monastic orders, the general diffusion of the common

[1] Freeman, *Norman Conquest*, vol. i. p. 31 : "In England, alone in the West, a purely national Church arose. One great error indeed was committed : the vernacular tongue did not become the language of public worship."
[2] Troeltsch, *Die Soziallehren der Christlichen Kirchen*, p. 196.

European enterprise of the Crusades, and the growth of universities as places of international resort—the Church Universal (and with it the primacy of the universal Pope) triumphed over the practice of territorial churches. The formulation of canon law in the received text of Gratian of Bologna (1150 A.D.), and its eventual codification by the great lawyer Popes of the thirteenth century (Innocent III, Gregory IX, Innocent IV, and Boniface VIII), consolidated the influence of the mediæval Church. The canon law which was administered in mediæval England was perhaps the greatest of the direct influences on national life which proceeded from the Church. It controlled the law of marriage ; it affected the disposition of property ; it vindicated, to some extent, the rules of morality. But it was not a native body of law ; and, what is more, some of the most important cases which came under its cognizance were never brought before the native courts of the English Church.[1] The law administered in England was the law codified by the Popes, and common to Western Europe ; and the graver cases of that law were often reserved for papal commissions, which, even if they sat in England, acted not in the name or on behalf of English bishops or the Archbishop of Canterbury, but in the name of the Pope. It was the same in other reaches of ecclesiastical organization. From the beginning of the thirteenth century appointments to Sees and higher preferments were more and more drawn, by way of " provision," into the hands of the Pope ; and though he had to reckon with the King, and to admit a virtual system of sharing appointments, he kept a large measure of actual power. The universities, again, were a single clerical system : one speech prevailed, and a single method of training was followed, in Oxford and Paris and Prague ; and in education, as in other spheres, the Church was an international society.

Thinking, therefore, in terms of the universal Church, we may seek to trace the action of that Church upon our country and our countrymen, first in the five centuries which precede the Norman Conquest, and then in the five centuries which follow. The great gift of the Church, in the earlier stage, was the Latin tradition and the genius of Rome, expressed in an organization and concrete in a body of law. Inheriting the old Empire, and being, as it were, in itself the old Empire in a new and spiritualized form (" the Papacy," said Hobbes, " is none else than the ghost of the old Roman Empire, sitting on the grave thereof "), the Church inherited and continued its political organization and its legal tradition. The system of Pope and patriarch, of

[1] See Maitland, *Canon Law in the Church of England*, and Ogle, *The Canon Law in Mediæval England*. See also H. W. C. Davis, on " The Canon Law in England," in the *Zeitschrift der Savigny-Stiftung für Rechtsgeschichte*, 1914.

metropolitan, archbishop, and bishop, was a reflection of the system of administration bequeathed by Diocletian to his successors ; and the forged Donation of Constantine expresses a deep truth, when it makes Constantine the Great bequeath to Sylvester I the imperial insignia, and to his clergy the ornaments of the imperial officials. The Church which came to England with St. Augustine, in 597 A.D., was already an organized and centralized Church ; and what it had received itself from the developed lay Empire of Rome it gave back again to the struggling and embryonic communities of the Anglo-Saxons. When Theodore of Tarsus, as Archbishop of Canterbury, vindicated the primacy of his See, erected a permanent synod, and achieved some regular division of dioceses, he supplied a model which would help to produce the primacy of an Anglo-Saxon king, the rise of an Anglo-Saxon Witan, and some regular division of Anglo-Saxon England in shires. Ecclesiastical unity preceded, and by preceding it aided, political unity. But it was perhaps the law of the Church, and its system of discipline, which exercised an even deeper effect than its methods of organization. The Church had not yet distinguished definitely between legality and morality. Its law was the word of the Lord, an undefiled law, converting the soul : it was the voice of morality, commanding righteousness. In virtue of that law the Church gave to the raw and untutored Germanic peoples the drill of moral habituation.[1] It imposed a definite discipline on a rude, heavy-drinking, vendetta-loving, primitive people. " With the law came sin "—and a sense of sin and a struggle for deliverance. The agents of the Church in its work of deliverance were the system of penances (of which there is already no little mention in the correspondence of St. Augustine with Gregory the Great), the confessional, and the judicial power in " pleas of Christianity " exercised by the bishop sitting in shire-court by the side of the ealdorman. (The separate courts of the Church in England belong to the period after the Norman Conquest.) The discipline of the mediæval Church—particularly, perhaps, in its early stages—has its analogies with the " holy discipline " which Calvinism practised afterwards in Geneva and in Scotland ; but in a later age a system may be pronounced inquisitorial, and prove unsuccessful, which in an earlier age could command a ready allegiance. It is curious to reflect that the penitential system, under which the penitent confessed his offence, professed his contrition, received absolution, and was assigned a " satisfaction " which he must subse-

[1] The law of the Church produced effects in the legal, as well as in the moral sphere. The first code of lay law in England belongs to the reign of the first convert—Ethelbert of Kent. The landbook, which created a new species of property, held by written title, and therefore readily transferable, was equally the gift of the Church and its legal knowledge.

quently discharge, was eventually to prove the stumbling-block of Germany in the age of the Reformation. It had been a gift and a benefit to the Germanic peoples at the beginning of the early period of the Middle Ages : a thousand years later, when indulgences had entered, and the noble idea of a " treasury of merits," vested in the Church from the works of supereroga-tion of its past saints, and available for the penitent sinner's need, had been turned into the practice of a bank on which all could draw in return for a consideration, it was rejected by them as the " filthy rags " of a mere gospel of " works " and a financial imposition on the poor. But whatever might be the revolutions of a cycle of a thousand years, the Germanic peoples, and not least our own, owed much in their beginnings to the power of Latin Christianity. Christianity, which had come to the old and civilized peoples of the Mediterranean area when they were made, came to the peoples of Northern and North-Western Europe while they were still in the making ; and it stamped them all the more deeply.[1] It crossed the native tradi-tion of Northern stocks with the fruitful strain of a great Hebrew spiritual tradition, which itself had already been blended, partly with Greek philosophy, but especially and particularly with the genius of Latin organization and law.

The work of the Church in the early Middle Ages was con-tinued and deepened in the later half. The Church now sought, and sought in a double sense, to be universal. It would embrace the whole world in its extension as a single Catholic society under a single œcumenical head. It would also penetrate the whole world by the intensity of its operation, seeking to bring every walk of life and every human activity under the control of the law of Christ entrusted to its charge. The attempt of the Church to control life at large by Christian principles, and to make religion not only an " influence," but the actual rule of daily action in every sphere, is a fascinating record in the history of human struggle.[2] Not only was knowledge systematized by the schoolmen, *ad majorem Dei gloriam* (whereby, it must be admitted, it lost its power of growth) : an attempt was also made to bring the course of trade into conformity with Christian rules which prohibited the taking of interest and enforced a " just price " for the exchange of commodities ; and not con-tent with regulating the life of the trader, the Church also sought to direct the life of the feudal knight. If it could not stop war, it would at any rate limit its ravage by the rules of the " truce of God," and it would prescribe such methods and objects—

---

[1] R. W. Church, *op. cit.* p. 229.
[2] See the chapter in F. S. Marvin's *Unity of Western Civilization* on " Unity in the Middle Ages." The *locus classicus* is the section of Troeltsch's great work which deals with the Middle Ages.

the method, for example, of chivalry, and the object of the Crusade—as would ensure the "just" conduct of hostilities. The churches to-day are still seeking to make their principles into rules of economic action and standards of international relations ; and it is still a moot question whether the teaching of our Lord can be translated by its ministers into rules of applied religion, which may regulate economics and politics, or whether the Kingdom of Heaven is a kingdom which cannot be realized to the letter in an imperfect and transitory world. It is certain that trade escaped from the control of the mediæval Church ; that the later history of chivalry is a history of etiquette and amorous escapades ; and that the end of the Middle Ages and the beginnings of modern history are marked by wars—such as the Hundred Years War, or the French invasions of Italy after 1494—which, if they sometimes use the name of Crusade, are naked wars of aggression. But the great attempt of the mediæval Church cannot altogether be written down as failure. In our own country, as elsewhere, the Church courts, administering a law of marriage which, with all its imperfections, was none the less something more than an accommodation to existing practice, sought steadily to maintain a standard of purity.[1] The Church courts had many abuses ; and the confessional, even if it enabled parish priests to give some guidance to their flock, had to contend against facile "pardoners" and venal salesmen of indulgences. But the notion of a moral law, and some practice in a discipline of life according to that law, never disappeared ; and the nation was gradually imbued with something of a spirit of law-abidingness, not only to the common law of the realm, but also to the general law of the Christian Commonwealth.

There were other ways in which the clergy of the Middle Ages served their country as well as their Church. There is a passage in the Vulgate which they remembered : "Est vir fortis, et pugnemus pro patria et pro civitate Dei nostri." They fought for the city of God in ways which benefited the nation ; and even in their very clericalism they helped to make the love of liberty an integral element in national character. Standing for the rights of their order and corporation, under the name and style of *libertas ecclesiæ Anglicanæ*, they challenged the Plantagenet kings who invaded their "liberties," and united with barons and commons to curb their power. Men such as Thomas Becket or Stephen Langton, and even lesser men, such as Peckham and Winchelsea in the reign of Edward I, must count with Simon de Montfort among the founders of English liberty. There were many Liberals among the mediæval clergy. Lord Acton spoke of St. Thomas Aquinas as the first Whig (the name

[1] See A. L. Smith, *Church and State in the Middle Ages.*

might also be given to St. Thomas of Canterbury) ; and Dr. Figgis, following in his steps, defined political liberty as " the residuary legatee of ecclesiastical animosities "—the extension, as it were, to a nation of a privilege originally vindicated for itself by a clerical corporation.   The tendency of the Church to promote the growth of liberty was common to the countries of Western Europe ; but while in France the clergy were not sufficiently strong to check the King to any considerable extent, and while in Germany they were so strong that, in alliance with the Papacy, they broke his power, in England they were strong enough to check without being, or wishing to be, so strong as to break the power of the Crown or destroy the growth of national unity.   It was thus their function, in the sphere of politics, to aid the growth of limited monarchy and a parliamentary system. It may be contended that they aided the growth of Parliament not only negatively, and by helping to check the Crown, but also positively and by the direct incentive of their own assemblies.   Stephen Langton summoned a representative convocation of the Church as early as 1225, exactly seventy years before the Model Parliament of Edward I.   It is true that the growth of the representative system in the Church during the course of the thirteenth century proceeded, on the whole, *pari passu* with its growth in the State.   But it is also true that the clergy were far more skilled than the laity in the conduct of elections, the vesting of representatives with regular (or " procuratorial ") powers, and the conduct of debate ; and it can hardly be doubted —the less when we remember that down to the end of the first quarter of the fourteenth century they continued to sit and to act as members of national Parliaments, before they withdrew to their own Convocation—that they contributed in their measure to the formation of those habits of collective mental action which are the foundations of parliamentary life.   In this way they aided the education of the nation at large—just as, through the universities and the chapter and monastic schools, they provided the main substance of education for individual Englishmen.   Nor should it be forgotten that mediæval literature is largely the work of the clergy.   Chaucer, indeed, remains the great poet of the Middle Ages ; and Chaucer was a layman.   But it was under the inspiration of religion, and generally by clergy, that nearly all our literature of the Middle Ages (as also of Anglo-Saxon times) was written ; and those who have read the beautiful elegy called " Pearl," or the " Piers Plowman " of Langland, will readily recognize the debt which letters owe to the mediæval Church—the universal mother, gathering *in gremio suo* not only the religion of the nation, but also its education and its literature.

III

The Reformation of the sixteenth century made religion a new factor in the life of nations when it introduced the conception and the practice of national churches. But the Reformation was a multitudinous and varied movement ; and it worked in different, and what almost appear to be opposite ways, in the different countries in which it triumphed. Among the Anglicans and the Lutherans it produced a national Church,[1] so adjusted to the national State, and so much co-extensive with it, that the prince was both *supremum caput* or *summus episcopus* of the one, and *rex* or *princeps* of the other. Among the Calvinists, however, it produced a voluntary religious body, which, voluntary as it was, was highly organized, and tended either to displace the State in favour of a system of theocracy, or to limit its power and curtail its functions. In the one case the Reformation was an ally of the cause of monarchy : in the other it may seem, at first sight, to be an ally of the cause of democracy, though when we reflect that the organization of Calvinism concentrated power in the hands of ministers and elders, and that it could readily join forces (as it did in France and Scotland) with the cause of municipal privilege or feudal ambition,[2] we shall prefer to call it the ally of aristocratic tendencies. From this point of view, and in its relations to the State and political order, Calvinism seems closely akin to high Catholicism, which has often shown the same tendency to challenge or check the State ; and Sir Robert Filmer pithily remarked, speaking of the doctrine of the Social Contract and the contractually limited State, " Calvin and Cardinal Bellarmine both look asquint this way." But if, on one ground, we may trace an analogy between Calvinism and Catholicism, and if, on that ground, we may distinguish both from Anglicanism and Lutheranism, there are many more grounds on which Calvinism blends with the other Reformed Churches of the sixteenth century ; and these are grounds of a deeper importance and a profounder influence on national life. The Reformed Churches were united, even if they differed in the degree of their emphasis, in recognizing the responsibility of the individual Christian, in preaching the necessity of individual faith, and in encouraging the direct relation of each individual soul with God. Priestly mediation, and with it (except among some of the Calvinist congregations) the system of religious discipline, became things of less account ; and a new and stronger fibre was added to character when each

---

[1] The Lutheran Churches in Germany should perhaps be rather called territorial, as they covered a given territory (*e.g.* Brandenburg or the Electorate of Saxony) rather than the body of the nation. *Religio* was a matter of the *regio* rather than the *natio*.

[2] See E. Armstrong, *French Wars of Religion*.

man was required to possess his own soul and to justify himself by his own inner faith. The age of the social drill and discipline of an organized Church, mediating spiritual life through its officers, began to pass into an age of responsible self-discipline and self-control.

The influence which a Reformed Church could exercise on the temper of a whole nation was nowhere more vividly shown than in Scotland. Calvinism here came upon a divided and disunited country, in which a clerical clergy, isolated and self-contained boroughs, and a turbulent feudal nobility, contended with one another.[1] It brought in its train a long and bitter struggle. Passionate for the union of a whole people in a single faith under Christ the King, the Calvinistic preachers fought against the monarch at Edinburgh (and, after 1603, in London), and against a self-seeking nobility. The course of the struggle itself affected the temper of the nation, which it steeled and hardened " as by fire "; but its final issue and achievement produced a still profounder effect. Scotland attained an independent unity by the establishment (or " recognition ") of Presbyterianism in 1690 ; but it attained that independent unity as a Church, and not as a State. The Scottish people became at last a single nation ; but the essence of their nationality was a national form of religion. That form of religion united internally a variety of elements which had before been engaged in strife; and externally it served to distinguish and separate a united Scotland from its chief neighbour nation in the south. The Union of 1707—which the Scottish people could never have accepted unless they had felt that they were already safeguarded by the independence of a national Church—removed a Parliament which had never been an effective centre of national life, and left the General Assembly of the Church, which from the first had been national and now stood alone, as the one representative of the whole nation. If England lived in its Parliament and the quarter-sessions of its Justices of the Peace, Scotland lived in its General Assembly and its kirk-sessions ; if England lived by its common law, to Scotland " the Calvinistically interpreted Bible was the divine rule of life."[2] In a word, if English nationality issued in a State, Scottish nationality issued in a Church, and became the animating spirit of a people united under God by a solemn Covenant after the manner of the Old Testament.

The results upon Scottish national character were deep and lasting. Foremost among them was a passion of liberty—a passion which was, indeed, a legacy from an earlier turbulence, but was at once refined and strengthened by the influence of

[1] S. R. Gardiner, *History of England*, vol. i. pp. 44 *sqq.*
[2] *Ibid.* p. 47.

Calvinism. The genius of Calvinism tended, as we have seen, towards an ideal of theocracy, or (failing the attainment of that ideal) towards the stringent limitation of the powers of the State in the interests of confessional liberties and the rights of private judgment. Andrew Melville had stood for theocracy ; and in 1596 he had spoken to James VI, as Hildebrand in 1076 had spoken to Henry IV (the genius of high Calvinism echoing the genius of high Catholicism, and both being united in a desire to make the *lex Christi* triumphant by means of the power of a Church) : " There is Christ Jesus the king, and his kingdom the Church, whose subject King James VI is, and of whose kingdom . . . but a member." Theocracy never established itself in Scotland ; but even to-day the attitude of the convinced Scottish Presbyterian towards the State cannot but impress any English observer. The State appears to him something dim, something remote—hardly seen, because it is shrouded in mist ; hardly heard, because the mist dulls the sound of its operation. The Church is vivid and near ; it has a spiritual independence ; and that independence issues in autonomy of action, and is sustained by " inherent rights." These ideas, which are expressed in the Schedule to the Act of 1921, are perhaps all the more readily entertained because the pageantry and many of the organs of the State reside in another " country." But the Scottish attitude to the State is even prior to the Union of 1707 ; and indeed it is even prior to the migration of the Scottish Kings to London in 1603. It is the inheritance of the Covenanters of the seventeenth century, and beyond that it is the inheritance of Knox and Melville in the sixteenth century. The tradition of the Covenanters, in particular, has influenced England as well as Scotland. It was not idly that, when a party arose in England, during the reign of Charles II, which took the defence of liberty for its province, it assumed the name of Whig—a name derived from the Covenanters of the Western Lowlands. The Covenanting spirit, allied to the spirit of English Puritanism, was the basis of resistance to absolute monarchy and the foundation of Liberalism.

Another result which Calvinism produced in Scotland was achieved through the discipline of life which naturally issued from its tenets and was regularly enforced by its organization. The power of discipline was vested not in the clergy alone, but in the kirk-session, in which the minister sat side by side with associated lay representatives (or " elders ") elected by the congregations of the church or parish. Republican in its form, and resting on the social standard and the general opinion of the parish, as expressed by its own elected leaders, the spiritual supervision of the kirk-session was none the less effective. Village opinion is readily censorious of any irregular conduct ;

and when the rigour of a strict faith was added to the natural pressure of that opinion, the mildest of nonconformity might easily provoke :

"Rumores . . . senum severiorum."

We must set to the credit of the kirk-session the work which it did in sweeping away the anarchy and turbulence of mediæval Scotland ; and no man can readily condemn a system which was the parent of orderly home-life, of intellectual rigour, and of a grave and steady conduct of business affairs. Even in the terms of this world, and the field of material prosperity, the discipline of the session was not unrewarded. On the other hand, intolerance, and even persecution, were fostered by the prevalence of a general spirit of supervision. Lecky has remarked that it was in Scotland, in 1697, that the last execution for heresy on British soil took place, and in Scotland again, in 1727, that the sin of witchcraft was last punished with death by any British authority.[1] It may also be remarked that the more rigorous the prohibition, the greater is the temptation to lawlessness and evasion. The puritanism which has inspired a drastic system of Prohibition in the United States has not escaped the evils of boot-legging and rum-running ; and the Presbyterian discipline of Scotland had for its shadow a spirit of anarchy, which could long be traced in the statistics of illegitimacy (though it must be admitted that these statistics raise difficult problems), and in the records of convictions for drunkenness—though here again climatic factors, and the social conditions of an area such as that of the Clyde, must also be taken into account.

One of the most definite and remarkable results of Calvinism, all over Scotland, was the large liberation of mental power which it helped to produce. The preaching and the disputations of ministers were themselves an education ; and it has often been observed that the deep problems of Calvinistic theology— problems of fate, free will, fore-knowledge absolute—were the training-ground of a metaphysical nation, sometimes pragmatical and angular in a stiff adhesion to its principles or preconceptions, but loving the course of argument and genuinely addicted to philosophical inquiry. The very contentions between Church and State were whetstones of a critical intelligence. "We were indeed amazed," wrote Burnet in his *History of My Own Times*, under the year 1670, being then the Professor of Divinity in the University of Glasgow, "to see a poor commonalty so capable to argue on points of government and on the bounds to be set to the powers of princes in matters of religion." But Calvinism provided more directly for Scottish

[1] Lecky, *History of England in the Eighteenth Century*, ii. p. 331.

education than by the incentive of its theological problems or the stimulus of its political principles. The Calvinistic clergy were from the first desirous of a national system of education, at once for its own sake and in order that it might prepare the nation for a fuller understanding of the principles of its faith. There was something of a previous basis ready to hand. In the fifteenth century the universities of St. Andrews, Glasgow, and Aberdeen had been founded ; and Scotland, small as it was, could already boast three universities to the two of England and Wales. The Scottish Parliament had passed an Act in 1496 providing that barons and substantial freeholders should send their eldest sons to grammar schools till they " got Latin," and, after that, to schools of arts or laws in the universities. On this basis Knox had already proposed to erect a general system of national education in 1560 ; and soon after 1641, during the first beginnings of the Civil War, an attempt was made to found parochial schools and regular bursaries to carry students to the universities. It was an Act of 1696 which finally instituted parochial schools throughout the country. It was on the basis of these national schools, and the national universities to which they led, that Scottish thought flourished so vigorously in the eighteenth century, and that Scotland was able to become the teacher in moral and metaphysical philosophy not only of England, but also of France and Germany. It is a sufficient illustration of the philosophical glories of Scotland in that century to mention the names of Hutcheson, Adam Smith, and Reid, who all held the Chair of Moral Philosophy in the University of Glasgow which has since been adorned by the names of Edward Caird and Henry Jones.

In this way the Scottish nation found itself, not only as a Church, but also, through the influence of the Church, as an educational society, united in a common devotion to knowledge and pure thought. It realized, in a measure, what Plato had desired and prophesied in his *Republic*—the ideal of a community transcending those acquisitive instincts of the mind which constitute economic association ; transcending, too, those defensive instincts, and that readiness to take a point of honour, which issue in military organization ; and basing itself essentially on that intellectual passion for divine wisdom which produces the educational society. The philosophy of Plato was a philosophy not of nations, but of cities. It has none the less its relevance to the modern nation, as well as to the ancient city. In the light of that philosophy we may say that a nation may not concern itself greatly with the expression of the national mind through the organization and in the form of a State, because it prefers to seek its expression through the organization and in the form of a spiritual society—a society which is at once a church and a school.

The formation of national character in Scotland has been treated with the more detail, as it affords, in two ways, a peculiarly admirable example. In the first place, we can trace with a special clearness, and against a definite background, the building of that spiritual superstructure which is the essence of national character. The building is historically recent : it is achieved by conscious acts of ecclesiastical and social legislation ; [1] and the two factors of religion and education exercise a definite and measurable influence. In the second place, Scotland provides a peculiar case of a strongly marked national character, and a high degree of nationality, expressing itself not in the usual form of a national State, but in that of a national Church and a national system of education. To complete the story of the making of Scotland (which lies outside our province) we should have to trace the operation of the economic factor, which, if it was last in the field, was by no means (as those who know Scotland best will most readily confess) the least powerful in its operation. Scotland, indeed, had in one sense long been shaped by the steady pressure of that factor. It had always been a poor country ; and poverty had been the parent of a thrifty and sparing temper, which in turn found a foster-parent in the ascetic genius of Calvinism. But the economic factor assumed a new importance in the course of the eighteenth century. It united Scotland with England, as nothing else would have done, in the enjoyment of a common commerce and the common pursuit of industrial occupations.[2] Within Scotland itself, it united the Highlands with the Lowlands—as, again, nothing else could have done. It introduced into the Highlands, made pervious by a new system of roads, a new view and use of land, which ceased to be the feudal basis of personal power for a handful of chieftains, and became the economic basis of a common profit for landlords and tenants alike. The abolition of hereditary jurisdictions in the Highlands, in 1746, was the complement of the Union of 1707 ; and both were the products of a new economic temper which they both helped to foster. The union between the Highlands and the Lowlands was perhaps an even greater influence on Scottish national life and character than the union of Scotland and England. The Highlands brought a strain of romance to blend with the logic, and a temper of loyalty to colour the passion for liberty, of the Lowland Scotch ; and the mixed genius of the Scottish people, which curiously unites the sentimental

[1] See Lecky, *History of England in the Eighteenth Century*, ii. p. 320.
[2] See Galt's *Annals of the Parish*, which is an admirable document for the progress of the Industrial Revolution in Scotland.

13

with the practical, is largely the result of this blending and colouring.[1]

There are thus two stages in the formation of Scottish national character during the centuries of modern history—the stage of a storm-tossed religious and educational development, from 1547 to 1696 ; and the stage (which may be said to begin with the Darien Scheme in 1693) in which Scotland, retaining the religious and educational essence acquired in the previous stage, added to it, by a conscious process, the outer casing of an economic framework and habit of life. The first stage is marked by a struggle against the State, which disappears, as it were over the border, and fades away into the south. In the second stage, with the Church " recognized " in 1690, and a national system of schools established in 1696, the State ceases to be attacked, and comes, on the whole, to be simply ignored. It is set in a far background ; and religious life, philosophical thought, the literature of Scott and Burns, and the general process of a free social development, are the large and sufficient interests of the nation. It is in this way that we may perhaps explain the quality of self-consciousness which marks Scottish nationality. It reflects upon itself, and consciously cultivates itself, because it is not embodied in an external political order of life. In the same way we may also explain the inarticulate and unconscious character of English nationality. Embodied in a system of institutions, and visible to the very eye in an ordered country-side marked like a garden with the impress of the possessor's mind and ideas, English nationality is never reflective, because it is so simply and obviously a fact. What is deep in the bone does not hover about the lips, or rise to that level of conscious-ness which excites reflection and speech. A Scotsman, a Welshman, a Jew, may become the political leader of the English people ; an Irishman like Wellington may command its armies, and another Irishman (a Swift or a Shaw) may lash its foibles by his satire. It remains the same ; and if it attains to so much reflection, it will only murmur to itself that " the English con-stitution might be worse, and England, after all, is not a bad country."

IV

The Reformation in England presents more than one curious aspect. It gropes along a slow course from what seem accidental beginnings (the want of an heir ; the caprice of a king ; the whim of a lady-in-waiting) to conclusions which were certainly unpremeditated. It was not the fruit of any national spiritual movement (as it was in Scotland) ; and yet it became a national movement, and it attained, alike in the Anglicanism of Andrewes

[1] See Lecky, *op. cit.* ii. 343.

and Laud and the Puritanism of Barrow and Bunyan, a spiritual majesty. Nationalism was certainly a part of its substance; and the nationalization of religion, which it brought in its train, may sometimes almost seem to mean a nationalization of God. More than one French writer has sought to detect this strain in English religious conceptions. Boutmy, in his work on the political psychology of the English people, refers to the " national God," and again to the " English God." [1] Professor Legouis, in his history of English literature, quotes the Elizabethan Lyly as having expressed the current idea of his age in the phrase " the only true God is the English." What Lyly actually said was that " the living God is only the English God," [2] and all that he meant was that the English worshipped only the living God. Yet it must be admitted that there has been a certain tendency in our thought, if not to claim God for our nation, at any rate to vindicate the claim of our nation to be regarded as belonging peculiarly to God. There is a tradition of God's Englishman, on whom He calls for any work of special difficulty.[3] It is a tradition exemplified in a story which is told of a Tyneside skipper, who, losing the wind to a rival, as he was trying to beat up stream into port, exclaimed: " This beats cockfighting: there's God Almighty gone and given the wind to a . . . Dutchman instead of His ain countryman." There is nothing, however, in such an attitude which is peculiarly English. It is natural to an untutored intelligence in any country; and the Dutch farmer of South Africa may equally feel that he is the special care of God and his language the language of Paradise.

There were two Reformations in England—the Reformation which issued in Anglicanism, and that which issued in Nonconformity; and the dualism of the two—reflected, from the end of the seventeenth century, in the opposition of our political parties—has been one of the most peculiar and one of the most potent influences in our national life. It has not only reflected itself in the political organization of parties: it has also appeared in a social division. Anglicanism has been the religion of the gentry, the land, the villages: Nonconformity has been the faith of the middle classes, of commerce and industry, of the towns. The one has fostered the love of tradition, the sense of historical continuity, the passion of national unity; the other

---

[1] Boutmy, *op. cit.* (Eng. trans.), pp. 192, 261.

[2] Lyly, " Euphues' Glass for Europe " (part of *Euphues and his England*); see R. Warwick Bond's edition of Lyly's *Works*, ii. pp. 205, 210.

[3] Milton, towards the end of his *Areopagitica*, wrote : " God is decreeing to begin some new and great period in His Church, even to the performing of Reformation itself : what does He then but reveal Himself to His servants, and as His manner is, first to His Englishman : I may say as His manner is, first to us, though we mark not the manner of His counsels, and are unworthy."

has cherished an ideal of the purity of original Christian truth, a belief in the need for basing religious order newly and freshly upon that truth, a doctrine of the indefeasible right of the individual soul to make its own peace with its Maker. To the one the past has been sacred ; to the other it has been suspect. The one was naturally drawn to a belief in two parallel and interconnected divine rights—the divine right of the king and the divine right of the bishop. It stood for authority, and it believed that authority, alike in Church and in State, had two attributes—the attribute of a divine origin and the attribute of a continuous historic tradition. It was God who had given to Adam a patriarchal power, which had then descended continuously, by a sort of patriarchal succession, until it was now vested by right of descent in the king : it was our Lord who had given to St. Peter a pastoral power, which had also descended without interruption, by an apostolic succession, until it was now vested in bishops. The figures of king and bishop were thus irradiated, as it were, by the divine origin of their office (like a stained window casting a glow on those who stood in its light) ; and who could offer them a shadow of violence, when behind them there stretched, in majestical series, the long unbroken line of their precursors ? The philosophy of Nonconformity was colder and more rational. The foundation of authority, ecclesiastical or political, was human institution. It was men who had erected presbyters or kings, for ends of edification or protection : it was on a compact between men that their authority rested ; and if that authority were not duly used for the ends prescribed, the compact was null and void, and what had been given by men could by men be taken away. There was here no anointing, and no anointed of the Lord who might not be touched. At the most there was a solemn appointment ; and there might be equally a solemn dismissal.

In the Anglican system the king was more than parallel with bishops. He was the bishop of bishops—the supreme head on earth of the Church as well as the State—or at any rate (in Elizabeth's milder phrase) " the only supreme Governor of the realm . . . as well in all spiritual or ecclesiastical things or causes as temporal." Royal supremacy is thus of the essence of the Reformation. The king adds a new province to his existing territory, by acquiring control of things ecclesiastical (hitherto subject to the Pope) in addition to the things temporal which he has always controlled ; and he gains at the same time a new consecration for his whole state and position, and a new appeal to the hearts of his subjects, by becoming, as it were, the chief priest of his people. Loyalty assumes a new fervour : " God bless the King " comes from men's lips with a deeper resonance ; " Church and King " is a compelling toast ; the principles of the Cavaliers, which became the principles of the Tory party, are launched on their long voyage. The conception and practice of royal headship, which may seem to lower the Church, had for its complement the fact of Establishment, by which the Church was exalted. If the king, who is the symbol of the State, is also the head of the Church, it is inevitable that the Church should be brought into a special relation with the State. On the one hand, the State will guarantee and protect the Church, by acts of legislation or executive process, in its powers and its properties ; on the other, the Church will consecrate the State, and, as it were, hold up its hands, in the course of its earthly activities. Establishment means both of these things ; but it means particularly the latter. The public recognition and profession of the principles and order of the Church, wrote Burke, " hath solemnly and for ever consecrated the commonwealth, and all that officiate in it. This consecration is made, that all who administer in the government of men, in which they stand in the person of God Himself, should have high and worthy notions of their function. . . . This consecration of the State, by a State religious establishment, is necessary also to operate with a wholesome awe upon free citizens." [1]

The conception which underlies establishment is a conception of a single society, which in one aspect we call a State, and in another we call a Church, but which in itself is one and undivided. " We mean by the Commonwealth (or State), that society with relation unto all public affairs thereof, only the matter of true religion excepted ; by the Church, the same society, with only reference unto the matter of true religion, without any other affairs besides." [2] Before the Reformation there was an English nation, and that nation was organized as a State ; but in matter of religion its members belonged to another and wider society, which was the general society of the Latin Church of the West. After the Reformation the nation, instinct with a greater degree of national consciousness, continues to be organized, and is organized even more closely, in the form of a State ; but it is henceforth also organized as a Church which is co-extensive with that State. The nation, in a word, is now conceived not only as a State, but also as a Church. It receives a new consecration ; and the State, as the secular expression of its life, shares with it in that consecration. Organized hitherto as a political society of subjects united in one allegiance, the nation is henceforth organized also, and co-extensively, as a Church of worshippers united by a single creed—or, at the least, in a single ritual.

[1] *Reflections on the French Revolution.*
[2] Hooker, *The Laws of Ecclesiastical Polity*, viii. (quoted in R. H. Tawney's *Religion and the Rise of Capitalism*, p. 166).

This was an ideal; but it never became a fact. Two grave questions occupied the minds of the leaders in Church and State as soon as they attempted to translate the ideal into practice. What was to be the basis of religious unity, and how much was it to include? What was to be done with the dissidents who refused to accept the basis and declined to belong to the single national society in its form of religious expression? Many attempts were made, from the beginning of Elizabeth's reign to the reign of Charles II, to find a formula of definition for the basis of religious unity—a formula which should at once comprehend all essentials and all believers. They were not successful. But if they could not find the one basis, statesmen and churchmen still clung to the conception of the one society. Elizabeth and Clarendon were equally clear that no man could be a loyal subject of the nation organized as a State unless he were also a conforming member of the nation organized as a Church. Citizenship involved the corollary of churchmanship; and as men might be made to discharge civic duties, so they might be compelled to fulfil religious obligations. In this way it became the policy of the State to enforce the regular attendance of its members (because they were also members of the Church) at the services of the Church, "upon every Sunday and other days ordained and used to be kept as holy days, . . . upon pain of punishment by the censures of the Church, and also upon pain that every person so offending shall forfeit for every such offence twelve pence . . . for the use of the poor." [1] In the same way the State sanctioned an ecclesiastical discipline of life according to the canons—a discipline enforced by the church courts (or, in minor matters, by the rector and churchwardens)—in the interests of Christian morality. The whole policy of religious uniformity attained its zenith in the days of Archbishop Laud, who laboured hard that "the external public worship of God— too much slighted in most parts of this kingdom—might be preserved, and that with as much decency and uniformity as might be." Acknowledging Aristotle as his "master *in humanis*," he threw a mantle of Aristotelian philosophy around his policy. Aristotle had believed in the "habituation" of men by a social drill which insensibly imbued them with the spirit of the society in which they lived. Laud similarly believed in the habituation of men by a religious drill which would insensibly imbue their minds with the spirit of true religion. "His love of outward observances, of the beauty of holiness, as he fondly called it, was partly founded . . . upon the recognition of the educative influence of regularity and arrangement." And so he set himself, with all the tenacity of his mind, "to form the

---

[1] The language is that of the Elizabethan Act of Uniformity of 1559. The penalty was varied and increased by subsequent legislation.

habits of Englishmen in order that there might be peace amongst them," and that they might be one Church and one faith, as they were one nation and one State under the supremacy of their king. . . . *Une foi, une loi, un roi*—it is an old aspiration.

The attempt to make the Church coextensive with the nation, and to use external religious observance as a drill to form the habits of Englishmen and to shape national character, encountered an invincible opposition. The ideal of uniformity was answered by the fact of Nonconformity. The Church could not be coextensive with the nation, when a large part of the nation refused to belong to the Church ; and there could be no general external drill when thousands insisted upon a free right of internal choice. Nonconformity had always before it the example of Scotland, where, instead of the nation being drilled by external rule into a single religious society, religious society, regarded as something independent and prior, shaped a nation by its inner spirit in the image of its own unity. Too weak to control the State in the Scottish manner, but too strong to be controlled by it, nonconformity seceded to the *Mons Sacer* of its own inexpugnable doctrine. As the *plebs* established itself in ancient Rome by the side of the *populus*, so the Nonconformist congregations established themselves in England by the side of the Established Church. Like the plebeians in early Roman history, they suffered grave disabilities. They could not hold office, municipal or national ; and by various statutes they were deprived even of the social right of maintaining schools and giving instruction. They were not dismayed ; and from the year 1662, in which the Caroline Act of Uniformity finally enforced a Prayer Book which they as finally rejected, the opposition of an irreconcilable nonconformity to a Church which had failed to achieve comprehension is a cardinal feature of English life. Henceforward the Church is not the nation, or coextensive with the State : it is partly, in respect of its own inner life, a privileged society within the nation, and partly, in its bearing and influence on national affairs, the cardinal principle of a national party. It is the Church—the Establishment of the Church, and the Royal Headship of the Church—that is the essence of the Tory party which came into being during the reign of Charles II, just as it is the voluntary religious society, the independence of its congregations, and the general conception of the free Church in the free State, that is the essence of the Whig party which came into existence at the same time. Assuming the guise of parties, the two confronting traditions became elements which deeply affected English life alike by the influence on their adherents of their different principles, and by the influence on the whole nation of the process of struggle and conflict which they could not but stimulate. Our party system, almost to the end of the nineteenth century, and until a new third party emerged under the name of Labour, was a legacy of ecclesiastical policies which, whatever the conscious design on which they were based, contributed the principles and methods of party organization to that long process of debate and discussion which fills the political history of our nation.

If the Church, seeking to be the nation, had become a party, it did not cease to be a religious society. It ceased, indeed, to exert any real power of formal discipline over its members : canons and church courts were of small account after the Restoration ; nor could a Church which had ceased to be the nation continue to drill the nation in godliness. But the bishops still maintained a control of education ; [1] and the Church at large, through the Society for the Promotion of Christian Knowledge (1699), and by means of Charity Schools, attempted to train the minds and to form the character of the children of " the labouring poor." In other and larger ways its ministers realized their social duty to the community ; and they never declined into any belief that they were only intended to maintain a cult or could content themselves with a perfunctory recital of services. The advertisement which Arthur Young had " heard of " in eighteenth-century England—" wanted a curacy in a good sporting country where the duty is light and the neighbourhood convivial "—may have been an excellent jest ; but it would be difficult to find its basis in contemporary practice. The parson was the centre of village life ; the vestry was the parish parliament ; the pulpit was a place of simple and homely guidance ; and the sermons of the eighteenth century, which on the lips of Bishop Butler could rise to the heights of moral philosophy, were not destitute of moral prudence even when they fell from the lips of country clergy. It is not within our theme to recite what the Evangelical movement did for the Church, or a Church stirred by the Evangelical movement did for the nation. It is sufficient to say that the Church at the end of the eighteenth and the beginning of the nineteenth century did not fail to express the feelings of the acutest social conscience of its day, and that it played its part in the abolition of slavery, the reform of prisons, and the spread of education alike by Sunday schools and the founding of " national " day-schools. The same conception of social duty came to inspire the Oxford movement, which, however far it might depart from Evangelicalism in other ways, continued its tradition of the social mission of the Church —devoting its energies to social service among the poor, and preaching the Church's duty to face, and to help to solve, the problems of an industrial society. It has indeed been a feature

[1] See below, pp. 241, 252.

common to the Evangelical and the Catholic sections of the English Church—and, for that matter, a feature common to both with the various Nonconformist societies, which in this respect have followed the same tradition and adopted similar methods—that they have all sought to make religion a general social force. One of the deep differences between the churches and chapels of England and the churches of the Continent (at any rate in Latin countries)—a difference on which foreign observers in England have always remarked—is the tendency of the former to regard themselves, and to act, as social centres, and the tendency of the latter to be places of a separate religious cult and ceremonial. In England, church and chapel alike have sought to give guidance from the pulpit ; they have alike drawn members of their congregation together, not only on Sunday, but also during the week, in various forms of social union ; they have alike gone out—radiating, as it were, their influence abroad —to undertake social service by the founding of clubs and the institution of settlements. It is perhaps in this way that they have both done their greatest work, during recent years, in influencing and helping to shape the character of the nation. It is no little thing that the members of a congregation should thus have had their lives enveloped in the general social atmosphere of their church ; and it has been a service to the nation that clergy and lay workers should have carried their banners outside the walls of their churches into by-ways and alleys and slums. Nor has the work been left only to the old and established religious societies. New organizations, such as the Salvation Army, the Church Army, and the Young Men's and the Young Women's Christian Associations, have taken their part ; and the general social duty incumbent on all who call and profess themselves Christians has been more and more widely recognized.

If we seek to explain why our English churches and chapels and religious societies have all shown this practical trend, we can hardly ascribe it to any general genius of Protestantism. Protestantism has many varieties ; and in some of its varieties it may confine itself, no less than other forms of religion, to the pure cultivation of a doctrine and ceremonial. We have partly, perhaps, to take into account the general diffusion in England of an interest in social problems, which has affected religious and other organizations ; but we may also remark on a tendency— nowhere more marked than it is in our country—in virtue of which a society, once it is rooted and established, goes beyond the particular purpose of its origin, and attempts a general scope of activity. How far a society can carry that attempt, without losing the essential quality of its own nature, is a grave question which each society has to face. Whether religious societies, in embarking on a career of general social activity, may not sacrifice, to some extent, the achievement of their essential religious aim of converting the soul, is a problem which confronts our religious societies to-day. The solution of that problem is their matter. From our point of view, which concerns the influence of religion on the formation of national character, it is enough to say that the Church of England, in line and in unison with other churches, is still a shaping force. If it has lost the control of education which its bishops once exercised, it is still deeply concerned in the education of the young. If it has lost the power of discipline which it once exercised through its canons and church courts, it has still a power of suggestion and of influence which it wields alike through the social activities which it encourages, and through the voice and opinions of those of its leaders who seek to aid in the solution of social problems.

V

Nonconformity, like Anglicanism, bequeathed a political party to the nation ; and like Anglicanism, but in its own way and with its own quality, it has been a social force in the process of national development. Any foreign observer—and not least, perhaps, the French critic of English life, from Voltaire and Montesquieu to Taine and Boutmy—is drawn by a mingled feeling of attraction and curiosity to this most peculiar, and yet most effective, of all the elements in English character. It has spread itself over the world, and made its home in the meeting-houses of Massachusetts no less than in the austere chapels of England ; it has steeled our qualities, and accentuated our angularities ; it has affected our economic life, and influenced the direction of our foreign policy ; it has done much to determine the aspect we have presented to the world, and the judgment which the world has passed upon us.

English Nonconformity has two main streams. The first we may call by the general name of Puritan. Its great period runs from the accession of Queen Elizabeth to the Revolution of 1688. It included (down to 1662) Low Churchmen as well as those who were definite dissidents from the Church ; it is represented to-day by Presbyterians, Congregationalists, Baptists, and Quakers. Perhaps its numbers were never very great during the seventeenth century ; and when William III attempted a religious census, immediately after the Revolution, he only enumerated 108,000 male Nonconformists to nearly 2,500,000 Conformists.[1]

---

[1] Dalrymple's *Memoirs*, Part II., Book I., Appendix. At the present time, according to figures given in the *Statesman's Year Book* (1926), the number of full members of the Church of England (in England and Wales) is 2,300,000 ; of Wesleyan Methodists, Primitive Methodists, United Methodists, and other

The volume of Nonconformity was greatly increased in the eighteenth century, when the stream of Wesleyanism was added to its current ; and at the present time the Nonconformists of England and Wales (who taken together are almost equal in number to the members of the Church of England) are evenly divided between societies which took their origin from the Puritan movement of the sixteenth and seventeenth century, and those which are derived from the Wesleyan movement of the eighteenth.   Remembering this division, and the successive stages in which Nonconformity has played its part and exerted its influence, we must distinguish between the effects of the first and fundamental, and those of the later and secondary period.

Puritanism was rooted and grounded in a positive belief ; but there is a sense in which we may say that, in English history, it has been the spirit " which constantly denies."   From its first beginnings it was engaged in a protestation against the State and a negation of its claims in matter of religion.   The Antigone of our national history, Puritanism has defied the edicts and canons of powers temporal and spiritual, and claimed the liberty of the spirit to obey only eternal law.   It has been, in this way, an apostle of freedom ; and yet freedom was not in the breath of its nostrils.   The Puritans demanded freedom, as passionate minorities always will, because they disliked the opinions of the majority too intensely to consent to be overborne by the weight of numbers.   They were no lovers of toleration for its own sake, and where they controlled the State, as they showed in New England, they were ready to enforce conformity to their own views, and to exert a discipline no less drastic than that of their enemies.   Roger Williams and the community of Rhode Island were a minority among their fellows ; and even Cromwell, a large-hearted lover of toleration, who called God to witness that " no man in England doth suffer for the testimony of Jesus," was unable in his hour of triumph to grant freedom to Anglicans and Catholics.   But if Puritanism loved liberty not in itself, or at all seasons, and worshipped it only with the passing love of a minority, it was condemned by the process of history to become a permanent minority, and it was thus elevated, even while it was condemned, to a permanent advocacy of religious freedom.   It has thus been a steady influence making for the limitation of the State.   It has said to the State, in the sphere of religion, " Thus far and no farther " ; and by a natural contagion of sympathy it has been led to set bounds to its interference on other grounds and in other spheres.   Even in their hour of

Methodists, nearly 900,000 (with nearly 200,000 Calvinistic Methodists in Wales) ; and of Congregationalists, Presbyterians, Baptists, and Quakers, nearly 1,000,000 (of whom 450,000 are Congregationalists and 415,000 Baptists).

triumph under the Commonwealth, the Puritans held, and in the Instrument of Government they laid it down, that there were "fundamentals" which Parliament itself might not touch or vary. In the long winter of their defeat they went beyond any doctrine of the limitation of the State, and they raised the deeper problem of resistance. They could not stop short at a theory of limitation, when the State refused to acknowledge limits; and prohibited by its laws from actions to which they felt themselves bound by the law of God, they acted in the risk of consequence. They met for worship in spite of the State, which forbade their conventicles; they made provision for the education of their members, and entered the teaching profession, in the teeth of laws which sought to attach the penalty of ignorance to the offence of nonconformity. There was nothing of lawlessness or anarchism in what they did: there was no parade of defiance, though there was an obstinate clinging to the principle, which Russell in 1683 died rather than abandon, that in extreme cases it was lawful to resist authority; and except for some turbulence in the reign of Charles II, there was nothing in the nature of insurrection. Nor, indeed, was the hand of the Government very heavy upon the Nonconformists, even in their breaches of the law. Statutes were inscribed in the Statute Book, but their enforcement was fitful; there were no dragonnades; and the officers of the boroughs, in which Nonconformity was strong, were not too ready to promote proceedings. Perhaps it was because the struggle was not à l'outrance, and because there was no quick or stern suppression, that the effects on general opinion and attitude were what they were. There was a long, but not a desperate contention, in the course of which a habit of challenging the State (without any expectation of the direst consequences) was gradually formed. There was no explosion, but there was a constant discontent; and the State lost more in authority, by the steady sapping of a challenge which it became more and more reluctant to answer by overt measures, than it would have lost by a general rebellion. It is to this gradual undermining of the old authoritarian State that we may partly ascribe the eventual triumph of democratic self-government. Puritanism not only inspired the Whig party: it also inspired more radical ideas of political progress which transcended the conceptions of Whiggery.

There were other ways in which Puritanism fostered political liberty. Its basis was religious individualism; and it fostered a general temper of individualism. Its doctrine of the responsibility of the lonely soul for its own salvation readily allied itself with parallel tenets of secular philosophy, and it helped to encourage their general diffusion. It was the air in which ideas of the Englishman's legal "birthright and inheritance," and even more drastic ideas of the natural rights of all men, flourished in the seventeenth century. It was the soil in which Bentham's utilitarian philosophy, that made each man the best judge of his happiness, and Adam Smith's political economy, with its insistence on the free course of trade under individual management, germinated and grew to strength. Puritanism and political economy (the political economy of the classical period) had indeed a close affinity ; and there is, as we shall see, a sense in which the English Antigone was also an English Midas, which turned what it touched into gold. All in all, we may say that Nonconformity served as a gathering ground of the various influences (religious, political, and economic) which produced the Liberal or Manchester philosophy of the nineteenth century— a philosophy which not only inspired a party, but determined in no small measure the general life and aspect of Victorian England. "Way for individual enterprise"—this was its teaching ; and backed by the manufacturing and commercial classes, which had always been the stronghold of Nonconformity, its teaching triumphed. The reluctant Peel, a Conservative and a Churchman, bowed to its logic ; the subtle mind of Gladstone, nurtured in the same tenets as Peel, came under its influence and became its chosen apostle. The England which presented itself to the Continent—the England which the Continent still sees (though it is passing or passed)—was the England of this tradition : not the England of Church and King, the "land" and loyalty, but the England of chapel and counting-house, the factory and self-help. The philosophy of England which travelled abroad was the philosophy of John Stuart Mill and Herbert Spencer ; and both, whatever their religious views, were deeply imbued with the Nonconformist tradition. Spencer, as he writes in his autobiography, sprang from a family "essentially dissenting" ; and his Nonconformist instincts and early training left an abiding mark, which appears in his opposition to any scheme of State education, and in the title and whole argument of *The Man versus the State*.[1]

If the Puritans were driven, as a tenacious minority, in opposition to the State, to develop the more negative qualities of a minority, there was none the less in their creed a positive quality which was the ground and the rock of their resistance. Puritanism was something more than a challenge to the State. It was the practice of a firm and resolute will (" will . . . is the essence of Puritanism "[2]), set sternly to the kingdom of God and His righteousness ; it was a rigour of self-control, and an unrelenting process of self-discipline, by which the will of man

---

[1] See the writer's *Political Thought in England from Herbert Spencer to To-day*, pp. 120–122.
[2] R. H. Tawney, *op. cit.* p. 201.

was made to fulfil the apprehended purposes of God. It was not for the Puritan to steep his mind in the warm comfort of historic tradition ; nor could his spirit float suspended in a cloud of encompassing witnesses, sustained by the communion of an inspired and inspiring Church. His was a new and solitary soul, projected into a bare world for an arduous and lonely struggle ; and he must wrestle alone, in the night, with the angel of the Lord. He lived in a spiritual solitude ; but he was not a solitary. He could not renounce the world and its works, or embrace the life of the hermit or anchorite ; he had been sent into the world to do his Master's business and to fulfil his calling ; and it would have seemed to him a surrender of the will and an act of cowardice to flee temptation or to shun struggle. The Puritans were strong " not in the spirit of the mediæval ascetic, because they despised the world, but because they looked upon the world as a kingdom of God, in which . . . they would do their Master's will." [1] Stoics of the religious world, they relied on no process of " habituation " by any form of social discipline, such as Laud had dreamed of enforcing : they wrestled, each for himself, to attain a responsible righteousness, proceeding not from without, or from any form of organized Church, but from the inner fountain of a pure heart and a firm will.

Loneliness was one of the Puritan virtues, as it was also one of the Puritan defects. They dared to be alone, and they cultivated the high virtues of solitude. Solitude is the preparation and the parent of achievement. There is a sense in which great religious movements come from the desert. Judaism sprang from the desert ; and our Lord went into the desert before the beginning of His ministry. Puritanism took England into the desert—as it were "on a journey to Damascus" ; and England came back from the desert with a new vision and a new purpose. In a merely temporal sense, the solitary habit of the Puritan was rich in large results. The growing period of Puritanism was also the growing period of English colonization. The bugbear of colonization is solitude ; and the nation which can best endure solitude is equipped in advance for colonial expansion. The English colonization of America was largely a Puritan achievement ; and this was a reason of its success. Volney remarked on the difference between the French and the English colonist. "To visit his neighbours," he wrote, "is so imperious an habitual necessity to the Frenchman that we cannot find a single instance of a colonist belonging to our nation settling out of hearing and sight of others, on any of the borders of Louisiana and Canada." He contrasted the English farmer of the backwoods, who, "if he has an opportunity will sell his farm and go into the woods ten or twenty leagues from

[1] S. R. Gardiner, op. cit. vol. iii. p. 242.

the frontier, and there make for himself a new habitation."
Puritanism taught Englishmen many things. It was not the
least of these that it taught them to live quietly in lonely
New England homesteads. "In your patience possess ye your
souls."

But the loneliness of the Puritan was also a defect. He
carried a lonely self-reliance to the verge of a lonely selfishness.
He rejected any comfort or consolation of society, because
he desired to lean on nothing but his own strong will; but he
also forgot the just claims of society. "A spiritual aristocrat,
who sacrificed fraternity to liberty, he drew from his idealiza-
tion of personal responsibility a theory of individual rights,
which, secularized and generalized, was to be among the most
potent explosives that the world has known."[1] He was ready
to ascribe the success which he achieved to his own right hand,
and to claim it as his now inalienable possession; nor was it
easy for him to say *Non nobis*, or to recognize the framework of
social co-operation in which we all do our work and achieve our
measure of triumph. He could readily ascribe failure to moral
failings, and condemn poverty as the result not of circumstances
but of character. Absorbed in himself, his struggles, and his
standards, he was led to expect of others what he demanded of
himself—not so much from pride, or a belief in the superiority
of his own standards, but rather from a conviction, which had
its modesty, that his standards were the least that were tolerable
in any decent community. If he had been less lonely, he would
have had more sympathy; and if he had had more sympathy,
he would have been less of a stern Sabbatarian, less of an enemy
to simple traditional pleasures—in a word, less set upon exer-
cising, in the moral sphere, that tyranny of conformity to which
he himself refused to bow in the sphere of religion. Loneliness
nerves the will; but it may paralyse the imagination. It
fosters a stern sense of personal responsibility; but it may also
develop a spiritual egoism which invades the whole range of
personality, and makes the general character self-centred and
self-opinionated.

Besides the practice of will, and the cultivation of solitude,
the Puritan had a passionate zeal for work which, acting upon
an energy natural, as we have seen, to the English stock, and
fostered, as we have also seen, by the conditions of the English
climate, raised it to a height at which it may sometimes seem
almost dæmonic. Work was conceived as something sacra-
mental — the outward and visible sign of an inward and
visible struggle to do the will of the Lord. The Parable of the
Vineyard and the Parable of the Talents were ever before
the Puritan's eye. He did not love the Book of Common

[1] R. H. Tawney, *op. cit.* p. 230.

Prayer, but there was one of its phrases which he took to heart ; and he set himself, with all his power, " to learn and labour truly to get his own living in that state of life to which it should please God to call him." The doctrine of Calling, as Mr. Tawney has pointed out,[1] was a cardinal doctrine of Puritanism. God had called and " elected " men spiritually to the grace which comes by faith. He had also called and chosen them temporally for some particular employment or business, in which they must labour with diligence, making themselves known by their fruits. Where the old Church had preached the necessity of " works "—the *opera injuncta* prescribed by the priest as a " satisfaction " to be performed by the penitent—the Puritan minister preached the necessity of work, as an appointed material struggle which was the corollary and complement of the spiritual struggle of the elect. Work was thus spiritualized, and made an end in itself. " To neglect this," wrote Baxter, " and say, ' I will pray and meditate,' is as if your servant should refuse his greatest work, and tie himself to some lesser, easy part." Spiritual life is in this way translated and hardened into material effort ; and production becomes, as it were, the law of life. It is in this emphasis on production, as well as in its stern and solitary individualism, that Puritanism shows its affinity with the tenets of classical political economy (especially in the form in which they were preached by Mill, the apostle of production) ; and it is here that the English Antigone becomes an English Midas. It is for this reason that more than one writer has regarded Puritanism as the parent of capitalism. Set together (the argument runs) the Puritan emphasis on work and production, and the Puritan challenge to the State with its consequent claim of a free way for individual initiative—and you have compounded the elements which constitute the capitalist system. The argument has been challenged by Mr. Tawney on two main grounds. In the first place, we can trace the origins of capitalism back to an earlier age than that of the Puritan Revolution, and we can find its spirit and its methods already present in the Italian cities of the later Middle Ages. In the second place, Puritanism, in its earlier phase, and down to 1660, opposed itself to the unlimited accumulation of wealth, and its preachers maintained the old mediæval doctrines of " the just price " and the prohibition (or at any rate the strict limitation) of interest. But if capitalism was earlier than Puritanism, and if Puritanism, in its first beginnings, challenged its methods and its principles, we must also admit (as Mr. Tawney readily admits) that the spirit of later Puritanism was an air congenial

---

[1] R. H. Tawney, *op. cit.* pp. 240 *sqq.* He refers to Weber's Essay, " Die protestantische Ethik und der Geist des Kapitalismus," in which this conception was first elaborated.

to the accumulation of wealth. It was not only that the Puritans were devoted to production in virtue of their doctrine of work and calling. Their discipline of daily life, in itself, and apart from doctrine, was calculated to lay the foundations of success in commerce and industry. They mortified themselves of joys—of luxuries and even of comforts; and a sparing habit of life was productive of saving, which led in turn to banking and the accumulation of capital. The regularity of Puritan life, its stern economy of time, the sense with which it was vested of working in the Great Taskmaster's eye, all tended to produce men of business capacity, ready for the management of affairs and the conduct of large undertakings. In both ways—by supplying the means and by providing the men—Puritanism prepared the way for commercial and industrial greatness, and was a forerunner of the Industrial Revolution.

But the Puritan zeal for work, like the Puritan cultivation of loneliness, had its defects as well as its qualities. If work was a moral end, and work could be measured by its "fruits" of success, it followed that wealth which had been earned by effort was a proof of moral desert; and upon that again it followed that poverty, unless it had been incurred by pure misfortune, was an argument of moral failing. Puritanism helped to dig the gulf—which is apparent in the history of English thought, and not least of English education,[1] from the end of the seventeenth century onwards—between a possessioned class, regarded as justified in its possessions by its moral and spiritual merits, and a class of labouring poor conceived as condemned to poverty by its moral and spiritual defects. In this temper poverty came to be regarded as possibly a misfortune, but more probably a fault; if poor relief was still granted, it was mixed with the bitter savour of deterrent methods; and if attempts were made to provide for the education of the masses, they were made to wear the guise of a work of reformation. And yet, in any just reckoning, and with every allowance for the element of acidity which it carried, there was an astringent quality in the Puritan temper which strengthened the whole of the nation. Work is not the whole of life, nor is it an end in itself. But it is a large part of life, and when it is practised as a spiritual exercise it is dignified and ennobled. To work steadily, with the will taut and braced; to work quietly, not for the approbation of others, but because you must be about your appointed business; to go through to the end, without shirking or trembling—these were no ignoble lessons. They were not perhaps altogether new lessons in the long record of English history. In the early glimpses which we have of the old English, in *Beowulf* and in other relics of their poetry and their thought, we

---

[1] See below, p. 249.

14

may trace, as we shall see, a sad and sober gravity ; a resolution " to fetter up the will " ; a readiness to fight against odds undismayed. When the pool of a nation's life is stirred, old and hidden things may come to the surface again ; and the grave and even melancholy temper of stern righteousness, which animated the nobler spirits of Puritanism, was a revival and reconsecration of the best elements in the old national tradition. Nor was that revival and reconsecration confined to England or the British Isles. It crossed the seas, and it controlled the birth of a nation in North America : it inspired a Lincoln no less than a Cromwell. Perhaps it is in the United States that we may trace the effects of the Puritan spirit most clearly to-day, alike in its strength and its weakness ; and here we may see writ large the figure of the struggling Samson—tenacious of expressed ideals, resolute to repress the evils of this world (be they slavery or alcohol), and anxious to establish the Kingdom ; but sometimes letting practice fall behind ideals, sometimes obscurantist in its clinging to imagined " fundamentals," and sometimes tyrannous in its passion for uniformity.

VI

Down to the end of the seventeenth century Nonconformity was a leaven, small in amount, which yet stirred and moved the whole nation. It grew in volume during the eighteenth century, when Calvinistic Methodism spread through Wales, which in the seventeenth century had been Anglican and Royalist ; when Wesleyanism began to count its adherents in hundreds of thousands ; and when the Nonconformist bodies generally, by their labours among the new population which was pouring into industry, began to make the volume of their membership more nearly equal to the settled Anglicanism of the countryside. Nonconformity, as we have seen, had always been strong in the towns, among the commercial and industrial classes ; and the growth of industrialism and of urban life, which marks the latter half of the eighteenth century, was naturally favourable to the growth of Nonconformity. In that growth it was Wesleyanism which played the greatest and most conspicuous part, affecting not only its own immediate adherents, but also a large section of the Anglican body from which it sprang and which it eventually left. The social influence which it exercised was profound and far-reaching. Wesley and his followers consciously carried their mission among the working-classes, and especially and particularly among the miners. They carried it in the form of a gospel of " enthusiasm " (detestable to the colder and more cultivated intelligences of an age of reason) which caught the popular imagination and stirred a popular emotion. But neither their mission nor their influence was confined to a single class. If they went to the poor, they also made converts among the upper classes, and they had their stronghold in the middle class. They gave to that class, which might otherwise have stayed complacent in a fat and dull prosperity, the stimulus of ideals—the aiding of missions ; the spread of education ; the reform of prisons ; the abolition of the slave-trade and of slavery itself. They knitted the middle to the poorer classes in the common bonds of a religious organization: they united them both in the services of the chapel, in which laymen might play their part, and in the common social gatherings of which the chapel was a centre and focus. In this way Wesleyanism stopped the widening of that social gulf which had existed, it is true, before the Industrial Revolution, but which the Revolution, without any counteracting influence, might have made both broader and deeper. By what it did to draw classes together, and by the fact that it supplied a religious channel for the satisfaction of cravings and demands which might otherwise have run into the secular channels of French Revolutionary doctrine, Wesleyanism helped to keep the nation stable in the period of convulsion which marked the passing of the eighteenth into the nineteenth century. But it was not merely a stabilizing force, nor was it content that the comfort of religious enthusiasm should serve to divert men's minds from a sense of social injustice. It supplied, especially from the ranks of its lay preachers, men who led and spread working-class movements for better things—men who could rise above hatred or materialism, and connect ideas of social reform with a keen religious faith. The strength and the hold of the Trade Union and the Labour movement have depended, in no small degree, upon this connection. In other ways it has to be admitted that Wesleyanism inherited and accentuated national defects. It had some of the intolerance of the older Puritanism. It had something of its anxious discipline of life ; and it diffused the same cloud of painful observance of the rules of external religion. It did not love the free course of thought, and it was dubious of human science. The tradition of the letter was strong in its teaching ; and if the righteousness which it sought to teach was beyond that of the Scribes and the Pharisees, the enlightenment which it attained provoked Matthew Arnold to the adjective " Philistine."

It is possible that the Christian Churches will not exercise in the future the direct influence on national life and character which they have exercised in the past. In particular the influence which Nonconformity in its various forms has exercised during the last three centuries—an influence particularly deep and pervasive—is not likely to be so marked in this century.

(What the remoter future may bring, and whether, in the process of the incessant movement of man's mind, a new floodtide of his undefeated religious impulse may not recur—that is another matter, which lies outside our scope.) It is not that Nonconformity has lost ground to the English Church, or, again, that both are losing ground to another Church : it is rather that both have handed to the teacher, and to the school, a torch which was once kept burning by the preacher, and uplifted in church and chapel. When schools and teachers were few, religious bodies had a double duty. They had to mould the characters and to awaken the intelligence of men by their teaching, as well as to touch and move their spirits by their preaching. The spread of a general system of national education may be said to relieve the churches of a part of their ancient duty. It was they who laboured first at the institution of that system ; and its foundation stones were laid, over a hundred years ago, by Anglicans and Nonconformists alike, when the different voluntary societies set their hands to the provision of Sunday schools and the founding of day schools. They still contribute to the working of the national system, as it stands to-day, both through the " non-provided " schools which they manage and through the provision which they otherwise make for religious instruction. But it is now the duty of teachers in their several stations—in universities ; in " public " and secondary schools ; and, above all, in all forms of elementary schools—to make their contribution, in this present century, to the formation of national character. They have the new instrument of a national system of education ; they have the new technique of regular methods of instruction ; they have in their charge, week by week and year by year, the precious and crucial years of adolescence. *Ad vos, dominos doctores et magistros, res redit.*

The Churches have still a work to do for the nation—a work no less arduous, and no less embracing, than any they have attempted before. They have to find, by the toil of their thinkers, a vision of eternal and immutable truth which they can commend, without reserve or qualification, to the growing demands of a more critical age and a more awakened intelligence. They have to escape from the shadow of unreality which lies heavy upon religious confessions, in days in which ancient formularies have not yet been revised to meet the growth of historical knowledge and scientific discovery. That is one work —*periculosae plenum opus aleae.* And there is another. They have to consider the bearing of Christian principles on social problems and policy. It is no easy matter of consideration. Is the economic life of nations a matter which can be regulated on any principles which the Churches can formulate? The mediæval Church sought to formulate principles, and to enforce the principles which it formulated. It did not succeed. Puritanism, in its early phase, attempted a discipline which embraced the regulation of buying and selling, of letting and hiring, of interest and price. In its later phase it abnegated the attempt. To-day there is more than one attempt being made to formulate the rules by which Christian order can be made to prevail in the political and economic life of nations. He would be a bold man who, in the light of history, would prophesy their success. And yet the attempts must be made. Christianity is not a religion of dualism; and it would be a form of dualism to believe that there is one rule in the world of religious life, and another in the world of economics or of international relations. Whatever the prospects—success or failure, praise or blame—a Christian Church is bound by its nature to seek " to reduce to the One " the tangled skein of human life.

LIST OF BOOKS

BUCKLE, H. T.—*History of Civilisation in England*, 1867.
CHURCH, R. W.—*Christianity and National Character* (in *The Gifts of Civilisation*), 1880.
KIDD, B.—*Social Evolution*, 1894.
LECKY, W. H.—*History of England in the Eighteenth Century*, vol. ii. 1892.
LEVY, H.—*Economic Liberalism*, 1913.
MACDOUGALL, W.—*The Group Mind*, 1920.
PEARSON, C. H.—*National Life and Character*, 1893.
SMITH, A. L.—*Church and State in the Middle Ages*, 1913.
TAWNEY, R. H.—*Religion and the Rise of Capitalism*, 1926.
TROELTSCH, E.—*Die Soziallehren der Christlichen Kirchen*, 1912.
ZIMMERN, A. E.—*Nationality and Government*, 1918.

CHAPTER VIII

LANGUAGE, LITERATURE, AND THOUGHT

I

W E have seen, in a previous chapter, that a race and a language group are two separate and different things. A race is a classification on the basis of physical type, and those who belong to that type may speak different languages. The members of the Alpine race speak French in the Cevennes, Italian in Lombardy, German in Bavaria, and Czech in Bohemia. A language group is a mental classification ; and those who are united on the basis of this classification may belong to a number of different physical types. The members of the Romance language group are Nordic in the north of France ; Alpine in central France, northern Italy, and part of Switzerland ; Mediterranean in southern France, southern Italy, Portugal, and most of Spain. There is a further point to be noticed. The racial character of a language group may change in the course of history. The original Celtic language group was apparently formed by a conquering Nordic strain which had subdued, and imbued with its language, a large part of the Alpine population of Central Europe. The Celtic language group to-day, which is mainly to be found in Wales and Ireland, would seem to consist of members of the Mediterranean race, whose ancestors were conquered by, and received their language from, the Celtic-speaking invaders who entered the British Isles before the Christian era. A language group, therefore, not only consists, as a rule, of different races : it may also, at different times, consist of different racial factors.

It is the quality of a race that its members constantly and regularly inherit certain physical features ; and it is possible, though far from certain, that they also inherit certain mental characteristics which are the concomitants of these features. It is certain that the members of a language group, as such, do not receive by inheritance, in the strict and proper sense of that word, any common characteristics either of body or mind. There can be biological inheritance of physical features, and possibly also of mental characteristics which are cognate with those features : there cannot be biological inheritance of a mental acquirement such as language, or of any characteristics which may be cognate with that acquirement. There can only be at the most a process of social transmission—a process, that is to say, which operates from mind to mind, and not from body to body. But it seems difficult to believe that there can even be social transmission, within a language group, of any common mental habits or characteristics. The process of social transmission implies the existence of a society which transmits some tradition of its common life to generation after generation of its members. A language group is not a society. It is simply a philological classification by which a number of languages are grouped together, mainly for scientific purposes, in virtue of the common elements which they all possess. It would not appear therefore that the language group in which a nation is included transmits anything to that nation, or in any way affects its habit of mind or character. If this be so, it is irrelevant to our national life that we are included in the Teutonic group of languages ; it is irrelevant to the life of France that it is included in the Romance group ; it is irrelevant to the life of Wales that it is included in the Celtic group.

Such a conclusion, however, is perhaps too drastic. We somehow feel (though we should all admit that feeling falls a long way short of assurance) that there are Teutonic qualities, Latin attributes, and a Celtic genius. It is possible that we are guilty of confusion. What we call Teutonic qualities may belong not to the Teutonic language group, but to the Nordic race, which we are confusing with the Teutonic language group. Similarly what we call Latin qualities may belong to the Mediterranean race as it has developed in France and Italy ; and what we call the Celtic genius, by which we mean a melancholy brooding over the chronicles of wasted time, may belong to the Mediterranean race as it has developed itself, among old rocks and barren wastes, in isolation and under a sense of defeat, in Brittany, Cornwall, Wales, and the south-west of Ireland. If, however, we consider a language group not as it exists to-day, but as it originally developed in the past, we shall recognize that in its beginnings it was possibly something more than it ultimately became, and that it even approached the nature of a political society. There was once a Celtic Empire in Central Europe, some centuries before the Christian era, and the vogue of Celtic speech proceeded from the conquests and assimilations of that Empire. There was a Roman Empire, which held together in a political unity all the nations which now form part of the Romance language group ; and what we call Latin attributes may very well go back to the days in which Rome diffused a common Latin speech, and with it a common stock of Latin ideas, through the southern half of Western Europe. On this basis we may argue that there may after all be some survival, by a process of social transmission which has continued separately in each nation, of characteristics common to all the members of a language group—characteristics which were originally acquired when they all lived together as a single society and possessed some form of organization that permitted the formation of a common language and a common stock of ideas. Such a survival of the influence of an original unity, with its common characteristics, may encourage in each nation of a language group a feeling of connection with the other nations ; it may lead to a sense of kinship as something existing not only in philology, but also in fact ; it may induce the different nations, in the strength of a sense of connection, to draw upon and borrow from one another freely ; and it may thus tend towards some assimilation of their development and character.

These, however, are vague and speculative conceptions. We can perhaps assume, with some degree of certainty, the existence of a common Latin fund in the Latin-speaking peoples which have inherited, along with the language, something of the tradition of Rome. We cannot safely make a similar assumption of a common Celtic or a common Teutonic fund. Even if there was once a Celtic Empire, the peoples who speak Celtic languages to-day were not parts of it ; and it has perished as if it had never been. There is no record or tradition of any single Teutonic society ; but there may have been such a society, and indeed we can hardly explain the existence of a single original Teutonic language, from which the different Teutonic languages have subsequently branched, unless we suppose a single original society in which it was spoken. But that society, if it existed, has left no traces ; and in any case it must have been too early and too inchoate to bequeath any definite body of tradition. The most we can say is that there is a kinship of Teutonic languages ; that words are not only words, but vehicles of associations ; and that the bond of common words and their common associations can not only be a link between peoples in the present, but may even suggest the transmission to those peoples of some common substance of thought from a dim and forgotten past in which they once lived together.

II

The English language has a peculiar characteristic, which prevents us from ascribing it entirely to any single language group. It is a mixed language—in structure and part of its vocabulary, Teutonic ; in a large and important part of its vocabulary, Latin. The Teutonic words generally express simple facts and the simpler feelings : the Latin words belong to a later and more reflective stage. Our forefathers brought a Teutonic language and Teutonic ideas to England fifteen hundred years ago ; [1] but they brought them to a land which already bore traces of a Latin invasion and occupation, and which was to be invaded and occupied by Latin influence again and again in the future. There was the religious occupation of St. Augustine and his Benedictine missionaries in 597 A.D., which made England a spiritual colony of the Roman Church. There was the political occupation of William the Conqueror and his Gallicized knights in 1066 A.D. : the Norman Conquest, it has been said, " marks the defeat . . . of the Teutonic conqueror by Latin civilization," and opens the door " for the entry of the Italian priest and Gallic legislator." [2] There was the cultural invasion of the Italian Renaissance and its votaries, in the reign of Elizabeth, which brought English literature back to Latin traditions of measure and form. A Latin strain has passed into us ; and it makes us, in a sense, neither Latin nor Teutonic, but a bridge between the two, touching on the one side France and Italy, and on the other Holland and Germany. We are a natural mediator in the differences and the rivalries of Latin and Teuton ; and we seem intended, by the nature of our language, to interpret the one to the other.

Our language has affected our literature, as our literature has in turn affected our national life. We may distinguish various effects which have been produced in our literature by " the double origin of our language, with its strange and violent contrasts between the highly coloured crudity of the Saxon words and the ambiguous splendour of the Latin vocabulary." [3] With a language which has drawn liberally and almost indifferently from two sources, we have necessarily a rich and abundant vocabulary. Our writers are not committed to any set stock of words and expressions : they can draw freely on the riches at their command, and they can frame the very texture of their vocabulary by their own choice. Sir Thomas Browne lived at the same time as Dryden, and Carlyle was a contemporary of Matthew Arnold ; but they almost seem to use different instruments of expression. An individualism of style, which corroborates a passion for individuality fostered in the national character by many other causes, flows naturally from the rich supply of our vocabulary ; and you may find among our writers Asiatic gorgeousness side by side with Attic austerity, and village simplicity cheek by jowl with urban sophistication. It must be admitted that liberty has not seldom become licence.

---

[1] " Hoc anno," it is written in the *Chronica Gallica* under the years 441-2, " Britanniae . . . variis cladibus eventibusque latae sub dicionem Saxonum rediguntur."

[2] H. W. C. Davis, *England under the Normans and Angevins*, p. 2.

[3] Lytton Strachey, *Books and Characters*, p. 11.

The abundance which permits choice demands also taste and discretion ; and not all who have chosen have chosen wisely. English has always been a difficult language to use ; bad English has often tended to drive good English out of circulation ; and not every age has had its Johnson to castigate offenders.

One of the features of our language which is due to its double origin is an abundance of apparent synonyms which on investigation are found to be distinguished from one another by fine shades of difference. We have a Teutonic word to express an idea ; we have often also a Latin word ; and we may sometimes have in addition a word derived from the Greek. *Fellow-feeling, compassion,* and *sympathy* seem very much alike ; but *fellow-feeling* is different from *compassion,* and *compassion* is not the same as *sympathy.* The English language is thus a subtle instrument, which can convey fine shades of meaning and makes possible delicate nuances of expression. There is little to be said for those who would austerely preserve the purity of a Saxon vocabulary. Those who refuse to play on more than a third of the keys of a piano will make little music. The Latin words are sonorous ; they are often words of " romantic " suggestion ; they are not seldom words of philosophic reflection. It would be difficult to write a philosophic work in pure Saxon ; and two of the most wonderful lines in English poetry :

> " Magic casements, opening on the foam
> Of perilous seas, in fairy lands forlorn "

contain Greek and Latin words (made more beautiful by passing through mediæval France), as well as words of Teutonic origin. In any case, our language has now been mixed for centuries ; and why should we fly in the face of an old tradition by rejecting a large part of its content ? We shall be wiser to love our riches, and to seek to elicit, as our great writers have always sought to elicit (Shakespeare in his English style was no small Latinist [1]), the wealth and the subtleties of expression implicit in a many-coloured and many-sounding vocabulary.

The range of our vocabulary, which permits individuality and encourages subtlety of expression, will not readily suffer either the nationalist regimentation current in Germany or the academic control traditional in France. We cannot be severely and austerely nationalist, because we have not, in that sense, a " national " language. We cannot be resolutely Anglo-Saxon, even if we would, and even if we were willing to lose the gifts of individuality of style and delicacy of expression, because the

---

[1] " The multitudinous seas incarnadine . . ."
 " And like an unsubstantial pageant faded . . ."
 " Violets
The perfume and suppliance of a minute."

loss of our Latin would leave us paupers. Perhaps it is no small benefit, in other than literary ways, that our language is essentially impatient of any exclusive nationalism. It is equally impatient of the control of any academy. It would need several academies, in constant session, to cope with the rush of would-be immigrants into the English language. There has been speech of an English academy of letters from the days of Bolton,[1] in the reign of James I, to the days of Matthew Arnold. The speech has not prospered. In some ways we have suffered from the want of any standard of usage. An academy which fixes a tradition of right words and permissible forms of expression, encourages lucidity and fosters good taste. All writers are led to use a common and uniform vehicle of thought, which makes their writings readily intelligible to others ; and all are induced to conform to a canon of propriety which, if it imprisons liberty, may also banish the baser sort of " poetic licence." The absence of an academy may mean the presence of obscurity and bad taste. But where all are free to express themselves freely, each may express himself more from the heart, and affect more deeply the hearts of his readers. The strong traditionalism of French language and literature has perhaps influenced the French nation less than the loose individualism of our language and literature has influenced us. There was only a single tradition in France, from the end of the Pleiad to the beginnings of romanticism : there has always been a various and manifold exuberance in England—except perhaps in the Augustan age ; and even the Augustan age had its rebels. As a nation, we have cared less for literature in general than France ; but we have had a richer variety for which to care, and about some of it we have cared a great deal. The freedom which permitted each writer—Donne equally with Bunyan, and Byron no less than Blake—to find his own audience was a freedom which increased the influence of literature. A Racine or a Molière running in harness will not go as far as a Shakespeare or a Swift running wild.

III

The literature embodied in the language of any nation is one of the moulds of its life, and one of the influences which shape its development. It flows into the national genius, and affects its substance. The reverse is also in some measure true ; and it may be argued, as it is argued by Professor McNeile Dixon in his Rede lecture on *Poetry and National Character*, that litera-

---

[1] Bolton, who had contributed to *England's Helicon*, presented a scheme for a royal academy to James I, who listened gladly. How happy the royal Johnson would have been in presiding over its deliberations, if ever it had been instituted !

ture takes the colour and expresses the temper of national life. But there are poets and men of letters who seem independent of any country and any age ; and this independence has been particularly marked in many of our writers, from Vaughan to Shelley and Blake, and from Shelley and Blake to Francis Thompson. Rising from original springs of inspiration, which seem to flow outside space and time, such writers have none the less flowed into the current of the national tradition ; and little as they seem to be affected by *it*, it has certainly been affected and influenced by *them*. There are many ways in which the body of national literature may help to determine the course of national thought and the currents of national feeling. There is the moral view which it expresses ; the attitude to life which it shows ; the problems it seeks to handle, and the spirit in which they are handled. Any body of literature, taken in the mass, is instinct with some sort of philosophy. The literature of ancient Greece was imbued with a philosophy of limit, of modera- tion, of " nothing in excess " ; the literature of modern France— in some respects similar, but in others widely different—has been penetrated by a spirit of order, lucidity, and logic. It is less easy to express in any phrase the general spirit of our English literature, partly because its volume is so large, and partly because its writers are so various ; but we may perhaps say that a predominance of ethical interest, and an absorption in character and its development, are the two related and general attributes of most of our writers. There are few English men of letters of whom we can say that they were simply dominated by the artistic impulse. John Milton and William Morris (and Milton even more than Morris) were great artists ; but they both descended into the struggles of their times, and they both sought to be teachers of their fellow-countrymen. It does not, indeed, matter very greatly whether a poet or writer cherishes a direct and conscious purpose of teaching (except that, in virtue of a paradox of literary · art which is a commonplace of literary criticism, the more he cherishes a didactic purpose the less his actual influence is likely to be) ; the real question is whether he has the gift of suggestive power and practical inspiration, which makes him able to " teach in song " the lessons which he has " learned in suffering."

In another and a simpler way the literature of a country may become a general influence by means of the view which it gives, and the picture it draws, of the process of national history and the character of national life. The view of national history which is enshrined in chronicle or drama, in legendary cycles or in historical narrative, becomes, in proportion to the vogue which it attains, a force in the further shaping of national history. In this sphere the legendary figure may be greater than the historical : Roland may outshine Charlemagne, and Robin Hood matter more than the greatest of the Plantagenets. The Arthurian cycle of Malory and the pageant of English history in Shakespeare's plays, from *King John* to *Henry VIII*, are historical influences, even if they are not historical documents ; and whatever criticisms we may pass on the Whig bias of Macaulay (which did not prevent him from being perhaps the greatest of English historians), we must admit that his *History* and *Essays* have helped to determine our ideas and even our action. Literature which is purely imaginative may be equally an influence with literature which deals with legend or history. The great imaginary figures thrown on the screen by the dramatist or novelist may catch the imagination to which they are presented ; and seizing and acting on what is presented, men may unconsciously conform themselves to the image of an image. It has often been remarked that when Mr. Pickwick kept Christmas, he set a fashion. M. Finot has said that the Parisian woman models herself on the pictures of Parisian women which she finds in French literature. It might also be said that Mr. Kipling's pictures of the men who have made the British Empire have helped to make the men who have made the Empire. It is easy for a reader of books (and still more for a writer) to exaggerate the influence which books may exercise ; and we have to remember that the imaginary figures of the artist may be copies as well as creations. But even a copy, when it has been transfigured by the artist, may become a model ; and a literary gallery of imaginary portraits has again and again shown its power of becoming a gallery of models for the imitation of a nation. There is the gallery of figures in Homer, which affected both the religious and the ethical ideas of the Greeks ; there is the gallery of the Arthurian cycle ; there is the gallery in Shakespeare's plays ; there is the gallery in the *Pilgrim's Progress*. There are laws of imitation in virtue of which we tend to follow the suggestion not only of actual, but also of imaginary persons ; and this is one of the causes of the power of literature. Plato was well aware of this power, and he exaggerated its influence, when, in the *Republic*, he sentenced the drama to banishment from his ideal city. Anxious to maintain the principle that each citizen should have a single station, and be devoted in singleness of mind to its duty, he believed that the drama, by its pictures of the lives and ways of many different types, and through the suggestion which those pictures conveyed to the general instinct of imitation, would make " all the world a stage," and every man a player " of many parts." We need not follow Plato in the severity of his logic ; but we may admit that the premise on which he argued was not altogether unfounded.

Literature may also influence life through the magic words and phrases with which it stores the mind and by which it moves the imagination. Such words and phrases become encrusted, by frequency of use and the passage of time, with glittering associations ; and it is not only what they are, but also what they evoke, which gives them potency. This is one of the secrets of all religious liturgies ; and we may say of the great passages in a people's literature that they form, as it were, a national liturgy. There are passages in the Authorized Version, speeches and lyrics and single lines in Shakespeare, stanzas of Gray's *Elegy in a Country Churchyard*, and verses in some of our hymns, which exercise a dominion over the mind. They cannot be dismissed as " tags," even when they are trite with repetition : they are rather " as goads, and as nails fastened by masters of assemblies." They have the currency of proverbs ; but they are different from proverbs, which at the best are canny country wisdom, and sometimes are only the smartness of market-places. Proverbs are bandied from mouth to mouth ; but the great passages of a national literature are like voices which echo on and on, in comfort or encouragement, along the valley of a pilgrimage.

Above all, literature may give to the national mind—or, to speak more accurately, to the minds of the members of a nation— a common content or substance of thought which makes for unity. The literature of a nation is a part of the tradition which constitutes its spiritual being ; and along with religion, and like religion, it belongs to the noblest and highest part of that tradition, because its concern is with eternities. The more the literary tradition of a nation becomes a common content of the minds of its members, through the diffusion of education, the more is that nation united, and the more homogeneous is its life. What divides a nation internally may be even more differences in culture than economic differences. They are, it is true, connected with one another ; and the economic differences which are expressed in the system of classes tend to promote differences of education, appreciation, and enjoyment. But we have allowed this tendency to go much further in England than ever it need have gone. With a system of law and a set of institutions which make, more than most, for national homogeneity, we have nevertheless developed grades and varieties of culture which are more divergent and discrepant than those of France or Germany or any other country in North-Western Europe. If games and sports still draw us together, we have no national theatre or opera ; and if we have a great body of national literature, we have not made it a national possession. English literature is the birthright of all who speak English ; and those who cannot enter into the enjoyment of it are losing their inheritance. In Ancient Athens, all Athenians, of all professions and classes, could sit in the theatre of the city, and enjoy in a common understanding the plays of the great Athenian dramatists.   It is only in such conditions that literature can exert the full measure of its influence in uniting and uplifting the people to which it belongs.   And until we are united by our literature, and can share Milton and Shakespeare together as the Athenians shared Æschylus and Sophocles, we forfeit, in one of its most precious spheres, the full enjoyment of the national tradition.

From these general considerations we may now turn to investigate the special and peculiar features of our literature which are most intimately connected with our national life and temper. The literature of any country may be said to fall into two divisions, according as it is concerned with creative imagination, or with philosophic inquiry and reflection.   The one we may call by the name of Art : the other by the name of Thought. The distinction is artificial, and the two divisions blend and overlap.   Art is the expression of Thought ; and Thought which is to be effective must be clothed in some form of Art.   But even if it is artificial, the distinction may none the less serve to determine the order of our investigation ; and we may accordingly begin our inquiry with that divison of English literature which belongs more especially to the sphere of Art.

The conception of Art which is generally accepted and practised by the great imaginative writers of a country is a matter of the very first moment.   Does Art result from an impulse—which in moments of ecstasy may be a blinding and tyrannical impulse—driving an artist to express, simply for its own and his own sake, and without regard to any other thing or person, some vision of beauty in a perfect " form " which then becomes, by virtue of its perfection, the essence of his achievement ?   And is Art accordingly, as Pater once suggested, always tending to reduce itself to music, in which "form" appears at its purest and is most nearly divested of matter ?   Or is it a juster view that Art issues from a contemplation of human life, leading the artist to seek to interpret some phase, for the help and sustenance of others as well as for his own satisfaction, in a form of beauty which clothes and dignifies the interpretation, but remains after all but a vesture—the essence being, from first to last, the interpretation itself ?   If we answer in the former sense, we shall say that Art is expression, and we shall join the school of " expressionism " : if we answer in the latter, we shall say that it is interpretation, issuing, as such, in communication. On the one assumption it is a matter for the individual artist ; on the other (which was the view of Plato) it becomes a social fact, and a contribution to the general life of society.   From the one point of view æsthetics is in another world from ethics ; from the other the two touch and blend, and the work of the artist enters the moral sphere side by side with that of the teacher or legislator. Whatever the choice which should ideally be made between the two *sub specie æternitatis*, we can at any rate say that the actual and historic tradition of English literary art has steadily moved in the directiom of interpretation, of social communication, of moral purpose. Our poets in particular, from Spenser to Shelley, have consciously connected their art with ideas of moral discipline and human betterment ; and it was one of our poets, Matthew Arnold, who defined literature as the application of ideas to life—an application proceeding, at its best, from men " who saw life steadily and saw it whole," and resulting in criticism and interpretation of the thing seen. The theory of some of our poets has been the actual practice of many of our writers. From *Beowulf* to the *Dynasts* of Thomas Hardy their writings have dealt with human life, showing its struggles, and seeking to reconcile on some basis (even if it be only that of a resigned pessimism) its enduring conflicts. Nor have they been only concerned with the problems of individual life. The problems of social life and order have never been neglected even in our imaginative literature, from Langland's *Piers Plowman* and More's *Utopia* to William Morris's *Dream of John Ball* and his *News from Nowhere*. And if it be said that human and social life are the necessary staple of all literature, in all countries, it may also be said that the definite effort of interpretation (which reaches its height in Shakespeare), and the clear light of a moral purpose (which shines most brightly in the poetry of Milton), are peculiarly marked in English literature.

From the conception of literary art as " an application of ideas to life " we may readily pass, by a natural transition, to consider the place which the study and description of human character have occupied in our literature. Perhaps varieties of character are strongly marked among us. In the view of neighbouring peoples, at any rate, we are a people of " characters," and even of " humours " or splenetic " vapours " ; and an American observer has remarked that " each of these islanders is an island." Among ourselves we readily cherish a particular regard for those who are characters ; and it is perhaps this ready observation of personal idiosyncrasy which has made English literature so largely concerned with living and breathing characters. There is the Elizabethan drama, with its figures of terror and humour and beauty, and its plots which deal (as in *Julius Cæsar*) with conflicts of human life set in terms of conflicting characters. In the seventeenth century there are Ben Jonson's comedies of " humours," succeeded, after the Restoration, by comedies of " manners " : there are descriptions of types, on the plan of Theophrastus, in the writings of Hall and

Overbury and Earle ; and above all there are the noble descriptions of historical characters which we find in Clarendon's *History of the Rebellion* and Burnet's *History of His Own Time.*[1] Finally, there is the novel of character, which English writers added, as a new and original style, to the French romance and the picaresque fiction of Spain—the novel of Fielding and Dickens ; the novel which, refined by a woman's delicate gift of social observation, attains its height in the pages of Jane Austen. In this interest in character our painting is parallel to our literature. The great English product—apart from landscapes, which are themselves, as it were, portraits of an aspect of scenery—is the portrait of a Reynolds or a Gainsborough.

A literature which is an application of ideas to life, and is informed by an interest in character, will also tend towards a moral interest. It will be " busied about things human and moral "—περὶ τὰ ἠθικὰ πραγματευόμενος—as Aristotle said of Socrates, contrasting him with his forerunners. We may carry the parallel further. Just as Socrates and his disciple Plato both sought to make their philosophy a " way of life," which men must be taught to follow and which would lead them towards " a conversion of the soul," so many of our great writers, starting from a similar concern with human and moral things, have similarly attempted to make their art a moral power. The names of Milton and Wordsworth readily spring to the mind ; and both Browning and Tennyson, in their different ways, were teachers of an age which was not ignoble. They were all masters of a school—but it was a school of moral discipline rather than a " school of art " : they were all makers— and that not only in the old Scottish use, which calls the poet a " maker," but also in the sense that they were, to the best of their power, the makers of their nation and generation. It is a commonplace of classical scholars that the poetry of Homer was a bond of Greek unity, a Bible of Greek religion, and a source of Greek education ; that it went far to make a Greek nation, so far as such a thing existed in ancient times, and to inspire a national tradition. It is no great extravagance to claim something similar for the general body of our English literature, and not least for our poetry. Our English literature is not indeed our Bible—and yet even our Bible, in the Authorized Version, is an integral part of it—but it has its own inspiration and its influence ; and it has been in its measure, and still remains, a bond of unity and a fountain of instruction.

[1] Some of these descriptions are collected in D. Nichol Smith's *Seventeenth Century Characters*.

IV

There is something of a miracle in English poetry. In its variety and its riches it stands supreme ; and yet we are otherwise a people of a severely practical utilitarianism, who in other arts (such as the arts of music and sculpture) have achieved but little. What is the explanation ? Matthew Arnold had recourse to the influence of the Celtic genius ; but to explain the wonder of English poetry by that influence is to explain something obscure by something obscurer. Professor M⁰Neile Dixon, in the lecture on *Poetry and National Character* to which reference has already been made, suggests two explanations. In the first place, our poets drew the inspiration of their poetry from looking directly at life itself on their own account. They did not follow the tradition or imitate the manner of a school : they listened to the rebuke :

" Fool, said my Muse to me, look in thy heart and write." [1]

In the second place, they drew the art which could clothe a native inspiration in a form of beauty from a contact and crossing with the Latin tradition of Italy and France—a tradition already expressed in the very vocabulary of the language, and readily passing, from that basis, into the higher reaches of style and expression. If this be so, and if our poetry is the issue of a happy marriage of native inspiration to a Latin tradition of art, we may thank particularly the quality of native inspiration for the influence which poetry has exercised—or at any rate attempted to exercise—among us. Because they looked into their own hearts and at life, our poets sought to touch men's hearts and to affect their lives ; and there has always been in them an ineradicable trend—in none more conspicuous than in Milton, a born artist, who had steeped himself in the art of Italy—towards a dedicated life of service. We have never thought of the poet as

" The idle singer of an empty day " ;

and he who proclaimed himself to be no more was in actual life the busiest of social teachers and workers. We have rather thought of

" The God-gifted organ-voice of England,
Milton, a name to resound for ages."

The sonnet of Wordsworth on Milton is famous :

" Milton, thou should'st be living at this hour,
England hath need of thee : she is a fen
Of stagnant waters . . .
We are selfish men :
O raise us up, return to us again,
And give us manners, virtue, freedom, power."

[1] Sir Philip Sidney's *Astrophel and Stella*, Sonnet 1.

Wordsworth himself was a preacher, who could sometimes fall into the " articulate monotony " of a prosy sermon ; but when he attired himself in brightness—as in some of his sonnets, in his *Ode to Duty*, or in his *Happy Warrior*—he could become the inspiration and the consolation of statesmen and men of affairs.

Poets are as prone to magnify their office as other men ; and we may perhaps discount their testimony. But the theory of English poets about the nature and office of poetry is too uniform, and too continuous, to be neglected. It appears in the *Defence of Poetry* of Sir Philip Sidney, to whom poetry is a thing designed " to lead and draw us to high perfection." It inspires the lofty purpose of the *Faerie Queene*. " The general end therefore of all the book," Spenser writes in the preface, " is to fashion a gentleman or noble person in virtuous and gentle discipline." [1] When Shelley ended his *Defence of Poetry* with the words, " Poets are the unacknowledged legislators of the world," he followed the same tradition. Shelley, indeed—not only in his theory, but also in his life and his poetry—is the most striking example of the practical trend of English poets. He was neither the beautiful and ineffectual angel of Matthew Arnold,[2] nor the inspired child of Francis Thompson. He had all Plato's zeal for action ; he wrote and distributed political pamphlets in Ireland ; and if his art sometimes reduced itself (in Pater's phrase) to the purest form of the purest music, his thought was inspired by a perfectly practical passion for human justice, and he interweaves a definite teaching of his dearest convictions among the splendours of the *Prometheus Unbound*.

There are several themes, recurrent in English literature, and particularly in English poetry, which are significant of its current and trend. One is the historical theme. National history, legendary or actual, has again and again caught the imagination of a writer ; and he has sought to clothe the memory of the past in a form of beauty which will help to make it an inspiration in the life of the present. This is true of Tennyson, in the *Idylls of the King*, even if the record of which he treats is the Celtic record of the Arthurian cycle ; for that record had been generally adopted, and had received a general vogue, under the name of " the matter of Britain," ever after the composition, early in the twelfth century, of Geoffrey of Monmouth's *Historia Britannorum*, " the fountainhead of mediæval romance." It is especially true of the writers of the Elizabethan age. There is history—veiled, it is true, in allegory—in the *Faerie Queene*.

[1] The words remind one of that doctrine of courtesy, based on *Il Cortegiano*, which was current in the sixteenth century. See below, Chapter IX. p. 261.

[2] Matthew Arnold thought that he ought to have been a musician rather than a poet. He might have mastered sounds ; he had neither the force nor the sanity to master the more difficult medium of words. Mrs. Campbell's *Shelley and the Unromantics* gives a very different impression.

Drayton, who wrote a poetical topography of England, "the much blessed," in his *Polyolbion*, versified the histories of Robert of Normandy and Piers Gaveston. The drama became historical in the hands of Marlowe ; and Shakespeare, drawing on two Tudor chronicles—Hall's *Union of the Two Noble Families of Lancaster and York* and the *Chronicles* of Holinshed—produced the series of historical plays which have made for so many their conception of the English past. The Elizabethan version of national history was coloured by a strong nationalism. Another version which was long in vogue, and which began to be formed soon after the Restoration, was imbued with the principles of a party. From the reign of Charles II onwards the members of the Whig party began to produce a version of English history which would justify its politics, and to search for precedents, more particularly in the troubled reign of Richard II,[1] which would vindicate its ambitions. It may seem curious to speak of such an antiquarianism in the same breath as Shakespeare's plays. But in the pages of Macaulay the Whig version of the past attained an artistic presentation and a glow which was almost poetic ; and a moving story of the past working of Whig principles was so admirably narrated that it became a living power in English life.

Another theme which is recurrent in our literature is that of religion. It has been constantly present ; and poets as well as preachers have again and again carried the message of religion into the national life. The theme of religion was the inspiration of much of the poetry of the Anglo-Saxon period. Cædmon is only a name, and nothing remains of his poems ; [2] but the anonymous *Genesis* and *Exodus* are the precursors in temper, and sometimes in power, of *Paradise Lost*. The Puritan age, and the later age of the Evangelical movement, drew from the same fountain of inspiration as the Old English writers before the Norman Conquest. (It may almost be said, as we have already had reason to suggest, that there was a recurrence of the Old English strain in the Puritan period.) In the one there are the poems of Milton and (almost greater in its general range of influence) the *Pilgrim's Progress* of Bunyan : in the other there are the great hymns—and the hymns of a people are no small part of its tradition—of Watts, the Wesleys, and Cowper. Perhaps no part of our literature has been a greater power than this for the whole of the nation at large, or grooved the national temper more deeply. But there is a literature of the religious theme which lies outside the range of Puritanism and Evan-

---

[1] There is a history of the reign, by "a gentleman of quality," which was written about the middle of the reign of Charles II, and shows the trend of inquiry.

[2] I accept, as an obedient disciple, what seems to be the current view. But I am told that there is something to be said to the contrary.

gelicalism. There are the poets of the devout life—Herbert and Vaughan and Crashaw (whose *St. Theresa* ends in one of the highest flights of English poetry), not to mention the curious religious poetry of "emblems" in Quarles and Christopher Harvey. There are the English mystics, from Richard Rolle of Hampole and the Lady Julian of Norwich to William Law and William Blake. Above all, there is the Authorized Version of the Bible (and, in its measure, the Book of Common Prayer) with its noble vocabulary, its splendour of phrase, and its echoing cadences. How different would English and Scottish life have been if we had not had that book in that form of beauty ! A monument and a model of style, it has influenced writers and orators for three centuries ; and the influence of its substance on English thought, since it first became a general national possession in 1611, goes deeper than any calculation can sound.

Another theme or note which is from first to last characteristic of our literature, and a secret of its influence, is one which we may call by the name elegiac. It is a sadness which is not weakness, and a lamentation which is not unmanly ; a melancholy which is mixed with endurance, and a brooding on the passage of time which never becomes despair. It appears again and again in Shakespeare—not only in *Hamlet* but in the Sonnets ; not only in the spirit of a play or a poem, but in a phrase or a turn of words. " Life's but a walking shadow . . . and like an unsubstantial pageant faded . . . the chronicles of wasted time . . . the wreckful siege of battering days . . . bare ruined choirs, where late the sweet birds sing." It is not an admixture of any Celtic strain ; it goes back to the earliest Old English literature. " The Anglo-Saxon genius for poetry," wrote W. P. Ker, " is best known in the elegies—*The Wanderer, The Seafarer*, and others—to which there is nothing corresponding in Germany or Iceland. The English invented for themselves a form of elegy. They seem to have been more readily touched by motives of regret and lamentation than other people." [1] This elegiac note transcends private affection and private loss ; it is broader and more impersonal ; it springs from the feeling :

> " Since brass nor stone nor earth nor boundless sea
> But sad mortality o'ersways their power,
> How with his rage shall beauty hold a plea,
> Whose action is no stronger than a flower."

It is a note which appears not only in elegies, but in other forms. *Beowulf* is an heroic poem ; but it has the elegiac note. The figure of " sad mortality," which the poet calls by the name of Wyrd, lowers over its action. A man thinks of his friends, and the thought comes to his mind, " Wyrd swept them all away."

[1] *The Dark Ages*, pp. 265–266.

But there is no pessimism in the thought, and it breeds no counsels of despair. One can be a man, and stand up against outrageous fortune ; for " Wyrd often saves an earl undoomed when his courage avails." The general moral of Old English literature, even in the definite elegies, is manful and undismayed. " Fetter up the heart " is a saying of a good courage which comes in *The Wanderer* ; and the refrain of the *Lament of Deor*, reinforcing the comfort of each example, is a challenge rather than a lament. " That old distress passed over, and so may this woe have ending." [1] And thus there emerges the idea of the fight against odds without flinching—an idea which seems to be indigenous in all early Teutonic literature, and became a peculiar and permanent tradition of our own. It is present in the ballads of *Robin Hood* and *Chevy Chase*. It rings in the sayings of the Elizabethan mariners. It appears in the *Samson Agonistes* of Milton and in Bunyan's Mr. Greatheart. It reappears, as something more than merely a literary reminiscence, in Tennyson's " Ballad of the Revenge," in Doyle's " Private of the Buffs," and " The Loss of the Birkenhead," and in Newbolt's " He Fell among Thieves." The literary critic may smile at the *lyra heroica* of the nineteenth century, and say that it was played by a public-school muse to the tune of " Play the Game." It is true enough that the public schools applied to their games a tradition, which they may have vainly imagined that they had themselves invented, of fighting hard to the end without caring for the chance of defeat. But it is a tradition which is older in our literature, by many centuries, than the oldest of public schools.

There are other and deeper manifestations of the elegiac note in English literature. It stirs religious thought, from Bede's fable of the sparrow that flies through the lighted hall [2] to Newman's *Dream of Gerontius*. It appears in Langland and the popular poets of his time, brooding on the Ploughman and his misery and the tangled perplexity of social life :

> " All singing one song that was sorrowful hearing,
> For they all cried one cry, a sad note of care." [3]

---

[1] I owe the passages quoted here to Dale's *National Character in English Literature*, pp. 52–53 ; cf. also p. 195.
[2] Bede, *Ecclesiastical History*, ii. 13. When the adoption of Christianity was in question, before the Northumbrian Witan, one of the thegns rose and said: " Such is the present life of men on earth, O king, in comparison with the time to come which is unknown to us, as when thou art sitting at table with thy captains and servants, in winter-time, and the fire is lit and the room is warm, and a storm of snow or rain is raging outside, and a sparrow comes and quickly flies through the hall, entering in at one door and going out quickly through another. . . . Out of the winter it comes, and into the winter it returns, and is vanished from thy eyes."
[3] *The Plowman's Crede.*

It inspires a series of noble elegies, from the anonymous but beautiful *Pearl*, of the fourteenth century, through *Lycidas*, to *Adonais* and *In Memoriam* and *Thyrsis*. But in all its manifestations it seldom becomes sentimental ; and the elegy itself can become an ode of victory. To face the facts ; to be honest with life and your own heart ; to grieve, and yet to endure and conquer—this is the teaching (and it is neither unworthy nor has it been ineffective) of one of the most characteristic and continuous themes of our literature.

It is a curious and perhaps a fanciful speculation, but it may none the less illustrate and enforce the trend of the argument, to inquire what are the dozen books, or poems, or passages of literature most likely to be chosen, by common consent, as those which have established themselves definitely as a national possession or influence. The canon of such a list will be neither artistic excellence nor fidelity in the expression of the national genius (though some element of both, and especially of the former, is obviously necessary to give general influence to any achievement of literary art) : what matters most is rather the range and vogue of acceptance, and the degree of the effect produced on social thought and imagination. First in such a list would come the Authorized Version of the Bible—the Psalms and the Book of Job ; the Gospels and some of the great Epistles of St. Paul. (For many in the south the Book of Common Prayer, and for many in Scotland the Shorter Catechism and the metrical paraphrase of the Psalms, would be pendants and corollaries of the English Bible.) The *Pilgrim's Progress* might come next ; and after it the tragedies and histories of Shakespeare, and especially, perhaps, *Hamlet* and *Julius Cæsar* and the plays of the Falstaff cycle. Milton might be counted fourth, with the figure of Satan in *Paradise Lost*, and that of Samson, and that of the Lady in *Comus* ; and after the poems of Milton we might reckon some of the earlier sonnets and some of the odes of Wordsworth. Then, in a place by themselves, there might come the great hymns of the Wesleys, and Watts, and Cowper ; and after them (though of a different order) the social poems of Burns. The *Pickwick Papers* of Dickens might be given the next place ; and Defoe's *Robinson Crusoe*, with its taste of the sea, and its picture of the lively and ingenious colonist, would have to be included. At the end of the list, and when it comes to the last three places, choice becomes difficult. But there is Gray's *Elegy in a Country Churchyard* (if one small perfect poem can be set by the side of its more massive companions) ; there is Boswell's *Life of Johnson* ; and who would exclude Sir Walter Scott or forget the *Heart of Midlothian* ? The list is full ; and how much is left outside—stirring ballads and noble elegies ; Foxe's *Book of Martyrs* and Hakluyt's *Navigations of the English*

Nation; the oratory of Burke and the *Letters* and *Speeches* of Oliver Cromwell. And yet, if one thinks of the figures which inhabit these books, what a gallery they make—Mr. Greatheart, and Hamlet, and Falstaff; the Happy Warrior of Wordsworth and the Cottar of Burns; Pickwick, and Crusoe, and Samuel Johnson; the Lady, and the wife of Christian, and Jeanie Deans.

There are other arts than literature; and music and song are influences in national life as well as the written word. In England we lost the inheritance of music in the course of the seventeenth century. Tallis and Byrd had written noble music in the reign of Elizabeth; John Dowland had published books of Songs and Airs for the lute, which wedded poetry to music; Thomas Campion, poet and musician, had written lovely poems and books of airs. It was not Puritanism that killed this promise, for many of the Puritans, like Milton himself, were lovers of music; but except for the untimely genius of Purcell (1658–95) it passed away, and England took little or no part in the development of a richer and more complicated music after the seventeenth century. Music ceased to be a substantial part of our life: the old popular songs, the ballads which had stirred Sir Philip Sidney, the carols, the mummings, and the folk-dances fell asleep. It is difficult to explain the causes of our loss. It can hardly be maintained that we are a nation that has no music in its soul: there was an abundance of music in Tudor England. Perhaps Puritanism may have aided, if it did not cause, a decline of national taste; perhaps, too, industrialism, and the shifting of the population to new and alien homes in crowded towns, may have helped to destroy a gift which could only flourish in the congenial soil of a traditional environment.[1] Whatever the reason may have been, we certainly lost a precious thing; and the nation at large—in its taste, its capacity for delight, and its power of adorning leisure— was all the poorer for the loss. It is true that there is a form of music which can flourish without relation to national life, and can thrive (as it has thriven in Vienna or in Munich) under the patronage of courts and princes. But there is also music which is a necessary part of national life and a necessary influence in the formation of national taste and character; and the want of such music has long been one of our defects. It makes us the readier prey to the boredom which so easily besets us; it makes us less apt in all matters of taste; it makes us less able to win the respect of other nations, which is given most easily and most readily in the field of artistic achievement. Music is an international art which crosses all boundaries; and a nation which

[1] Professor Buck has suggested to me that musicians have to live, and that if there are no patrons to encourage them, they cannot write music. The argument seems very sound; and there certainly were few patrons after 1660.

would play its part in the world must make its own contribution. There are signs of revival among us ; and not least among these is the new place which music is beginning to take in our system of education. If our schools can spread a deeper love of music through the length and breadth of the country, they will have done much to remove a national defect, to improve the national taste, and to refine the national character.

V

It remains, in conclusion, to examine the influence on national life of the literature which is rather Thought than Art, and is expressed less in the medium of beauty than in the direct and austere form of truth—the literature which is immediately addressed to the problems of life and society, and affects the nature of both, to a greater or less extent, by the influence of its suggestion. The thought which is most effective over the general range of national life will necessarily be that which deals with ethics and the related studies of economics and politics. There is a certain congruity in the trend of English thought in all the three fields of study. The moral philosophy of English thinkers has been based on the foundation of individual duty and individual perfection, whether it takes the form of Bishop Butler's somewhat facile enthronement of individual conscience over passions and affections, or that of the Utilitarian claim that the perfection of man is an individual happiness to be attained by an individual application of the calculus of pain and pleasure. The political philosophy of English thinkers has followed a similar line. Locke proclaimed against the State the natural right of the individual to enjoy the property with which he had mixed his own labour. Bentham, even if he regarded natural rights as " a kind of fiction " which might be " the greatest enemy of reason and the most terrible destroyer of governments," none the less vindicated against all governments the " greatest possible latitude " for individuals, as " the best judges of their own interests," in securing their own happiness by their own free action. When political economy became an independent study, it inherited, and it expressed with a new force, the current conceptions of individual autonomy. Adam Smith was the critic of that " policy of Europe " which, by limiting individual enterprise, diminished the wealth of nations. " He contended that even when government acted with the best intentions, it nearly always served the public worse than the enterprise of the individual trader, however selfish he might happen to be " ; [1] and if he insisted that private interests might conflict with public good, and that there were cases in which

[1] Marshall, *Principles of Economics*, i. ch. iv. § 3.

" defence, not opulence," should be paramount, he also enunciated that general doctrine of the harmony of individual interests, which cleared the way for the free course of individual competition.

The congruity of these conclusions is partly due to the fact that they belong to a common age, and are inspired by the general fashion of thought which was dominant in that age. The Restoration of 1660 and the Revolution of 1688 are landmarks in our social and political development. There was now a new business class, largely trained in Puritan ideas of individual responsibility; there was also a limited monarchy, against which Parliament had vindicated both its own privileges and the rights and liberties of all subjects; and the eighteenth century saw further changes, alike in the management of land and the conduct of industry, which sprang from the enterprise of individual landowners and private " undertakers." The philosophies of Butler and Bentham, of Locke and Adam Smith, flourished readily in such an environment; and it may well be contended that such abstract thought as we have produced has been more the product of its own than an influence upon later generations. Such a contention has its force. Pure speculative thought, working without conscious regard for time or place, has been rare and infrequent in England. We may count the names of Bacon and Newton; but Bacon was a Lord Chancellor and a politician as well as the author of the *Novum Organum*, and Newton, the most modest of scholars, was also the Master of the Mint. Our thinkers have been drawn into practical life; and our thought has generally been of the type we may call " immersed." [1] It has been plunged in practical issues: it has been directed to practical solutions. This has increased its immediate influence: it has also, perhaps, diminished the range and the permanence of its effects. Our thought does not travel well. It is too insular for exportation, and little of it (except the theory of Locke and Adam Smith, and the Scottish philosophy of the eighteenth century) has attained any vogue on the Continent; and even at home it is generally too much of its age to affect succeeding ages to any considerable extent. If we have shown a gift for practical discussion which has been the very nerve of our politics for many centuries, it is the reverse side of that gift that we have shown but little aptitude for the heights of any discussion of abstract principles.

What has been said of the trend of English thought—of its individualistic turn and its immersion in actual life and

---

[1] In the same way it may be observed that English historians have often been men immersed in affairs. Gibbon not only served in the militia, but sat in Parliament and served as a Commissioner of Trade and Plantations; Macaulay was a Cabinet minister; Grote was a banker and a member of Parliament; and Froude was a lively publicist as well as an historian.

current affairs—may suggest a reflection, which is also, it must be confessed, of the nature of a digression. There is not only a congruity in the trend of our thought in the various fields of ethics and politics and economics : there is also a certain homogeneity of texture in *all* the various manifestations of the national mind.   It is possible for a nation to develop on different lines in the different fields of its growth.   In Germany, for example, Lutheranism, with its strong insistence on the priesthood of each Christian man, is a different thing from the old Prussian spirit of government, with its rigorous sacrifice of the citizen to the iron necessity of the State ; and the philosophy of Kant and Hegel, though it may sometimes seem to touch both,[1] is again a separate development, moving on its own lines, and borrowing, if it borrows at all, from earlier philosophy, whether in Greece or France or Scotland.   In England it would rather seem as if there were a steady tendency to a general unity.   One of the most characteristic expressions of English religious life is Puritanism ; and Puritanism lays the same emphasis on individual autonomy which appears in English political theory and political economy   English law is a law of the liberty of the individual subject ; and English literature, as we have noticed earlier in this chapter, has never admitted the rule of a uniform style, the control of an academy, or even the dominance of a " school."   A sociologist may suggest that there must be in us some basic quality of racial individualism, which acts in every field as a selective agency, choosing for survival the philosophies, the forms of religion, the law, and the literature which are most adapted to its own nature.   Such a suggestion, however, is something like the invocation of a mystery to explain a fact ; and it is not ascertained that any race, or any racial blend, possesses a peculiar quality of individualism.   It is simpler to suggest that in a small country, which secured at an early date, and continuously maintained, a scheme of political unity, the expression of national life attained in each sphere tended to provoke some analogous expression in others by a natural sympathy.   Puritanism, for example, affected the course of political theory and the bias of political economy ; and Puritanism itself perhaps owed something to earlier legal doctrines of the rights and liberties of the subject.   If we follow this line of thought, we shall not say that some unknown foundation of national life produced a general uniformity in all its manifestations, but rather that the known factors of national life (law and literature, religion and social thought) interacted on one another in the favourable environment of national unity, and reacted with their joint force on the nation from which they had sprung.

[1] Kant may be said to be closer to Luther, and Hegel to Prussia.

But in spite of this homogeneity (or perhaps by reason of it) we have to admit that the influence which pure thought has exercised on the action and disposition of Englishmen has been less than it has been with the French. France has been passionate, especially in the great crises of her history, for general ideas pretending to universal validity ; she has sought to give them effect within, and to spread them, by arms or example, without ; she has been the logician among the nations, and the apostle of her own logic. It would surprise the world if we showed passion for an idea ; [1] and we should be surprised ourselves—and perhaps also disconcerted—if ever we lapsed into logic. Theory has little chance with us, unless it chimes with the practical instincts by which we prefer to act, or attaches the halo of a generalization to some tradition of which we are fond. We like to mix the empiric with the traditional, and to grope our way tentatively forward by the alleged light of some precedent. We have clung to political documents or practices of our own ; we have been content to let them " broaden down," while pretending that they remained the same ; and without vindicating any apostleship, we have rather cherished a Hebrew conception that we are an elect and particular people. An insular position and a legal temper have combined to make us practical traditionalists, wedded to the legal lore of our island experience. Set in the angle of the Continent, and touching Germany and Switzerland, Italy and Spain, France has received and radiated the thought of Western Europe. The French, to use a distinction made by M. Tarde, have followed *imitation-mode* ; the English have followed *imitation-coutume*.

Theory with us has thus followed and justified rather than guided practice : Locke, for example, consecrates the practical expedients of the Revolution of 1688 in his *Treatise on Civil Government*. In some of the great movements of our history we can hardly even say that theory was active enough to provide an *ex post facto* justification. The one great theorist of the age of the Puritan Revolution, Hobbes, was a cynical eccentric who " built a Tory consequence of passive obedience on a Whig foundation of the original contract." If there were also practical theorists abroad in that age, such as Sexby, who preached the principle of manhood suffrage, and Lilburne, whose theory included annual parliaments and complete religious liberty, they were not effective. It was on legal precedents that Pym ʻand Hampden took their stand ; and Cromwell, though upon occasion he " swore roundly at Magna Charta " (a good stick

---

[1] And yet it may be said that, even if there has not been passion, there has been tenacity. Cromwell and Milton clung to the idea of freedom of worship ; and the whole people clung to the idea of the suppression of the slave-trade a hundred years ago.

with which to beat the king, but a sore annoyance to a man who was seeking to keep order in " this poor parish "), was guided by what he called the " dispensations " of events rather than by any theory. The Reformation of the sixteenth century was equally free from the guidance of general ideas. It had no Luther or Calvin or Knox. It was a revolution achieved to give a king a divorce and a nation less clericalism ; but what it meant in doctrine and general thought was a matter left for succeeding ages to seek, if haply they might find it.

The one epoch in English history during which theory exercised the greatest effect on the social and political life of the nation was the epoch which began in 1776, with the publication of Bentham's *Fragment on Government* and Adam Smith's *Wealth of Nations*, and ended in 1859-60 with the publication of Mill's *Essay on Liberty* and his treatise on *Representative Government*. The new and industrialized society, with its large population and its great towns, which was coming into existence when this epoch began, was unable to fit itself into the general framework which it had inherited from the thinly populated and mainly agricultural England of the past. The procedure of the law, alike on the civil and on the criminal side, contained antiquities which went back to the reign of Henry II. The distribution of constituencies, unaltered (except for very minor changes) since the reign of Elizabeth, had become an anachronism ; the parliamentary suffrage in the shires was still regulated by an Act of 1430, and that in the boroughs was a mosaic of varieties which local custom and a series of parliamentary decisions in cases of disputed elections had both combined to produce. The economic system of mercantilism, based on " the policy of Europe," belonged to an agrarian age which was being steadily left behind. The " territorial constitution " of the past belonged to the past ; and a new " industrial constitution " was needed. It was the work of Bentham and Adam Smith, and of John Stuart Mill, the heir and successor of both, to give to the ministry, the parliament, and the people the ideas and the formulas which would help to recast the law and the Government and to readjust the system of economics. The influence of the trend of thought which they represented has been admirably traced by Professor Dicey in his work on *Law and Opinion in the Nineteenth Century*. It affected the younger Pitt in his earlier and brighter years, before the waves of the French Revolution broke over England. It affected the Conservative Peel, who made important reforms in the criminal law when he was Home Secretary (1822–27), and made a great breach in the old agrarian system of economics at the end of his ministry in 1846. It affected the whole career of Gladstone ; and it was the inspiration of the great Victorian age.

We have now entered on a new phase, in which we are finding that the ideas and formulas of utility and individual autonomy are themselves becoming out of date. We are beginning to see that the fully-grown industrialized society has developed a multiplicity of contacts, and even collisions, which demand some scheme of social regulation that goes beyond the tenets of individualism and free competition ; and we are beginning to recognize that there is such a thing as over-industrialization, that the balance of national life requires some defence of interests other than production, and that such defence can only be achieved by new measures of social control. Society, after all, is not merely composed of individuals : it is also composed of groups (such as organized employers and organized workers) which can hardly be left to compete in freedom, because the shock of their competition affects all the general fabric of life. Nor is society merely concerned with utilities : it is also concerned with the higher interests of social justice and national culture. A new social constitution, which is neither "territorial" nor "industrial," must slowly be made ; and the ideas have to be formed and enunciated which will aid in its making. It cannot be said that any theory has yet been formed in England which is likely to control the future ; and perhaps no theory is likely to be formed. We have borrowed the German theory of Marxianism, and given it the English dress of Fabianism ; we have borrowed the French theory of Syndicalism, and given it the English dress of Guild Socialism. Neither dress seems to fit. We are too individualistic to wear with any grace the garments of State Socialism ; and we are too nationalist (as perhaps all nations are) to split into autonomous industries organized in the form of guilds. Some may borrow from Russia, as others have borrowed from France or Germany ; but even if they could frame any tolerable English version of Communism, the original is too peculiar a mixture of the revolutionary methods of Nihilism with the autocratic dictatorship of the Tsars for any conceivable version to obtain vogue in a country which has long respected law and cherished liberty. It is difficult to believe that any of these philosophies (if they can properly be termed philosophies) will greatly determine or affect our future. But their presence may remind us that it is not only by the thought which it takes itself that a nation may add to its stature, and that the thought of other nations has always in some measure been, and is becoming more and more, a factor in the life and development of each of the nations of Europe. Our insularity may triumph in the end over all importations ; but the thought of revolutionary France moved us more than a hundred years ago, and it may be some wave of thought from another nation which will move us again in the present century.

LIST OF BOOKS

DALE, E.—*National Character in English Literature*, 1907.
DIXON, W. M.—*Poetry and National Character*, 1915.
KER, W. P.—*The Dark Ages*, 1904.
  „   „   *Mediæval English Literature* (Home University Library).
LEGOUIS, A., and CAZAMIAN, L.—*Histoire de la littérature Anglaise*, 1924.
TAINE, H.—*History of English Literature*.

CHAPTER IX

IDEAS AND SYSTEMS OF EDUCATION

I

" ANY educational system corresponds to a set of ideas, consciously or unconsciously entertained, about the order of society and the arrangement of men within that order. Where there is a set of ideas based on the assumption of different social strata, one rising above another, in the manner of a pyramid—with the members born in each stratum tending to follow their fathers, by a kind of hereditary succession, in the same or a similar calling—you will have an educational system in which there are different and stratified types of schools, each preparing its pupils for the different stations in life to which they are destined by birth. Where, on the other hand, there is a set of ideas based on the assumption of an homogeneous society—in which talents indeed may differ, because natural endowment differs, but all alike are to have their chance of development—you will have an educational system in which there may still be different types of schools, but those different types will not be stratified to suit social position and the accident of birth, but varied to suit various talents and the varieties of natural endowment. Strata, and hereditary status within the different strata—that is the one set of ideas : diversities of gifts, and diversities of ministrations according to gifts, but one and the selfsame Spirit, dividing to every man severally as He will—that is the other set of ideas. Different schools for different classes form the educational system which corresponds to the former ; different schools for different aptitudes, in whatever class they are found, constitute the educational system which corresponds to the latter." [1]

If educational systems are thus influenced by contemporary social ideas and the current form of social organization, they also influence, in their turn, the trend of those ideas and the development of that form. In one sense they are mirrors which reflect an existing social order : in another they are burning-glasses, which affect by the heat they transmit the system on which

[1] The passage is taken from an address, on *Social Ideas and Educational Systems*, given by the writer to the Co-operative Congress at Blackpool in 1925.

they are turned. A scheme of education based on traditional ideas and practices will tend to preserve and stereotype a static society of fixed positions ; a scheme resting on new ideas and tendencies—such as those which inspired the French Revolution—may help to create a dynamic society of moving capacities. The one is the product, as it is the producer, of class distinction and an aristocratic temper : the other issues from a belief, which it also helps to inspire, in the equality of men and the free movement of talent.

The extent to which education can affect social organization and national character depends on the extent of its diffusion ; and that in turn depends on the authority by which it is administered. If education is left to voluntary agency, a little will be given here, and a little there, as benefactors arise or societies extend the scope of their work ; but the results will be sporadic and accidental. If, on the other hand, a Church which is as wide as a nation makes education its care—as the mediæval Church, and the Anglican Church after the Reformation, attempted to do—the results which it achieves are likely to be more general, more deliberate, and more profound. The interest of the Church in education may, however, be limited. It may, like the mediæval Church, concern itself mainly with the education of clergy, in schools attached to cathedral-chapters and monasteries ;[1] or, again, with the training of choristers in " song-schools " or " almonries." If it goes further, and concerns itself with the laity, it may, like the Church of England after the Restoration of 1660, desire mainly to impart " education in the knowledge and practice of Christian religion as professed and taught in the Church," and to encourage the power of simple reading in order that laymen should master for themselves the Scriptures, the Catechism, and the Creeds. It was perhaps only in Scotland that the action of the clergy resulted in a national and general system of education. Elsewhere the educational work of the Church tended to be ancillary to ecclesiastical purposes. It would be unfair to criticize the Church for limiting the scope of its work. It was natural that it should seek particularly to do what was particularly necessary for its own purposes. The Church only became open to a just criticism when it sought (in virtue of the power of licensing schools, which bishops in England, as elsewhere, long claimed and exercised) to control or to check the growth of other forms of education.[2] Nor must it be forgotten that, apart from the specific work which it did in education, the Church in itself, as

[1] It is a moot point how far laymen (or *externi*) were taught in monasteries. See J. Adamson's *Short History of Education*, pp. 10–11 ; and G. C. Coulton's *Mediæval Studies*, No. 10, on Monastic Schools in the Middle Ages.

[2] It was, however, held in Cox's case (1701) that the bishop's licence was only required for grammar schools, and not for other schools.

an organized body, was a great educational force which sought to form character and to impart a discipline of life to its members. None the less, though the limitation of its educational work was natural, and though, outside the limits of that work, it was always labouring as " a schoolmaster to bring men to Christ," it remains true that education only became a great national force affecting national life and character when it ceased to be regarded as the province of the Church, and came to be conceived as the duty of the State. The educational revolution which made the State responsible for the training of child-life was comparable in its sphere to the Industrial Revolution in economics and the French Revolution in politics ; and indeed, as we have already had occasion to remark, it has its intimate connections with both of those revolutions. In a sense, it is true, an educational revolution was part of the Reformation of the sixteenth century, which, as it tended to secularize charity, and as it instituted a lay system of poor relief in place of ecclesiastical almsgiving, tended also to secularize education, and led naturally to a lay system of " grammar " and " parish " schools. But though the consequence was realized in Scotland (by the Act of 1696), it was not recognized in England, where the Church still maintained its position ; and in France and other continental countries (whether, like Prussia, they embraced the Reformation, or, like Austria, they held fast to the Roman Church) the old ideas and the old practices continued to prevail. But by the middle of the eighteenth century a revolution in education had begun on the Continent ; and it had begun in Austria and Prussia. Maria Theresa, after suppressing the Jesuit order, which had largely controlled education, created elementary, higher elementary, and normal schools in 1774. Frederic of Prussia declared, as early as 1763, that children from the age of five to that of thirteen should attend schools ; and in 1771 his minister Zedlitz began, though he did not carry to completion, the founding of a national system of education. In France, where La Chalotais had advocated national education in his Essay of 1763, it was left for the Revolution to attempt, and for Napoleon to achieve, a system of State education. England was last in the field. The Church was indeed losing control by the end of the eighteenth century ; and Parliament had granted freedom of teaching to Nonconformists and Roman Catholics by Acts passed in 1779 and 1791. But Englishmen hoped that voluntary societies ("National" or "British and Foreign") would do the work which the State was attempting to do abroad ; and in a generation of *laissez-faire* there was a widespread belief that it was the birthright of an English parent to provide at his own discretion for the education of his own children. Clinging to voluntary action, and dreading any system of national education as inimical to national liberty, England waited until the Industrial Revolution was a hundred years old, and the second Reform Bill had been passed, before she finally recognized, by the Act of 1870, that an industrialized country must educate its workers, and a State organized on the basis of a wide parliamentary suffrage must " educate its masters." By the end of the nineteenth century the educational revolution had been accomplished—even in England ; and the new and potent agency of a national system of education had been added to the forces by which national character is moulded.

In addition to the idea of social organization which it expresses, and the nature of the authority by which it is administered, we have to reckon with a third factor which determines the influence of any system of education. What is the idea of human development on which it is based, and which it seeks to realize ? There is an " ancient division " in the world of education between those who want to make the scholar, with the tool of books, and those who want to make the man, by all the exercises of spirit and body which foster " human excellence." The division appeared during the Middle Ages, in the distinction between a " clerkly " system of education, pursued in universities and schools, and the " knightly " system practised in the castle, which was directed (if we may use the old Greek terms) to giving both a " gymnastic " of the body, for sport and for war, and a " music " of the spirit which tuned it to notions of honour, gave to it grace of manners, and adorned it with the accomplishments of song and poetry. In its mediæval form, the division corresponded to a division of classes, and reflected the difference between the training natural to the clergy and the training proper to the baronage. But it is not confined to its mediæval form ; and it appears again and again in the history of education without any reference to class. We may distinguish two different ideas of human development, which are both independent of social differences, and either of which may be advocated for members of every class—the idea of the book, as against the idea of practical work : the idea of pure reason, mental awakening, and intellectual acquirement, as against the idea of practical reason, the unfolding of active faculty, and the development of character. The teacher will always feel the attraction of the first of these ideas, and the natural bias of education will thus deflect it towards the clerk and the book. Students of books themselves, and devoted to the pursuit of pure knowledge, teachers are apt, unconsciously and unintentionally, to form their pupils in their own image ; and, in any case, books are easy tools, and pupils are readily assessed in terms of the proficiency with which they use them. On the other hand, the practical genius of our people, their instinct for character, and their sense of the fundamental importance of action, have steadily influenced education in England ; and it has thus shown a peculiar national quality which has made it, in its turn, a peculiar national influence. Our public schools, especially since the days of Arnold, have proved that they have inherited the " knightly " tradition without forgetting the claims of the " clerkly." If for long years they were less successful than the schools of France and Germany in giving a mental discipline, they atoned for any defects by the quality of a vivid interest in personality. Masters sought, in form-rooms and " houses," to make their boys men ; and boys were encouraged, through organized games and by methods of self-government, to work together loyally and to look responsibility in the face. Like Sparta of old, the public schools have sometimes run to pattern ; and as Sparta was criticized by Plato and Aristotle for producing only the virtue of courage, they have been criticized for producing the stock virtues of " good tone " and *esprit de corps*. But they have made men, if they have made them according to type ; and they have cherished an ideal of general human excellence. Partly under their influence, and partly under the direct influence of the same national genius which affected them, our county and municipal secondary schools and our public elementary schools are coming to cherish the same ideal ; and they too are seeking to affect character, and to stimulate practical interests, as well as to awaken and train the intelligence. Apart from its intrinsic value, such a conception of the teacher's duty and function is a force which makes for social stability. There is a certain danger, in modern times, of what may be called the clericalization of society. The general spread of education, if it works by the book and directs itself only to the intelligence, readily produces a great supply of would-be clerical workers, which pours in a flood towards every grade of clerical service. The channels are not adequate for its flow ; and the discontented product of a clerkly system of education, destitute of congenial employment, may become a revolutionary force. In any case, the growth of an *intelligentsia*, technically accomplished in its particular field, but without the ballast of principle or the corrective of other interests, disturbs the harmonious development of national life. It is not likely that we shall see such a growth in England—at any rate if we hold fast to a broad conception of " the whole duty of teachers."

Three questions emerge from the considerations which have just been raised. In what ways has education, regarded as the expression of a social ideal, affected the system and relation of classes in England, and what effects has it thus produced on general social development ? What have been the different consequences which have flowed from different methods of administering and controlling education ? To what extent have current conceptions of the purpose of education determined its nature and its results ?

II

There are still two different systems of education in France, intended for two different classes. There is the primary system, meant for the general mass of citizens. A child who begins in this system normally remains in it for the whole of his educational life. He may rise to a " higher primary school " ; he may pass to a " primary training college " ; he may even enter a " higher primary training college," intended to provide the teachers of training colleges ; but he is still included in the primary system. By its side there is the secondary system, which is meant to produce an intellectual élite, and leads to the university. It is a separate system ; those who are to receive a secondary education begin it in tender years ; they are from the first, as the students in the primary system are till the last, pledged and ascribed to a single channel. On the whole, there is no transference from one system to another ; and the determination of the system to be followed is made at an age too early to allow any judgment of the bent of native ability. There is nothing in the organization of State schools in England which is so clear-cut or rigid. We have, it is true, a number of public schools, under private management, which mainly draw on the children of the upper and professional classes—just as we have also a number of preparatory schools, also under private management, which prepare the children of the same classes for entry into the public schools. They stand apart ; and the State is directly concerned with " public elementary schools " and with the " secondary schools " which are maintained or aided by local authorities. There is no great gulf between the two ; but equally there is no clear conception of their relations. We are still in a haze. On the one hand, there is a constant crossing of the boundaries and a ready transference. Children who have been taught in public elementary schools pass readily, by winning scholarships at the age of eleven, to secondary schools ; and teachers who have received their training in secondary schools and universities become members of the staffs of public elementary schools. On the other hand, there is still a tradition that public elementary schools were originally devised, and are still intended, for the children of the labouring poor, who will find their fulfilment in them ; and it is still the case that the majority of teachers in these schools have themselves been educated in them, and have received their further training in colleges devoted to the production of elementary teachers. A tradition of the past still cuts across the tendencies of the present. The tradition presents us with the idea of a special type of elementary school, for the children of a particular class, staffed by a special type of elementary teacher. The tendencies are towards an elementary school which is elementary only in the sense, first, that it is preparatory to a further or secondary education, to which more and more children will proceed at the age of eleven or twelve if they show the necessary capacity, and secondly, that it is staffed by teachers who are in a preliminary stage, from which, if they prove their ability, they too will move to other and further stages. Relics of a system based on differences of class are thus mixed with the beginnings of a system based on differences partly of age and partly of individual capacity.

It cannot, however, be said that the doctrine of education according to classes was ever clearly entertained or rigidly practised. It was the tradition and practice of the mediæval Church, anxious to recruit itself freely, and offering within its fold a career always open to talents, that ability should receive its chance without any regard to class ; and the foundations of William of Wykeham at Winchester and Oxford were definitely intended for " poor and indigent scholars." A statute of 1406 proves that the policy of the State was not different. It enacted that every man and woman, of what estate or condition whatsoever, should be free to set son or daughter to learn " letters " at any manner of school that pleased them within the realm. But the sixteenth century shows trace of other feelings and a different order of ideas. There is a passage in Strype's *Memorials of Cranmer*, under the year 1542, which has often been quoted. A question had arisen of the admission of boys to King's School, Canterbury. Several of the electors would have confined admission to the sons or younger brothers of gentlemen. " It is meet for the ploughman's son to go to the plough, and the artificer's son to apply the trade of his parents' vocation ; and the gentlemen's children are meet to have the knowledge of government and rule in the Commonwealth . . . all sorts of men may not go to school." Cranmer held stoutly an opposite view ; and he carried the majority with him. " I grant much of your meaning herein as needful in a Commonwealth ; yet utterly to exclude the ploughman's son, and the poor man's son, from the benefits of learning . . . is as much to say, as that Almighty God should not be at liberty to bestow His great gifts of grace upon any person . . . who giveth His gifts both of learning, and other perfection in all sciences, unto all kinds and states of people indifferently . . . wherefore, if the gentleman's son be apt to learning, let him be admitted ; if not apt, let the poor man's child that is apt enter in his room." This was the practice actually followed in the " free " grammar schools, which were able to dispense with fees ; and we may even say that Cranmer enshrined his views for the future in the words of the Catechism (already to be found in the First Prayer Book of 1549), in which Englishmen were bidden to do their duty " in that state of life to which it shall please God to call them "— words which run contrary to the idea of fixed station and to any doctrine of education based upon that idea. But such an idea is tenacious in its grip ; and though it be driven out by a catechism, *tamen usque recurret.* A farmer told Hannah More at the end of the eighteenth century that he " did not want saints, but workmen " ; and his wife, with a woman's plain speaking, added that " the poor were fated to be poor and ignorant and wicked, and we could not alter what was decreed."

There had been something of a revolution in English life, between the time of Cranmer and the days of Hannah More, which may help to explain the ideas of the farmer's wife and the progress (or rather the regress) of English education. A State system of poor relief had been introduced by Elizabeth ; it had been placed by 1700 under the control of the Justices of the Peace, who were thus tempted to regard themselves as a local providence ; it had been vastly increased in volume, by a lavish system of outdoor relief, in the middle of the reign of George III. Under the influence of this system and its development, the working classes came to be regarded as a mass of dependent poor, distinct from the rate-paying, well-to-do sections by which they were aided or even maintained. Puritanism, in the guise which it had come to wear about 1660, sanctioned this order of things as a form of divine dispensation. God had prospered the prosperous in reward for their merit, and He had put down the poor according to their deserts.[1] Under the double influence of poor relief and Puritanism the Beatitudes were inverted, and the Magnificat was drastically revised. It was inevitable that educational ideas and practice should be affected by the change. For about two centuries after 1660 there was a general conviction that there ought to be a separate and lower form of education for the " labouring poor." There were two reasons for this conviction. One was a reason of economy : unless the poor were trained to some calling, they would fall into indigence and " come on the rates." The other was, or professed to be, a reason of religion : unless the poor were taught to read the Bible and recite the Catechism, they would walk in ignorance of Christianity and fall into sins even worse than the sin of poverty. The connection between education and the system of poor relief is one of the peculiarities of England. It may seem at first sight curious that a system of national education should in Scotland have been the creation of the Kirk, and in England a

---

[1] Locke's theory of property gives a similar sanction of philosophy to this order of ideas.

sort of by-product, slowly and reluctantly developed, of a State scheme of poor relief. But the scheme of poor relief was a cardinal element of English life. It was not only the one form of social policy which the nation could devise to meet social problems : it was also, as we have seen, the origin of local self-government ; and it was natural that it should also be the source of any scheme of general education.

Such schemes were at first, and for many years, attempted on a voluntary basis. Towards the end of the seventeenth century there was a movement for the general foundation of " charity schools." This was the work of the Society for the Promotion of Christian Knowledge ; and the schools which the Society founded were intended "for the education of poor children in the knowledge and practice of the Christian religion " and " to fit them for services or apprenticeship." Towards the end of the eighteenth century appeared the " schools of industry," which mixed the " labour " of manual work, intended to lead to some vocation, with the " learning " of the elements of religion. It was in 1802 that legislation was first introduced for instituting a measure of compulsory education ; and the legislation, as we might expect, was intended to secure the proper training of pauper apprentices [1] who had been sent into industry by the Poor Law authorities. By Peel's Act of 1802 their employers were required to provide instruction (including some elements of religious teaching) during four of the seven years of their apprenticeship. The State went a step further in 1833, when it began to aid from its funds the voluntary schools (whether " British " or " National ") which had arisen early in the nineteenth century under the influence of Lancaster and Bell.[2] Apart from an isolated experiment in 1649, this was the first recognition of the principle that the duties of the State towards its members included something more than the provision of poor relief. But even in 1833, and indeed for many years afterwards, the contributions of the State to the cause of

[1] As early as 1723 there are provisions for education in the Act which made possible the institution of workhouses. London had been able under an Act of 1662 to resolve to give elementary and industrial education to a number of poor children ; and a private Act of 1769 permitted the education of poor children in London to be defrayed from the rates.

[2] Lancaster was the moving spirit. The society which sprang from his efforts—the British and Foreign School Society—was founded in 1814, and aimed at teaching general Christian principles on undenominational lines. The National Society with which Bell was connected, and which was founded in 1811, was Anglican. In other respects the two men and their two societies differed little. Both men were convinced that the necessary teaching could be given by " monitors " who had received a little training. Both Societies were intended for the poor. The National Society existed " for promoting the education of the poor." The original name of Lancaster's society was " the society for promoting the Royal British or Lancasterian system for the education of the poor."

education were still regarded as a form of charitable gift to the poor. The private charity of individual subscribers to voluntary schools was being met, it was commonly thought, by a measure of public charity. The grant of 1833 was made "in aid of private subscriptions for the erection of schoolhouses for the education of the poorer classes in Great Britain." "The object of the grant," it is still stated in the Code of 1860, "is to promote the education of children belonging to the class who support themselves by manual labour."

It would thus appear that from 1660 to 1870 the trend of educational ideas and practice in England expressed, and helped to perpetuate and deepen, a cleavage between two classes. On the one side stood the propertied classes, ready to relieve the indigence of the poor by the payment of rates, and to remove their ignorance by the foundation of voluntary schools ; on the other side stood the labouring poor, who, if they were not "fated to be ignorant and wicked," seemed fated to need assistance and suitable schooling. There was a good deal of genuine philanthropy on one side of the gulf ; there was also, among many who stood on that side, a genuine ardour for spreading true religion :

"Tendebantque manus ripae ulterioris amore."

But there were none the less "two nations" ; and the two nations had existed side by side, in the prevalent world of ideas, for many years before Disraeli proclaimed their existence. It was not the Industrial Revolution which created them, or first opposed them to one another: it was the old agricultural and trading England of the later Stuarts and the early Hanoverians. The Restoration of 1660 had enthroned the landed interest and given the management of the Poor Law (and thereby the control of local government) into its hands ; and it was the gulf between squirearchy and peasantry, rather than that between industrial magnates and artisans, which was at once reflected in, and accentuated by, the theory of charity schools, schools of industry, and the early stages of elementary education. Industrialism, at any rate in its early stages, and before the days of great undertakings and large companies, is seldom marked by any great difference between masters and men in social position or intellectual habits. So far as it has any educational tendencies, it makes for the general diffusion of a common technical training. The idea of a separate system of education for the class of the labouring poor was an idea bequeathed by an earlier agrarian England—an idea which was neither natural nor suitable to the new industrial England of the nineteenth century, but which long continued to survive, as a belated anachronism, partly perhaps because we are naturally tenacious of old ideas, but partly also because we were too much occupied with the other legacies of the past (a protectionist system, for example, and a narrowly limited franchise) to " repeal " or " reform " the educational legacy as we were repealing or reforming the Corn Laws and the Suffrage.

Whatever the reason of the delay, education was a laggard in an age of general reform. It lagged behind the principles and practice of our common law, with its guarantee of the equal rights of all subjects of the Crown ; it lagged behind the extension of the suffrage ; nor did it in any way rise to the needs of an industrial development which had largely changed social relations and altered human needs. It was particularly the change of social relations, and the alteration of human needs, in a new industrial society, which at length introduced a new movement of ideas, begun by the Education Act of 1870, and continued by the Education Acts of 1902 and 1918. Because an industrial society is a moving society, without fixed and stereo-typed classes, in which men may rise by capacity, and in which efficiency depends on the discovery and use of every capacity, we are recognizing (as Cranmer already recognized in his day) that education cannot be based on any scheme of different hereditary classes, but must start from the same conception of equality which governs our law and our suffrage ; and we are realizing that, if there are to be different types of education, they must express and elicit the different types of human capacity which are to be found in " all kinds and states of people indifferently." In the same way, because an industrial society is a society of specialized workers, and creates a human need for the more general development of the mind and its various powers, we are also coming to see that education must be directed to the making of a " full man," who has interests outside his work, and can adorn his leisure by the play of faculties which find no scope in his occupation.

These are both large changes. With the second of them we shall be more properly concerned when we come to consider the idea of human development which inspires educational effort. The first of them means a revolution in the ideas of society and the social order which lie behind educational organization. The ideas of the later seventeenth and of the eighteenth century had postulated a stratified society, in which a lower labouring class had been imbued with the elements of knowledge and the temper of mind suited to its condition by the philanthropic zeal of an upper leisured class—the State either standing aloof, or, at the most, aiding by its contributions the charity of one of the classes of the community. Traces of these ideas still survive ; but we are now moving fast to the idea of a single society, in which all the members must be treated as equally worth while, and in which the State, acting on a principle of equality (alike in its law, its suffrage, and its system of education), shoulders the burden of responsibility for the education of its members. But equality is not the same as identity ; and civic equality in the sphere of education does not imply that every citizen receives the same type of education. It means, rather, that each member of the community is given the same opportunity of developing his faculty as others ; and if we assume (as we are bound to assume) that there are differences of faculty, it follows that the same opportunity will only be given if there are different methods of education suited to different faculties. Equality of opportunity, secured by differences of method (literary, scientific, technical, and manual) which are adjusted to differences of bent and capacity—such, in brief, is the general basis on which our education should rest, and on which it is coming to rest. And a national system resting on that basis will help to produce the ideal on which it is based— that of an homogeneous society, permeated by a temper of equality at once consistent with, and only to be realized through, the recognition of a large " diversity of gifts" among its members. Education in its true nature is the greatest of levellers, because at its best it levels men up to a common standard, and enables them all to share alike in the intangible and invaluable riches of a common culture. But it will only level men up, and enable them to share alike, if it provides different ways of ascent to the common standard, and different avenues of entrance into the common treasure-house. On that basis—the basis of a recognition of equality combined with a recognition of differences—we may expect that education, which once recognized a difference of class and accentuated it by its recognition, will help to create a single society in which men are knit together as a single body " through that which every joint supplieth."

III

The provision and the control of education will normally be vested in either the Church or the State. There is, however, a form of compromise, which England characteristically invented about 1700, developed largely just after 1800, and has continued to maintain under the provisions of the Act of 1902— that of the voluntary educational society, resting on the support of a church or a number of ecclesiastical societies, but in time receiving aid (as it began to do after 1833) from the resources of the State. The history of education in England since the Reformation is a history of the action partly of the Church, partly of the voluntary Society, and partly of the State.

The Reformation increased the number of lay schools ;

but it left the Church still in control of education.　The licence of the bishop continued to be required for teachers ; and to make assurance doubly sure, the restoration of the Church in 1660 was accompanied by drastic statutes which prohibited Nonconformists from teaching—a prohibition which was only removed in 1779.　The Nonconformist " Academies," which arose in the latter part of the seventeenth century, were thus outside the pale of the law ; and indeed any dissenter who sought to teach in any institution, or even in a private house, was liable to fine or imprisonment.　It was not that the Church provided education itself ; it was rather that it controlled the provision of education by others.　It was left by the State to supervise, and it was armed by the State with penal powers in its work of supervision.　The fact that the Reformation, in its peculiar English form, issued in a State Church, with an established position, which the State was able to dominate and could therefore afford to trust, will readily explain why the State itself left education unaided and unconsidered.　It is significant that it was in the days of the temporary fall of the Anglican Church, and in the beginnings of the Commonwealth, that the State first showed any sign of a direct interest in education.　A group of thinkers, possibly influenced by the *Great Didactic* of the contemporary Czech reformer Comenius, were advocating State schools and a system of compulsory attendance ; and in 1649 the Long Parliament voted an annual sum of £20,000, partly to increase the incomes of the heads of Oxford and Cambridge Colleges, but mainly for the maintenance of ministers and schoolmasters.　In this, as in other respects (for example, the reform of parliamentary representation contained in the Instrument of Government), the Commonwealth anticipated the measures of the nineteenth century.　But the anticipations were banished to the limbo which awaits precocious growths by the Restoration of 1660 ; the Church returned with even larger powers ; and education was condemned to be the prey of ecclesiastical rancours which even in our own day have not yet vanished entirely.　Nor, indeed, is it wonderful that the educational disabilities from which Nonconformity so long suffered should have left, even after their disappearance, the legacy of tenacious and bitter memories.[1]

　　The two centuries after the Restoration were centuries of the activity of voluntary societies—the Society for the Promotion of Christian Knowledge, the National Society, and the British and Foreign School Society.　At first the voluntary

---

[1] It was the law courts, by their decisions (especially in Cox's case), which secured liberty for teachers even when the trend of legislation seemed to run in a contrary direction.　The English judges, in this and other respects, have rendered a very great service to the cause of liberty—a service which deserves to be remembered.　See Adamson, *op. cit.* pp. 195-196.

society was Anglican ; but by the beginning of the nineteenth century the Nonconformists had founded the most vigorous and flourishing of these societies. The result was that both were united in claiming education for the sphere of free voluntary effort. The Church had no desire to relinquish to the State a field of work which it long regarded as its own ; and the Nonconformist bodies, even if their members had adopted the idea of State schools in the days of the triumph of Nonconformity, were in their days of depression inspired by a general distrust of the State and a general passion for liberty in all its forms. The general trend of English opinion moved in an opposite direction from that of French thought. La Chalotais, in 1763, was writing : " I claim for the Nation an education dependent upon the State alone, because education belongs essentially to the State ; because every nation has an inalienable and imprescriptable right to instruct its members." In reaction against the clericalism of the Jesuits, he was urging that religion, far from being the sum and substance of education, was a matter only for the family and the parish church, and lay entirely outside the school ; and he was arguing, on the other hand, that " the teaching of morality belongs, and always has belonged, to the State." His ideas were generally followed, and French thought adopted the conception of a national system of education, administered by the State—a system which included moral instruction and the shaping of character, but left religious teaching entirely aside. The essence of this conception is, in a word, nationalism ; and the peculiar insistence of its advocates is on the value of imbuing the young with the particular inheritance and the special tradition of their nation. It was not, they felt, the universal truths of a common Christian society which concerned the national State (*they* were a matter for the Church) ; nor was it, again, the common beliefs of a general European enlightenment : it was the feelings and sentiments of a national society, expressed in a national tradition. There is here a certain return to the ideas of education which were expounded by Plato and Aristotle ; and the return is particularly apparent in those thinkers who, desirous of making good citizens, argued that in every State the education of youth should be particularly " formed and adapted to the nature and end of its government," and that " the principle by which the whole community is supported ought to be most strongly inculcated on the minds of every individual." [1] The general body of English thinkers stood at the antipodes to such ideas ; and the more advanced they were,

[1] The writer here quoted was (curiously enough) an Englishman, Thomas Sheridan, who published in 1756 a book on *British Education*. His principles are exactly those which Aristotle applies to the Greek city-state in the seventh book of the *Politics*—that education should be directed to inculcating the spirit of the constitution.

the less did they believe in any national system of education administered by the State. Priestley and Godwin might on other grounds sympathize with French radicalism, but in this respect they departed from its principles even more drastically than the sternest of English Conservatives. Priestley, who had begun life as a tutor in a Nonconformist academy, and was inspired by the Nonconformist passion for individual liberty, was contending, in 1768, that education was " a branch of civil liberty " which ought to be " inviolably preserved to individuals " ; that the State had no more right to educate children than to fix their dress ; and that a balance could only be preserved between the several religious and political parties if all were free to provide for the education of their own children.[1] In much the same sense Godwin argued, in 1793, that " national education ought uniformly to be discouraged on account of its obvious alliance with national government." Priestley and Godwin (whose tradition was continued by Herbert Spencer) did much to determine the ideas and the practice of the first half of the nineteenth century. Priestley's idea of a balance of voluntary organizations was realized in the division between the National and the British Schools. Godwin's fear of the alliance between national education and national government corroborated a general distrust of State interference, and identified the cause of the free school with that of the free church and free trade. It was something of a paradox, and no little of a misfortune, that the most advanced thinkers in England were the most opposed to the inevitable line of any real advance in education, and the most inimical to the assumption of any responsibility by the State. Their theory postulated more from the working of the voluntary principle than it could ever, under any conditions, have supplied ; and in the actual conditions of the time they simply supported a system under which the private subscriptions of one class—largely given for denominational reasons —were used to provide the education of another, which, by the mere fact of receiving aid, naturally came to be regarded as a class of dependents. They dreamed of " balance," and they actually promoted the rivalry and the jealousy of different religious bodies ; they hoped for " freedom," and they found that they had encouraged class differences.

There was a mixture of good and bad in a scheme which made education a charitable service rendered on voluntary lines. There was a resolute and sturdy independence, mixed

[1] The notion of " balance " was a current English notion, especially among the Whigs. There must be an economic " balance " between agriculture and industry. There must be a political " balance " between local self-government and the central authority. In the same way there must be a " balance " in education, on the lines of *laissez-faire*, between the different parties (Tory and Whig, Anglican and Nonconformist) who desired its promotion.

with a certain condescension; there was genuine religious feeling, blended with something of a spirit of philanthropic superiority. By 1850 the scheme had proved its inadequacy; and there was a growing recognition of the principle that education was a proper public responsibility and a necessary State service. If in 1833 the State had only made a subscription in aid of private subscriptions, it had soon found that it was necessary to create a public department to superintend the expenditure of public moneys; and in 1839 there was created a Committee of the Privy Council on Education. The die was cast when the State created the germ of a public educational authority; and Kay-Shuttleworth, secretary to the Committee for its first ten years, was able under its shelter to lay down the lines of a national system of popular education. Development along these lines was slow and gradual. In 1870, public elementary schools were established by the side of the voluntary schools; in 1880, attendance was made compulsory for children under the age of thirteen; and in 1891 the payment of fees in public elementary schools was abolished. By the Act of 1902 a further step was taken: secondary schools, maintained by counties or county boroughs, were added to the provision already made for elementary education; a system of scholarships and free places was developed, by which the abler children in elementary schools were enabled to carry their education further, to the age of sixteen or even eighteen; and elementary schools, instead of being schools for children of a given class, who never went beyond their range, tended more and more to become schools for children of a given age, who might pass in maturer years to other schools for higher education. When secondary schools were added by the State to elementary schools, and when, at the same time, the State began to aid universities, it could be said that a national system—covering alike the primary, the secondary, and the university stages of education— had at last been instituted; and the institution in 1900 of a Board of Education, to act as a single authority for all educational purposes,[1] provided an organ for the administration of that system. In a sense we may say that the ideas of La Chalotais and of France had triumphed, and the ideas of Priestley, Godwin, and Herbert Spencer had disappeared. But in several respects (and they all touch matters of fundamental importance) the English system remains unique, and bears large traces of the English past. In the first place, and contrary to the practice of France (or, again, of the United States), religious instruction is an integral part of the teaching given

---

[1] The Committee of the Privy Council on Education had not been the only organ. There had also been a Science and Art Department; and the Charity Commissioners had been vested with the care of educational endowments.

in our elementary schools, whether public or voluntary. In the second place, the voluntary elementary schools retain their place and their function ; and since 1902 they have been regularly aided from public rates. In the third place, there is a large element of local self-government in the administration of the schools (elementary or secondary) which belong to the public authority. The Act of 1870 instituted local School Boards, elected by ratepayers, to administer the public elementary schools which it created ; the Act of 1902, while it abolished the School Boards, instituted still more powerful local education authorities, in the form of committees of County and County Borough Councils, for the administration of public elementary and secondary schools. These authorities, which have appointed their own directors of education and (in some cases) their own inspectors of schools, exercise very large powers and a very considerable influence. The control of education is in no sense centralized in the Board of Education. The local Education Authorities are perhaps the most powerful organs of local self-government in the country ; and those who know their powers will readily recognize that the principle of " balance " is still maintained (in another sense than that of which Priestley wrote) by the *condominium* which associates the local authorities with the central Board in the administration of education. It remains to be added, if we would understand fully the differences between the practice of France and that of England, that we have a great number of private schools exempt from public control—" public schools," such as Eton and Harrow, and free grammar schools, which are managed by their own governors ; schools managed by private associations, such as the Girls' Public Day Schools or the Woodard Schools ; and preparatory and other schools belonging to private persons. There is, in a word, a system of national education ; but while it is a system, it is blended and intertwined with the three elements of voluntary association, local self-government, and private enterprise, and while it is national, it has not forgotten to recognize the religious principles which the different religious bodies profess. There is a system, but it is not systematized ; and there are reasons, as we shall see, why we may hope that it never will be. It is incomplete ; and it will be necessary, in the near future, to devise other methods and institutions for post-primary instruction, side by side with the " secondary," which will enable a vastly greater proportion of children to receive some further training, over and above that of the ordinary elementary school. The " central " schools, which some authorities have instituted, and which provide a four years' course, partly humane and partly practical, for children who come at the age of eleven and leave about the age of fifteen, suggest a line along which there may yet be large developments.[1]   But as it stands, unsystematized and incomplete, our system suggests reflections.   The assumption by the State (whether directly or through its local organs) of a general responsibility for the education of its citizens is a fact of profound importance, and it is likely to be the dominant factor in the shaping of national character for many generations.   When the State assumes such a responsibility, it is beginning to act directly, as a formative influence, on the minds and the characters of its members.   In a democratic community, in which the State is the general body of the voters, such action must necessarily take the form of a conscious self-determination, proceeding from the community, and directed by it towards the realization of an ideal self.   A national community which can attempt such self-determination has reached a new stage.   It is in the position of the grown man, when, from the stage of social drill (acting upon him externally by virtue of its prestige, and yet, at the same time, appealing to him within by virtue of its accord with his own higher impulses), he passes into the stage of free moral self-direction.   It has come of age : it has begun to bear on its shoulders the orb of its fate.   The formation of national character has now become a new matter. The old factors still remain operative ;   race and environment still count ;   the volume of population, and the variety of its occupations, are still an influence ;   the system of law and government, the genius of language and literature, and the spirit of churches and creeds, still shape and mould men's minds. The factor of a national system of education does not abolish these older factors ;   and it may even serve to strengthen their operation—as when (for instance) it is directed towards the teaching of national literature, or includes within its scope the work of religious instruction.   But if it does not abolish, and may even incorporate and corroborate old forces, a national system of education is something new.   Its schools are a new institution, added to the old institutions of courts and parliaments and churches ;   it is new in itself as a focus, which gathers together many of the influences that play on national character ;   and it is new, above all, in being inspired by a consciously entertained purpose of shaping and forming men's minds.   The nature of that purpose we shall have to discuss at the end of this chapter.   What matters here is the simple fact that the agents of the purpose are consciously seeking to exercise an influence directly on national character.   It is this which distinguishes education from the other spiritual factors whose operation we have sought to trace in previous chapters.

The obvious danger of a general system of State education

[1] See the last report of the Consultative Committee of the Board of Education, on the Education of the Adolescent.

17

is that it may produce uniformity of type and discourage both local and individual variety. This was the argument urged by Priestley, Godwin, and Herbert Spencer, and it is the theme of a fine chapter, entitled " The Decay of the Family," in C. H. Pearson's book on *National Life and Character*. Will the family continue to be a responsible moral institution, he inquires, when the State school looks to the health and physique, as well as the mind and the character, of its members ? " We may imagine," he writes, " the State *crèche*, and the State school ; and the State doctor, supplemented, it may be, by State meals ; and the child, already drilled by the State, passing out from school into the State workshop." [1] There is some justice in Pearson's fears, and his imaginings were prophetic. It is true that teachers may be rivals, and even supplanters, of parents ; it is true that there are fewer real homes, and less of family life—though the reason is hardly the growth of State schools, but rather the premature employment and precocious independence of children, coupled with conditions of housing which make home life very difficult. But the indictment against State schools goes far beyond any matter of their effect on the family. Godwin's fear of the alliance of national education with national government touches profounder issues. A system of national education is, as it were, a new tool in the hands of the State ; and it may use the new tool for what it imagines to be its own ends. It may attempt a uniform prescription, from a central office, of a single code intended to realize a national ideal conceived in the brain of its own officials, and it may thus seek to defeat the right of self-determination which, in education no less than in other matters, is inherent in any democratically governed community. It may attempt, through the teaching of national history, and through the organization of the life of the school, to enforce the negative form of patriotism which is chiefly occupied in crying down the achievements of other nations. Political parties may seek to make schools partisan, seeing a ready way to victory in an alliance with teachers and an indoctrination of the young. Such possibilities are all conceivable ; but any new tool, and any special gift, has always its possibilities of abuse. Man has the special gifts of reason and speech, and he can use them, as Aristotle long ago remarked, either to lift himself in the scale of creation by rational discourse, or to sink below the beasts by the subtlety of his deceit ; [2] but reason and speech are not condemned by the fact that they can be abused. Science has found out many inventions (in the air, on the land, and under the water), which can be used to destroy

---

[1] Pearson was writing in 1893. Infant schools, and school officers of health, and the provision of meals in schools, no longer need to be imagined.
[2] Aristotle, *Politics*, i.

human life as well as to promote human progress ; but science is not condemned thereby. In the same way a national system of education may be used to produce a community rich in manifold diversity [1] or to create the mechanical uniformity of a termite-heap. It is an edged tool, but edged tools are needed for any deep grooving ; and it does not follow that there is anything wrong in a tool because there may be something wrong in its use. We can only judge tools by the efficiency with which they fulfil the purposes for which they are used ; and if we pass any moral judgment, it can only be passed on purposes.

The purposes for which a national system of education is likely to be used in our country will hardly be the production of a mechanical uniformity or the creation of a negative patriotism. It is true that State schools are likely to increase in number ; but their creation will be the duty of different local authorities, reflecting differences of local feeling and environment. Meanwhile voluntary and private schools continue to flourish ; and we may even say that the action of the public authority, far from supplanting, is rather intended to supplement the existing provision of schools. No doubt more and more of the voluntary and private schools will be driven, by lack of adequate means, either to transfer themselves entirely to local authorities, or to seek financial aid which will involve some amount of control : but where there are hundreds of local authorities, there cannot be any great uniformity. Above all, the free initiative of the teacher in planning his course of instruction is likely to remain undiminished. This is a factor of the first importance ; and the freedom of our teachers is a precious thing. The Board of Education may issue " suggestions for teachers " in various subjects ; the inspectors of the Board, and those of the local authority, may both advocate their particular methods ; but the independence of the headmaster and his staff in the sphere of curricula is already large and is not likely to be diminished. Teachers, indeed, have in recent years gained a higher standing and a more assured position. Organizing themselves on the basis of their occupation, they have formed powerful associations ; and the National Union of Teachers, for example, is a body which negotiates on almost equal terms with the Board of Education and the Local Authorities. There is not only a " balance " between the central administration and the organs of local self-government ; there is also a balance between both of these and the teachers' associations. Some may even say that the real danger in education is not that of State regimenta-

---

[1] Von Humboldt, quoted in Mill's *Essay on Liberty*. All individuality of power and development, he argued, had two requisites—freedom, and variety of situations. From the union of these arise individual vigour and manifold diversity, which combine themselves in originality.

tion, but rather that of " occupationalism." Teachers, zealous for their profession, may regulate only too strictly the conditions of entry and the terms of service ; and they may erect a code of " professional conduct " to which a general conformity may be demanded. There has been a swing of the pendulum ; and where Pearson and others, thirty or forty years ago, feared " State socialism," those who are anxious for liberty to-day may fear instead the growth of professional regimentation. Even in this matter, however, we should be foolish to be unduly alarmed. It is never very easy for all the branches of a profession to be united. In the teaching profession there is a certain cleavage of interests between different branches ; and in the elementary branch there is also something of a division between men and women teachers. But it is the strength of teachers, rather than their weaknesses, which gives ground for the surest hope. They care for their children ; they care for their school ; they care for their subject. They serve their children not only in class-rooms, but also in playing-fields and in holiday camps ; and they readily attend summer schools and vacation courses to refresh their minds and to learn new methods. Anyone who knows our State schools, elementary and secondary, will be proud of the work which their teachers are doing to enrich and deepen national character, not only by what they teach, but also by what they do and by what they are. They are bringing the family into touch with the school by the establishment of parents' unions, which draw parents into the school, and enable them to discuss with teachers the work which it does. They are experimenting not only in new methods (of which the number is legion) for the teaching of old subjects, but also in the teaching of new subjects such as arts and crafts and music and painting, which not only give a new dexterity to the fingers, but can provide occupations for leisure in older years, and even create a cultured taste alive to the play of beauty. In all this there is much more of " manifold diversity " than there is of running to type ; and on this basis a State school, guided by its teachers and co-operating with the parents of its children, may make a new generation of which older men may say, " Now lettest Thou Thy servants depart in peace, for our eyes have seen Thy salvation." We may yet see the teacher, by the power of suggestion which his personality carries to the young, and through the organized life of the school and its various studies and games and societies, making a nation which has learned to correct the narrowness and the routine of specialized industry by the development of general faculty and the cultivation of general interests, has escaped from feverishness into a quiet steadiness, and has risen from follow-my-leader habits to the heights of collective endeavour.

IV

What has just been said leads naturally to a consideration of the purpose of education, as it has been conceived in our country, and as it has inspired our schools. And here we have to note an element which, as we have seen, has always been steadily prominent in our national tradition of education. English schools, and English teachers, have been concerned with the making of men and the shaping of character rather than with the making of scholars or the development of the intelligence. It is this which has been, and continues to be, the chief mark of difference, in the matter of education, between Great Britain and France or Germany. We have been deficient in the encouragement of pure study ; we have excelled, if we have excelled at all, in the general development of human power. It is partly perhaps that we have clung with a natural conservatism to a tradition which was common throughout Western Europe in the Middle Ages, and partly, it may be, that we have followed, and strengthened by following, a national tendency towards practical work and the gaining of practical results.

In the knightly education of the Middle Ages, a boy passed at the age of seven from his home to a castle for his training ; and he stayed there for his first seven years as a *damoiseau* or valet, and for another seven years as a squire. There are two things which may be noticed in this fourteen years' apprenticeship. In the first place, it was all spent away from home. This is a practice which has always survived in England. It is remarked in an Italian Relation of 1500 A.D. that, when they attain the age of seven or nine, the Englishman " puts away his children into the houses of others " ; and the system of preparatory schools to-day may still suggest a similar observation. In the second place, the fourteen years were all devoted to a general training, in the giving of which the ladies of the castle shared with the men, and which, if it was largely a training in sports and martial exercises, included also reading, music, singing, and the practice of social accomplishments. The passing of the Middle Ages did not end the knightly ideal. It only suffered a change ; and it was transformed, under the influence of the doctrine of courtesy, which was expanded in Castiglione's *Il Cortegiano* (translated into fine Tudor English by Sir Thomas Hoby about 1560) [1] into the ideal of " the gentleman." This ideal, which was developed in the sixteenth century, spread from Italy into France and England and Spain. In France there arose, in the seventeenth century, a number of academies for the training of gentlemen in manners, statesmanship, and war ; and these academies attempted to introduce

[1] See Sir Walter Raleigh's preface to Hoby's translation.

what we may call a modern curriculum, including some natural science, the study of foreign languages, and political philosophy. A number of schemes for English academies were projected; but the only definite result was the foundation, towards 1700 A.D., of several Nonconformist academies, which were partly intended for the training of ministers, but partly also to prepare young men of Nonconformist families for commerce or private life.

The tradition of knightly education, modified by the " doctrine of courtesy " and the practice of academies for the training of gentlemen, recurs in the system of education developed in England, during the nineteenth century, for the sons of the upper and professional classes. The knight of the thirteenth century, and the gentleman of the sixteenth, passes into the public school and university man of the nineteenth. There are three stages in his education—the preparatory school, the public school, and the university. Like his forerunner in the Middle Ages, he has a fourteen years' apprenticeship, which lasts from the age of eight to that of twenty-two; like him, he goes away from home; but unlike him, he divides his apprenticeship among three different institutions. Throughout his apprenticeship he is under the guidance of teachers who take a personal interest in the development of his character. We have already remarked that one of the marks of English literature, which appears particularly in the drama and the novel, is a strong trend towards the description of character, the study of its development, and its exhibition in action. English schoolmasters and tutors have steadily shown a similar trend. They have often been men of distinctive personality and definite character (sometimes, indeed, to the extent of being " characters "), who could not but affect the boys and young men, with whom they lived in daily intercourse, by the mere example of their tastes, their pursuits, and their general behaviour. Living among growing youth, and watching its growth, they have also been drawn into seeking to influence that growth by active co-operation; and the best of them—studying, as any observer with a lively mind cannot but study, the little shades of difference which make each person something unique—have learned to apprehend, and have sought to encourage, the growth of individuality. Some of them have perhaps been too painfully anxious, and have forgotten that watched kettles refuse to boil. Many of them have tended to sacrifice the natural development of boys on the altar of *esprit de corps*, and have not remembered that *esprit de corps* is only a means to something higher than itself, and in any case is something more than regimental buttons and abundant pipeclay. But there are few who have not laboured truly according to their lights; and our national character is the stronger and richer for their labours.

The English public-school [1] tradition was not the creation of Arnold of Rugby; but it was deeply affected by his influence. Already in 1837, at the age of forty-two, he was clear about "what alone is education—the forming of the moral principles and habits of men." He put those subjects first at Rugby which would most "enlighten and sustain the moral nature"; and this explains his interest in history. "What I have often said before," he declared in a confession of his faith, "I repeat now: what we must look for here is, first, religious and moral principle; secondly, gentlemanly conduct; thirdly, intellectual ability." The order in which Arnold placed these three things may seem curious; but it is characteristic not only of Arnold, but also of England. Equally characteristic was the close alliance which was formed at Rugby and in other public schools between the central authority of the headmaster and the system of self-government among the boys. There had been prefects before Arnold's time, just as there had been games of football in schools before a Rugby boy (over a hundred years ago) had the audacity "to take the ball in his hands and run"; but definite self-government, partly through prefects lawfully armed with large powers, and partly through regular games managed by boys under rules of their own making, was something new in its scale and importance. The result of the scheme of education which Arnold did so much to promote was the production of a type of character, with certain traits, which came to influence the army, the public services, and the professions, and influenced, through them, the nation at large. To play the game fairly according to its rules; to play for the side, and not for your own hand; to play to the end of the hardest-fought struggle, without slackening effort till the whistle blows; to fear sentiment; to hate exaggeration; to let your highest praise be "Not bad," and your worst blame "A poor sort"—these are some of the rules of the unwritten code. They have inspired the soldier at his post, and the civil servant at his desk; they are the rules of an aristocratic system of ethics; they emphasize the virtues, to which the members of any aristocratic society naturally cling, of sticking together, never "letting another fellow down," and fighting "in the last ditch" to the last gasp. They produce a steady fidelity in any collective enterprise, and they have aided accordingly the working of our party system of politics; but they foster tradition at the expense of initiative and the spirit of the "team" at the cost of individual responsibility. Behind the gallant figures of Good Form and Esprit de Corps may sit the darker shadows of uniform type and tame

[1] I have not attempted to treat of preparatory schools. Their ideals are set out in the *Master and his Boys*, by the late S. S. Harris—a great athlete, a true Christian, and a fine example of the English schoolmaster.

conformity. But the system, at its best, can send into the world young men of a gentle courtesy and a stern sense of duty—half mediæval knights, and half (in some of their rigours) stoical Spartans who will let a fox gnaw at their vitals rather than betray any sign of weakness. The Public Schools Commission of 1864, while it criticized their courses of study as " wanting in breadth and flexibility," and while it noted that too many men " of idle habits and empty and uncultivated minds " came from the schools, could yet fairly set to their credit " the creation of a system of government and discipline which had greatly influenced national character and social life." [1]

It was the function of the older universities, in the general practice of the last century, to receive the product of the public schools—or such part of it as did not pass directly into the Army or some other form of immediate occupation—and to give it a final form and direction. The colleges of Oxford and Cambridge, once clerical, and devoted to the clerkly type of education, had moved towards the other tradition. The development of a tutorial system produced the college tutor, who was not merely a teacher in the field of studies, but a friend and guide in the general growth of pupils to whom he stood *in loco parentis*. Early in the nineteenth century there was a change which deepened and broadened the university courses of study ; and in Oxford in particular there was instituted, soon after 1800, the curriculum called by the name of Literæ Humaniores, which included ancient history and philosophy along with classics, and sought to give not only learning, but also an outlook on life and something of a philosophy of conduct. On the basis of the tutorial system, and of the " schools " (or courses of study) to which it was applied, there arose an idea of the university as a place of preparation for public life—an academy, as it were, in the old French sense. The idea was fostered by the debates of undergraduates, conducted on parliamentary models, in their Unions ; and it was encouraged by the influence of tutors such as Jowett, who inspired their pupils with notions of public duty and the stirrings of public ambition. In this way the work of the university largely became the production of a governing class, from which Parliament and the Civil Service might both be recruited ; and a temper and type of character were developed—in the field of classical studies not less (and perhaps, indeed, even more) than in those of history and law—which affected not only the legislature and the administration at home, but also India and the Empire at large. A single name—the name of Lord Milner—will perhaps indicate sufficiently the nature of this temper and the type of this character.

The education given at public schools and in the old univer-

[1] Adamson, *Short History of Education*, p. 314.

sities may seem, at first sight, to be confined to a narrow class, and therefore limited in the range of its national influence. There are, however, two things which we must remember. In the first place, the inherent influence of the public schools and the older universities has affected thousands who have never themselves been members of either. Their code was one of the most definite things in the nineteenth century ; it was carried into public places and institutions — the Army, Parliament, the Civil Service of the Crown—by men who also carried prestige ; and it was a leaven which largely worked on the general mass. It is hardly fanciful, for instance, to trace in the English conduct of the Great War some of the influences of this code, alike for good and for evil. Nations show the stuff of which they are made in the way in which they wage war ; and the fight between the English public-school tradition and the tradition of the German General Staff illuminated the nature of both. In the second place, the tradition of the public schools, in its better features, has now become the inheritance of the numerous " secondary " schools, maintained by the public authority, which have arisen in the last twenty-five years—just as it has also become the inheritance of the old " grammar " schools, and of girls' schools, and of many other sorts of schools. Masters have carried with them the seeds of their own training ; and whether schools were " day " schools or " boarding " schools, whether they were independent of public authorities or managed by them, whether they were for boys or for girls, they have equally adopted what seemed to them good. They have followed the same organization of " houses," engaged in friendly rivalry with one another ; the same system of prefects, with its lessons and practice of responsibility ; the same method of eager games and of school societies—in a word, the same scheme of a general development of body and mind and character.

But what of the mass of the population, and the schools in which they get their training for the business of life ? The old schools of " Charity " or of " Industry," with their emphasis on religious instruction, were not destitute of the idea that education must be concerned with character as well as intelligence. The Sunday schools, which from 1780 to 1840 perhaps provided more children with elementary instruction than any other form of school, and often attempted to give evening instruction during the week, followed the same idea still more directly ; and it was also present in the work of the National and the British and Foreign Schools Society. The religious basis on which the provision of elementary education long rested, even if it was productive of religious jealousies, and though it has left a legacy of difficulties to the State in its administration of elementary schools, has kept alive the conception that education is some-

thing broader than instruction. Along with its legacy of difficulties it has bequeathed to the State a legacy of value. Our
system of State education has never dispensed with some
element of religious teaching. And because that element has
always been present, it has been all the easier for the State
gradually to elevate its general scheme above mere instruction,
and to lay emphasis on the moral purposes which, side by side
with the intellectual, a system of national education has to
serve.

It was with Robert Owen that the clear conception of the
moral purpose of elementary education first appeared, and it
was he who first regarded the training of character as something which stood by itself, and was not merely implied by
a general religious purpose. Deeply interested in the welfare of
the children whom he employed at his factory in New Lanark,
he founded, about 1815, a " New Institution for the Formation
of Character." It included an infant school ; a day school for
children between the ages of six and twelve ; and a system of
evening lectures for adults. Believing that the community
might be reformed if character were " formed for, and not by,
the individual," he sought to use education as a means to that
end, and to form the character of the young by setting their
life in a proper environment. Other factory owners, such as
Thomas Ashton, of Hyde in Cheshire, followed a similar policy.
When the State, from the beginning of the reign of Queen
Victoria, began to regulate elementary education, and to attach
conditions to the grants which it made, it set back the clock by
the regulations it issued and the conditions which it imposed.
Anxious to secure " results," and to secure them in the visible
form of a proper accomplishment in reading, writing, and arith-
metic, Robert Lowe, as Vice-President of the Committee of
Council, introduced in 1862 a system of payment by results,
which, if it produced a mechanical proficiency, " diverted attention from the moral function of the school," [1] and tended to
sacrifice the general development of faculty (moral as well as
mental) by concentrating attention on purely " clerical " powers.
The system lasted till 1890 ; and the twist which it gave to
elementary education is responsible for many of the criticisms
which are still directed, by those who have not forgotten the
past but are not acquainted with the facts of the present, against
our elementary schools. By the beginning of the twentieth
century, however, a great change had taken place. There is a
brief document, of a single page—the Introduction to the Code
of Regulations for Public Elementary Schools—which admirably
explains the nature of the change. It was first issued at the
beginning of this century ; and it was (one may conjecture) the

[1] Adamson, *op. cit.* p. 308.

work of the Parliamentary Secretary to the Board of Education (Sir William Anson, the Warden of All Souls College, Oxford), and of the Secretary, Sir Robert Morant—men who knew the best elements in the public schools and the old universities, and knew, too, the lofty conceptions of education to be found in the old Greek philosophers. It sets out that the purpose of the public elementary school " is to form and strengthen the character as well as to develop the intelligence " ; that " teachers can do much to lay the foundations of conduct " ; that " the discipline of the school can implant habits of industry, self-control, and perseverance " ; that " the corporate life of the school, especially in the playground, should develop fair play and loyalty " ; and that in all its work and all its efforts the school should enlist the co-operation of parents and the home.

Here the ideals of the public school—and, behind them, the ideals of the old " doctrine of courtesy " and of the knightly system of the Middle Ages—are extended to the public elementary school. It is not to be a place of " clerkly " education : it is to be a place of the making of men and of general manly excellence. To enunciate a programme is not the same thing as to give it effect ; and there is much to be done in our public elementary schools before any full effect can be given to these ideals. Not to speak of the need for providing some further education, to which children can go forward, at the age of eleven or twelve, from the elementary school, there is a need, in the elementary school itself, for smaller classes, in which the personality of the teacher can tell more directly, by individual methods, upon his pupils ; there is a need for playing-fields, in addition to playgrounds ; there is a need for a steady recruitment of devoted teachers, who have not only technical training, but also full minds. But, at any rate, the ideal is there ; and its realization will mean the making of national character, by conscious effort, on a new and greater scale. There are struggles to be fought in our national life, and battles to be won (cleanly, and without rancour or resentment) in time of peace, which have to be fought and won in the classrooms and on the playgrounds of our public elementary schools.

There is one thing which is already being added in practice, here a little and there a little, and which needs to be added as a clear and conscious conception, to the aims and purposes of our national system of education. Besides the forming and strengthening of character, and the developing of intelligence, there is also the awakening and the guiding of taste. The young have to be trained to seek not only goodness and truth, but also beauty. The growth of instruction in music and singing, in painting and drawing, in wood work and metal work, and in arts and crafts generally, shows how we are feeling our way towards such a conception. The addition of these things is not the addition of fringes or mere accomplishments : it is a definite enriching and strengthening of our national life. It corrects, in the first place, a defect in our national genius, which, whatever it may attain in the region of conduct or even in the field of scientific inquiry, is seldom effective in matters of art, and does not readily turn to the appreciation of beauty. It remedies, in the second place, the defects of the industrial specialization which marks our country. The single faculty development, of which we have already spoken, receives its best corrective when men learn in their youth interests, which may become the hobbies and delights of their maturer years—the interests of music and art and creative craftsmanship. If we only add the education of the " book " to the narrow specialization of industrial life, we simply add one specialization to another, and we give to a growing mind something which it may never really incorporate. If we can add an education in the liberal practice of beautiful arts, we are adding something which is at once broad in itself and likely to enter readily into the mind. Finally, we may say of any form of education, which is directed in its measure to the awakening and the guiding of taste, that it recognizes the claims, and prepares men for the use, of leisure. This is a grave and serious matter in an industrial community. In such a community the working day is filled with a recurrent round of similar manipulations ; and it is only in hours of leisure that men are free to seek some larger development. Any system of education in such a community should thus be directed not only (or so much) to the preparation of men for the efficient doing of work, but also to the training of men for the happy and fruitful use of their leisure. Leisure is not easily used, unless we have learned to feel interests with which we can readily fill it ; and it has often been remarked of our nation that, if it has any special attribute, it is that of a peculiar genius for being bored. There are few interests that fill leisure more readily, or are better prophylactics against the boredom which so easily besets us, than those interests of Art which can at once quicken the eye, and make the hand deft, and refine the taste. All in all, the training of men to use their leisure is one of the most necessary duties of all industrial communities.

V

Here we must end a large and stirring theme. We have traced three main movements in the development of English education. We have seen it, first and foremost, ceasing to be the ally of a fixed system of classes, and becoming a power which makes for social equality—just as, since women began, about 1850, to found their own schools and to vindicate their right of instruction, it has also made for sex equality. We have seen it, in the next place, passing gradually from churches and voluntary societies into the sphere of the State ; and, finally, we have seen that the conception of its purpose entertained by the State, however narrow it may on occasion have been, has attained a breadth and a scope which may make us hope that national life will profit more and more from the work of our national schools. In all the change there has been no break or clear revolution ; and abundant elements of the past still survive in the present. Some of these elements constitute problems which have still to be solved. Our public elementary schools, for example, still bear traces of a time in which they were the schools of a particular class ; and we have still to decide whether in the future they are to be primary schools—and, as such, intended not for a class, but for an age—from which children will normally pass to other forms of post-primary instruction, or whether they are to remain what they are. But many elements of the past which still survive are elements of permanent value. It is all to the good that the element of religious instruction has not disappeared from our schools ; and whatever may happen in matters of administration—whether the different religious bodies retain their schools or transfer them to public authorities—that element seems sure to remain. It is all to the good, again, that not only has the old English principle of local self-government asserted itself largely in our national system of education, but that the principle of voluntary enterprise and private initiative has still continued to operate. We may well hope that that principle will never disappear. The private munificence, which helped to found, and continues to support, many of our schools and all our universities, is more than a private virtue : it is also a public service. It is a salt which gives savour. Freedom of experimentation, and the striking out of new lines of development, depend upon it. The State intends the best, but it can only act uniformly by general rules. The gifts of private munificence add experiment to uniformity ; and they serve to maintain that freedom of action, in matters of the mind, which the State, bound to impose rules and to attach conditions to the expenditure of all its monies, cannot, even if it would, respect in equal measure.

LIST OF BOOKS

ADAMSON, J.—*Short History of Education*, 1919.
DOBBS, A. E.—*Education and Social Movements*, 1919.
HARRIS, S. S.—*The Master and his Boys*, 1924.
PEARSON, C. H.—*National Life and Character*, 1893.

CHAPTER X

THE SIGNS OF THE TIMES

WE can experience the character of a nation, as we can experience the personality of an individual ; but to describe either, as we can describe a natural object, in terms which will command universal assent, is a task beyond our powers. Individual personality is an opal of many lights, which varies as it is turned to this or that object or person ; and national character is no less many-coloured. A nation can hardly see or describe objectively another nation—or indeed, for that matter, itself. The character of the English nation is one thing when it is described by a French writer such as Boutmy ; it is another thing when it appears in the pages of a German writer such as Treitschke ; it is still another thing when an Englishman seeks to paint the portrait of Englishmen. Prejudice clouds the vision ; but prejudice is not the only cloud. There is, or there may be, a bewildering difference between national character as it appears in the individual specimen, and national character as it appears in the conglomerate body of the whole nation. It is less so in France, where an intimate social life and the regulative tradition of the nation have shaped the individual specimen in their own image. It is more so in England, where individual eccentricities of every pattern may play freely around the deep but hidden core of the national being. There *is* a rock on which we stand and from which we are hewn ; but we keep it shyly secret in mists of reserve, and it is only in some destined hour of national crisis, such as came to us in the midsummer of 1914, that we can see for ourselves, and show to others, the stuff of which we are made.

Yet we can trace, however dimly, some characteristics of our nation. There is a characteristic of energy, partly drawn from the race which predominates in our national blend of races, and partly developed by the influence of the climate in which we live. There is a characteristic of initiative, which a variable climate may have helped to encourage by its shifting demands, but which has been raised to the higher power of a free individuality by a system of common law which has respected the rights of the citizen, a trend of religious thought which has emphasized individual responsibility before God, and an economic doctrine and practice which have remitted to voluntary enterprise the direction of national trade and industry. There is a characteristic of liberty, which our law has at once ensured and amicably yoked with a spirit of law-abidingness, and which our constitutional development has elevated into a system of government by organized discussion—a system which produces a habit of compromise, a temper of moderation, and a capacity for collective mental work according to settled rules of procedure. Upon these earlier and more fundamental characteristics the great revolution in our national life which began about 1760 has superimposed new habits and tendencies. The urbanized life of a vastly greater population, engaged in the clamour and routine of industry, has produced febrility of temper and gregariousness of behaviour. The multiple contacts and conflicts of a great and complicated society have inevitably involved an ever-increasing volume of State-regulation ; and an acuter social conscience, more and more alive to the sad and recurrent accidents of large-scale industry — unemployment and injury, sickness and a destitute old age—has appealed to the State for the mercy of a control which the State is more and more seeking to provide. The regulative spirit has gained on the spirit of individual liberty. If, as some have laughingly said, our weather has produced a habit of patience, tempered by "humorous grousing," with our inevitable sky, it may also be said that the new dispensation of our social and economic life has produced a similar habit of patience, similarly tempered, with what seems an equally inevitable Government. The old liberal tradition of criticism of the State and magnification of self-help seems weak and dwindling ; and we chew the thistles of a patient resignation with a melancholy placidity. Yet there are still reformers and even revolutionaries in the land ; and no man yet knows what our new and comparatively untried system of national education may do to lift up our hearts and rekindle our spirits —to chasten our febrility, to sublimate our gregariousness, to ennoble our leisure, to elevate our characters, and to

"Give us manners, virtue, freedom, power."

Every present is also a crisis, in the true and proper sense of that word—a "time of decision," in which we have to make the future by our choice. In every present men may well be alarmed by the crisis, and not least in ours to-day, wherein we may see, like the prophet, "multitudes, multitudes in the valley of decision." What will they make of the future ? Who shall say ? But at any rate we may seek to discern the signs of the present, and we may ask, and seek to find, what is the nature of its economic position ; what is the course of its social tendencies ; what is the volume of the international influence in which it is set ; and what is the direction of its educational trend.

I

We surrendered, nearly two hundred years ago, a system of national economy in which we lived both by industry and by agriculture, and even more by agriculture than by industry. We pinned our future to the production and marketing of coal, iron, cotton, and other industrial commodities ; and since a great population was at once made necessary, and made possible, by this policy—since men must be there for the work, and the work was there for the men—we produced a great population to produce a great sum of industrial commodities. This great population now tends to be stationary at the size which it has already attained ; and we need feel no serious apprehensions about its future growth. What we have to ask is whether the resources which we possess for the production of coal, iron, cotton, and other industrial commodities are sufficient to support our existing population—or, at any rate, to support it on the basis of our old individual system, under which each producer managed his business on his own account. Such a system, it is readily obvious, requires some margin or reserve to meet the possibilities of waste. In times of scarcity, as we learned in the war, the State must ration and control. It is only in times of comparative plenty that it is ready and glad to leave matters alone to the free course of trade. Have we resources enough, with a sufficient margin of reserve, to maintain our old individual system —and the type of national character which was its corollary ?

Cotton is now being manufactured in the countries in which it is grown. Our coal, if it is not by any means exhausted, is less of a marketable export than it was. Within our borders two of our main pivots are weakening : in the world outside we have seen already, and we may expect in the future to see, new resources being explored and exploited, and a large fund of human labour mobilized, or ready to be mobilized, especially in Oriental countries, to compete with us on the basis of a lower standard of living. Even in our old, more balanced, and less delicate system of economy, we had to expend large funds on a system of poor relief intended to aid unemployment and destitution ; and in the reign of Charles II the poor rate almost amounted to one-half of the revenue of the Crown. The Victorian age of prosperity seemed to alter the whole situation ; but our own age, in which, it is true, we perhaps live under abnormal conditions, shows a new volume of provision for unemployment, often miscalled the dole, which is so far good as it rests on payments made by employed and employers as well as on the contributions of the State and augmentations provided by local authorities, but which, in view of the effects it must tend to exercise on the fibre of our people, can hardly be welcomed as a permanent institution of our national life. Meanwhile, the outlet of emigrations seems narrower and more restricted ; and even if it were wider and more free, we cannot provide from the population of our great towns the human material which new countries need, nor can we expect from our townsfolk any alacrity in abandoning the organized pleasures of an urban civilization for the rawer and more solitary life of prairie or veldt or bush. It would almost seem as if our vast population, in the present conjuncture of the stars, and unless new possibilities are discovered and utilized, must entail one of two results—either a restriction and diminution of numbers, or a regulation and rationing of wealth by the State (as in a time of siege or under pressure of war) with a view to a different and more equal system of distribution. Either result, and more particularly the latter, will produce in its turn a trend of character towards a different type—less adventurous, less self-reliant, less ready to shoulder the divine burden of responsibility ; more expectant of aid, more querulous about privation and effort.

But are there no new possibilities to be discovered and utilized ? That is the question of questions. We have seen that a territory is never a destiny which determines in a constant and identical way, from generation to generation, the fortunes and the character of its inhabitants ; we have seen, on the contrary, that it is a sum of possibilities, among which men are free to choose, in the light of their knowledge and insight, according to the given conditions and the current needs of the hour. We have to discover by a thorough inquiry the full possibilities of our territory—the territory not only of Great Britain, but also of the British Dominions beyond the Seas. We need statistical data ; we need long-time forecasts ; we need long-time policies based upon both. Two hundred years ago we could afford to leave to the chance of individual discovery the possibilities of coal and iron and cotton. To-day we must use, as it were, a collective prescience ; and even if we do not socialize the means of production, we must at any rate socialize our thought, and by a collective and organized inquiry discover the possibilities of a higher economic development. What such inquiry may suggest in the way of agriculture, of afforestation, of the use of water-power, of the development of imperial resources, it would be idle at this moment even to attempt to guess.[1] We may hope, not in the interests of any party, or of

---

[1] There are, perhaps, large possibilities of biological research, in the matter of the proper breeding of animals and plants, which may conceivably add a new sum of possibilities to our resources.

any particular policy, but in the general interest of the whole nation, that some new possibility for the restoration of agriculture may be discovered—not so much because it will diminish, to any great degree, the volume of unemployment, but because it will add a more adequate quantity of a very necessary ingredient —the ingredient of a sound agricultural stock and tradition—to the forces which determine our national policy and character. A balanced national character demands a ballast of agriculture.

But above and beyond all the possibilities which are inherent in material resources there is the great and cardinal possibility which is inherent in human capacity. If coal and cotton and iron fail, men are still left ; and there is no resource which is more worth exploration than the hidden and unelicited powers of human material. We do not yet know what we can make of ourselves, or how much more fully we can utilize even our existing resources by a more intense cultivation of our own minds. There is surely human material running to waste in our present dispensation. If we can mobilize that material, by a training which fits it more adequately for industry without sacrificing general culture or the claims of pure intelligence, we can stand in the valley of decision undismayed, for all our multitudes.

Two conclusions emerge in regard to the economic position of the present hour, in its bearings on national character. In the first place, it may be possible, by thorough and collective inquiry, to discover possibilities in our island and our Empire such that we can still support a great mass of population, at the same or a higher standard of comfort, on the same system of individual management which has been the corollary, and has helped the maintenance, of our old national characteristics of energy, initiative, and liberty. In the second place, it is possible, and it is very desirable, that we should so understand and enhance the possibilities of human capacity in all our population, that we should not only maintain, but even advance, the old characteristics which we cherish, and that we should even add new characteristics of forethought and planned design in which we have hitherto failed.

II

One of the deepest social tendencies in our long history has been that which sets towards voluntary organization. Our country, above all countries, has been a paradise of guilds and clubs. In our Middle Ages there was an abundance of merchant guilds, craft guilds, religious guilds ; there were Inns of Court for the lawyers, and free Universities, which were guilds of masters, or scholars, or both, for the body of students. The same sort of abundance marks our modern history. The law of trust, under cover of which property can be held by trustees for a voluntary organization which cannot, or does not, itself hold property, has co-operated with our native tendency to produce a network of free social groups. By its aid, Nonconformist congregations and societies have organized themselves; great companies have arisen which have helped at once to extend our commerce and to found our Empire; and trade unions have grown and grown until they have come to embrace the majority of the working classes. It is the last development which may well arrest our special attention.

In a great industrial society the unit of the club tends to become co-extensive and synonymous with the unit of the occupation. The reason is simple. As the practice of division of labour establishes itself further and further, and occupation is separated from occupation, each occupation tends to become the permanent and the exclusive interest of a body of men who in turn tend to organize themselves for all purposes—whether of friendly benefit, or of politics, or of economic defence of their interests—on the basis of the occupation which has become the essence of their lives. It is true that the extent of the occupation, as a unit of organization, is not yet clearly defined. Sometimes—more generally in the past than in the present—men have taken the craft or process as a unit, and formed craft unions: sometimes (and this seems to be the dominant tendency of the present) they have adopted the general and wider industry—mining, engineering, the railway—and formed industrial unions. In either case, but particularly in the latter, the organization based on the occupation is growing into new and consolidated power. The voluntary society of the occupational order is becoming so strong that it is, as it were, over-leaping itself; and falling on the other side it is ceasing to be voluntary. The old club is turning into the new State. Thinkers have arisen who would turn the occupation into a guild, and the guild into a sovereign over its particular industry: who would set the guild in the foreground of our national organization, and relegate the national State to a background of residuary duties.

The philosophy of occupationalism—or, if you will, vocationalism—involves two consequences. In the first place, it involves a challenge to the State—the State which is based on the nation, and therefore on the territory or region which is the hearth and home of the nation. The organ of the national and territorial State, in an age of democracy, is Parliament. More than one force is now arrayed against Parliaments. There is the strong man armed, impatient of cliques and peculation, and rejoicing in the black shirts of a purer order of Fascism. There is the Marxist in a hurry, disdainful of bourgeois culture and slow evolution, and dictating behind a red guard in the interests of the proletariate. Not the least serious among these forces, at any rate in our own country, is an occupationalism which is entrenched in professions as well as in trades, and may inspire the teacher, for example (not to mention the doctor), as well as the worker. But occupationalism is not only a challenge to the State : it also entails another and equally vital consequence. The philosophy of occupationalism is a philosophy pivoted upon work—upon a conception of work as engulfing life, so that life must be organized for the sake of work. " We are workers," the philosophy runs ; " we must work freely ; and to work freely we must control our work freely by our workers' organizations." May it not be maintained that we are men as well as workers ; that as men we have leisure to use, as well as work to do ; that leisure is greater than work, because it is the growing-time of the spirit ; and that life must therefore be organized as much, or more, for the sake of leisure as it is for the sake of work ? Whatever the answer we may return to these questions, it surely matters, and matters profoundly, for the future of our country, that we should have a just appreciation of the exact claims of leisure upon our life. Men may talk of class-consciousness and class-war as the mark of our times ; but the real struggle is perhaps that in which vocation challenges, not only the sovereignty of the nation, but also the claims of leisure.

The nation is not to be discredited because there is much false nationalism abroad. I have sometimes thought that there are three sovereigns which dispute our allegiance. One is blood—or the idea of a nation as a group of kinsfolk, united by an intimate consanguinity within their gates, but divided from the stranger without by an impassable barrier of difference. That is false nationalism. Another is contiguity—the sweet ties of neighbourliness, strengthened by old and common tradition, which unite the racial blend that inhabits a given territory, and make it a nation of the spirit—which is a reality, and not a nation of the body—which is a simulacrum. That is true nationalism. A third is occupation—the bond of a common profession, which unites its members by the daily and homely ties of common work and interest. This may be, and tends to be, though it need not be, a principle which we may call by the name of anti-nationalism. To prefer the second of these sovereigns, which we have called by the name of contiguity, is not to fall into any worship of the State, or to subscribe to any patriotism of flags and " days " and power and victories. It is simply to cherish a loving sense of the community of the spirit in which we live, with its manifold and immemorial tradition— a community wider than all our individual interests ; a community not only of to-day, but also of yesterday and to-morrow —a community that lifts us with wings up into its riches, above and beyond the individual and immediate interests of ourselves and our profession, our kinsfolk, and our blood. A patriotism of this order is not a patriotism which is externally directed, either against other nations or against the great cause of internationalism, of which it is rather the ally and the necessary condition : it is a patriotism that is internally directed to the chastening and sublimation of all that is small or mean. It is the patriotism which Mazzini preached, when he taught that a nation was a God-given unit, with a duty to God which was its mission, so that it laboured within and without to realize His will by the light of its own particular vision. It is the patriotism which he set over against what he thought to be the false sectionalism of French thinkers, who would split the nation into communist societies, and the no less false internationalism of German reformers, who would sink the nation, with all its precious freight, in the barren sea of an international socialism. In his faith, which was a fine faith, we may believe that a true patriotism, based on the conception of national mission, necessarily issues in a true internationalism, which is the co-operation of patriotisms for the realization of the common and universal ends embedded in the genius of each—the ends that live in the ideal realm of justice, duty, and righteousness. And we may equally believe that a true patriotism cannot be inimical to a true individualism of conscience and character. We are all indeed citizens of the ideal realm ; and by reason of that citizenship we may sometimes be bound to resist a State which makes claims that conflict with universal and immutable duties. In such a case patriotism is not enough. But the national State, even when it is imperfect, remains an actual and concrete realm of the spirit ; and even in our resistance we have to remember that the ends for which we strive will remain bare and ghostly, unless by our protestation, and even if need be our martyrdom, we can secure their incorporation in that actual and concrete realm. In this sense resistance, at its highest power, is a tribute and offering to the State which we resist, and it may even be called the finest flower of patriotism. And if resistance, the supreme effort of the individual, is no negation of the nation or of patriotism, who will deny that the nation, and the call of patriotism, which lift the individual from the torpor of routine and the bondage of immediate interest into a realm of the spirit, are a fulfilling, and not a negation, of the individual's essence, which is, in a word, the power of spiritual development ?

If the power of spiritual development be the essence of the individual, and if, as I have said, it is leisure which is the growing-time of the spirit, should not our social philosophy be directed to a consideration of leisure and its uses ? There are those who think of man as essentially creative ; who regard him as creative in and through his work or occupation ; and who demand, in order that he may be truly creative, that he should have a free and full voice in the control of his work. Man is indeed a maker ; but the supreme thing which he makes is himself. If his making were only in the field of external work, his soul would get but a dusty answer to life and its problems. Work is a matter of daily rubs : work is a matter of daily and, it may be, deadening routine. Can we really pivot our hope of a better life on a new organization of work, by some form of occupational control, in days in which work is becoming more and more unskilled, more and more a matter of routine and repetition, and less and less a matter of creative energy ? The greater the mass of inventions of the human mind, the less the amount of mind required from the great majority of workers for the performance of their particular process. It is not wrong to look forward to a state of society in which men shall be provided with congenial work by equality of opportunity, and shall be given a field of creative energy through a share in control of their labour. It is not wrong ; but is it enough ? Work, and creative energy applied to work, are part of life, and go to the making of man ; but a full life contains other things, and a full man can only be made if those other things are also present. Even in the field of creative activity we pour out our souls not only in the work which we do, but also in the leisure we enjoy, the music we play, the words we write, the hobbies we pursue. But man is essentially contemplative, as well as essentially creative ; and there are many who would contemplate rather than create, because being rather than doing is their interest, and by contemplation they pass into the being of beauty, or truth, or goodness ; and such as these wait upon leisure, that therein they may have their enjoyment and fruition. In a people of a restless practical energy, such as ours, the ideals which need to be emphasized are the ideals of leisure ; of creation which is not work but a lovely play ; of serene contemplation. We have to learn, in a word, not only to organize work, but also to cultivate leisure. This is a matter of education and of schools ; but it is also a matter of public policy and of public institutions—national galleries, national academies of music, national opera-houses, national theatres. Our State, like the Athenian State in the days of Pericles, must set beauty in public places, and make beauty a public cult. We are behindhand in this matter—far behind the ancient Athenians, and well behind our neighbours to-day in France and Germany. Beauty is only one side of the matter, and it is not only the eyes of our taste that need to be opened. There is also truth, and the passion of pure curiosity for truth, whether it serves to help us to make some new order of society or to achieve some other result of utility, or whether it simply begins and ends with itself. It is not an occupational society which we need to achieve in this country, but rather what I would call an educational society—a society set, as Spinoza would say, to the cultivation of the true life which is the life of the mind ; a society which erects and endows beauty, loves truth for itself, prepares the young to enjoy their leisure in days of maturity, and furnishes the mature with noble means of enjoyment. It was such a society which Plato saw, as in a vision, in his *Republic* : it is such a society which we must seek to see, as in a vision, in our future. This educational society, if it ever comes down from the heavens, will fire our minds to a ready patriotism ; for who can fail to say in his heart, " Dear city of Athens," if Athens be after this pattern ? And because its nature is that of an educational society, it will train and perfect the character of the nation in which it is set, " blotting out this, and writing in that, until it makes the characters of men, as far as may be, pleasing to God."

III

The growth of international influence upon national character is a mark of our times. From the earliest times, indeed, nations have always been formed in contact with one another. France has been formed by her relations with Germany and England, and affected in different ways and to different issues by her relations with either. England and Scotland have both been deeply affected by France. We have borrowed from her genius a fine tradition of measure and taste in literature, and of grace in manners, which has influenced in its degree alike our thought and our action. The progressive industrialism of the nations of Europe in the nineteenth century has made them at once more like in their features, and more interlocked in their relations. Methods of government have assumed a common type : English parliamentarianism, French methods of administration, the social legislation and educational system of Germany, have all made, as it were, a tour of the world. The economic interdependence of Europe is shown alike in the internationalization of business and in the spread of international organizations of the working classes. There is, too, the internationalism of science, and of religious thought in the various Christian Churches ; and not least, because it may be a harbinger of great things in the future, there are the growing connections which the students of European universities are knitting with one another. But we cannot be blind to the powerful factors which make in an opposite direction. There is the survival, and even the renaissance, of separate national traditions embedded in separate languages which are more and more sedulously cultivated. Language is being confounded, that we may not understand one another's speech ; and yet a common understanding based on some commonly accepted vehicle of speech is a necessary condition of any enduring internationalism. The sensitive spirit of corporate national pride was perhaps never more sensitive ; and protectionist policies, linguistic restrictions, and prohibitions of easy intercourse, all readily flow from such a spirit.

In the disturbed and heaving waters on which we are now being tossed it is not easy to see beyond the moment. But there are deep human necessities which make for the increase of international life. There is the passion for prosperity, which involves friendly dealings with other nations if it is to be satisfied. There is the passion for security, which, in a combustible system in which any fire may spread to the furthest confines, involves some system of mutual insurance against the outbreak of fire. Under the influence of these necessities—not to speak of other and higher reasons—nations are being drawn into a relation which is no longer that of mere contact, but becomes more and more that of co-operation. Each nation, we realize, has not only to live for itself, but also to live for others—if only in order that it may be able to live for itself more freely. To realize this fact is to realize also the truth of Mazzini's saying that nation is mission, and that each nation must contribute, by some discharge of its mission, to what Dante called " the total civility of mankind." One of the noblest aspects of this new realization of the doctrine of mission is the system of mandates —the system under which a nation takes for its mission, in the interest alike of the inhabitants and of other nations, the government of some area which is not yet ripe for self-government. We may claim for our country that its law of trust, by which a trustee administers property without profit for the benefit of another, has helped to produce the system of mandates : we may claim, indeed, that it was in the spirit of a trust, or a mandate, that we long ago learned to administer the parts of our Empire which were not self-governing. We have here given something to the world ; but we owe far more than we have given, and we have to learn so to shape the character and temper of our nation that we may be cheerful givers. And not only for us, but for all nations, there is now established a new form of international organization to influence, and a new conception of international duty to stimulate, the making of national character. Nations have now to train themselves to co-operate, and to school themselves to see and undertake missions. The societies that built themselves in isolation, or in conflict, or at most in contact, have now to build themselves in co-operation, with a new gravity and sobriety of temper, and a new habit of ordered mutual adjustment. There is nothing which more broadens or deepens the character of the individual than the learning of the adjustments which, in the co-operative life of the family and of other institutions, he is bound to make for the sake of the happiness and the well-being both of others and of himself. May we not anticipate a new depth and a new breadth of national character as nations learn the adjustments which they are bound to make, for their own sakes and for the sake of other nations, under a system of international co-operation ?

IV

I have said so much already, in other connections and in dealing with other themes, about matters of education, that I only need, in turning to consider the educational trend of the present hour, to draw into a summary what I have already said.

A democratically organized national State, governing itself by its own national will, and training itself by its own national system of education, is something new, and something of very great power. In the field of individual moral growth Aristotle long ago distinguished three stages. There was the stage of natural endowment, or φύσις ; there was the stage of social habit and drill, or ἔθος ; there was the stage of responsible individual action by the light of a moral consciousness, which he called by the name of φρόνησις. In the field of the growth of national character we may distinguish similar stages. A nation has its natural endowment of racial blend and territorial environment. A nation undergoes the drill, and is shaped by the habit, of its system of law and government and its mode of religious thought and life. A nation, when it attains a national system of education inspired by a moral purpose, begins to enter the stage of responsible self-direction.

The grave and solemn responsibility of national self-direction opens before our view in many directions. A nation may seek to control and direct the proportions of its racial blend, as the United States of America is now attempting to do. It may seek to influence, directly or indirectly, on eugenic principles, the rate of reproduction in the various classes or elements of its population. In the economic sphere, it may attempt some nationalization of the production and distribution of wealth; or, short of that, it may undertake a deliberate review of all its resources and possibilities, and it may determine by an act of choice what resources it will exploit, and what possibilities it will prefer. But of all the areas in which a nation can choose, and of all the means by which it can determine its future, there is none that matters more, or indeed as much, as education. It touches the mind ; and the mind is the life of man. It touches the mind on many sides ; for it stimulates the intelligence towards truth, both practical and theoretic ; it awakens the taste to beauty—beauty of bright sight and murmuring sound ; it shapes the will toward goodness, and forms and strengthens the character. And since it touches the mind, and touches the mind on many sides, it may do many things for our future. It may check and steady the fever and fret of our urban life ; it may chasten, and sublimate to a noble fellowship of common achievement, the gregarious and follow-my-leader habit of our urban population. It may help us to mobilize to the highest reach of their capacity, by a practical training in general skill, all the human resources by which we can best ensure the economic future of our country. It may teach us to cultivate our leisure, and to make ourselves at home in all those broad spaces of the spirit, with all their possibilities of fine enjoyment, that lie outside and around the area of daily work. It may lift men to international conceptions of the past history and the future policy of their nation, and open their eyes to the ways of international co-operation and the duty of national mission. But to shape the mind of a nation is a work of many days ; and for all these things we must wait patiently—patiently and faithfully—on the working of slow time. " Shall the earth be made to bring forth in one day ? Or shall a nation be born at once ? "

INDEX

PRINTED BY MORRISON AND GIBB LTD., EDINBURGH

For Product Safety Concerns and Information please contact our EU
representative GPSR@taylorandfrancis.com
Taylor & Francis Verlag GmbH, Kaufingerstraße 24, 80331 München, Germany